CHRISTIAN CONVERSION

A DEVELOPMENTAL INTERPRETATION
OF
AUTONOMY AND SURRENDER

Walter Conn

PAULIST PRESS
New York/Mahwah

ACKNOWLEDGMENTS

The author thanks the editors of the following journals and books for use of material which originally appeared in different form in their pages: *Contemplative Review* 17/3 (Fall 1984); *Cross Currents* 32/3 (Fall 1982) and 34/3 (Fall 1984); *Human Development* 3/3 (Fall 1982); *International Philosophical Quarterly* 21/4 (December 1981); *Journal of Religion* 65/4 (October 1985); *Perkins Journal* 36/4 (Fall 1983) and 37/4 (Summer 1984); *Religious Education* 76/1 (January-February 1981); *Thought* 58 (June 1983); *Creativity and Method,* ed. Matthew L. Lamb (Milwaukee, WI: Marquette University Press, 1981); *The Pedagogy of God's Image,* ed. Robert Masson (Chico, CA: Scholars Press, 1982); and *The Westminster Dictionary of Spirituality,* ed. Gordon S. Wakefield (Philadelphia: Westminster, 1983).

The Publisher gratefully acknowledges the use of excerpts from *The Seven Storey Mountain* by Thomas Merton, copyright 1948 by Harcourt Brace Jovanovich, Inc.; renewed 1976 by The Trustees of the Merton Legacy Trust. Reprinted by permission of the publisher.

Library of Congress
Catalog Card Number: 85-62937

ISBN: 0-8091-2783-0

Published by Paulist Press
997 Macarthur Boulevard
Mahwah, New Jersey 07430

Printed and bound in the
United States of America

CONTENTS

iii

DEDICATION

To Fran

In memory of our father
Earl F. Conn
who showed us the heart of Christian conversion

PREFACE

Conversion has recently been rediscovered by Christians. It has even become fashionable. This should be good news. The problem is that—in its popularity—conversion means almost anything anybody wants it to mean. The skeptic must be excused for wondering if it is really the *metanoia* of the Gospels that has become such a hot news item.

Despite the manifest importance of conversion as a personal, cultural, and political phenomenon in contemporary life, there is yet no critical, foundational study of it. Theological discussions of "born again" faith and sociological analyses of conversions to "new religions" abound, but there exists no critical way of evaluating conversion claims. This book, an interdisciplinary study which combines a philosophy of self-transcendence with a critical interpretation of developmental psychology, attempts to establish a criterion for such evaluation of Christian conversion. My purpose is not to assess various conversion claims, but to provide the critical basis for such discussion.

In several previous works I have presented a developmental interpretation of Christian conscience as the radical personal drive for self-transcendence realized in creative understanding, critical judging, responsible deciding, and generous loving. Here, after a brief recapitulation of that thesis, I extend the developmental interpretation to the reality of Christian conversion.

My basic strategy, as outlined in Chapter 1, is threefold: (1) to disclose the fundamental connection between an adequate understanding of conscience and a normative interpretation of conversion; (2) to situate the various dimensions of conversion within a pattern of personal development; (3) to show how a *critical* understanding of conversion can be philosophically grounded in a theory of self-

1

transcendence and empirically controlled by a psychology of development.

In the developmental sections of Chapters 2 and 3, I build principally on the work of Erik Erikson, Jean Piaget, Lawrence Kohlberg, James Fowler, and Robert Kegan. I bring the basic elements of their theories together in a single integral model of personal development as self-transcendence, with the strengths of each theory criticizing and compensating for the weaknesses in the others. Having enjoyed a recent popularity of its own, developmental theory is now itself the object of some controversy as the winds of fashion change. Fair use of developmental theory today, then, demands that the author provide his or her own interpretation. Thus, in Chapter 2 I present the theories as I understand and use them, and in Chapter 3 I confront several of their problematic aspects. Both suspicion and retrieval have their moments, then, as I spell out my critical interpretation and constructive appropriation of developmental theory.

Development functions as the book's middle term between conscience and conversion. Chapter 3's interpretation of conscience as developmental leads directly to Chapter 4's consideration of developmental transitions as conversions. Moral, cognitive, and affective conversions are delineated as key dimensions of a fundamental shift from an instinctively spontaneous to a personally reflective patterning of the drive for self-transcendence.

Once the main lines of the stages of development and the dimensions of conversion are sketched, I turn to the life of Thomas Merton for a concrete example rich in the complexities and depth of Christian conversion. First, in Chapter 5, I consider Merton's early conversion experience as a Christian version of moral conversion (including cognitive and affective components). Then, in Chapter 6, after introducing the notion of a distinctly religious conversion, I examine Merton's mature Christian experience in its light. Thus Christian conversion is viewed not as one more conversion to be added to the moral, affective, cognitive, and religious quartet, but as the specific shape these conversions take when focused on Jesus in the symbolic context of the Christian story.

From this consideration emerges the personal measure of Christian living: the conscience which has experienced the fullness of Christian conversion—the loving, compassionate conscience rooted in Jesus' God and structured by universal principles of justice. This is the morally autonomous conscience that has completely surrendered itself in religious conversion.

Any endeavor like this generates much gratitude. For generous assistance at various phases of research and typescript preparation I am in debt to Geraldine Bloemker, Teresa Byrne, Patricia Fry, Chris Heverin, Marie Lovera, Francesca Maiorana, Melchior Masina, Joan Phillips, and Corinne Weaber. For critical reading of earlier drafts I must thank Maryanne Beckford, John Carmody, Bernard Cooke, Lawrence Cunningham, Charles Curran, Donald Gelpi, Margaret Gorman, Paul Knitter, Paul Philibert, Lewis Rambo, and Norbert Rigali. Each helped enormously. I am also grateful to Robert Daggy, Curator of the Thomas Merton Studies Center at Bellarmine College, Louisville, Kentucky, for his careful guidance during my research visit. I also want to thank Frederick Crowe for the generous support of the Lonergan Trust Fund. The friendship of colleagues and the cooperation of administrators at Villanova University lightened the burden considerably over the past several years of writing.

This book is dedicated to my sister, Fran Gilchrist. Twenty wonderful Christmas days with Fran, Charlie, and their family have symbolized the continuing love our father gave us. Fran knows conversion the way it should be known. My first book on conversion was dedicated to my mother, Ethel Conn, and my aunt, Mary V. Keough; in this one too I continue to be indebted for all they have given me. Beyond our families, we are inspired by good teachers, and, if we are teachers, by good students. At Boston College, I was blessed in both ways. Joseph Flanagan has been introducing students to themselves for over twenty years; I was lucky to be one of the first. Jane Hanson was in the first class I taught in 1966. Her lively response assured that it was not the last. Shared Thanksgivings with Jane and Chuck and Emily are perfect symbols of the loving support that continues, as the copy of *Insight* Jane keeps next to the bed in the guest room is a reminder of the encouragement she once gave a novice teacher. And if I needed one, it would also be a reminder of the debt I owe to Bernard Lonergan, who died as this volume was being completed. His profound influence will be apparent on every page.

Finally, in everything I do I am sustained by the loving care of Joann Wolski Conn. This book is no exception; she has contributed her interest, her insights, and her critical literary eye.

Eagles Mere
January 31, 1985

Conscience manifests itself as a summons of the Self to its ownmost potentiality-for-Being-its-Self.

Heidegger

1

CONSCIENCE AND CONVERSION

CONVERSION

Ever since Jesus first went into Galilee, proclaiming the good news from God, conversion has been fundamental to Christian life. The Christian understanding of conversion as a moral-religious reality finds its roots in the Old Testament: the history of Israel is the story of a people repeatedly being called to conversion, called to turn back to its covenant with the God it has adulterously abandoned. David is the model of how this call to conversion works in the individual sinner's life (2 Sam 11—12). The story of Job, who comes to recognize the mystery of God, underscores the fundamental truth that even the just person is called to conversion.

John the Baptist continues the prophets' call to conversion in the New Testament. And after John's arrest, Jesus takes up the call and makes it central to his preaching: "The time has come . . . the reign of God is at hand. Be converted and believe in the good news" (Mk 1:15). The key biblical words for conversion are *nacham* and *shub* in Hebrew, and *metanoia* and *epistrophe* in Greek.[1] If conversion means a radical turning, or a redirection of one's life, the first word in each pair, emphasizing repentance, specifies a turning *from* (sin), while the second indicates a turning *toward* (God). Emphasis on conversion as repentance for sin has probably kept Christians from thinking of Jesus as having experienced conversion, even though he did present himself to John for baptism. It has been the extraordinary experience of Paul on the road to Damascus, rather, that has dominated Christian thinking about conversion in the New Testament (especially accounts in Acts).[2] Many contemporary theologians, however, realizing the full *religious* depth of conversion beyond the moral, recognize in Jesus' response to crises in his life and ministry a transformation of faith, a rethinking of his relationship to the Father that defines the very essence of religious conversion.[3]

Though rooted in the prophetic call of the Old Testament, and absolutely fundamental to New Testament teaching, conversion was by no means an exclusively Judeo-Christian reality. Indeed, the early Christian meaning of this fundamental reality was elaborated in a cultural context of mutual influence where it shared the term *epistrophe* with Middle- and Neo-Platonism as well as with Stoicism and Gnosticism.[4] Judaism and Christianity might have been alone among ancient Mediterranean religions in demanding conversion, as A.D. Nock claims, but philosophic conversion as the object of education, a moral-intellectual "turning of the soul," was already established with Plato (*Republic* VI, 518D).[5]

The philosophic search for truth becomes the Christian yearning for God in St. Augustine, whose *Confessions* recount his intellectual, moral, and religious conversions.[6] Indeed, the *Confessions'* eloquent articulation of the profound *experience* of interior transformation has given St. Augustine a preeminent place in Christian spirituality. Though medieval spiritual writers like Meister Eckhart continued to focus on the experience of Christian life, the dominant Scholastic mode of theology effectively lost the experience of conversion in the metaphysical analysis of faith, grace, and justification. Luther best marks the return of conversion as experienced to a central place in reflection on the Christian life. However else they differ, Luther and St. Ignatius of Loyola share the reality of conversion in their personal experience as well as in their analyses of the spiritual life.[7] Despite the enormous influence of Ignatius' *Spiritual Exercises* on individual lives, however, it would be some four centuries before formal Roman Catholic theology was ready to recognize in the experience of conversion the significance which had become a primary characteristic of Protestant theology.

Philipp Spener and Pietism in Germany, John Wesley and the founding of Methodism in England, and Jonathan Edwards and the Great Awakening in New England are only three of the many names and events that would have to be mentioned in any complete survey of conversion in Protestantism.[8] More than anything else, perhaps, these were responsible for the popular religious revivalism that carried into and through the nineteenth century.

It was in this revivalist context at the beginning of this century, then, when psychology was still in its infancy as a science, that William James' classic *Varieties of Religious Experience* (1902) established the pragmatic view that has dominated much of contemporary thinking on the topic: conversion is essentially a psychological process of unifying a divided self.[9]

During the twentieth century, it is true, conversion has not consistently been a primary concern of theologians. But in recent years many theologians, interested in taking the concrete experiential dimension of Christian life very seriously, have begun to pay special attention to the personal experience of conversion.[10] In fact, some prominent theologians have recommended that we look to conversion as the basis of theology. Bernard Lonergan, for example, has proposed that reflection upon conversion can provide an appropriate foundation for a contemporary empirical theology.[11]

While this suggestion is valuable insofar as it would root theological reflection firmly in concrete personal experience, it is not without difficulties. Primary among these difficulties is the ambiguity of "conversion." The meaning of conversion has never been particularly clear, but today the problem is compounded. For just when theologians have begun to take conversion seriously as a theological reality, conversion phenomena are blossoming across the religious countryside in ever greater profusion and variety. Conversion stories have become newspaper and magazine staples over the last decade: a "born again" President and his faith-healing sister; famous convicts who are "convicted" once again in prison—this time by Jesus; Christian entrepreneurs who bring their religious zeal to the marketplace; cult members kidnaped by de-programmers; the child whose faith demands the rejection of life-saving therapy. All these are converts, as are those who give up comfortable lives to devote themselves to the oppressed of the world. Indeed, conversion is a highly confusing and controversial issue today largely because the term "conversion" refers not to one reality but to an enormously wide range of very different human realities.

In a very ordinary sense, conversion can mean the social fact of someone joining a traditional Christian church. Conversion from one Christian church to another has been questioned as the goal of a church's missionary enterprise in an ecumenical age. But these conversions obviously continue, as do the conversions of non-Christians to Christianity. In the Roman Catholic Church, for example, fewer conversions may be occasioned by a young man's desire to marry a "Catholic girl," but John Henry Newman and Dorothy Day continue as models for many Catholic converts. Of course, the conversion door swings both ways, and others have found a model in Charles Davis.[12]

Within a church, conversion can also mean a Christian's deeply emotional experience of being "born again" in turning to Jesus as a personal Savior. Today, sophisticated Christian media campaigns of buttons, bumper stickers, and billboards try to do for mass audiences what fundamental Christian churches have long been trying to do in simpler and smaller ways: bring about a sense of forgiveness for sins and personal salvation through profession of faith in Jesus Christ.

Conversion also means the just and loving dedication of one's life to one's neighbor called for in the Gospels. And today, when some Christians hear this call as a demand to work for the liberation of the oppressed through the transformation of unjust social, economic, and political structures, others insist that Jesus was no social revolutionary but the proclaimer of a kingdom not of this world. So Christians disagree radically over the social relevance of Jesus' call to conversion. Is conversion entirely a personal experience of the heart, or does it have an essential social dimension? Is personal conversion authentic if it does not work for the transformation of unjust social structures? Is the transformation of unjust social structures possible without personal conversion? What is the proper relationship between these personal and social transformations?

Again, conversion may not lead to following a "way" modeled on the life and teachings of Jesus at all, but to a way or discipline of some other spiritual master or tradition. Krishna Consciousness and the Transcendental Meditation of the Maharishi are only the best known of a vast array of choices available to the spiritual seeker.[13]

Some of these ways, along with groups like the Children of God and Sun Myung Moon's Unification Church, have aroused the greatest controversy and confusion over conversion.[14] They have done this by giving conversion the added implications of a cult because of their total (some would say, blind) commitment to an authority figure. So there are not only questionable methods of conversion, but also responding attempts by families to forcibly "de-program" their converted children, whom they see as "brainwashed" victims.[15]

In the midst of this confusion and controversy, therefore, when a theologian proposes that reflection on conversion can provide theology with an adequate foundation, the reader quite rightly asks, "Reflection on what kind of conversion?" Among all the species flourishing in today's culture, what kind of conversion is the theologian recommending as the experiential foundation of a contemporary theology? Very simply, the question is, just what is religious conversion?[16] And perhaps most importantly, what, among the mystifying array of competing claims, are the criteria for discerning authentic conversion?

These are among the most fundamental theological questions of our time, but they certainly do not represent the first attempt to understand the reality of conversion. So they must be raised within a context of earlier interpretations—interpretations which have inevitably added a further set of questions to the conversion issue.

Are conversions sudden events or gradual processes? Is conversion a single, once-and-for-all event in a person's life? Or may a person experience two, three, or more conversions at different points in life?

Is religious conversion primarily an adolescent phenomenon, as William James and other early psychological investigators proposed? Or is mid-life a more likely period for a radical personal conversion, as the Jungian perspective suggests?[17] Is there some context in which these different views can be understood as compatible and complementary? Is religious conversion always a positive experience which contributes to personal growth and maturity, or is conversion sometimes regressive?[18] If the latter, is it possible, even necessary, to distinguish between descriptive and normative meanings of conversion? For example, given the recruitment practices of many cults, in what sense can commitment to these groups be called a religious conversion?

From this psychological perspective, perhaps the basic and most important question emerges as: Is there such a thing as an essentially religious conversion? If so, how can it be distinguished? Is there a difference, for example, between an essentially religious conversion on the one hand, and a religiously-colored psychological conversion which brings some unity and harmony to a troubled person's life, on the other? Will even a genuinely religious conversion be linked to some particular psychological problem or crisis in a person's life? For instance, are religious conversions to be expected at critical points in adult life like those described in *Passages*?[19]

The same kind of questions are involved in the distinction commonly made between religious and moral conversions. Does this distinction have a biblical basis? If the "unjust man" is converted from sin, from what is Job, the "just man," converted? And is there a distinctively Christian conversion? If so, how is it related to a more general religious or moral conversion? Does every Christian experience a Christian conversion? *Should* every Christian experience such a conversion?[20] These are just some of the ways in which the basic question of the nature and criteria of religious conversion can be specified.

The conviction underlying this study is that any foundation for a contemporary theology rooted in conversion will be only as solid and stable as the answers to these questions are precise and profound. The aim of this study, then, is to clarify the issue of authentic religious conversion by analyzing the human person's basic conversion possibilities. The primary point is not to survey the various manifestations of conversion in contemporary life, but to work toward a normative interpretation of conversion.

Such an analysis of basic human conversion possibilities can be carried out successfully, however, only within the context of an adequate fundamental interpretation of the human person, especially of that dimension of the person oriented toward value and realized in decision. For even a preliminary and tentative notion of conversion suggests a change based on a decision about the fundamental values in a person's life.

Traditionally this value-decision dimension of a person has been designated in western culture by the metaphor of "conscience."[21] Thus, the basic strategy of this study is the construction of an adequate interpretation of conscience as the necessary context for attempting a fundamental understanding of personal conversion.

CONSCIENCE

Conscience, of course, has had no less an ambiguous career than conversion. While it has not been featured in as many sensational headlines in recent years, conscience, and especially the question of its freedom, is never out of view. The issue may be the legitimacy of conscientious objection to military action, Amnesty International's concern for the fate of prisoners of conscience, or the freedom of religious conscience sometimes invoked in the current abortion controversy.

But if conscience has caused its share of controversy in the political life of western society from Antigone to Thomas More and from Anne Hutchinson to Solzhenitsyn, it has also been at least as troublesome in the theoretical realm. For, while conscience has never lacked commentators, as a group its commentators, psychological as well as philosophical and theological, have been notable, above all, for their lack of consensus on just what conscience is.[22] It has been suggested, in fact, that conscience suffers from the same social disease that Augustine diagnosed in the case of "time": overfamiliarity.[23] Everyone knows what conscience is until asked for a definition of *exactly* what it is. This is where the confusion begins.

As is often the case when a definition is requested, what seems obvious and simple enough one minute can become rather complicated and confusing the next. Still, definitions come forth, usually focusing on one particular element in the complex reality of conscience. For some, conscience is identified with a specific human power, or faculty, or act, be the act one of direct intuition or of more complex judgment. For others, conscience is simply a vague sense of guilt, or just another word for the unconscious superego of psychoanalytic theory. For some, conscience is innate, for others, it is the result of the socialization process. To appreciate the enormous variety of meanings in English usage alone, one need only turn to the two-page entry in the *Oxford English Dictionary*, which offers the nicely understated judgment that "opinions as to the nature, function, and authority of conscience are widely divergent, varying from the conception of the mere exercise of the ordinary judgment on moral questions, to that of an infallible guide of conduct, a sort of deity within us."

Diversity on some minor or obscure moral point may be taken in stride. There is reason for some concern, however, in the face of so little common understanding of such a fundamental moral reality as conscience, which all acknowledge, and which many regard as the final and supreme authority in the moral life. "Follow your conscience" has become for many something of an absolute in an otherwise relative world. Conscience has always been normative within Protestant Christianity, where it was given foundational status in the program of the Reformers. In recent years, moreover, the central role of conscience as the "subjective norm" of the moral life has been effectively acknowledged in the teaching of Roman Catholic Christianity. Despite the Catholic insistence on hierarchical authority, the Second Vatican Council recognized conscience as "the most secret core and sanctuary of a man," where "he is alone with God, whose voice echoes in his depths."[24]

Given the prominent status and fundamental moral authority accorded to conscience, then, it is crucial to understand precisely what is meant by this conscience which is appealed to so often as the last (or, sometimes, first and only) moral word. If few contemporary Christians would be willing to accept "spontaneous personal feelings" as an adequate definition of conscience, fewer still would agree that conscience is a "command to unquestioning obedience to authority." But what *does* constitute an adequate understanding of conscience for contemporary Christian life? This is the question which will focus the present study's attempt to construct an interpretative context for assessing basic human conversion possibilities.

Centuries of persistent use in both Christian and secular western culture, by scholars and simple folk alike, have established a primacy and centrality of place for the term "conscience" in the moral vocabulary and, therefore, life of the contemporary Christian. The theologian ignores this fact at the risk of abstracting ethics from concrete Christian experience. Despite the term's serious difficulties, then, "conscience" will be employed as a fundamental category here in order to maintain continuity with the history of Christian moral experience and ethical reflection.[25]

Thus, the strategy of focusing on "conscience" is a practical one. The point is not that "conscience" has some intrinsic significance for the Christian life, nor that it is an absolutely indispensable category in theological ethics. Rather, it is simply a matter of recognizing the fact that, whatever philosophers and theologians may think about it, the term "conscience" is embedded in concrete Christian living. It is here to stay for a good while, and thus must be dealt with clearly and systematically. Still, if "conscience" is durable and pervasive, its meaning is ambiguous and its theoretical status problematic.

Any new attempt to deal with the ambiguity of conscience must take into account both its historical development and its present theoretical discussion. The next several pages, therefore, will map a route through some of the significant recent literature which has brought reflection on conscience to its present point. By attending to the strengths as well as the weaknesses of the present theoretical discussion about conscience, it will be possible to specify the precise contribution which this study will make to a more profound and comprehensive understanding of both conscience and conversion.

The problematic status of conscience in contemporary Christian theology has been indicated with the starkest possible clarity by Paul Lehmann: "Ethical theory must either dispose of the conscience altogether or completely transform the interpretation of its ethical nature, function, and significance." After some three hundred pages of historical analysis in Lehmann's 1963 *Ethics in a Christian Context*, conscience emerges as the central question for contemporary ethics. Lehmann's diagnosis is pointed and his prescription abrupt: "The semantic, philosophical and theological pilgrimage of conscience begins with the Greek tragedians of the fifth century before Christ and ends with Sigmund Freud. It is a moving, tortuous record of decline and fall which forces upon us in our time the frankest possible facing of a sharp alternative: either 'do the conscience over' or 'do the conscience in'!"[26]

For Lehmann, two key points highlight this history of decline and fall. First, Kant replaced the classical human significance of conscience as the judging "link between the internal nature of man and the order in which his life is sustained" with the "legal significance of conscience as an internal [juridical] voice of an external authority." And it is this authoritarian conscience which ethically is so conspicuously unpersuasive today. But if Kant is responsible for the decline of conscience, Lehmann argues that credit for its fall must go to Freud, who exchanged conscience's ethical role for a psychoanalytic one by identifying conscience with the negative, aggressive censoring function of the superego, which he viewed as ethically impotent and useless.[27]

Lehmann sees this fall as a possible prelude to conscience rising again, on the condition that conscience, now freed from its dehumanizing context, can discover a context in which its ethical potential could be realized. In Lehmann's view the appropriate context is the *koinonia*, the community of Christian believers, for here conscience is transformed theonomously to forge a "link between what God is doing in the world and man's free obedience to that activity."[28]

Lehmann makes a persuasive argument for the centrality of conscience in the Christian life, as well as for its need of theonomous transformation in the context of the *koinonia*. Still, his attempt to "do conscience over" results in a radically inadequate understanding of the very reality of conscience which stands in need of a transforming context. The difficulty is that Lehmann never goes beyond a *descriptive* approach to the phenomenon of conscience. With Paul and the Reformers he helpfully associates conscience with the "heart" of which the Old Testament and Jesus speak. But after the spell of its affective coloring and poetic overtones fades, there remains the task of specifying the precise nature of this heart which, as he says, "knows by a kind of sensitivity at once central and total which marks the person as a whole."[29] Such a task requires a cognitional theory capable of providing an *explanatory* understanding of conscience in its relation to the full human person. In short, conscience needs a *philosophical* interpretation as well as a theological context.

One clear indication of Lehmann's failure to really "do conscience over" in the sense of providing it with an adequately foundational interpretation is the basic ambiguity of a recent book by C. Ellis Nelson, *Don't Let Your Conscience Be Your Guide*.

Writing fifteen years after Lehmann, Nelson is thoroughly familiar with his work, and shares his basic interest in the Christian transformation of conscience. In Lehmann's language, Nelson sets out not to "do conscience in" but to "do it over" by explicating the possibility of its "inversion" (conversion) through faith. For Nelson, only the faith received from God through an experience with Christ constitutes an authentic Christian guide.

Nelson's first step is to show that conscience, which he understands as the childhood internalization of negative and positive social norms represented by the Freudian superego and ego-ideal, is an unreliable and inadequate norm for Christian life. He then attempts to "do conscience over" by showing how faith can bring about an "inversion" of conscience, in which the "positive conscience" (ego-ideal) becomes dominant and is transformed through attachment to Christ. Nelson has hardly mentioned this "inversion of conscience," however, when "conscience" virtually disappears from his analysis in favor of faith and the "conscious I." In effect, then, conscience is not so much inverted by faith as replaced by it. The conscience which Nelson, as Lehmann before him, set out to "do over" has been effectively, if unintentionally, "done in."

The problem is not that Nelson has insufficient appreciation of the importance of conscience for the Christian. Indeed, he asserts that because "conscience . . . penetrates all our decisions and ceaselessly monitors our thoughts and wishes . . . we who claim the Christian religion must have some idea of how it relates to conscience, or our faith will not be connected to the practical issues of life." The difficulty, rather, is that from the start Nelson locks himself into a radically inadequate understanding of conscience by identifying it with a dimension of the self-system outside the "conscious center of the self" (i.e., the superego and ego-ideal).[30]

When Nelson then comes to speak of the conscience being "turned upside down" through experience with Christ, he seems to realize implicitly that conscience as the internalized social norms of childhood is simply incapable of being transformed by the fully personal reality of faith. So he quietly drops, not only this inadequate understanding of conscience, but conscience altogether, and shifts his attention to the more suitable "conscious I," without offering any adequate explanation of the relationship between the conscious and unconscious dimensions of personal moral life. Nelson has been aiming at Lehmann's theonomously transformed conscience, then, but discovers that his understanding of conscience will not bear the weight of such transformation. He has correctly rejected the Freudian superego and ego-ideal as inadequate Christian guides, and, from a practical perspective, he has accurately recognized the need of establishing a truly Christian understanding of conscience, but he has not provided one. His intuition is correct, but he has no theoretical interpretation of the human person powerful and comprehensive enough (1) to properly relativize the moral significance of the unconscious, or (2) to take full account of the moral dimension of the conscious "I," as well as its possibilities of transformation through faith, or (3) to explain all this precisely in terms of conscience. A major aim of the present study is to do just that—in short to "do conscience over," without ambiguity, by providing just such an interpretation of the human person.

If the ambiguity of Nelson's work makes it clear that a successful interpretation of conscience requires an adequate starting point, a recent study by Daniel Maguire, *The Moral Choice*, goes a long way toward providing such a starting point.

While Nelson subverts his own attempt to transform conscience by taking the unconscious processes of the superego and ego-ideal as his basic understanding of conscience, Maguire unambiguously opts for the conscious self as the key to an adequate interpretation of conscience.

Maguire does not develop an interpretation of conscience in *The Moral Choice;* his primary purpose is to present a theory of moral knowledge, an ethical method. The elements of his ethical method are essentially the personal and communal resources which individuals bring to moral situations, including an exhaustive questioning process, principles, reason, affectivity, and creative imagination. After completing a thorough analysis of these and the many other components of his method, Maguire looks back and asks why such an obviously important moral reality as conscience is not among them. His answer is that conscience is not an element in method; conscience, rather, is the *whole* of ethical method as embodied in a valuing person. Conscience is ethical method incarnate.

For Maguire, then, conscience is quite simply "*the conscious self as attuned to moral values and disvalues in the concrete.*" It is the person, the morally conscious self, "in his actual state of sensitivity or insensitivity to the worth of persons and their environment." According to this view, conscience is grounded in the common, human "appreciation of the value of the self, the value of others, and an awareness of the connection between the two."[31] Each conscience grows out of this "foundational moral experience" in its own unique fashion, according to the various concrete ways that cultural/social/interpersonal factors influence and shape personal history. Conscience, then, is neither innate nor artificially added on from the outside. It is, rather, the personal, historically conditioned result of an individual's interaction with other naturally social beings who share a common core of the foundational moral experience of value.

As such, "conscience is not so much one of the parts of ethics as it is that which ethics should serve, critique, and seek to perfect. Ethics should seek to purify not just reason but all that a morally evaluating self is . . . and that means more than reason. It means conscience with all that that entails."[32]

Although Maguire does not offer an explicitly developed interpretation of conscience, he does contribute to such an interpretation by locating its appropriate starting point. This study will attempt to make some significant advance toward a fuller interpretation of conscience by explicating the most fundamental dimensions of the "all" that conscience entails, including the question of its development, its relationship to the unconscious, and its structured drive for self-transcendence.

Despite the real value of Maguire's approach to conscience in terms of the conscious self, its deliberately limited character becomes apparent when compared with the view presented by John Macquarrie in *Three Issues in Ethics*. Like Maguire, Macquarrie offers no formal, developed interpretation of conscience. But his brilliant sketch of conscience does outline some of the most important elements which any adequate interpretation must include.

Macquarrie suggests a basic threefold notion of conscience, distinguishing the following "levels": (1) concrete deliberation on a specific moral question in a particular situation; (2) knowledge of general moral principles; (3) a fundamental mode of self-awareness. To these he adds knowledge of a particular code or set of rules, which mediates between the first and second levels.[33]

In terms of these levels or dimensions of conscience, Maguire's understanding is focused primarily on the first level. Conscience is the conscious self precisely as existentially engaged in concrete moral deliberation. Of course, Maguire's analysis also makes it clear that principles are central to ethical method, and thus to ethical method as embodied, i.e., conscience.

It is at Macquarrie's third level of conscience, the "fundamental mode of self-awareness," that the limitations of Maguire's approach become apparent. Because Maguire discusses conscience only as it is related to his analysis of ethical method, his "conscious self" is quite appropriately presented not in terms of an "awareness of self" but as an "intentionality" directed toward objects of deliberation.

Maguire's approach suits his specific purpose quite well, and does make the contribution of restoring the conscious self in a very concrete way to the center of the discussion about conscience. Still, if one is to interpret conscience accurately and fully, the conscious "awareness of self" must also be revealed as the dynamic and foundational core of conscience at the center of the morally deliberating conscious self.

For Macquarrie, the basic function of conscience is self-disclosure. Specifically, conscience discloses the "gap between our actual selves and that image of ourselves that we already have in virtue of the 'natural inclination' toward the fulfillment of man's end." Thus, radically understood as a fundamental mode of self-awareness, conscience is not only a disclosure; it is also, as Macquarrie insists with Heidegger, a call or summons. It is a call to authentic personhood, a summons to that "full humanity of which we already have some idea or image because of the very fact that we are human at all, and that our nature is to exist, to go out beyond where we are at any given moment."[34] It is precisely conscience in this fundamental sense of a radical drive for self-transcending authenticity which this study will explicate as a context for understanding the basic conversion possibilities of the human person.

The great virtue of Macquarrie's view is that it identifies conscience not only with moral deliberation, but at the deepest level with the call to authentic personhood. To recognize a gap between the self one is and the self one could and, indeed, ought to be is to recognize the need for change. For some, the change may be only one of *degree*, a question of further growth or development. But, for others, the required change will be much more fundamental. At the heart of the Christian Gospel is the call to a radical conversion, a change not simply of degree, but of basic *direction*, a fundamental reorientation of the total self, a personal revolution.

Macquarrie does not discuss conversion himself, but by recognizing the depth dimension of conscience, he opens the possibility of grasping the intrinsic connection between conscience and conversion.[35] From one side of this connection, the claim has already been made that a foundational understanding of conversion requires a fully adequate interpretation of conscience, of the valuing dimension of the human person. At this point, it should be clear that this claim is rooted in the judgment that a conversion is authentic insofar as it is a response to a fundamental personal demand, which, because conscious, both is, and is revealed by, conscience in its most radical meaning.

From the other side of the connection, it has now become apparent that an understanding of conscience in its depths points to the necessity of radical conversion. If we are to understand conscience in its fullness, then, and especially as a norm for authentic decisions, we must understand the conversion which it demands of the personal subject, as well as the way the conversion, in turn, transforms the subject's orientation, and thus conscience. In short, conscience and conversion can be adequately understood only in relationship to each other.

If we begin with conscience, we can discover that it points to conversion, which in turn demands a life of fidelity to conscience. If we begin by trying to understand conversion, we realize the necessity of a fundamental interpretation of conscience, which in turn points to conversion. This, then, is the virtuous circle of conscience and conversion which the following chapters will explicate in detail, while presenting a distinctive interpretation of each of these fundamental human realities. But before proceeding any further, it is important to explain the meaning of "authenticity" as it is used in the present context. This explanation will lead through "responsibility" directly into the study's basic thesis on self-transcendence.

AUTHENTICITY AND RESPONSIBILITY

It was Lionel Trilling who pointed out how "authenticity" emerged during this century, especially in existentialist thought, as the dominant criterion of the moral life. Though more demanding than the notion of sincerity which it replaced, authenticity, as Trilling has shown, is not entirely unambiguous, sometimes giving moral authority even to such traditionally condemned realities as violence and unreason. The difficulty with authenticity is that it is not a criterion of the moral life, as Trilling suggested it is, but is an ideal which stands in need of a criterion.[36]

This difficulty accounts in large part for the emergence in recent decades of "responsibility" as a dominant concept in philosophical and theological considerations of the moral life, principally in the seminal work of H. Richard Niebuhr.[37] For, without rejecting the gains realized in the ideal of authenticity, the focus on responsibility attempts to reestablish concern for the "other" as a criterion at the center of moral consciousness. Though fundamentally arbitrary, the ideal of authenticity did recognize that one cannot be true to one's self simply as a means to, and for the purpose of, avoiding falsehood to others (as Polonius classically expressed the ideal of sincerity). The concept of "responsibility" goes beyond this insight in its realization that one can only be true to one's self insofar as one is true to others. One can be true to one's self, in other words, only insofar as one reaches out and goes beyond one's self in responding to the values in each human situation in a manner that is at once free and creative, critical and fitting. Insofar as a person goes beyond, transcends himself or herself in response to value, then, authenticity is not arbitrary. The *criterion* of human authenticity, therefore, is the very *self-transcendence* which is effected in the realization of value through critical understanding, responsible decision, and generous love.

If "self-transcendence" is to function well as a criterion, however, it must be specified precisely, for the term is used in many different ways, some of them quite vague and mysterious. In this study "self-transcendence" refers to the threefold achievement, just mentioned, of "moving beyond one's own self," cognitively, morally, and affec-tively. For example, self-transcendence is realized when one person, truly understanding another's need, reaches out and, in a warm em-brace, makes a serious commitment of support. Such self-transcend-ence must be distinguished very clearly from both self-fulfillment and self-sacrifice.[38]

SELF-FULFILLMENT, SELF-SACRIFICE, AND SELF-TRANSCENDENCE

Self-Fulfillment

If this is the century of the ego, as Norman Mailer suggested some dozen years ago, it might well have reached its culmination during the 1970's, the period Tom Wolfe has tagged for posterity as the "me" dec-ade. This was the time when self-fulfillment, self-enhancement, self-promotion, self-liberation were promoted from the paperback racks of every supermarket in America.

This contemporary search for self-fulfillment has more recently become a favorite target of social and cultural critics. Christopher Lasch's devastating critique of what he calls *The Culture of Narcissism* is only the best known of several attacks.[39] Paul Vitz, in his *Psychology as Religion*, argues that humanistic psychologists Abraham Maslow, Erich Fromm, Carl Rogers, and Rollo May have supplied the theoretical jus-tification for what he calls "The Cult of Self-Worship."[40] And, most recently, social researcher Daniel Yankelovich points to the inherent contradiction he finds in the search for self-fulfillment—a search he characterizes as authentic grass-roots experimentation, involving in one way or another perhaps as many as eighty percent of adult Amer-icans. While the traditional ethic of self-denial and sacrifice has been replaced by an ethic that denies people nothing, Yankelovich found in his interviews that "many truly committed self-fulfillment seekers fo-cus so sharply on their needs that instead of achieving the more inti-mate relationships they desire, they grow farther apart from others."[41] This reflects something of "the narcissistic character disorder" of cur-rent psychiatric literature—the self-centered affliction, as Robert Coles describes it, of "one whose central, controlling ways of getting on give evidence of a strong avoidance of lasting attachments to other people, accompanied often by a hunger for just such human bonds. . . . "[42]

Insofar as critiques of self-fulfillment are aimed at the pseudo-humanism of consumer oriented "pop psychology," they seem entirely appropriate. For while the explicit goals of many self-fulfillment therapies appear humanistic in their interpersonal and social orientations, the implicit understanding of the human person informing the starting points of these approaches is self-destructive in its naive individualism. The self of "pop psychology" is essentially a bag of desires, and self-realization means fulfilling as many of these desires as possible. "You can never do enough for yourself." The pervasiveness of this view in the mass media would be laughable if it were not tragic. People throw themselves into intense, self-absorbed navel gazing, run off in every direction (sometimes at once) to gratify their every impulse, and end up deeply frustrated. Yankelovich cites countless divorces and wrongheaded career changes as part of the confusing fall-out from the very risky search for self-fulfillment. Unfortunately, people fail to perceive the paradoxical truth that authentic realization of their deepest human desires occurs only when they turn their primary attention from their own interests and desires and genuinely involve themselves in the needs and desires of others. Everyone would be a big-game hunter in the jungle of life; to appreciate that the prey of self-realization and happiness is lost in the kill is a difficult lesson.

Self-Sacrifice

The "pop-psychology" of self-fulfillment, of course, is only the latest edition of the guide for the self-seeker. Through the ages there have been as many versions as there are forms of self-delusion. And the traditional Christian response has always been the one rooted in the Gospel injunction to renounce oneself and take up one's cross in following Jesus (Mk 8:34).

Unfortunately, the Gospel call to follow Jesus has too often been misunderstood as requiring the sacrifice or denial of the self's authentic realization. Indeed, several recent studies argue that this misinterpretation of the Gospel has been involved in legitimating the traditional relegation of women to subordinate roles of passive, obedient service: self-sacrifice is holy; self-assertion is sinful.[43] It takes the artistry of a Mary Gordon to begin to do justice to the ambiguity of this reality. The heroine of her *Final Payments*, Isabel Moore, has sacrificed her young adulthood to the care of her invalid father, and does not regret a moment of it. Though adolescent guilt over a discovered fling with a boyfriend plays a key part in her relationship to her father, Isabel looks back on her sacrifice "not with self-pity but with extreme pride." Gordon, in fact, sees sacrifice rooted in affection as having an immense importance in life, though she is at the same time deeply intrigued by the phenomenon of otherwise powerful women who suddenly buckle to the authority of a male.[44]

If a misunderstood sacrifice of self has proved devastating for centuries in the lives of women, the effects on the preaching of the Gospel have been equally severe. For many men throughout the western world, Christianity is a "woman's religion." And what else can a patriarchal society expect after using a distorted Gospel to glorify women in a state of passive, obedient subjection for so long? Beyond male and female relationships, the distortion of the Gospel has been extended as an ideological justification to every situation of oppressive servitude. As long as this perversion of the Gospel for the justification of oppression continues, Nietzsche's judgment will stand: Christianity is a religion for slaves.

This is precisely the kind of interpretation of self-sacrifice which must be rejected as anti-Christian. Jesus calls us to loving service of the neighbor as friend, not to self-destructive servitude to a master as slave.[45] Indeed, no authentic Christian interpretation can recommend the denial or sacrifice of the self as the conscious, creative, critical, responsible, free, and loving personal subject. Such a policy would have Jesus being followed by an army of robots. No, to follow Jesus genuinely in his life for others requires the commitment of the very self such sacrifice would destroy. To follow Jesus, of course, means to live one's life as authentically as he lived his. It has nothing to do with being a "follower," everything to do with being a leader. A reader of the Gospels need not "psychologize" Jesus to realize that the Christian life of creative and responsible love requires courageous assertiveness as much as realistic humility.

What, then, is an authentic Christian understanding of self-sacrifice, if it is not the sacrifice of the self? Quite simply, Christian self-sacrifice consists in the denial of all those (otherwise perhaps quite legitimate) desires, wishes, and interests of the self which interfere with the singleminded commitment to follow Jesus in love. Such commitment demands not the sacrifice of the self or its authentic realization, but the sacrifice by the self of anything which stands in the way of loving the neighbor (in the extreme, even the sacrifice of life itself). From the viewpoint of Christian commitment to the neighbor and genuine self-realization, the "to-be-filled-bag-of-desires-self" of "pop psychology" is really a bag of snakes. The list of possible desires is endless, and particular desires are often mutually contradictory. Many of the goods sought by seekers of self-fulfillment, of course, are not only legitimate but positively worthwhile. Part of the grace of the Gospel, however, is the insight that the search for such genuinely personal goods through focusing on the self is fundamentally illusory. Indeed, it is precisely the renunciation of such fulfillment-seeking that allows the possibility of authentic self-realization in a loving service which makes no demands and draws no lines, the service to all which Jesus calls us to join him in.

Self-Transcendence

If self-fulfillment and self-sacrifice, as commonly understood, are deadly for the authentic Christian life of loving service, a living image has been drawn from the tradition by such contemporary theologians as Reinhold Niebuhr, Paul Tillich, Karl Rahner, Bernard Lonergan, John Macquarrie and David Tracy: the dynamic exigence of self-transcendence.[46]

As an image suggestive of the authentic dynamism of the Christian spiritual life, self-transcendence stands in total opposition to the image of self-sacrifice understood as a denial, renunciation, abnegation, repudiation, sacrifice, or other negation of the true self. Only a self affirmed in the reality of its subjectivity, and realized in its essential potentiality for objectivity, is capable of transcending itself. In the simplest terms, without a transcending self, there is no self-transcendence. The self is not negated through transcendence; rather, it is realized in its authentic being. Self-transcendence is authentic self-realization.[47] Understood as a sacrifice of the self in its essential dynamism for an intelligent and responsible life of loving service, the image of self-sacrifice must be rejected by an understanding of the Gospel in terms of self-transcendence.

At the same time, as a critical response to value, self-transcendence rejects the illusion that narcissistic self-fulfillment constitutes self-realization. It stands firmly against any image of self-fulfillment which focuses on the self as a collection of desires to be fulfilled. Whatever the appearance of surface activity may be, the image of the self whose desires are to be fulfilled is essentially a passive receptacle, a self whose happiness consists in being filled "to the brim." Even if this image were accurate, in a limited world of finite persons such a self would condemn most people to anxious frustration. The cruel truth, of course, is that from the point of view of fulfilling desires the self is not a receptacle, but a bottomless pit. Thus even the most talented and successful elite will find only endless frustration in the search for self-fulfillment. In contrast, the self implicit in the image of self-transcend-ence, exactly the opposite of a passive receptacle, is a dynamic spring, a self that is realized only in its active movement beyond itself. Freed from the illusion of quantitative fulfillment, such a self senses the peace of authentic realization in the very activity of realistic knowing, responsible choosing, and genuine loving.

Like the Gospel, the image of self-transcendence suggests the par-adoxical view that authentic self-realization results not from a self-cen-tered effort to fulfill one's desires, but from a movement *beyond* oneself in an attempt to realize the good of others. Indeed, such realization of the self through transcendence is a form of self-fulfillment. But it is a fulfillment of the fundamental desire for truth, value, and love con-stitutive of us as distinctively personal beings. While its fulfillment in self-transcendence brings a sense of peaceful happiness, the very na-ture of this basic human desire defies any self-centered striving for happiness through fulfillment. In fact, the fulfillment proper to the radical personal desire or drive for self-transcendence can require that one "empty" oneself in the sense of sacrificing the fulfillment of oth-erwise legitimate desires. In the ultimate case, as we have already noted, this self-emptying can mean the giving of one's very life for the neighbor. One will save the life of one's true self, the Gospel makes clear, only if he or she is ready to give up everything else, even life itself, in loving service of the neighbor.

Though self-transcendence has been developed most extensively as an image of authentic personhood by theologians, its reality can be found in the works of many psychologists, most explicitly, perhaps, in that of Viktor Frankl. Frankl discusses self-transcendence throughout his many works, but even in his early treatment of the fundamental human dynamism, *Man's Search for Meaning*, we find an arrestingly di-rect statement of one of this book's basic theses: "Human existence is essentially self-transcendence rather than self-actualization. Self-ac-tualization is not a possible aim at all, for the simple reason that the more a man would strive for it, the more he would miss it." For only to the extent that a person is committed to life's meaning, Frankl as-serts, is he or she actualized. In other words, "self-actualization cannot be attained if it is made an end in itself, but only as a side effect of self-transcendence."[48]

Even when the reality of self-transcendence is not named as such, it can play a central role in the interpretation of human existence. From the particular perspective of Christian spirituality, Henri Nou-wen conveys the dynamism of the different dimensions of self-tran-scendence through the image of "reaching out." For Nouwen, the spiritual life is the relationship between three constant movements of reaching out: to ourselves (moving from loneliness to solitude), to others (moving from hostility to hospitality), and to God (moving from illusion to prayer).[49]

Perhaps the most detailed and comprehensive articulation of self-transcendence is that of Bernard Lonergan. Over the course of a professional lifetime Lonergan has attempted to map the route of self-transcendence in its many dimensions.[50] This is not the place to examine his charts in detail, but a brief reconnaissance of the main lines of Lonergan's analysis will throw some preliminary light on the reality of self-transcendence which underpins this study's interpretation of conscience and conversion.

For Lonergan, self-transcendence occurs in our effective response to the radical drive, the dynamic exigence of the human spirit for meaning, truth, value, and love. Though single in source and ultimate goal, this questioning drive of the human spirit manifests itself in multiple, interconnected questions: the drive for understanding seeks meaning in questions for intelligence; but not any meaning, for once attained, meaning is critically scrutinized by the drive for truth in questions for reflection heading toward realistic judgment. And when understanding and judgment are within a practical pattern oriented toward action, there follows the further moral question for deliberation: given my judgment of the situation and required action, what am *I* going to do about it? Finally, this practical questioning oriented toward action occurs within—and is permeated by—a matrix of affectivity which must be strong enough to support the required action over the obstacles of conflicting interests. What, in the last analysis, am I going to commit myself to in love?

In this view, every achievement of creative understanding, realistic judgment, responsible choice, and genuine love is an instance of self-transcendence. Among all the possible realizations of human potential, such cognitive, moral, and affective self-transcendence is the criterion of authentic self-realization. The Gospel demand calling us to intelligent, responsible, loving service of the neighbor requires no more and no less than the fulfillment of this fundamental personal drive for self-transcendence. As the criterion of personal authenticity, self-transcending love is also the norm by which every other personal concern, interest, need, desire or wish must be judged—and, if necessary, sacrificed. Fidelity to this law of the human spirit, this radical dynamism for self-transcending love, sums up the demand of the Christian life because it is a response to the divine within us—God's gift of love.

In contrast to interpretations of conscience embedded in essentially compartmentalized or reductionistic views, an approach to conscience deep and comprehensive enough to allow a full understanding of conversion must be developed within a holistic and emergent interpretation of the personal subject; in short, within a theory of self-transcendence. Indeed, conscience must be understood, not only as the morally conscious self or as a fundamental mode of self-awareness, but precisely as the dynamic core of conscious subjectivity which constitutes the very being of the person, driving him or her toward the authenticity of self-transcendence. Conscience and conversion, then, can be most adequately understood as intrinsically connected in a normative theory of self-transcendence.

CONSCIENCE AND DEVELOPMENT

Because the great advances in psychology of the last half century have added enormously to our knowledge of moral-religious consciousness, demonstrating conclusively that it must be understood developmentally, Chapters 2 and 3 will root this study's interpretation of conscience and conversion in a psychological context of personal development drawn from the research findings and theories of Erik Erikson, Jean Piaget, Lawrence Kohlberg, James Fowler and Robert Kegan. They will show how these psychological theories implicitly use self-transcendence as a criterion of mature personal development. They will also argue that these psychological theories establish the normative *meaning* of self-transcendence in a concrete and especially illuminating fashion, and thus provide an integrated model of self-transcending subjectivity.

Erikson makes a significant contribution to the understanding of personal subjectivity by focusing his developmental theory on the reality of psychosocial identity. The issue of personal identity will therefore be the principal point of interest in a consideration of Erikson's eight stages of the life cycle. These stages will be examined as moments in a process of self-transcendence, a process headed normatively toward the personal realizations of identity (fidelity), intimacy (love), generativity (care), and integrity (wisdom). Erikson's psychoanalytic view will also make possible a critical assessment of the relationship between the superego and conscience.[51]

Piaget's major contribution to an interpretation of conscience lies in his analysis of cognitive development from infancy through young adulthood. Building on Piaget's stage theory, this study will explain how developing cognitive abilities gradually effect a liberating movement from radical cognitive egocentrism toward the self-transcendence of critical, realistic judgment.[52]

The psychosocial (affective) and cognitive dimensions of the person will then be brought together in specifically moral consciousness. It will be seen how the stages of moral judgment in Kohlberg's theory also move normatively in the direction of self-transcendence—from egocentric hedonism toward the true conscience of personal, universal principles.[53]

With Fowler we will examine how the personal subject's faithing— way of interpreting and relating to the ultimate conditions of existence—also develops normatively from an egocentric Intuitive-Projective Faith to a self-transcending Universalizing Faith.[54]

Finally, in Kegan's attempt to establish the fundamental unity of the self that is developing, we will see the possibility of integrating the affective, cognitive, moral, and faith dimensions of the personal subject in the radical meaning-constitutive activity that is the very motion of the self's development.[55]

Taking account of the fact that relatively few people ever reach Kohlberg's highest stage of principled judgment will give reason to turn to a philosophical analysis of moral consciousness, especially of the possibility of moral conversion. Thus the developmental theories will not only provide a model of self-transcending subjectivity, but also establish a radically developmental interpretation of conscience, and raise the question of the relationship between personal development and conversion.

CONVERSION AND DEVELOPMENT

A brief, proleptic consideration of the last four crises of Erikson's life cycle will provide a context for suggesting in outline form some of the relationships between development and conversion which we will be pursuing in Chapters 4 through 6.

First, Erikson's psychosocial interpretation of the *identity* crisis in terms of a commitment of fidelity to value specifies an intrinsically moral dimension in adolescent conversion. Second, the psychosocial crisis of *intimacy* in the young adult raises the question of a further conversion—of the possibility, even normative necessity, of the person, now secure in his or her own identity, risking that identity by falling-in-love. Third, Erikson's specification—at the adult crisis of *generativity*—of a fully ethical orientation of care and responsibility in contrast to the ideological orientation to value of adolescence points to a properly adult moral conversion beyond the possibilities of youth. Finally, Erikson's identification of a crisis of *integrity* vs. despair in the older adult suggests that the years after mid-life might be the occasion for a transformation of life radical enough to truly be called religious. Taking these four psychosocial clues from the stages of Erikson's life cycle, we might now consider the possibility of the following fundamental conversions: (1) moral conversion; (2) affective conversion; (3) cognitive or critical moral conversion; (4) religious conversion. Each of these conversions may occur in an explicitly religious context, but such a context is not necessary. When they occur in a Christian context, they are dimensions of a full Christian conversion.

Conversion is commonly understood as a change in the *content* of a person's faith or fundamental orientation. Thus, for example, a person in becoming a Christian adopts the Christian story as an orientation to life—or drops it for another master story in converting from Christianity to something else. If we say that a person's fundamental horizon is established by a set of existential questions, conversion as change of content may be understood as a *horizontal* conversion: new answers (content) to old questions within an established horizon.

As valuable as this content approach to conversion is, my principal focus here will be on a complementary approach suggested by structural theories of development, especially those of Piaget, Kohlberg, Fowler, and Kegan. In this approach, conversion is viewed from the perspective of structure rather than content, and may be understood as a *vertical* conversion: radically new questions creatively restructuring content (old or new) into a totally new horizon.

1. Moral Conversion

Lawrence Kohlberg is widely known for his six stages of moral reasoning development, which he divides into pairs on three levels: preconventional, conventional, and postconventional. Kohlberg gives no attention to conversion, but careful reflection on the nature of structural stages indicates that stage transition (especially between major levels) is a form of conversion. Here I will concentrate on the transition from preconventional to conventional moral reasoning. Kohlberg claims that this transition occurs, at the earliest, in the young adolescent, occasioned in part by the emergence of Piagetian formal cognitive operations.

Fundamentally this transition is a shift from a premoral to a moral orientation, that is, from a radically egocentric orientation in which the

criterion for decision is self-interested satisfaction to a social orientation in which the criterion for decision is value (in various convention-
ally defined forms). The actual realization of value in one's life is a
further issue, but this new criterion—rooted in the ability to distinguish the valuable from the valuable-for-me—establishes a new horizon, sets a new personal agenda. Content will vary greatly among
individuals, but morally converted horizons are similar inasmuch as
concern for value is their defining and constitutive character. When
structural and psychosocial stages coincide, moral conversion to value
meshes perfectly with the adolescent's discovery of self in fidelity.

2. *Affective Conversion*

Moral conversion to value calls us beyond ourselves; it is more of
a challenge than an achievement; it discloses the gap between the self
we are and the self we should be. The challenge to close that gap is the
challenge to move beyond ourselves not only in our knowing but also
in our deciding and our acting, the challenge to make our action consistent with our judgment of what we should do and be. But we meet
that challenge, we close that gap, we really move beyond ourselves with
regularity, insofar as—and only insofar as—we fall in love. For only in
such falling-in-love do our full persons escape the centripetal force of
our persistent egocentric gravity. Then we become beings-in-love, existential principles of responsible action consistent with our best judgment.

For many years Kohlberg's cognitive-structural perspective never
particularly focused on affectivity or moral action. In recent years,
however, the question of distinctively adult moral development has
prompted Kohlberg to look to Erikson's existential crises and psychosocial ego-strengths or virtues with renewed interest. In the next section we shall see how Kohlberg came to link postconventional moral
development with the generativity of Erikson's adult ethical orientation, characterized by care and responsibility. Here I simply want to
emphasize how the young adult's prior Eriksonian crisis of intimacy—
with its defining strength of love—may be the occasion of an affective
conversion, a fundamental relocation of the self's dynamic center of
gravity. That Kohlberg has not given any special attention to the crisis
of intimacy must be seen as an important oversight insofar as the structural decentering of the self in affective conversion is a necessary condition for the care and responsibility of the ethical adult's generativity.

Robert Kegan's analysis of the emergence at Stage 5 of a self capable of sharing itself while remaining distinct offers a structural inter-

pretation of affective conversion critically grounded in the key distinction between preidentity fusion and postidentity intimacy.

3. Cognitive or Critical Moral Conversion

For more than half a century Jean Piaget traced the course of cognitive development from the infant's sensorimotor activity, through the acquisition of language and symbolic functions in early childhood and the emergence of concrete operational thought in later childhood, to the appearance of formal operations in adolescence. Each transition to a higher stage introduces a significantly new element. Concrete operations *systematize* previously acquired cognitive activities. Formal operations give wings to operational thinking, freeing it from the here and now limitations of concrete experience. When it occurs, such liberation from the concrete inevitably becomes escape from the real, as the formal thinking of the idealistic adolescent revels in its new power of flight. Only the vocational experiences proper to the adult bring the winged perspective back to earth, integrating formal thought's universalizing abstraction with the empirical dimension of concrete operations into the power of realistic judgment.

While such development is obviously fundamental to one's understanding of the world, it is also crucial for self-understanding. For insofar as a person who has developed through concrete and formal operations to adult realistic judgment can reflect this power back on the self, precisely as a knower, there is beyond cognitive development also the possibility of cognitive conversion: the critical recognition of the constitutive and normative role of one's own judgment in knowing reality and therefore value. A person who experiences such critical understanding of self as knower ceases to look beyond the self somewhere "out there" for a criterion of the real or the valuable. For cognitive conversion consists precisely in discovering that criterion in one's own realistic judgment.

Kohlberg's third, postconventional level of moral reasoning, as rooted in self-chosen, universal ethical principles, requires exactly this kind of cognitive conversion in the moral dimension, i.e., critical moral conversion. Basic moral conversion to conventional morality is essentially uncritical, locating authority in absolutely *given* social values. To become postconventional, one must not only relativize conventional values, but one must discover the final criterion of value in one's own critical judgment, and thereby become the author of one's own moral life. Critical moral conversion to a postconventional stance goes beyond restructuring one's horizon in terms of value, then, by grounding that horizon of value in the reality of oneself as a critical, originating value. Kohlberg believes that, in addition to advanced cognitive development, postconventional moral transformation requires existential adult experiences of irreversible life decisions and of care and responsibility for others.

4. Religious Conversion

James Fowler's analysis of faith development presupposes—in its distinction between Stage 3 Synthetic-Conventional Faith and Stage 4 Individuative-Reflexive Faith—the same kind of cognitive conversion to a critical standpoint of being one's own authority. Fowler's analysis reaches beyond this critical stance, however, to a postcritical Stage 6 Universalizing Faith, whose felt sense of ultimate environment includes all being.

Indeed, even Kohlberg, after many years of research on moral reasoning development, has in recent years—within the context of considering development in older adults—raised the question of a seventh, religious stage. Kohlberg's point is that if a person reaches Stage 6 of moral reasoning, and seriously tries to live a life of principled justice for a number of years, that person will inevitably ask the most fundamental question of all: "Why be just in an unjust world?" or, most simply, "Why be moral?" In fact, in Kohlberg's view, only such a person can ask this question, which he regards as ultimately a religious question, in a psychologically serious way. In his speculations, Kohlberg sees a religious Stage 7 beginning in the despair of perceiving human life as finite from the perspective of the infinite—the meaninglessness of life in the face of death, for example. Continuation toward a more cosmic perspective in non-egoistic contemplative experience leads to identifying with the cosmic or infinite perspective. The structural result is a decentering figure-ground shift in which despair is overcome by the contemplative experience of cosmic unity implicit in the despair. For Kohlberg, this experience is correlative to Erikson's final psychosocial task of integrating life's meaning.

This decentering figure-ground shift, which Kohlberg says cannot be realized on purely rational grounds, is what Christian theologians mean when they refer to a religious conversion that is not just the joining of a new religious group but is the radical reorientation of one's entire life that occurs when God is allowed to move from the periphery to the center of one's being. When this radical religious conversion is seen from the perspective of total self-surrender, the relativization of human autonomy is stressed.

Properly understood, one surrenders not oneself or one's personal moral autonomy, but one's illusion of absolute autonomy. But such total surrender is possible only for the person who has totally fallen-in-love with a mysterious, uncomprehended God, for the person who has been grasped by an other-worldly love and completely transformed into a being-in-love. Such religious conversion is not only rare, it is not even religious in any ordinary sense. One need not be "religious" to experience it; indeed, when it is experienced by an explicitly religious person, such radical transformation might be best understood as a conversion from religion to God.

CONVERSION OF CONSCIENCE

Character: Structure and Content

The above reference to content and structure highlights the point that conscience, the radical drive of the personal subject for self-transcendence, always has a particular concrete shape, a specific horizon. This concrete shape of conscience constitutes the moral quality of a subject, the "sort of person" one is; in the fullest sense of the word, it is *character*.[56]

Conscience, then, is to be understood in terms of both structure and content. If conscience in the most radical sense is the developing *dynamism* of the person for self-transcendence, it is also *structure and content* in the sense of the specific concrete shape taken by that dynamism as it is formed by the discoveries, decisions, and deeds through which a subject creates his or her "second nature" or character as a particular "sort of person." It is in this concrete sense of conscience as character that a person's specific insights, judgments, and decisions have their source.

In fundamental conversion, then, there is both continuity and discontinuity. Conversion radically redirects and transforms the concrete shape and orientation of personal subjectivity, the structure and content of one's conscience as character; thus the discontinuity. But if conscience as character is changed in conversion, conscience as the person's radical drive for self-transcendence remains. Thus basic conversion, a transformation of the person's whole orientation, a radically new beginning, occurs within the continuity of the subject's fundamental dynamism for self-transcendence.

Concluding Questions

We have considered four types of vertical conversion—structural reorganizations and reorientations of personal horizons. Each may occur in either explicitly religious or non-religious contexts. But, as structural, when such conversion does occur it will necessarily be in the context of some particular content. In fact, vertical conversion as structural reorganization may occur together with horizontal conversion as content-change. On this point, it is important to ask whether specific vertical conversions of structure by their very nature require horizontal conversions of content. Kohlberg, for example, defines moral Stage 6 in terms of the universal principle of justice. He claims that only certain kinds of content are compatible with such a structure (opposition to capital punishment, for example). Fowler's faith Stage 6 also seems compatible with only the most profound religious content. And, finally, from the perspective of content, do some horizontal conversions of content, like Christian conversion, for example, require vertical conversions of structure if they are to involve serious personal transformation, and not just emotional "highs" and superficial language games?

These are the kinds of questions we need to confront if we are to understand what we mean when we talk about conversion—the kinds of questions we will wrestle with in Chapters 4, 5 and 6. After Chapter 4's initial discussion of conversion in the moral, cognitive, and affective dimensions, Chapters 5 and 6 will turn to the life of Thomas Merton as a concrete, personal context of character in which to pursue the specific meaning of Christian conversion, focusing on its moral and religious dimensions. But this is a developmental interpretation of conscience and conversion, so we must first lay the developmental foundation in Chapters 2 and 3. There a critical model of the developing *self* will provide the basis for our later specification of the moral and religious conversions of conscience in terms, respectively, of autonomy and surrender. The preceding pages have viewed the book's general outline from the air; now we return to the ground to follow that outline through the rugged terrain of stages and crises in search of conversion.

The perfection of human nature consists perhaps in its very growth in goodness.

Gregory of Nyssa

To live is to change, and to be perfect is to have changed often.

John Henry Newman

2

PERSONAL DEVELOPMENT THROUGH THE LIFE CYCLE

THE SELF-CONSTITUTING "I"

Conscience has been identified as the radical drive of the personal subject toward self-transcending authenticity. By the "personal subject," of course, is meant the concrete, conscious individual who is born and grows up, learns and works, loves and sins, becomes sick and, finally, dies. It is not some metaphysically defined substance named "person," abstract and static, angelically timeless without the human stuff of flesh and bones, needs and feelings, successes and failures. In order to interpret conscience (and thus conversion) adequately, then, the personal subject must be explicitly understood in the very concreteness of its consciousness and becoming. (In the interest of clarity, I am for the moment deliberately avoiding the ambiguous term "self," though its meaning remains our objective.)

A little etymological study tells us, in fact, that conscience *is* consciousness—the distinctive moral consciousness of the responsible, existential subject concerned with value, with moral judgment, decision, and choice.[1] Indeed, such activities as judging and deciding and choosing are among those which are *essentially* operations of the personal subject, in the sense that whenever they are performed the personal subject is aware of, is present to, or experiences himself or herself operating. Such personal operations not only intend objects, then, but

33

also render the operating subject conscious. Thus by their intentionality personal operations make objects present to the subject and in the very same act by their consciousness they simultaneously make the operating subject present to himself or herself. A person may, for example, be most intensely conscious, present to self while engrossed, even "lost," in a particularly fascinating novel. Such experience is puzzling, even paradoxical, for one who identifies consciousness not with the subject's self-presence in intentional activity, but rather with reflexive knowing. Reflexive knowing, however, is a second act which, in our example, the person may perform when, after putting the novel down, he or she perhaps thinks about his or her own life in the light of one of the characters' experience. In this case the subject is simultaneously present to herself or himself in two different ways: as subject by consciousness, and as object by the intentionality of the reflexive act. Such is the fundamental distinction Bernard Lonergan draws between the subject-as-subject (consciousness) and the subject-as-object (reflexive intentionality). Operations as intentional make objects (including the self) present to the subject; operations as conscious make the subject present to herself or himself. Thus, in "self" language, we have the interior duality of self-as-object ("myself") and self-as-subject ("I").[2]

Consciousness, according to Lonergan's theorem, not only reveals the subject-as-subject, but constitutes it. The subject experienced in consciousness does not exist without consciousness (in dreamless sleep or coma). The "I," the subject who feels, understands, and decides, is not only revealed to itself as such in consciousness, but is made capable of feeling, understanding, and deciding only through consciousness. It is constituted as an "I" by consciousness. In sum, all this adds up to the fact that in the reality of the personal subject, consciousness is not only cognitive, it is also constitutive.[3] Clearly, an appreciation of this radically constitutive nature of consciousness is central to an adequate understanding of the person as a free and responsible, existential subject, and thus of conscience.

But if the personal subject is constituted by consciousness, it is constituted as *this* personal subject only through the concrete particularities of its own history. For the existence of the personal subject is in process; its very being is becoming. And, as Lonergan further points out, in this process of personal becoming the subject's world changes— not *the* world, but the world correlative to the subject, the world in which *this* personal subject actually lives.[4] As a personal subject, the new Ph.D. astrophysicist is radically different from the little girl who played with toy rockets twenty years ago in kindergarden, and so are their worlds. Borrowing a visual-spatial image for a model of conscious subjectivity, then, we may speak of a personal horizon defined by two poles which condition each other: a subject-pole, or the standpoint of the consciously operating personal subject, and an object-pole, or the subject's world. As spatial horizons limit a field of vision relative to a person's given standpoint, so personal horizons define a subject's world of feelings and knowledge, interests and questions in relation to his or her present reality—a reality rooted in a structured context of past achievement and dynamically oriented toward the future. But if past achievement is the source of future possibilities, it also sets the limits to present capacities.[5]

Within the process of personal becoming Lonergan has specified general structural dimensions of the subject's world. First there is the infant's very limited world of immediacy—the felt and the sucked, the touched and the grasped, the heard and the seen—the world of immediate experience. But this tiny world of the infant begins to widen as the wings of language gradually emerge and expand, and before many years the growing child is soaring ever farther and higher in the world mediated by meaning. Through its seemingly infinite possibilities this world mediated by meaning transcends not only any one world of immediate experience but all the experience of every world of immediacy. Still, beyond this world we know, the world mediated by meaning, there is the world we construct by meaning. First, and most obviously, there is the world of technology which has transformed our natural environment. But beyond our transformation of nature, there is the less obvious but even more significant transformation of ourselves. So beyond the worlds mediated or even directed by meaning, therefore, there is the world of the subject that is constituted by meaning. This is the fully human world of community, the world of common meaning, created over the millennia through that educational process of the human family called tradition, and embodied in its culture as well as in its social, political, and economic institutions.[6]

Something of this common history of constitutive meaning is recapitulated in the socialization of the individual, a process which, at its best, is an education that fully liberates the personal subject for responsible, creative participation in a freely constituted world of meaning.

The world of the personal subject, then, is a world not only mediated but also constituted by meaning. And since this is the subject's only world, the personal subject, too, is constituted by meaning in his or her very reality as a conscious, luminous being. This is possible because the radical core of conscious subjectivity itself, in its dynamism for self-transcendence, is self-structuring, self-constituting. At both the subjective and objective poles of personal horizon, then, the conscious person becomes himself or herself through a radical, self-creating drive for meaning and value. Any adequate interpretation of conscience, therefore, must take full account of this self-constituting process of becoming, which is the very being of the self-transcending personal subject.[7]

It will be helpful, therefore, to place conscience in a context of personal development based on the psychological perspectives of Erik Erikson, Jean Piaget, Lawrence Kohlberg, James Fowler, and Robert Kegan, since these psychologists use self-transcendence implicitly as a criterion of mature personal development. Once this criterion is made explicit, their theories can provide a normative, integrated model of self-transcending subjectivity. Ultimately, this developmental perspective will raise the question of the relationship between the development of personal conscience and its conversion.

It should be noted that the two basic psychological approaches discussed here—the cognitive developmental and the psychosocial developmental—focus in large part (though not exclusively) on *unconscious* personal structures: the Piagetian approach shared by Kohlberg and Fowler is principally concerned with explicating unconscious cognitive development just as the psychoanalytically inspired approach of Erikson objectifies unconscious affective development; Kegan's neo-Piagetian perspective focuses on disclosing the development of the unconscious structure of the self underlying both cognition and affectivity.[8] While these developmental structures can profitably be brought to explicit, conscious light through various reflexive techniques of self-appropriation, optimal personal living requires that they function effectively in their proper unconscious dimension. The essential point to be grasped is that such development goes forward spontaneously or unconsciously as an ongoing adaptational effect of the subject's conscious, deliberate, step-by-step attempt to make sense of its natural environment as well as to enter into and continue creating a human world of meaning. In Chapter 4 we will see how at key points in the transformation process conversions constitute the conscious counterparts of unconscious developmental stage transitions.

It is also important to note that while developmental theories specify development in terms of stages, the emphasis in this interpretation of the developing self will be on the unifying *movement* through the stages, especially the major transitions between stages which will be correlated with conversions. If conflict is the usual developmental ex-

ERIKSON	PIAGET	KOHLBERG	FOWLER	KEGAN	CONVERSIONS
8) Integrity/Despair Wisdom		7) Religious			Religious
7) Generativity/ Stagnation Care		6) Universal Principles	6) Universalizing		Critical Moral
	Contextual-Dialectic		5) Conjunctive		
6) Intimacy/Isolation Love		5) Social Contract	4) Individuative-Reflective	5) Interindividual	Affective
		4½ Relativist			
5) Identity/Confusion Fidelity	Full Formal	4) Authority-Social order		4) Institutional	Moral
(Affiliation/ Abandonment)	Early Formal	3) Interpersonal Concordance	3) Synthetic-Conventional	3) Interpersonal	
4) Industry/Inferiority Competence	Concrete	2) Instrumental-Relativist	2) Mythic-Literal	2) Imperial	
3) Initiative/Guilt Purpose	Preoperational	1) Punishment-Obedience	1) Intuitive-Projective	1) Impulsive	
2) Autonomy/Shame, Doubt Will					
1) Trust/Mistrust Hope	Sensorimotor	0) Amoral	0) Undifferentiated	0) Incorporative	

planation for stage transition, I interpret it here in terms of the deepest human motivation: the experience of a person struggling for self-transcendence and finding his or her present, concrete horizon inadequate to meet the complex reality of the natural, interpersonal, socially structured human world that is life.

This chapter will present a brief exposition of the developmental theories, organized to emphasize their interrelationships in an integrated model of self-transcendence. With this basic model in place, the following chapter will then offer a critical discussion of these developmental theories, and finally a specification of conscience precisely as developmental.[9] The second and third chapters' overall goal, then, is a developmental understanding of conscience as the radical drive of the personal subject for self-transcendence—an understanding rooted in a critical appropriation of both cognitive and psychosocial theories of development. This understanding of conscience as the concrete, structured dynamism of the self-transcending subject will ground our interpretation of conversion.

PERSONAL DEVELOPMENT AS SELF-TRANSCENDENCE

To demonstrate how a criterion of self-transcendence operates implicitly in the concrete specifics of the different developmental perspectives, this chapter will briefly sketch the theories of Erikson (psychosocial/affective), Piaget (cognitive), Kohlberg (moral), Fowler (faith), and Kegan (self). By integrating these theories in a single sequence of personal development, it will show how they interrelate and complement each other.[10] While the focus here will be on our central explanatory category of self-transcendence in the developmental theories, I will anticipate our discussion of conversion by noting those key developmental transitions which will later be correlated with basic conversions.

To maximize clarity amidst complexity, this sequence of development will be divided into the three basic periods of childhood, adolescence, and adulthood, with each theory considered at each period (i.e., three parts, each with five sections). Specific crises or stages of each theoretical perspective will be discussed at the period of their earliest appearance and optimal correlation (e.g., identity and Stage 3 Synthetic-Conventional Faith at adolescence). The simplified chart on p. 37 can serve as a map; but remember that its ideal alignments do not mean "always" or even "usually."

Childhood

Affective. Erik Erikson has analyzed the course of personal development as a life cycle of eight psychosocial stages. Each stage is marked by a definite crisis and is, hopefully, productive of a specific virtue or psychosocial strength. The first four of these "eight ages of man" correlate closely with the psychosexual stages in Freud's analysis of sexuality in infants and children. With Erikson, however, the emphasis is on the development of the individual in the context of his or her social environment. During what Freud called the oral period, Erikson stresses the fundamental struggle between basic trust and mistrust. "The mother must represent to the child an almost somatic conviction that she (his first 'world') is trustworthy enough to satisfy and regulate his needs." Emerging from a successful resolution of this first crisis— a balance favoring basic trust—is the psychosocial virtue of hope, "the enduring belief in the attainability of primal wishes in spite of the anarchic urges and rages of dependency."[11] Because Erikson regards such rudimentary trust and hope as the foundation and possibility of even the most mature and lofty religious faith, it is clear that, in his view, self-transcendence is a critical issue from the very beginning of personal development. We will see later how central adult trust is to the very possibility of radical religious conversion.[12]

Corresponding to the Freudian anal, phallic, and latent stages are Erikson's next three psychosocial stages. In each of these stages Erikson delineates further childhood crises revolving upon the issues of *autonomy* versus shame and doubt, *initiative* versus guilt, and *industry* versus inferiority. From their successful resolutions come strengths of will power, purpose, and competence. Like hope, these strengths are themselves realizations of self-transcendence. They are also foundational elements that make possible the various adult forms of personal self-transcendence—trusting hope, autonomous will, initiating purpose, and industrious competence.[13]

Within this early childhood development, of course, there also emerges what Erikson calls "the great governor of initiative," the superego. Now the child not only fears being found out by others, but also "hears the 'inner voice' of self-observation, self-guidance, and self-punishment," which creates a radical division and estrangement within the self.[14] Though the narrowly moralistic superego is a necessary foundation for the mature adult's ethical conscience, the development from immature superego to self-transcending conscience is inevitably difficult and painful. Mark Twain gives a memorable example of the promise as well as the pain of this development in Huck

Finn's struggle between his love for Jim, his slave friend, and the law he broke in helping Jim to escape. After much soul-searching, and sure that he will go to hell for wickedly refusing to turn Jim in, Huck decides, "All right, then, I'll go to hell. . . ."[15] But we are ahead of the developmental story: if the older but still confused Huck thinks he will go to hell for doing what he judges right, the younger child is unable even to distinguish what is right from the interiorized rules of the superego.

It seems to be no accident, but rather the wisdom of life's ground plan, that the psychosexual period of latency and the psychosocial stage of industry and competence coincide. It is no accident, either, that Erikson's school age of industry and competence is the occasion, in Piaget's theory, for one of the most decisive breakthroughs in the entire course of cognitive development—the emergence and logical grouping of concrete operations. Let us shift, then, to Piaget's analysis of these concrete operations in their context of previous cognitive development. For it is important to understand how intimately related and interdependent the basic areas of development are. In fact, cognitive, affective, moral, and faith development are only facets of a total development of the concrete person.

Cognitive. Cognitive development, according to Piaget's analysis, is dominated by a dialectical movement from cognitive egocentrism toward a decentered objectivity. Four basic stages mark the course of this development: sensorimotor (approximately 0–2 years); preoperational (2–7 years); concrete operational (7–11 years); formal operational (11–15 years).

The first, or sensorimotor, stage sets the pattern of later development toward decentered objectivity in a strikingly clear way. The titles of two key volumes by Piaget on this early period illustrate well the bi-polar character of cognitive development: *The Origins of Intelligence in Children* in reference to the subject-pole of personal horizon and *The Construction of Reality in the Child* in reference to the object-pole.[16] These two aspects of cognitive development occur together in the one interaction between the individual and the environment. As the infant adapts in a very practical way to its surroundings (seeking equilibrium through assimilation and accommodation), it begins to discover itself and its cognitive operations. At the same time the infant also "organizes reality by constructing the broad categories of action which are the schemes of the permanent object, space, time, and causality, substructures of the notions that will later correspond to them."[17]

Piaget points out that these categories are completely absent at the beginning, when "the child's initial universe is entirely centered on his own body and action in an egocentrism as total as it is unconscious (for lack of consciousness of the self.)" He goes on to explain that "in the course of the first eighteen months, however, there occurs a kind of Copernican revolution, or, more simply, a kind of general decentering process whereby the child eventually comes to regard himself as an object among others in a universe that is made up of permanent objects (that is, structured in a spatio-temporal manner) and in which there is at work a causality that is both localized in space and objectified in things."[18] So, for example, we have the familiar instance of the baby that pursues the ball even when it has rolled out of sight, because "out of sight" is no longer "out of existence" as it was just a few months earlier. From the psychoanalytic perspective this is the cognitive condition for affective object-choices.[19]

As this line of thought indicates, Piaget—though widely known for his descriptive analysis of the development of children's thought, particularly in its pedagogical application to curriculum planning—is essentially interested in questions and issues that are best described as epistemological. And it is the explanatory, theoretical power of his genetic epistemology, worked out in a critical, empirical context, that constitutes, in my judgment, the real and lasting contribution of his work.[20] This is especially true in the relation of developmental moral psychology to religious ethics. The major contribution of the descriptive analysis in his classic *The Moral Judgment of the Child* notwithstanding, Piaget's critical significance for religious ethics lies in his theoretical analysis of cognitive development and the explanatory epistemology derived from it.[21] It is appropriate here, therefore, to stress again that Piaget's general epistemological thesis of development from egocentrism toward decentered objectivity is evident even in the first year and a half of life, as the infant begins to discover itself and create its world in a self-transcending process of equilibration.[22] Indeed, to properly emphasize the major theme of construction in Piaget's view, we should say that the infant does not so much discover itself as it cognitively constitutes or creates itself as a self distinct from a world of objects.[23]

The second key period of cognitive development, in Piaget's analysis, spans the years approximately from two to seven. It is essentially a period of transition and preparation—transition from direct external actions of practical intelligence to the *internalized* actions of thought, and preparation for the emergence of the *organized* internal actions called operations that are marked by reversibility. As Piaget explains, during early childhood intelligence is transformed, through language and socialization, from simple sensorimotor or practical intelligence to thought itself. However, it is only vis-à-vis others that the young child is led to seek evidence for its thinking. The child is always satisfied with its own thinking until it learns to consider the objections of others and then to internalize such critical discussions in the form of reflection. But social relations are still rudimentary at this early stage, so even in the most reality-oriented thinking of the young child, says Piaget, one quality stands out: he or she constantly makes assertions without trying to support them with evidence.[24] Only gradually, then, does there appear the ability to distinguish clearly between fact and fiction, the ability, for example, to affirm accurately the existence of the Great Pumpkin, while recognizing Santa Claus as no more than a happy fantasy.

But at around the age of six or seven, according to Piaget, there begins to occur a fundamental transformation in the child's thinking which marks a key turning point in the course of cognitive development. There begins at this point a transition from the isolated intuitions of the preoperational period to concrete *operations* which are by definition *systematically* organized and interrelated in what Piaget calls *groupings*. Arithmetic provides a simple example of operations and their reversibility: addition and subtraction, multiplication and division.

Much could be said about the specifics of cognitional development during this period. The important point to be stressed here, though, is the further decentering of the young child's egocentric viewpoint that is achieved through the emerging logical operations' power to situate the knowing subject within the much broader context of objective relations. The emergence of concrete operations is gradual, but by the time their development is completed at around the age of ten or eleven, the transformation of the child's world is nothing short of radical: a constitutive factor in the developing conditions for the possibility of cognitive conversion.[25]

Concrete operations, limited by their very concreteness, are not the last word in cognitional development (even the child who is brilliant in arithmetic will stall on the abstractions of the calculus). But as systematically organized logical operations which enable the child to move beyond his or her own viewpoint and take other perspectives into account, they constitute a springboard for cognitional self-transcendence that is totally beyond the horizon of the young child. And just as social interaction is necessary for this development of intelligence, so the arrival of these concrete operational powers seems to be the condition for the psychosocial achievements of industry and competence which Erikson highlights during the school age.

Moral. Having considered preadolescent development in the affective/psychosocial (Erikson) and cognitive (Piaget) areas, let us now turn our attention briefly to the specific question of moral development during this period. Our guide here will be Lawrence Kohlberg, whose work can be understood initially as a more empirical, second-generation version of Piaget's classic analysis in *The Moral Judgment of the Child*.[26]

Kohlberg charts the development of moral (justice) reasoning through six stages grouped in pairs on three levels: Preconventional Level (Stage 1 Obedience and Punishment Orientation; Stage 2 Instrumental-Relativist Orientation), Conventional Level (Stage 3 Interpersonal Concordance or "Good Boy-Nice Girl" Orientation; Stage 4 Authority and Social-Order Maintaining Orientation), and Postconventional Level (Stage 5 Social Contract, Legalist Orientation; Stage 6 Universal Ethical Principle Orientation).[27]

Clearly, Kohlberg's specification of the major levels turns on his meaning of "conventional": "conforming to and upholding the rules and expectations and conventions of society or authority just because they are society's rules, expectations, or conventions."[28] The levels can be understood, then, in terms of the self's socialization. The preconventional self is the egocentric individual, for whom social rules and expectations are entirely external (concrete individual social perspective). The conventional self is the social person who has internalized and thus identifies with the rules and expectations of others, especially authorities (member-of-society social perspective). The postconventional self is the autonomous social person who has differentiated itself from the rules and expectations of others and can thus accept (or in some cases reject) social rules on the basis of self-chosen general principles which underlie them (prior-to-society social perspective). Here we will focus on the preconventional level's Stages 1 and 2, which are characteristic of, but not limited to, childhood.

According to Kohlberg, the preadolescent child, whose social perspective is concrete individual, "has not yet come to really understand and uphold conventional or societal rules and expectations," which remain essentially external to the self.[29] At Stage 1 of the preconventional moral level, the child with emerging concrete operations is often "well-behaved" and responsive to cultural labels of good and bad, but understands these labels in terms of (1) avoidance of breaking punishment-backed rules, (2) obedience for its own sake, and (3) avoidance of physical damage to persons and property. Desire to avoid punishment and awareness of the superior power of authorities are reasons for doing what is right at this stage.[30] The child's social perspective at this first stage of moral development is still egocentric. Oblivious to the interests of others, and to the possibility they may differ from one's own, the young child is incapable of relating two points of view. As an example of Stage 1, Kohlberg offers the response of a ten year old boy to a question of whether a boy should tell his father about some bad thing his brother had done: "In one way it was right to tell because his father might beat him up. In another way it's wrong because his brother will beat him up if he tells."[31]

Three years later the same boy responds: "The brother should not tell or he'll get his brother in trouble. If he wants his brother to keep quiet for him sometime, he'd better not squeal now." The clear perception here of the brother's point of view and its relation to the subject's is illustrative of the social perspective at moral Stage 2: individualism, instrumental purpose, and exchange. Now aware that everyone has individual interests, and that these conflict with the interests of others, the older child understands right behavior as acting in one's own interests and allowing others to act in theirs. Sometimes this is accomplished through fair exchange—a deal: "You scratch my back, and I'll scratch yours."

Gradually then, along with and dependent upon the development in the cognitive and psychosocial dimensions noted above, three significant trends begin to manifest themselves in the child's moral consciousness: (1) intentionality of the agent becomes more important, merely physical consequences less; (2) relativism and awareness of possible diversity of views of right and wrong begin to replace a simplistic, totally right or totally wrong approach; (3) punishment begins to give way to recognition of harm done to others or violations of rules as reason for an act being wrong.[32] As Kohlberg sees it, these trends gradually progress during childhood to the point where their terminal qualities become dominant in the older preadolescent child.

Kohlberg's theory thus indicates that, even from early to later, preadolescent childhood, there is a measure of development in moral consciousness—development from an egocentric preoccupation with punishment and obedience toward the self-transcendence of reflective perspective-taking and equal exchange. We have noted that the cognitive self-transcendence achieved through the emergence and development of concrete operations during this period of middle childhood, though constituting a radical breakthrough, is, nevertheless, fundamentally limited by the intrinsic concreteness of the operations. The "reality" they constitute is too heavily dominated by the empirical. Similarly, the limited moral self-transcendence effected in the development from Stage 1 to Stage 2 is excessively oriented toward the concrete interests of the self. Not until adolescence do the roots of the movement toward self-transcendence really begin to take hold—with the cognitive transformation of concrete operations into formal, with the psychosocial crisis of personal identity, and with the emergence of a socially oriented morality and faith. Only then does moral conversion become a real possibility. Recall how Pinocchio needed Jiminy Cricket to act as his "conscience" until he became a "real boy" by caring for Geppetto.

Faith. Having seen how Kohlberg delineates the development of the preadolescent's moral reasoning, let us turn now to James Fowler's even more ambitious attempt to trace the development of the structure of personal faith. Faith, as Fowler understands it, is a knowing, a construing, or an interpreting of experience in light of a person's or community's relatedness to those "sources of power and values which impinge on life in a manner not subject to personal control."[33] In theological language, such ultimate conditions of existence would be called the transcendent. For Fowler, however, faith or, more accurately, active "faithing" is a universal human reality, and not necessarily religious in any ordinary, explicit sense. In "faithing" the total self is involved; the cognitive, affective, and evaluative are inextricably interwoven. Fowler's analysis focuses on the structural core of this faithing, on the patterned processes of faith as knowing and valuing rather than on the content of faith as knowledge and values.

Fowler's research and theorizing on faith development was inspired by and is heavily indebted to the Piagetian-Kohlberg structural approach. Consequently, we should understand the six stages of faith distinguished in his theory as including the cognitive, social perspective, and moral factors already considered, as well as reference to the psychosocial/affective component seen in Erikson. The six stages of Fowler's developmental model of faith, the first two of which emerge in childhood, are: (1) Intuitive-Projective, (2) Mythic-Literal, (3) Synthetic-Conventional, (4) Individuative-Reflective, (5) Conjunctive (Paradoxical-Consolidative), and (6) Universalizing.[34]

After the preconceptual and mostly prelinguistic period of infancy, when faith is undifferentiated from the earliest psychosocial strengths of trusting hope and willful autonomy described by Erikson, there emerges with the increasing use of linguistic and ritualistic symbols the first structural stage of faith. During this fantasy-filled, imitative stage of Intuitive-Projective faith, the child's dependence on parents for love, security, and nurturance "makes them prime authorities or references in his/her construction of a meaningful world."[35] Along with a greater awareness of self as separate from others during this stage comes an anxiety grounded in the new awareness of death, and especially fear of one's parents' deaths.

The special gift of this stage is the birth of imagination, the ability to grasp experience in powerful images "and as presented in stories that register the child's intuitive understandings and feelings toward the ultimate conditions of existence." Unhappily, the imagination that almost universally fears "lions, tigers, bears and monsters" can also be possessed by unrestrained images of terror and destructiveness or exploited in the reinforcement of taboos. As powerful as the child's imagination is, however, it is an egocentric imagination, as six-year-old Freddy reminds us when asked if everybody thinks God looks like his little statue of Christ: "Mmm—not when he gets a haircut."[36]

As concrete operational thought is beginning to emerge, and as the psychosocial focus is shifting from the issue of purposeful initiative to that of industrious competence, the second stage of Mythic-Literal faith begins to make an appearance. Here the preadolescent child appropriates stories, beliefs, attitudes, and moral rules of the community in an uncritical and quite literal-minded way. Beyond parents, authority is now recognized in teachers, religious leaders, customs, traditions, the ideas of peers, and the ever present media.

The distinctive new strength of this stage is the ability to narratize experience. In contrast to younger children who must depend on stories told by others, the preadolescent with concrete operations has the capacity to generate his or her own stories. And the ability now to take the perspective of others results in images of God more fully anthropomorphic than the younger child's vague images of God as being "like the air—everywhere." Still, the concreteness and literalism of the preadolescent mind dominates the anthropomorphic imagination, as ten-year-old Millie's description suggests: "God is like a saint. He's good and he like—he like rules the world, but in a good way. [How does he rule the world?] Well, he—not really rule the world, but um— let's see, he like—he lives on top of the world and he's always watching over everybody. At least he tries to. And he does what he thinks is right."[37]

Clearly, as in other aspects of personal development, the preadolescent, though still very limited, is beginning to reach further out beyond the self in "faithing," in construing experience in terms of its limits.

Self. Whereas Erikson, Piaget, Kohlberg, and Fowler focus on specific dimensions of personal development, Robert Kegan directs his theoretical efforts toward establishing the fundamental unity of the self that is developing. Working from a neo-Piagetian constructive-developmental perspective, Kegan finds this fundamental unity in the meaning-constitutive activity that is the very motion of the self's development or evolution. He understands this meaning-constitutive activity as not only the unifying but also the generating context of personality, that is, of subject and object as well as of thought and feeling.

Shifting the focus of the Piagetian processes of differentiation and integration from cognition to the prior reality of personality, Kegan sees the individual's radical developmental activity as both the very creation of the object (differentiation) and the subject's relating to it (integration). In this view "Subject-object relations emerge out of a lifelong process of development," in which a series of qualitative differentiations of self from world create an ever more complex object of relation—"successive triumphs of 'relationship to' rather than 'embeddedness in.' "[38]

This process is first manifested in the infant, which both Piagetian and psychoanalytic psychologies view as starting life in a world without objects, a world in which everything is an extension of the newborn. Whereas the infant's gradual development of object relations is interpreted primarily in cognitive terms by the Piagetian and in affective terms by the psychoanalytic view, Kegan's neo-Piagetian perspective reaches for what he regards as a "more basic phenomenon [than either cognition or affectivity], the evolutionary transition from an undifferentiated state to the first equilibrium." By the end of the first year and a half, with the balance established through the creation of the object relation, the pattern of developmental activity is set as "an activity of equilibration, of preserving or renegotiating the balance between what is taken as subject or self and what is taken as object or other." In this view, personal development is fundamentally a series of renegotiated balances which organize the individual's experience in qualitatively different ways. Clearly, such developmental activity is intrinsically cognitive: for the infant, the gradually evolving ability to relate to the object even when it is not present. But Kegan's basic point is also to insist that this activity is intrinsically affective, the felt experience of motion:

for the infant, the protest upon separation from the primary caretaker, which, more than the loss of an object, is really a loss of the subject's very organization of its center. In identifying the developmental
activity of decentration as the fundamental ground of personality, Kegan is suggesting that the source of emotion is the "phenomenological
experience of evolving—of defending, surrendering, and reconstructing a center."[39] Intrinsic to every decentering emergence from embeddedness to greater relatedness—which is experienced as a loss of
center, a loss of self—are first the emotions of anxiety and depression.
Then, as the balance begins to shift more decisively to the new self,
there is anger and repudiation of the former self (subject) that in the
developing balance is now at the object-pole. Only when the new balance is fully established can repudiation give way to positive reappro-
priation.

The radical differentiation and integration of subject and object
effected in infancy—the emergence from a primordial incorporative
stage (stage 0)—is only the beginning of a lifelong development which
Kegan traces in five major succeeding stages: (1) Impulsive, (2) Imperial, (3) Interpersonal, (4) Institutional, and (5) Interindividual.[40]
We shall now briefly consider the Impulsive and Imperial stages of
childhood.

If the initial underlying structure of infancy is embeddedness of
the self in its reflexes (sensing, moving)—the infant does not have but
is its reflexes—the basic differentiation and integration of self (subject)
and other (object) during the first eighteen months constitutes a radical transformation of this deep structure. Reflexes now become object
of a new organizing center, a new coordinating subjectivity. By thus
disembedding itself from its reflexes the self effects a transition to the
Impulsive stage, where it is no longer subject to its reflexes. Now the
two year old has its reflexes at the deep structure's object-pole. At the
subject-pole the new impulsive self is embedded in the impulses and
perceptions that now coordinate the reflexes: the self now has its reflexes and is its perceptions and impulses.

Kegan suggests that the plasticity or unstableness of the preschool
child is rooted in this new embeddedness of the self. Cognitively, the
child can recognize objects as separate from the self, but those objects
depend on the child's perception of them; if the perception changes,
so also does the object. The preschooler is subject to its perceptions.
Affectively the same is true of impulses. Control of impulses requires
mediation, but the preschooler is its impulses; they are immediate to
it. Just as the young child cannot hold two perceptions together, neither can it hold two feelings together; it has no capacity for ambiva-

lence. Thus Kegan suggests that the tantrum is "an example of a system overwhelmed by internal conflict because there is no self yet which can serve as a context upon which the competing impulses can play themselves out; the impulses *are* the self, are themselves the context."[41] Just as the young child is subject to its cognitive perceptions, so too is it subject to its affective impulses. Kegan sees "Sesame Street's" Cookie Monster as a brilliant character for the impulsive child, who can both identify with and gain a little scoffing distance from the Monster's uncontrollable urges: "Want cookie! *Take* cookie!"

The capacity to objectify impulses and perceptions not only ends the instability of the earlier subject-object relation, but establishes a new subject-object relation which creates a more enduring self as the child moves into school age. While the physical world is being conserved through Piaget's concrete operations there is also conservation of internal experience—the creation of a private world which the younger child does not have. With the constitution of an enduring disposition (needs, interests, wishes) at the subject-pole, the school-age child also develops a more consistent self-concept (*what* I am as distinct from the earlier *that* I am and the later *who* I am).

Central to this heightened sense of self that comes with the capacity to command one's impulses (to have them, rather than be them) is a new sense of agency: freedom, power, independence. Things no longer just happen; the new awareness of agency gives the child a sense of having something to do with what happens. All this also means a budding sense of one's own authority, which Kegan suspects effects the transition from Kohlberg's first moral stage, where authority is right simply by virtue of its existence, to the second, where the self's interests become primary. With the freedom and power of agency, of course, also comes a new sense of responsibility for what happens; and for the self now dominated by needs the threat of failure leads easily to imperialistic manipulation, as Lucy Van Pelt demonstrates to readers of "Peanuts" with fascinating consistency. The child at the *Imperial* stage projects its needs-embeddedness onto the other; it constitutes the other as the means by which its needs, interests, and wishes will or will not be fulfilled. Kegan gives the example of a child who betrays a confidence because it suits its needs to do so. Because the child understands that the other person has its own needs and interests, and how the other might feel about being betrayed, the child will experience concern about the consequences should the betrayal be discovered. But because how the other will feel is not part of the very source of the child's own feeling (which would require the rather complex integration of one needs-perspective with another that is beyond the self embedded in its own needs), the child experiences only practical concern about consequences, not a guilty conscience. The Imperial stage is specified precisely by the absence of a shared reality, of mutuality. Only the later ability to internalize the other's voice in the very construction of the self will free the child's feelings from an alienating dependence on the other's reaction.

Adolescence

Cognitive. As we have already noted, Piaget demonstrates that the child "thinks concretely, he deals with each problem in isolation and does not integrate his solutions by means of any general theories from which he could abstract a common principle." In striking contrast to this, he points out, is the adolescent's interest in problems not related to everyday practical realities. And what Piaget finds particularly interesting is the adolescent's "facility for elaborating abstract theories . . . that transform the world in one way or another."[42]

In his experiments, Piaget has discovered that at about the age of eleven or twelve there is a "fundamental transformation" in children's thinking—a transition from concrete to formal thinking. The concrete intelligent operations of childhood are concerned only with "tangible objects that can be manipulated and subjected to real (physical) action"; but with the advent of formal thinking, says Piaget, "the logical operations begin to be transposed from the plane of concrete manipulation to the ideational (conceptual) plane, where they are expressed in some kind of language (words, mathematical symbols, etc.), without the support of perception, experience, or even faith."[43] The adolescent, for example, who a few years earlier used concrete operations to set speed records solving the Rubik cube, may now be able—with formal operations—to explain those solutions systematically in mathematical equations.

This formal thinking is hypothetico-deductive, says Piaget; it allows one to draw conclusions from pure hypotheses as well as from actual observations—conclusions that have "validity independent of their factual truth."[44] The revolution effected by the emergence of formal operations finds its fundamental significance, then, in the fact that it liberates the adolescent's thinking from concrete reality by empowering it to build its own reflections and theories. As Piaget puts it, "with the advent of formal intelligence, thinking takes wings"; and he is not surprised that this new power is at first both used and abused.[45]

For, like other new cognitional abilities, formal thought tends to start off "by incorporating the world in a process of egocentric assimilation," and "only later does it attain equilibrium through a compensating accommodation to reality." That is, the power of formal operations to draw conclusions with a validity independent of factual truth, the power which allows formal thought to transcend the limitations of immediate concreteness, can construct an idealistic world of possibilities entirely separated from—and, indeed, opposed to—experience. In this sense formal thought can be egocentric. And, from the perspective of Piaget's epistemology, an equilibrium in touch with the real world is attained only when it is understood that the "proper function of [formal thought's] reflection is not to contradict but to predict and interpret experience."[46] Piaget suggests that such a realistic equilibrium requires some experience of responsibility in the adult world.[47] Formal thinking is itching for conversion, but it needs to get its feet on the ground.

Affective. Having sketched the broad outline of adolescent cognitive development as understood by Piaget, we can turn to the affective/psychosocial side of the adolescent's development. For Erikson, the key to development during adolescence is identity. Though Erikson focuses on identity throughout the entire course of personal development, adolescence is its time of crisis.

Psychosocial identity, as Erikson understands it, is "at once subjective and objective, individual and social." It includes a subjective sense—sometimes intense, even exuberant—of continuity as an active, alive individual. At the same time, the social side of identity development "presupposes a community of people whose traditional values become significant to the growing person even as his growth assumes relevance for them." An inner ego synthesis of the individual, then, is complemented by genuine role integration in his group (not a mere assortment of roles that can be interchangeably "played").

What Erikson calls an identity *crisis* is constituted by the fact that here in adolescence "persistent (but sometimes mutually contradictory) infantile identifications are brought in line with urgent (and yet often tentative) new self-definitions and irreversible (and yet often unclear) role choices."[48] Erikson insists that the "integration of an identity is more than the sum of childhood identifications."[49] The very newness and originality of this "more than," which must be worked out in the creative crucible of adolescence, seem to constitute the critical, self-transcending nature of identity.

To the degree that one is able to resolve this crisis of identity, there is generated the characteristic strength of adolescence: fidelity, the "ability to sustain loyalties freely pledged in spite of the inevitable contradities of value systems." Closely connected to and supported by this virtue of fidelity is what Erikson calls the fundamental *ideological* orientation of adolescence. Erikson suggests that "if the child learns to be moral . . . to *internalize the prohibitions* of those significant to him, his moral conflicts continue in adolescence, but come under the primacy of ideological thinking . . . *a system of commanding ideas* held together more (but not exclusively) by totalistic logic and utopian conviction than by cognitive understanding or pragmatic experience."[50] The close connection here between Erikson's understanding of the adolescent's moral (i.e., ideological) horizon and Piaget's explanation of the emergence of formal thought during adolescence seems clear and in need of little emphasis. We will see how both fidelity and formal thinking play key roles in basic moral conversion.

While identity as a crisis is typically highlighted during adolescence, identity is a central issue throughout the entire course of life and must be redefined at every stage. Indeed, as we shall see with Thomas Merton, even the crisis of identity is not always confined to adolescence, but can dominate the early adult years as well. Erikson's major study of identity, fidelity, and ideology, in fact, is *Young Man Luther,* where Luther's early adulthood in the monastery is interpreted not just as a great struggle for faith but also as a delayed moratorium in which he was negotiating his crisis of identity, searching for an ideology to which he could fully commit himself.[51]

Moral. In Kohlberg's analysis, adolescence is the time when maintaining the expectations and rules of family, group, or nation is first seen as valuable in its own right. There is now concern not only with conforming to the social order, but also in maintaining, supporting, and justifying it. During the first phase of this Conventional Level (Stage 3), good behavior means pleasing or helping others—seeking their approval by being "nice." Conformity to stereotypes of majority or "natural" behavior is important. But behavior is now also judged by intention—"he means well" is heard regularly. At this stage, then, the adolescent's social perspective clearly places the individual in relationship with other individuals. Shared feelings, agreements, and expectations take primacy over individual interests.[52] Caring for others, and the need to be a good person, in one's own eyes as well as others', is important.

Later, at Stage 4, a person behaves well and earns respect not only by doing one's duty and respecting authority, but by maintaining the given social order for its own sake. The older adolescent now takes the social perspective of the system that defines roles and rules, and views individual relations in terms of their place in the social system. Another response to the dilemma of the boy who must decide whether to inform on his brother can illustrate the interpersonal character of Stage 3: "He should think of his brother, but it's more important to be a good son. Your father has done so much for you. I'd have a conscience [sic] if I didn't tell, more than to my brother, because my father couldn't trust me. My brother would understand; our father has done so much for him, too."[53]

In contrast to this Stage 3 response which sees things from the perspective of shared relationships among individuals, the following response to the question, "Why shouldn't you steal from a store?" exemplifies the social system orientation of Stage 4: "It's a matter of law. It's one of our rules that we're trying to help protect everyone, protect property, not just to protect a store. It's something that's needed in our society. If we didn't have these laws, people would steal, they wouldn't have to work for a living and our whole society would get out of kilter."[54] In Chapter 4 we will correlate this transition to conventional morality with basic moral conversion.

Faith. With the emergence of formal operations and the extension of the person's world beyond the family and primary social groups, faith, according to Fowler's interpretation, "must help provide a coherent and meaningful synthesis of that now more complex and diverse range of involvements." Faith must also offer a basis for identity, ideological orientation, and commitment, which though deeply felt are still uncritical, as "coherence and meaning are certified, at this stage, by either the authority of properly designated persons in each sphere, or by the authority of consensus among 'those who count.' " The person's entire world of meaning, in fact, is typically mediated by symbols which are "dwelt in" in a precritical or naive way. In keeping with the interpersonal character of Stage 3 faith, images of God are no longer physically anthropomorphic, but personal—God is friend, companion, comforter, guide. And because faith is as derivative as identity at this stage, God often bears "the role of the 'collective other' who sums up the legitimate expectations and the individual loyalties of the significant others and groups in one's life."[55] Though Stage 3 faith first appears in and characterizes adolescence, it, like the stages of conventional moral reasoning, often best describes the stabilized personal development of even older adults. In fact, Fowler offers two adults as examples for our reflection on Stage 3. The first is a thirty year old Catholic mother, speaking about her image of God: "I picture God as the religion books say, an all-knowing and loving God . . . an all-loving and powerful person—and a person! The religion books point that out, but that's what I *feel*. I feel God *is* powerful and he's loving. . . . I believe there is a God and he hears what I'm saying and knows what I'm thinking and is there to help me. . . ."[56]

By contrast, Fowler's second example of Stage 3 shows the enormous range for variety of *content* in a structural faith stage. The example is Malcolm X as an adolescent and young adult. After discussing Malcolm's youth in terms of what Erikson calls negative identity, Fowler suggests that Malcolm's "years in the streets—as hustler, pusher, and thief—must be seen as a kind of Stage 3 phase." More than at any other period in his life, according to Fowler, "Malcolm was acting on unexamined and fatalistically accepted values. Barred from more constructive channels, he poured his tremendous energies and drives into the struggle for survival and significance in the tough, materialistic life of the streets."[57]

Here again, at the Synthetic-Conventional stage, we see how Fowler's understanding of faith development has moving beyond or transcending self for its criterion, as the new cognitive abilities and experiences of adolescence plunge one into a wider and deeper world to be faithed.

Self. In Kegan's view of the evolving self, adolescence typically witnesses the self's emergence from an embeddedness in its own self-interest needs. The self no longer *is* its needs (the Imperial self), it *has* them. Because it *has* its needs, and is no longer subject to them, the self can now coordinate them with the needs of others, and thus become "mutual, emphatic, and oriented to reciprocal obligation."[58] If such shared feelings are the strength of the new conversational self located in the interpersonal matrix, its limit lies in its inability to reflect on the expectations, satisfactions, obligations of that shared reality because it *is* that shared reality, and thus is subject to it. Conflicts at this *Interpersonal* stage are not so much between the self and the other as between the self as a part of one shared reality and the self as part of another shared reality. Without coordination of its various mutualities the Interpersonal self lacks the self-coherence that is the hallmark of identity.

Kegan emphasizes that the balance struck at this stage is "interpersonal" but not "intimate." Despite appearances, real intimacy is impossible because there is no self to share with another; the very existence of the interpersonal self depends on—is subject to—the other. Kegan thus insists on the fundamental difference between intimacy and fusion.[59] If the Stage 2 self imperializes the other as an instrument of its need-satisfaction, the Stage 3 Interpersonal self now needs the other not only to complete itself but even to know and define itself. Kegan tells us about twenty year old Diane, for example. Diane has a pattern of becoming dependent on a man very quickly, withdrawing from other friendships until her whole life is built around him. When he eventually finds the relationship too oppressive and begins to back off, Diane becomes despondent.[60]

The Stage 3 Interpersonal self *is* its relationships. What Kegan specifies as defining the movement to the fourth, *Institutional* stage is the self's separation from its relationships in the creation of a coherent identity of its own across the interpersonal context. Now, because the self is no longer parceled out among its various relationships, it has a sense of self-ownership. In *having* its relationships rather than *being* them, the self becomes something of a psychic institution at the subject-pole which coordinates the many facets of its interpersonal mutuality now at the object-pole. Interpersonal feelings remain important, but they are now relativized within the new ultimate context of the psychic institution that regulates them: the integral self-system (role, norm, self-concept, auto-regulation). The self transcends its interpersonal relationships, yet in a way that does not leave them behind but rather incorporates them into the balance of the new self-system.

As strong and as independent as the new Institutional self is, Kegan points out that in the very strength of its systematic structure lies its limit. Like the classic bureaucrat, the Institutional self is identified with its organization; its very meaning and being is derived from its organization; it *is* its organization. As a result, at Stage 4 there is no self before which the policies of the organization can be brought. Rather, the self is subject to those institutional policies, and thus vulnerable to the excesses of control characteristic of every unlimited organization. We get some sense of the way control can become excessive at this stage from Rebecca, who, in her mid-thirties, has too much of the self-sufficiency Diane needs so desperately. "I know I have very defined boundaries and I protect them very carefully. I won't give up the slightest control. In any relationship I decide who gets in, how far, and when." Rebecca values respect above all else: "You don't have to like me. You don't have to care about me, even, but you do have to respect me." She sees her "self" as "a steel rod that runs through everything": "What you just really can't be is weak."[61] Rebecca may not be typical of most women. Ordinarily, men are the ones who find Stage 4's sense of independent strength and control particularly comfortable, and easily take up permanent residence there, whereas women, because of their orientation toward attachment rather than separation, usually find Stage 3's dependent relationships very comfortable, and have difficulty moving from Stage 3 to Stage 4. For the same reason, however, those women who do reach Stage 4 may experience less of a problem than men typically do in moving beyond its independence to Stage 5's mature interdependence of intimate and responsible caring.[62]

Adulthood

Cognitive. We have noted that the egocentrism of the adolescent's formal thought gives way to a consistent pattern of genuine understanding and realistic judgment only when the logic of formal operations is adequately complemented by concrete experience in the social world. Such adult knowing can be powerfully systematic and reflective, but always in a creatively imaginative way that remains in dialectical tension with the conflicting realities of the concrete context. Adult knowing appreciates the relativity of context: historical, political, social, cultural, personal. It recognizes that reality—especially human reality—is ambiguous, that even the most blatant contradictions on paper—like love and hate—are not infrequent bedfellows in reality. Adult knowing decenters the flighty, totalistic logic of adolescence by bringing it back to the earth of complex situations, where the idealism of simplistic certitude gives way to the realism of nuanced probability.[63] Here, as we will see in Chapter 4, is the concrete possibility of cognitive conversion.

Affective. Similarly, the experimentation of the ideological orientation that Erikson sees succeeding the moral learning of childhood must also finally submit to the realistic demands and lessons of adult social experience. Thus, Erikson points out, "this ideological orientation as well as the moral one is, in turn, absorbed but never quite replaced by that ethical orientation which really marks the difference between adulthood and adolescence—'ethical' meaning a *universal sense of values assented to* with insight and foresight, in anticipation of immediate responsibilities, not the least of which is a transmission of these values to the next generation."[64]

Erikson's primary example of the ethical orientation, of course, is Gandhi, who, as we will later see, was Thomas Merton's principal model for the social-political transformation of personal spirituality. For Gandhi, truthful action was governed by the readiness to get hurt and yet not to hurt.[65] In the Gandhian principle of non-violence—"That line of action is alone justice which does not harm either party to a dispute"—Erikson saw the political counterpart to his own interpretation of the Golden Rule as mutual enhancement.[66] For Erikson, non-violence, inward as well as outward, becomes truly effective only when an ethics of insightful assent to values transmitted by informed persuasion replaces the moralism of blind obedience enforced by absolute interdicts.[67] As Gandhi embodied this truth for Indians, so did Martin Luther King for Americans.

We shall soon see how such an adult *ethical* orientation is characterized in Kohlberg's schema of moral judgment stages, but first we should consider very briefly how Erikson analyzes psychosocial/affective development in the adult years. For just as the adult ethical orientation in the above definition is clearly pointed in the direction of self-transcendence, the virtues which characterize, strengthen, and to a great degree constitute that ethical orientation are likewise the fundamental launching pads of self-transcendence.

Erikson sees young adulthood as characterized by the crisis of *intimacy* versus isolation. Consolidated identity, according to Erikson, "permits the self-abandonment demanded by intimate affiliations, by passionate sexual unions, or by inspiring encounters." A basic resolution of the *crisis* of identity in adolescence is necessary, then, for the young person to have the psychological strength and confidence to risk going out of himself to achieve the even fuller reality of personal identity that is found only in an intimate relationship of fidelity with another. The young adult, says Erikson, is "ready for intimacy and solidarity—that is, he can commit himself to affiliations and partnerships even though they may call for significant sacrifices and compromises." The specific strength of this period, love, serves what Erikson calls "the need for a new and shared identity in the procession of generations."[68] A clear sense of consolidated identity, of course, is entirely different from what in the everyday language of common sense we mean by a "strong ego," the kind of independence which asserts itself even in the autonomy of the very young child. An adolescent or even an adult can manifest great (even fiercely stubborn) independence, determination, discipline, and all the other marks of a "strong ego," yet still be radically dependent on others—a defensively oriented candidate for fusion and conflict, not intimacy and sharing. A person with what we popularly call a "strong ego," in other words, may have a very weak sense of self-identity. The strength of a "strong ego" is in its self-centeredness; the strength of self-identity is in its capacity to risk the self-transcendence of intimacy and generativity.

Though secured in intimacy, love, according to Erikson, finds its fulfillment in *generativity*, which is concerned first of all with establishing and guiding the next generation, but also includes productivity and creativity. Erikson names the particular strength of maturity, care, "the broadening concern for what has been generated by love, necessity, or accident—a concern which must consistently overcome the ambivalence adhering to irreversible obligation and the narrowness of self-concern."[69]

Integrity (versus despair) is the critical issue for old age, in Erikson's view. Strength at this stage "takes the form of wisdom in its many connotations—ripened 'wits,' accumulated knowledge, inclusive understanding, and mature judgment." Quite simply, "wisdom maintains and conveys the integrity of experience, in spite of the decline of bodily and mental functions." It loves life in the face of death. The wisdom of integrity is thus the natural expression of a life of self-transcendence, but it is also itself self-transcending and a promoter of self-transcendence in others in that "a meaningful old age (preceding terminal invalidism) provides that integrated heritage which gives indispensable perspective to those growing up, 'adolescing,' and aging."[70]

Erikson exemplifies these adult crises in the person of Dr. Isak Borg, the main character of Ingmar Bergman's film *Wild Strawberries*.[71] At age of seventy-six, and widowed for many years, Dr. Borg is to travel from his retirement home to the city of Lund where he will be honored with a Jubilee Doctorate in the ancient cathedral. Erikson notes "the old man's defensive voice and his punctilious manners that indicate with how much self-restriction he has paid for [his] seeming autonomy of proud withdrawal."[72] The day-long auto trip becomes—in Bergman's hands and Erikson's eyes—the opportunity for Dr. Borg to work through not only the crisis of integrity versus despair but also (in accord with the epigenetic principle) his earlier unresolved crises, especially those of intimacy and generativity. Indeed, the trip along familiar roads becomes a symbolic journey back into Dr. Borg's "childhood and deep into his unknown self," as he is confronted with disturbing truths about himself and his family by his traveling companion for the day, daughter-in-law Marianne, as well as by his "dreams." By the end of the day the ceremonial honor bestowed on Borg seems, to Erikson, "almost unreal or, at any rate, transcended by a certain simple depth of wisdom that he has gained—and by a decision through which he and his immediate family find themselves firmly and subtly united."[73]

In the adult strengths of love (affection), care (responsibility), and wisdom (sagacity), then, we can clearly recognize Erikson's understanding of human maturity as characterized by an intrinsic dynamism to move beyond one's self and to be concerned for others that I call the "radical drive for self-transcendence." Later we will specify intimacy, generativity, and integrity as the psychosocial correlates of affective, critical moral, and religious conversions, respectively.

Now, having considered Piaget's explication of the emergence of formal logical operations in adolescence and their realistic stabilization in young adulthood, as well as Erikson's understanding of the stages of psychosocial development during adolescence, youth, and adulthood, we can turn our attention to the more specific area of the development of moral judgment in the adult years—picking up Kohlberg's analysis again at the postconventional level.

Moral. For Kohlberg, the key element in Piaget's interpretation of adolescent development is the dramatic shift in cognition from concrete to formal operations already noted—a shift which creates a radically new world view. We have seen how the emergence of abstract, formal operations constitutes the cognitive ground of both the identity crisis and the ideological orientation of adolescence delineated by Erikson.

Perhaps this shift in the adolescent's cognitive horizon has been studied in as much depth in the moral realm as in any other. Kohlberg has shown that it grounds the member-of-society social perspective as well as conventional moral reasoning. But, Kohlberg also claims quite explicitly that "the shift in adolescence from concrete to formal operations, the ability now to see the given as only a subset of the possible and to spin out the alternatives, constitutes the necessary precondition for the transition from conventional to principled moral reasoning." He goes on to conclude, then, that it is not until adolescence that "the child has the cognitive capability for moving from a conventional to a postconventional reflective or philosophic view of values and society."[71]

In other words, formal operational thought plays two key roles in Kohlberg's understanding of the development of moral reasoning. First, its abstracting power constitutes the cognitive basis of conventional moral reasoning by enlarging the adolescent's horizon. In contrast to this "institutional" role, formal thought's reflective power also makes possible the "subversive," critical questioning that Kohlberg sees as a prerequisite for postconventional moral reasoning.

Clearly, Kohlberg's analysis of moral development places great weight on the cognitive factor. Kohlberg is not suggesting, however, that the development of moral reasoning is simply a matter of cognitive sophistication. His position, he says, is "not that moral judgments are cognitive—they are not the mere application of logic to moral problems—but that the existence of moral stages implies that [moral] development has a basic cognitive-structural component."[75] Cognitive maturity, then, to put Kohlberg's view in its most straightforward terms, is a necessary, but not a sufficient condition for mature moral reasoning. In other words, according to Kohlberg, "While formal operations may be necessary for principled morality, one may be a theoretical physicist and yet not make moral judgments at the principled level."[76]

This is a critical point because Kohlberg, on the basis of his studies, claims that most people (even those capable of formal operational thought) never advance to the principled stage of moral reasoning, and that those who do move on to postconventional thought do so, at the earliest, only in young adulthood.

What else, then, in addition to cognitive advance, does Kohlberg regard as necessary for moral development generally, and for development to principled, or postconventional, moral reasoning in particular? Since development through the first four moral stages involves wider role taking and a more adequate perception of the social system, Kohlberg suggests that, besides cognitive advance, "opportunities for participation and role taking in all the basic groups . . . appear to be important for moral development" at these stages.[77] However, while Kohlberg does not consider extensive personal experience of moral decision and choice as necessary for development from one stage to the next in childhood and adolescence, such is not the case for postconventional stages. For principled moral reasoning is "not a more adequate perception of what the social system *is;* rather it is a postulation of principles to which the society and the self *ought to be committed.*"[78]

Kohlberg mentions two types of personal experience which seem to be significant factors in the movement to principled morality. The first experience is that of leaving home and entering the life of a college community with its confusion of conflicting values. In the context of identity questioning, psychosocial moratorium, and the need for commitment, this experience can effect a relativistic breakthrough of the absolute givenness which the social system enjoys in moral Stage 4. Named Stage 4½, this period of radical relativism, in which the validity of morality—equated with Stage 4 reasoning—is questioned, may be a transitional phase to principled moral reasoning. If such a transition is to be achieved, Kohlberg suggests that in addition to the experience of identity crisis, moratorium, and commitment, in which new responsibility is only for the self and freedom is to make one's own choices for oneself, there must also be "experience of *sustained responsibility for the welfare of others* and the experience of irreversible moral choice. . . ."[79] These are the marks of adult moral experience, and are, as Kohlberg points out, central to the caring generativity of Erikson's ethical orientation. Such experience is the principal crucible in which the adolescent's abstract, idealistic thinking is transformed into the adult's contextual, realistic knowing. We will examine this more closely in Chapter 4 when we identify critical moral conversion as the conscious dimension of the shift to postconventional morality.

In the most general terms, Kohlberg understands postconventional morality as characterized by autonomous moral principles which have validity independent of the authority of any persons or groups. The social perspective here is a prior-to-society legal or moral point of view. As with the lower levels, Kohlberg here specifies two stages of development.

The first stage on this level is a social-contract orientation with legalistic and utilitarian overtones. Moral behavior is defined in terms of critically examined rights and standards commonly agreed upon by society. Because of a clear awareness of the relativism of personal values at this level, there is a definite stress on procedural rules for reaching consensus. At this stage the legal point of view includes the possibility of changing law in terms of social utility, rather than freezing it as at Stage 4.

From this contract viewpoint there may develop an orientation to internal decisions of conscience. However, this orientation (not a stage in the full sense) lacks the comprehensive, universal, and consistent ethical principles which finally constitute Kohlberg's sixth and highest stage of moral reasoning. The defining elements of this sixth stage are the "universal principles of justice, of the reciprocity and equality of human rights, and of respect for the dignity of human beings as individual persons."[80] It should be clear, I think, that by definition this highest stage of moral reasoning has self-transcendence as its basic criterion. Moral judgments are judgments of personal conscience, but a personal conscience consistently guided by universal principles and striving for as comprehensive a context as possible.[81]

In response to Heinz's famous dilemma about stealing a drug to save his wife's life, a twenty-four year old man illustrates an advanced Stage 5 moral orientation: "It is the husband's duty to save his wife. The fact that her life is in danger transcends every other standard you might use to judge his action. Life is more important than property." But Stage 5's lack of clear prioritization of the moral over the legal point of view is evident when he adds, in response to "Should the judge punish the husband?": "Usually the moral and the legal standpoints coincide. Here they conflict. The judge should weigh the moral standpoint more heavily but preserve the legal law in punishing Heinz lightly." In contrast, the following Stage 6 interview response to Heinz's dilemma is clearly rooted in the prior-to-society, strictly moral point of view: "It is wrong legally but right morally. Systems of law are valid only insofar as they reflect the sort of moral law all rational people can accept."[82]

For Kohlberg, then, maturity in moral reasoning is not simply a matter of development in cognitive structures. There is also the significant element of maturity in the affective patterns of feeling and valuing. To put it another way, Kohlberg's analysis indicates that maturity in moral judgment is not the maturity of something alongside of, or in addition to, cognitive structures and affective patterns of feeling and valuing, but is a manifestation in the moral sphere of an integrated personal (i.e., cognitive *and* affective) maturity.

Having reflected on the development of cognitive, affective/psychosocial, and moral reasoning patterns in adulthood, it is now possible to continue the demonstration of self-transcendence as the implicit criterion of personal development by examining the adult stages of faith.

Faith. Like the shift from conventional to postconventional morality, the movement from the Synthetic-Conventional Faith of Fowler's Stage 3 to Stage 4's Individuative-Reflective Faith involves a breakthrough. In this case it is a breakthrough to a new self-awareness and personal responsibility for one's commitments, life-style, beliefs, and attitudes. Movement to Stage 4 faith also forces the young (or older) adult to face, but not successfully deal with, certain unavoidable, universal tensions until now submerged in a conforming, member-of-society perspective: individuality vs. belonging to community; subjectivity vs. objectivity; self-fulfillment vs. service to others; the relative vs. the absolute. These tensions are usually collapsed into one side or the other during Stage 4. Similarly, multivalent symbols are typically translated (demythologized) into clearer, more easily managed conceptual meanings.[83]

One of Fowler's interview respondents, Mr. E., was asked: "How would you describe your religion, your life-style, or your system of values?" The high degree of reflective self-consciousness in his answer is characteristic of Stage 4. "Well, as for my religion, if you take it from the point of view of organized religion, there basically is none. I was born a Catholic but don't practice any formal religion, ritual, or anything like that. . . . I live my life the way I think I should—that doesn't depend at all on the religious formulations of any group or religious organization, and my values are just what seem right to me. I rejected the values of many organized religions and hold some values which are contrary to not only organized religion but to society as a whole."[84]

In Stage 4, the self-awareness and personal responsibility involved in defining and choosing one's identity and world view, and in making one's commitments, clearly indicates a significant measure of self-transcendence in breaking through the confinements of conventional role conformity and authority. But the transition to the Conjunctive (Paradoxical-Consolidative) Faith of Stage 5 represents an even more far-reaching transcendence of the self. Here, the adult—most appropriately in the thirties—recognizes the integrity and truth of other persons' positions in a way that earlier over-valued commitments excluded, and "affirms and lives out its own commitments and beliefs in such a way as to honor that which is true in the lives of others without denying the truth of its own."[85] This Stage 5 transcendence of earlier, inadequate resolutions of tensions based on one-sided reductions and exclusions clearly exemplifies how all personal development—from the simplest cognitive to the most advanced faith—is a response to the tension of conflict, crisis, and disequilibrium.

As part of the movement toward integrating what had previously been excluded by Stage 4's interest in conceptual clarity, neatness, and certainty, the adult of Stage 5 faith moves into a post-critical second naiveté which retrieves the dynamism of the symbol in a new and powerful way, ready to encounter the mysterious riches of the personal and social unconscious.[86] In sum, Stage 5 faith can be characterized as being radically open to the "other" in every sense; and this openness is in league with the mature, generative adult's attempt to risk living out a moral orientation committed to universal principles of justice, equality of human rights, and respect for the dignity of the human person, while knowing and being prepared to pay the cost of such commitment.

In an interview, Mrs. B., a Stage 5 woman of thirty-six years, was asked: "Did you feel, and do you feel, that your values *should* hold true for all other people as well?" Her response was: "No. And that's difficult, because I believe *some* of my values should hold true for other people. But I don't believe that I can *impose* my values on other people." Asked why, she continued: "Because *they* have as much right as I do to choose and decide their own course and what they value. I have no more right to impose on them than they do to impose on me. On the other hand, I have a responsibility—and this is a priority that increases as I grow older and know more, and learn more—I have an obligation to, to express my values and in a sense teach what I have learned from experience, as well as learned from other people. . . ."[87]

If the special self-transcendence of Stage 5 faith is found in its radical openness to the "other," the self-transcendent characteristic of Stage 6 Universalizing Faith consists in the fact that the Stage 6 person goes beyond the paradoxical balancing of "opposites" by transcending all dichotomies in identifying with all, including the transcendent, in a community of universal inclusiveness, of Being. As its description makes evident, Universalizing Faith is rare, and in any case should not be expected before mid-life. In Chapter 6 we will correlate it with radical religious conversion. At Stage 5, Fowler explains, "one acts out of conflicting loyalties. A readiness to spend and be spent on behalf of others is limited by concern for one's own, or one's family, or one's group survival. Perceptions of justice outreach the readiness to sacrifice self for the sake of justice and in the spirit of love." But now, at Stage 6, this conflict is overcome "through a moral and ascetic *actualization* of the universalizing apprehension." Without regard to personal risk, the person of Stage 6 faith "becomes a disciplined, activist *incarnation* of the imperatives of absolute love and justice. . . ."[88] Martin Luther King, whom Kohlberg cites as an example of moral Stage 6, may be illustrative here, too. The paradox of being-for-others disappears at Stage 6; now one is being most truly oneself in being for others. Full self-realization, in short, is found in full self-transcendence.

As an example of Stage 6 faith, we have part of the response of an elderly, celibate member of a religious order, who was interviewed by one of Fowler's students and asked what he saw as the purpose of life. "It's receiving from God what he wants to give. That is the purpose of human life," he responded. He expanded this by explaining that "we are constituted by an aspiration for union with God to the highest degree that we can receive him. That is what human life is all about. And we have that deep aspiration covered up with all of these ephemeral drives and looking here, there, and the other place for something that will fulfill us, and masking the deepest aspiration which is for God and for love of our neighbor, which is by a sacrificial love." Evidently appreciating the difficulty of understanding this kind of love, he added: " 'Sacrificial' does not mean giving up things: it means a unifying love which we receive only from God and his inner dynamism, because we are all selfish and sinful and therefore to love members of the human race who are not in themselves lovable. And growth is in the realization that we do this not through our own power, but through the transformation of our spirit by the spirit of God."[89]

Self. Kegan locates the last of his stages of the evolving self in the self's emergence from the psychic organization dominant at the Institutional stage. Where before the self *was* the organization, now the organization is shifted to the object-pole and the self directs and runs it. This Stage 5 capacity to coordinate the institutional allows the self to join others as fully personal individuals—"people who are known ultimately in relation to their actual or potential recognition of themselves and others as value-originating, system-generating, history-making individuals." At this *Interindividual* stage the self's "community is for the first time a 'universal' one in that all persons, by virtue of their being persons, are eligible for membership."[90]

If the Institutional self brought the "interpersonal" into itself, Kegan explains, the new Interindividual self brings the self back into the "interpersonal." Again, Kegan insists on the fundamental difference between intimacy and fusion. At Stage 5, unlike Stage 3, there is a self to be brought to others, not derived from them; Stage 5 allows the intimate sharing of distinct identities, Stage 3 only the clinging fusion of merely adumbrated identities. The Interindividual self is capable of genuine intimacy with others because it is for the first time capable of intimacy with itself, capable, that is, of not only recognizing but also tolerating emotional conflict within itself. Where the Stage 3 Interpersonal self is not strong enough even to admit the existence of emotional conflict within itself, but must keep it "out there," the Stage 4 Institutional self brings the conflict inside but sees it as intolerably dangerous to the smooth functioning of the organization (i e , the self), and thus something to be dealt with by an efficient institutional administrator in the least costly manner possible. Because the Stage 5 self no longer *is* the institution, but recognizes a plurality of institutional selves at the object-pole within the Interindividual self, it is freed from seeing emotional conflict as ultimately dangerous to the self and can therefore be open to it as an interior conversation. By breaking open the institutionality of the former balance, and locating itself now in the coordination of psychic institutions, the Interindividual self surrenders what Kegan calls "counter-dependent independence" for interdependence. In place of Stage 4's closed auto-regulation, the Stage 5 self's ability to share itself in intimacy allows the emotions to live in, and be "re-solved" at, the intersection of self-systems. This transcendence of the closed institution enables the self to "give itself up" to another, says Kegan, only to find itself as distinct in the sharing experience Erikson calls "a counter-pointing of identities."[91]

The Interindividual self that has a self to share with others is open, dynamic, flowing; it is not the closed end of a development toward isolated independence. Though not the end of development, it does represent a decisive point in the fundamental process of differentiating and integrating movements begun in infancy with the radical creation of self and other. While different points in the course of development emphasize either differentiation (Stage 2) or integration (Stage 3), the balance struck at the Interindividual stage creates a distinct (differentiated) self ultimately realized in the very sharing of itself (integration), and thus includes in creative evolutionary tension what Kegan takes to be the two greatest yearnings in human experience: the yearning for separateness or independence (differentiation) and the yearning for inclusion or connection (integration). This balance will be central not only to our understanding of affective conversion, but also to our interpretation of the relationship of autonomy and surrender in radical religious conversion.

SELF-TRANSCENDENCE AND THE DEVELOPING "I"

The basic and direct point that I have been endeavoring to establish in this chapter is that whether we look to Fowler's theory of faith development or to Kohlberg's analysis of the development of moral reasoning, or whether we examine the more fundamental development of cognitive structures as explicated by Piaget and of psychosocial patterns of affectivity as described by Erikson, we find in each of them one central and dynamic reality: *self-transcendence* (be it of objective knowing through contextualized formal operations; of the fidelity and intimacy in loving and responsible care; of the universal intent of a principled conscience; or be it of universalizing faith) as the normative direction of fully human development and therefore the key criterion of personal maturity. Kegan's understanding of the evolving self points to this same self-transcendence as the constitutive and unifying reality of personal development.

Indeed, it is precisely the various dimensions of the *unified self's* development—the self constituted in and through the radical drive for self-transcendence—that we have been examining in this chapter. It may be helpful as we bring this exposition of the self's development to a close, then, to underline with Erikson the centrality of the self's unity as realized and manifested in the sense of "I," just as we began with Lonergan's analysis of the self-as-subject.

Despite the insistence of Erikson the psychoanalyst on the importance of understanding the ego as primarily an unconscious inner organization of experience, he is equally clear on the significance of the conscious "I": "the ground for the simple verbal assurance that each person is a center of awareness in a universe of communicable experience, a center so numinous that it amounts to a sense of being alive, and more, of being the vital condition of existence." Erikson's reproduction of the following passage from William James' *Principles of Psychology* at the beginning of his discussion of the "I" suggests that he has in mind something very much like Lonergan's self-as-subject:

> Whatever I may be thinking of, I am always at the same time more or less aware of *myself*, of my *personal existence*. At the same time it is I who am aware; so that the total self of me, being as it were duplex, partly known and partly knower, partly object and partly subject, must have two aspects discriminated in it, of which for shortness we may call one the *Me* [only one of the things which the I is conscious *of*] and the other the *I* [which *is* conscious].[92]

For Erikson, this subjective sense of the "I" is perhaps the most obvious fact of existence, but also one of the most elusive. It dwells on the border of conscious existence, but is dependent on psychosocial qualities like the sense of identity for its vitality. Erikson even finds this subjective sense of the "I" in the inner light, the luminosity of awareness that Jesus refers to in Matthew's Gospel through the image of the eye as the lamp that fills the body with light (Mt 6:22).

This numinosity of the "I" is elusive precisely because it is subjective; it cannot be captured "alive" in reflection because reflection objectifies. One can reflect upon the self that is "me"; one can only experience the self that is "I." Still, indirectly, we get some better purchase on the "I" by considering what Erikson calls its "counterplayers." Indeed, the list of pronouns—from "I" to "They," "as each one first gets to be pronounced and understood correctly in childhood, and then is meaningfully experienced and reexperienced throughout life"—suggests a developmental map of the sense of "I" that summarizes in pronominal shorthand the course of personal development we have been tracing throughout this chapter.[93] The first sense of "I," Erikson proposes, emerges from the newborn's interplay with a sensed "You" in the maternal caretaker (a Primal Other). The mutually enriching relationship with this Other—and related Others—gradually empowers the original sense of "I" to recognize another fundamental counterplayer—almost an Inner Other, *my Self*. It also becomes the model for mutual recognition throughout life, including the expectation of that ultimate meeting which, as St. Paul says, we now only vaguely sense (the Ultimate Other). Beginning with "I" and "you," then, the system of pronouns reflects a ground plan ready to unfold in stages. The original dyad soon turns into a number of triads as a series of "he's" and "she's" (and "it's") become added counterplayers. And they, along with the plurals "we," "you," and "they," are not only verbal necessities but the bearers of important emotional involvements with complexly varied connotations that must extend to an increasingly widening range of counterplayers as one moves out from one's family and community. "And yet, throughout all these critical stages with all their involvements, there remains for the *I* a certain existential solitariness" which Erikson sees "as seeking love, liberation, salvation."[94]

Later, in our final chapter, we will return to this theme of the existential solitariness of the "I" when we consider Thomas Merton's lifelong search for God in his true self. For now, we can anticipate the later discussion of Christian conversion with Erikson's observation that Jesus' demand of active faith is both a therapeutic formula and an ethical message responding directly to the search of the solitary "I" for love, liberation, salvation. For to be *active* (along with numinous, central, continuous, and whole) is one of the most essential dimensions of a sense of "I." Thus Erikson can conclude that "repentance as an active choice (and the Greek word for it is *metanoia*, translated by Luther as 'Umkehr'—'turnabout')," not only makes one central to one's life-space, but, through liberation from the inactivation of a bad conscience and from banishment by divine judgment, brings one closer to the wholeness of the "I" 's numinosity—the full alertness called for in the repeated encouragement: "Be aware! Be wakeful! Watch!"[95]

Happiness is equilibrium. Shift your weight.

Tom Stoppard

3

DEVELOPMENTAL THEORY AND CONSCIENCE

Personal development is the ever greater realization of the radical drive for self-transcendence, for reaching out beyond oneself affectively and cognitively through critical, principled judgment and responsible, loving action. So far, our consideration of the developmental theories has remained expository, simply interweaving the theories in a way calculated to highlight the unity of personal development seen as self-transcendence. The aim was to make explicit and give emphasis to the developmental theorists' implicit use of self-transcendence as a criterion of movement to higher stages, a norm of maturity. This very argument, of course, eliminated from the beginning any possible claim to neutrality regarding the basic, overall thrust of the developmental theories. The general perspective of this study is one of enthusiastic but critical support. Still, there are clarifications, distinctions, qualifications, and criticisms to be made. The primary purpose of this chapter is to sharpen our focus on an integrated developmental model of self-transcending subjectivity as an explanatory understanding of conscience critically grounding the meaning of fundamental conversion. The first major section works through several problematic aspects of developmental theory toward a unified view of the developing self. The second section then distills the central elements of a developmental understanding of conscience from both Chapter 2's exposition and the present analysis.

DEVELOPMENTAL THEORY: ANALYSIS AND CRITICISM

Difficulties within developmental theory are numerous. While I cannot deal with all of them here, I will address those which pose the most serious questions for the construction of an integrated model of the self (a model of developing, self-transcending subjectivity). Toward a unified theory of the self (and, in the next section, conscience), then, this critical discussion will move through such key areas as the nature and relationship of stages, affectivity and imagination, and the relation of judgment and action. Such detailed analysis of the self is a *sine qua non* condition for our later discussion of conversion. For if conversion is a transformation of the self, our interpretation of it will be only as successful as our understanding of the self is accurate.

Nature of Stage Development

A basic question central to my thesis concerns the way different theorists understand the very nature of stage development, and thus the possibility of validly integrating their perspectives.[1] Clearly, Erikson's psychosocial approach and Piaget's structural approach are both developmental stage theories. Yet their meanings of development and stage are significantly different, despite the fact that in later years both Erikson and Piaget saw their independent theories—with their respective emphases on the affective and the cognitive—as mutually complementary.[2]

Erikson, working out of the psychoanalytic tradition, has a functional understanding of development in which stages are defined by psychosocial tasks and marked by ego crises. Every person who lives into old age develops through all the stages of the life cycle, meeting (and remeeting) each task more or less successfully. Stages are essentially critical periods in which lifelong tasks of ego identity are dramatically highlighted. Though linked to a biological process of maturation, each stage has an obvious, culturally defined psycho*social* component.[3]

In contrast, Piaget's stages are defined in terms of logical-cognitive structures. Each higher stage is a structurally different and more adequate (i.e., more highly differentiated and complexly integrated) organization of intelligence, realizing ever more successfully its invariant function of maintaining an active equilibrium with the environment (through assimilation and accommodation). These structural stages are invariantly sequential, hierarchically integrated, holistic, and universal.[4] Unlike the psychosocial stages of Erikson's life cycle, however, Piaget's highest cognitive stage of formal operations is not necessarily attained by every adult, regardless of age.[5] Structural stages are not maturational in that sense, though they may be linked to maturation of the nervous system during childhood and adolescence.[6]

Still, as previously noted, there is a positive correlation between the developmental sequences of psychosocial-functional and structural-cognitive stages: the blossoming of symbolic and imaginative powers during the play years of purposeful initiative; the emergence and development of concrete logical operations during the school years of industrious and skillful competence; and the appearance of formal operations just as the adolescent, moving into a more complex social world, is engaged in the difficult task of pulling together past identifications and projecting future possibilities as part of the attempt at establishing a workable (personally and socially meaningful) identity for the present. The point, then, is not to unify functional and structural theories in a simple fusion which ignores their differences, but to integrate them in a complex system which recognizes their complementary relationship. Thus, psychosocial development can be a necessary existential condition for structural development at some points (e.g., experiences of responsible caring for postconventional moral reasoning), just as cognitive development can be a necessary structural condition for psychosocial development at other points (e.g., concrete logical operations for industrious competence). While conceived in entirely different terms, then, the functional and structural stage theories do have one thing in common: focus on the person in transformation. They are connected in their attempts to explain (in methodologically different ways) distinct, but inseparable, dimensions of the one, concrete developing person.[7] Kegan's perspective on the evolving self clearly reveals this underlying unity, even as it highlights our focus on the dynamic self, not the stages it develops through.

Relationship of Stages: Hierarchy, Epigenesis, and the Imagination

Discussion of the nature of stages in the functional and structural theories leads to another question central to our understanding of developmental theory: How do stages relate to each other? What do Kohlberg and Fowler mean when they say that developmental-structural stages are hierarchical? Or what does Erikson mean by the "epigenetic" relationship between psychosocial stages? First a few words about the latter question; then we will consider the hierarchical relationship of structural stages, especially on the place of intuitive-symbolic knowing in cognitive development.

For Erikson, development through the life cycle is epigenesis. Transformed from its biological origins, the epigenetic principle states that "anything that grows has a ground plan, and that out of this ground plan the parts arise, each having its own time of special ascendancy, until all parts have arisen to form a functioning whole."[8] Stages, then, are successive differentiations of parts which exist in some form from the very beginning. While each developmental issue is highlighted at its point of crisis, they all exist in constantly changing forms from beginning to end throughout the life cycle. Intimacy, for example, does not just come into existence as an issue in young adulthood. Intimacy is always a fundamental psychosocial issue; in young adulthood it is highlighted at its critical phase.

The genius of Erikson's life cycle, indeed, is that epigensis leaves nothing behind as it moves forward. Every human issue (strength and weakness) is brought along in a transformed state from the very beginning. So, for example, while the basic crisis of trust/mistrust occurs in infancy, the issue of trust/mistrust and some degree of the virtue of hope is always present in some form throughout life. And, as Don Browning has rightly emphasized, the epigenetic principle keeps the earlier and later, the so-called "lower" and "higher," in the human person together. Indeed, while epigenesis specifies the meaning of life (including its beginning) in terms of the "higher" purposes of its end, it insists that the "higher" purposes will be effective only insofar as they have taken up and carried forward in transformed fashion the strengths of the earlier and "lower."[9] Reflective, responsible, purposeful activity, for example, to be genuinely human must always include the dimension of the playful, just as mature, adult conscience will never completely transcend the superego. Epigenesis is a developmental view not of angels but of total, historical, embodied persons.

For Kohlberg, the Piagetian notion of hierarchically integrated structural stages is paradigmatic. As Kohlberg explains this stage model, "higher stages displace (or rather reintegrate) the structures found at lower stages." As an example, he points out that "formal operational thought includes all the structural features of concrete operational thought but at a new level of organization. Concrete operational thought or even sensorimotor thought does not disappear when formal thought arises, but continues to be used in concrete situations where it is adequate. . . ."[10]

Simple as it seems, this basic point is extremely important for an accurate understanding of Piaget's view of cognitive development, and therefore of the cognitive-structural approaches of Kohlberg and Fowler. Piaget's analysis of cognitive development is often taken to be merely logical, to the detriment of other dimensions of knowing. And this is not without reason, as Piaget's focus, especially during later childhood and adolescence, is clearly on the development of logical operations. Still, as we have just seen in Kohlberg's example, if logical operations become the focus of attention as cognitive development progresses, the earlier sensorimotor and especially intuitive-symbolic patterns of knowing are not left behind but taken up and included in the more highly differentiated and completely integrated synthesis of a higher level. Knowing, then, even in Piaget's analysis, never develops to a point where it is only logical. Even the most advanced patterns of logical knowing are always rooted in sensorimotor activities and the symbolic-intuitive knowing which first appear in early childhood.

Clearly, Piaget's analysis of formal logical thinking is not the place to look for a rich interpretation of the mature forms of this symbolic-intuitive knowing. For this we would do better to turn to the recollective hermeneutic of Paul Ricoeur.[11] Piaget was, after all, always principally interested in the development of the logic of *scientific* knowing. Indeed, on the specific *development* of intuitive-symbolic knowing in patterns other than the logical-scientific, there is little systematic understanding. Howard Gardner has recently called attention to this gap in developmental understanding, and has even offered a suggestive sketch of the basic stages in the development of artistic understanding in children and adolescents.[12] And Hans Furth has suggested a linking of Piaget and Freud based precisely on the centrality of symbol in their complementary approaches.[13] This whole area of cognitive development plainly needs an enormous amount of research and analysis, especially for clarifying the foundations of moral knowing in its fullest human sense. Indeed, while the postconventional stages of Kohlberg's sequence require advanced formal logical operations for their critical ethical reflection, the heart of moral reasoning is in the fundamental symbolic-intuitive patterns of valuing which are at once and inseparably affective and cognitive.

While Piaget's analysis focuses on the logical patterns underlying scientific understanding, and not on the more holistic affective-cognitive patterns of personal understanding I would call *symbolic*, still his general approach to knowing is most helpful for appreciating the central and dynamic import of this symbolic pattern of imaginative-feeling. This is true particularly because of his critically realistic insistence that all knowing is constructive activity oriented toward creating reality, not the slavish copying of a naive realism geared to reproducing an already existing reality.[14]

If this creative dimension belongs to all knowing, for Piaget it is especially characteristic of the imaginative symbol. Though the creative aspect of the symbolic function is most obvious in the imaginative play of young children, Piaget maintains that it continues even after symbolic play is integrated into intelligence and the symbol becomes less distorted and more adequate to the reality symbolized. Creative imagination, he says, is the "assimilating activity in a state of spontaneity," and "does not diminish with age," but with the progress of accommodation is integrated into and thereby broadens intelligence. Piaget also understands the imaginative symbol as expressive of the affective life.[15] But because these two dimensions of symbols—creativity and affectivity—are present in Piaget's work only in principle, there still remains the further work in this area necessary for an adequate developmental understanding of personal knowing as *imaginative*.

In recent decades William F. Lynch has been one of the most persuasive advocates of the human importance of imagination. For Lynch imagination is linked radically to human hope, the sense that "there is a way out." Imagination envisions what cannot yet be seen, realizes that "the boundaries of the possible are wider than they seem." And here, in the realm of the possible, reality is discovered, created. For "the task of the imagination is to imagine the real." Its principal drive is "through fantasy and unreality into reality." In Lynch's view, then, imagination is not fantasy, but that total set of personal forces which "contributes to the formation of the full contextual image of an object."[16] In this sense, then, imagination is moral insight in operation—cognitively and affectively searching the possibilities and constructing a concrete context of value for creative action. This is why Daniel Maguire names imagination the supreme moral power.[17] Faced with two humanly unacceptable alternatives, moral imagination refuses to believe that it cannot transcend the situation, that it cannot create a third, human alternative. Thus Ray Hart suggests that at the heart of imagination is a "distrust of the 'given'."[18]

Like Lynch, Hart interprets imagination not as one power, but as a wide range of mental acts (including sensation and reason) which intend and move us into the "unfinished" realm of the "coming to be," the world of human creation which lies always before us. Indeed, if creation means anything, Hart asserts, it is that the imaging mind puts more meaning into reality than it takes out. But the meaning imagination creates is not just any meaning; it is the symbolic meaning which engages the mind as a whole. Through the concrete-universal character of symbols, imagination is able to remain close to the event while elaborating its feeling-tone in a universe of non-discursive discourse.[19]

If creative imagination moves us into the realm of the "coming to be," the central unfinished reality of that realm existentially is the self. As Paul Tillich explicated "ontological shock" as the jarring conviction that our disposition is cheating us of our ownmost possibilities of being, Hart speaks of the correlative "imaginative shock" that activates our feeling-imagination in quest of those possibilities. Such shock can open the self to new possibilities by breaking through one's historical selves and retrieving unrealized potencies; but the feeling-imagination can be put into such shock only by language spoken in its own tongue: the language of symbol. A work of art, for example, can terrify the "average feeling" of ossified imagination because of its power to shake the equilibrium of feeling-imagination. "Shock" in a work of art, says Hart, "is the breakdown of equilibrium in average feeling and its re-establishment at another level; in every great work of art, the felt world is at stake."[20] We can think, for example, of what *Guernica* has meant for (done to) so many people in the last half century. But art is only one of the forms in which the concrete-universal symbol drives to our imaginative-affective heart to shock us into greater reality; personal existence is shot-through with symbolic reality.

Indeed, so deeply does symbolism permeate personal existence that Howard Rugg maintains that creative imagination is primarily embodied in gesture. The felt-thought of imagination is gestural symbol rooted in tensed body movement. Like the modern classic interpreters of symbol, Ernst Cassirer and Suzanne Langer, Rugg uses the term "symbol" for every expression of human consciousness. But, as Langer, for example, distinguishes between discursive and presentational symbols, Rugg distinguishes between verbally-reasoned thought and felt-thought, and focuses on the gestural symbol that is felt-thought as the locus of creative imagination.[21]

William Van Roo makes much the same distinction in considering two modes of symbolizing: conceptual and intuitive. While all symbolizing begins in insight, its expression can either head for the clear and distinct ideas of abstract, univocal concepts, or seek appropriate concrete embodiment of its intuitive grasp of feeling in a sensuous medium tied to perception, memory, and image. Van Roo's general definition specifies symbol as a sensuous image which actualizes the symbolizer in the term of an intentional operation, reveals the symbolizer internally or externally or both, and may affect the human world, including, perhaps principally, the symbolizer.[22] It is not difficult to see how the elements of this definition are particularly appropriate to what Van Roo names the intuitive symbol, which embodies in its depth and fullness the complex reality of the symbolizing person.

Indeed, it is for this affect-laden image that actualizes, reveals, and influences the multidimensional person in its wholeness that I reserve here the term "symbol." For when our concern is the affective, cognitive, moral, and religious totality of the person, we must focus as sharply as possible on that communicator of human reality that best relates in an integrated way to the many dimensions of that totality. And this is that mode of affective understanding which various theorists name intuitive, imaginative, creative, presentational, gestural felt-thought, and which in this study I will simply call symbolic. It will be central to our interpretation of personal conversion.

Because Piaget is interested principally in the development of the logical organization grounding the scientific pattern of knowing, his analysis—like much of western culture and education generally—ignores the symbolic pattern of understanding once the discursive pattern differentiates itself from their common symbolic-intuitive base of preoperational activity and develops into organized structures of logical operations. Thus Piaget offers no analysis of symbolic-intuitive understanding as it develops into the more mature stages of the symbolic pattern. Despite his important emphasis on the creative dimension of the symbol, then, and on its role in expressing affectivity, Piaget leaves much analysis to be done on the development of that understanding which is at the heart of moral life: the symbolic pattern of affectively discerning value.[23]

While making this crucial qualification, however, we must note that though symbolic understanding may be central in our moral response to value, that response to value must be critically translated into the practical logic of action. Except in those relatively few instances when the logic of the discursive pattern is transported into the rarified atmosphere of scientific theory, then, the development of the logical pattern which Piaget stresses is an indispensable dimension of our self-transcending thrust into the complex human world as creators of value. Mature moral living demands the integration of the symbolic pattern of imaginative-affective understanding with the discursive pattern's logic of practical understanding. Kohlberg's analysis of moral reasoning takes a few tentative steps in the direction of this integration with its recognition of affectivity as a key factor in moral development. While this recognition of affectivity needs great expansion in a fully adequate analysis of moral reasoning, mature morality's requirement of the logic of practical reasoning clarifies Kohlberg's reliance on Piaget's analysis of logical development as a necessary though insufficient part of such an adequate analysis. And while Piaget's approach focuses on the logic of discursive reasoning at the higher stages, his hierarchical understanding of stages insists that the logical operations of the discursive pattern are rooted in the same symbolic-intuitive preoperational activities as the symbolic pattern is, and that their full realization in human life requires their reintegration with a developed symbolic pattern.

Are Kohlberg's stages of moral reasoning hierarchically related in the same way as Piaget's cognitive stages, as Kohlberg claims? In what sense can the higher stages of moral reasoning be understood as subsuming the lower into a more complexly integrated organization? Is there any way in which the egocentric structure of Stage 2 instrumental reasoning, for example, can be integrated into the reasoning of Stage 6 structured by the principle of justice? Higher stages, rather than taking up lower stages, would seem to reject them as inadequate moral orientations. And they clearly do. But lower stages are rejected precisely in terms of their *limitations* as moral orientations. Like early cognitive stages, lower moral stages represent positive advances as well as limitations. Because of their limitations, lower stages are rejected as inadequate orientations to the moral life. The limitations of lower stages, then, whether cognitive or moral, are not subsumed by and integrated into the higher stages. Egocentrism is characteristic of the lower stages of both cognitive and moral development. In neither case are egocentric limitations subsumed by higher stages. The positive cognitive gains of symbolic-intuitive intelligence, for example, are brought up into and reintegrated by the structures of formal logical thinking (which rejects lower stages as inadequate cognitive *orientations*, but not the strengths of their cognitive powers). In the same way, the moral elements of agreement and fairness at Stage 2 or of intentionality and mutual relationships (respect, loyalty, etc.) at Stage 3 are not rejected but clearly maintained and even transformed by higher stages. Indeed, in Kohlberg's view, such elements are only particular manifestations of the developing welfare and justice concerns which are present at every stage, and which "take on more differentiated, integrated, and universalized forms at each step of development."[24] Kohlberg's view on this point could not be a clearer statement of the drive for self-transcendence in the moral realm.

In this discussion of stages I have stressed the significance of imagination in moral reasoning, a significance we will later see personified in Thomas Merton. Because of the intimate connection between imagination and affectivity it is important that we now consider the controversial issue of affectivity in Kohlberg's theory.

Kohlberg on Affectivity

A recurrent criticism of Kohlberg's theory of moral development has emphasized its insufficient attention to the affective side of moral consciousness.[25] This criticism is not without grounds, for Kohlberg clearly and deliberately conceives his approach to moral development in the strictest Piagetian cognitive-structuralist terms. He is interested not in behavior, nor even in the content of moral judgments, but rather in the structure of justice reasoning behind moral judgments. In posing moral dilemmas to his subjects, Kohlberg is not primarily interested in their answers, but in the reasons they give for the answers when asked to explain them.

Because Kohlberg has defined the boundaries of his theoretical interest and research very narrowly, he presents only a small target for critics.[26] Despite this, many interpret him as claiming to explain *all* of moral development (motivation, behavior, etc.), and then go on to criticize his approach as inadequate for this purpose.[27] If Kohlberg escapes that kind of criticism, though, there still remains a key question. Is Kohlberg's cognitive-structural approach really adequate to do justice even to his narrowly defined issue of moral reasoning development?[28]

As noted in the presentation of postconventional morality, Kohlberg does not view cognitive development as sufficient in itself for moral development. His point is "not that moral judgment stages are cognitive—they are not the mere application of logic to moral problems—but that the existence of moral stages implies that [moral] development has a basic cognitive-structural component." And Kohlberg has consistently asserted that "cognitive maturity is a necessary, but not a sufficient condition for moral judgment maturity."[29] However, he has not been as consistent or clear in explaining precisely what this means. What, in addition to cognitive development, does he claim is necessary for moral development? Even an initial, tentative answer requires examining a complicated series of hints scattered throughout many articles.

In a comparatively recent article Kohlberg, immediately after making his "necessary but not sufficient" assertion, repeats in a newly organized way his standard position on the necessity of role taking ability for moral development: "Just as there is a vertical sequence of steps in movement up from moral Stage 1 to moral Stage 2 to moral Stage 3, so there is a horizontal sequence of steps in movement from logic to social perception to moral judgment."[30] Here, development in social perception (role or perspective taking) as well as development in logical reasoning is seen as necessary (and, since nothing else is mentioned, one might infer sufficient) for development in moral reasoning. Significantly, there is no mention of the affective dimension of the person in this horizontal sequence leading to and constituting moral reasoning. However, while social perception would seem to be a merely cognitive process, the fact that Kohlberg distinguishes it here from purely *logical* reasoning (and not from the more general cognitive capacity he usually refers to) raises a question about the way Kohlberg understands the nature of social perception, role taking, or perspective taking.

Usually, when Kohlberg discusses affectivity he refers to specific sentiments or emotions like guilt, fear, and shame which persons feel in moral judgment situations. And Kohlberg does not consider these feelings of essential moral import, for "the quantitative role of affect is relatively irrelevant for understanding the structure and development of moral judgment," and "the development of sentiment, as it enters into moral judgment, is . . . a development of structures with a heavy cognitive component."[31] In sum, with regard to moral emotion, Kohlberg's "point of view is that the 'cognitive' definition of the moral situation directly determines the moral emotion which the situation arouses."[32] All this is said, however, in the context of Kohlberg's assertion "that 'cognition' and 'affect' are different aspects of, or perspectives on, the same mental events, that all mental events have both cognitive and affective aspects, and that the development of mental dispositions reflects structural changes recognizable in both cognitive and affective perspectives."[33] For, basically, Kohlberg's position, like Piaget's, is one of "cognitive-affective parallelism," which holds that "the *development* of cognition and the development of affect have a common structural base."[34]

If Kohlberg's view on such narrowly moral and negative emotions as guilt, fear, and shame offers little opening to a positive place for the affective in moral reasoning, his discussion of empathy and justice in connection with social perception or role taking seems to offer greater possibilities.

In Kohlberg's view, "the primary meaning of the word 'social' is the distinctively human structuring of action and thought by role-taking, by the tendency to react to others as like the self and to react to the self's behaviour from the other's point of view."[35] Role taking has both affective and cognitive dimensions, and "when the emotional side of role taking is stressed, it is typically termed 'empathy.'"[36] If the highest development of this social process in the moral sphere is the reconciliation of conflicting claims through the principle of justice, its roots, according to Kohlberg, are to be found in the fundamental human reality of empathy, the awareness of other selves as having thoughts and feelings like one's own.

Kohlberg's studies in a variety of cultures indicate that the overwhelming focus of moral choice and feeling concerns the consequences of human action "for the pain and harm (or joy and welfare) to human (or quasi-human) beings." Such empathy grounds the child's entire social life. "Perceived harm to others is as immediately, if not as intensely, apprehended as is harm to the self. Empathy does not have to be taught or conditioned; it is a primary phenomenon."[37] Development and socialization merely organize this spontaneous empathy into consistent sympathetic and moral concerns. In Kohlberg's view, then, there is, from the very beginning of moral experience to its highest development, a "psychological unity of empathy and justice in moral role-taking."[38]

Martin Hoffman, in his attempt to ground altruism in sympathetic distress, has suggested a cognitive-developmental interpretation of empathy in which the development of a sense of the other transforms the child's self-oriented empathic distress into a true sympathetic concern for the other.[39] In this view empathic distress, an involuntary, at times forceful, experiencing of another's emotional state, is developmentally first. This is a global distress experienced by infants, who, without self/other differentiation, behave as though they themselves were experiencing any distress they witness in others. Hoffman explains that a major change in reaction to distress occurs when a child becomes capable of distinguishing between self and others. Now, when confronted with another in pain, the child still experiences empathic distress but recognizes that it is the other, not herself or himself, that is in actual pain. This recognition transforms empathy *with* the victim, a parallel affective response, into sympathetic concern *for* the victim, a more reciprocal response. The motive to alleviate the child's own distress gives way, to some degree, to the motive to alleviate the other's distress. Hoffman sees this transformation of empathic into sympathetic distress occurring in three stages correlated to developing cognitive apprehension of the other: (1) person permanence (without distinguishing others' inner states); (2) role taking (which appreciates others' feelings as other, and enables appropriate responses to alleviate others' distress); (3) identity recognition (which allows one to see others as continuing persons with histories and thus respond not only to immediate situations of pain but also to the distress embodied in their larger patterns of life, their general plight; further cognitive development can expand this comprehension of general plight to groups as well as individuals). Hoffman's thesis is that such sympathetic distress predisposes a person to act on the other's behalf, i.e., altruistically.

There is clearly a place in Kohlberg's understanding of moral reasoning, as we have seen, for this fundamental affective reality of empathy. That empathy's development, in Kohlberg's view, may be largely mediated by cognitive-structural development does not alter or minimize the importance of its recognition. When Kohlberg claims, then, that moral stages are primarily "the product of the child's inter-action with others,"[40] or, as we have seen, that development of moral reasoning presupposes (in a horizontal sequence) development of both logical reasoning and social perception, the affective reality of empathy is included, even if it is not emphasized or even made explicit. "Interaction with others" and social perception (role or perspective taking) are rooted in empathy, according to Kohlberg's view. Though clearly possessing a cognitive dimension, they are radically affective. Like every interpersonal reality, they are at once, and inseparably, af-fective *and* cognitive. Despite Kohlberg's cognitive-structural ap-proach to the development of moral reasoning, then, the reality of the moral reasoning at issue is, according to Kohlberg's own account, an irreducibly affective-cognitive unity. Moral reasoning, as Kohlberg clearly asserts, is "not the mere application of logic to moral prob-lems."[41] Logic, of course, is applied to complex moral problems, but the essence of specifically moral reasoning, leading to judgments of moral value, is evaluation, which is rooted not in the purely logical analysis of concepts, but in the affective-cognitive apprehension of concrete human values.[42] Even the most advanced formal logical op-erations, therefore, do not by themselves enable a person to make ma-ture moral judgments.

Given this analysis of Kohlberg's understanding of moral reason-ing as a fundamentally affective-cognitive unity, criticisms of Kohl-berg's approach to moral development as rationalistic must be judged as inaccurate. Kohlberg's approach needs to be filled out through greater attention to the affective dimension of moral reasoning, but the roots and theoretical justification for such a move are already pres-ent in his approach. In fact, as we have seen in his revised analysis of adult moral development, Kohlberg has recently begun to place em-phasis on the moral significance of certain specifically adult *experiences* of personal choice, seeing them as conditions for development to post-conventional moral reasoning. In so doing, he has suggested that an adequate account of development to principled morality, which we will correlate with critical moral conversion in Chapter 4, must integrate the functional stages of the Eriksonian psychosocial view and the moral judgment stages of the cognitive-structural analysis into a single whole.[43] Indeed, along with the parallelism of affective and cognitive functioning and development, Kohlberg had already identified as a basic assumption in his approach "a fundamental unity of personality organization and development termed the ego, or the self," whose various strands of development are "united by their common reference to a *single concept of self* in a *single social world.*"⁴⁴

In stressing the idea of a fundamental unity of personality, Kohlberg's thinking approaches the thesis of the present study, which envisions an integrated interpretation of the basic (affective, cognitive, moral, and faith) dimensions of the concrete personal subject in terms of its drive for self-transcendence. Central to this integrating perspective is the view that Erikson's psychosocial virtues—especially such preeminently moral ones as fidelity, love, and care—are developmental successors to the fundamental empathy which Kohlberg identifies as a basic component of moral reasoning. This is the reason for correlating Piaget's cognitive analysis and Erikson's psychosocial account from the beginning of the developmental process.

In this focus on the fundamental unity of personality, Robert Kegan's understanding of the self's developmental process is also helpful for relating moral reasoning and affectivity. As we have seen, for Kegan personal development is a basic process of self/object differentiation and integration. On the affective side, this means successive objectifications of increasingly complex personal needs: sensorimotor needs, impulsive needs, self-interest needs, interpersonal needs, identity needs. As part of the totality of personal development, the development of moral reasoning is intrinsically linked to this process of need differentiation and integration. The fact that moral reasoning is not merely cognitive means, in other words, that a person's level of moral reasoning will not rise above his or her successful negotiation of the various dimensions of personal need. As long as a person is *subject to* self-interest, for example, moral reasoning will be pervaded by those interests and tied to Stage 2. When those self-interest needs are successfully shifted to the object-pole, they no longer dominate the self and its moral reasoning. The self and its moral reasoning are no longer identified with self-interests; the self *has* its interests, and moral reasoning deals with them. Now moral reasoning, like the self, begins to be identified with—and limited by—interpersonal needs.

In Kegan's view the objectification of needs does not eliminate them, it merely puts them at enough distance for the self to control them, instead of being dominated by them. This perspective presents a systematic, structural way of understanding what Abraham Maslow means when—in discussing the hierarchy of human needs—he speaks of satisfying basic (deficiency-compensating) needs in order to be motivated by the growth-producing needs of self-actualization.⁴⁵ In this way it becomes clear that all the needs of Maslow's developmental hierarchy—from the rudimentary physiological needs of survival, through the needs for security, belongingness, and esteem, to the various forms of self-actualization—are constitutive elements in the very fabric of moral reasoning. That Kohlberg recognizes this fact is evident in the different types of motivation for moral action he has specified at the six stages: from fear of punishment and desire for reward, through anticipation of disapproval or censure, to concern about community disrespect and, finally, self-condemnation.[46] In sum, concrete persons, not abstract reasons, make moral judgments. And concrete persons are subject to various kinds of needs, ranging from survival to self-transcendence. Inevitably, then, moral judgments are intrinsically shaped by the needs those who make them are subject to.

We can continue our discussion of affectivity in Kohlberg and expand it to consider the place of affectivity in structural theory generally by shifting our focus in the next section to Fowler's "faithing."

Fowler on Affectivity

Fowler's stages of faith, which are explicitly modeled on the Piagetian-Kohlberg structural-developmental paradigm, can be understood to be hierarchically related in the same way as theirs, with the highest stage of universalizing faith taking up and transforming the positive, self-transcending elements of the lower stages.

However, while Fowler explicitly follows the Piagetian-Kohlberg structural approach in his analysis of faith, he makes a point of asserting that he "cannot adopt the Piagetian theoretical separation of cognition and affection, of reason and emotion, but rather must account for their interpenetration in the dynamics of faith." As Fowler understands him, "Piaget makes a rigorous distinction between *cognition* (the 'structures' of knowing) and *affection* (the 'energetics' or motive-force, of knowing)." Fowler sees Kohlberg maintaining this distinction with Piaget, but recognizes that Kohlberg "makes it clear that in reality the two interpenetrate and are inseparable."[47] In another place Fowler even recognizes that Kohlberg's approach is "pointing to *operations* or *patterns of thinking, feeling,* and *valuing* which *underlie* moral attitudes and behavior."[48] Despite this clear recognition, however, Fowler sees Piaget and Kohlberg as claiming "that cognitive structures tend to dominate the affective dynamics and that only the cognitive structures can serve as a basis for describing the sequence of developmental stages."[49] And this is good reason for Fowler to place Piaget and Kohlberg in the tradition not only of Kantian formalism but also of Cartesian rationalism. Without pursuing the issue of Fowler's accuracy in interpreting Piaget and especially Kohlberg on this point, we can ask whether Fowler, in fact, carries out in his own approach this point of difference he sees between his and the Piagetian-Kohlberg approach.

We can ask, in other words, how faithful, in practice, is Fowler to his conception of faith as "a structured set of operations in which cognition and affection are inextricably bound together," in which "the 'rational' and the 'passional' are fused"? Does Fowler's approach do justice to his notion of faith as "an active 'mode-of-being-in-relation' to another or others in which we invest commitment, belief, love, risk, and hope"?[50] Clearly, this is an extremely important issue in this study's attempt to construct an *integrated* model of the personal subject in its drive for self-transcendence, i.e., of conscience, the foundation for our interpretation of conversion.

We have noted how Kohlberg, though explicitly working within a narrow definition of moral reasoning, has, in principle at least, provided the theoretical opening for an interpretation of moral judgment in which cognition and affectivity are inseparably one. In contrast to Kohlberg's explicit emphasis on the cognitive, Fowler offers an expansive notion of faith in which knowing, feeling, and valuing form an integrated whole. Can a cognitive-developmental approach do justice to such a fully personal understanding of faith? Can Fowler use this approach without the cognitive dimension dominating, as he says it does in the analyses of Piaget and Kohlberg?

Fowler's approach, of course, is structural. It does not focus, therefore, on the content of faith, on faith as the particular beliefs, values, symbols, and cultic allegiances which give substance to a person's life. The primary and explicit focus of Fowler's approach, rather, is the inner structure of faith, and particularly of faith-knowing. Fowler deliberately parallels his focus on the "structural character of faith-knowing" with Piaget's focus on "patterns of thinking" and Kohlberg's focus on "the forms or structures of thinking" used in justifying moral choices.[51] Thus, despite his judgment that cognitive structures unfortunately dominate in Kohlberg's approach to moral development, Fowler himself seems to allow the cognitive to rule in his own approach by focusing on faith as a kind of *knowing*. And he does this while announcing his understanding that knowing, feeling, and valuing are inextricably fused in faith.

In fact, while discussing this fusion of the "rational" and the "passional," Fowler acknowledges his indebtedness to the "psychoanalytic tradition (notably through Erik Erikson's writings), which insists upon recognizing the sharp qualification of rationality by unconscious defenses, needs and strivings, and which recognizes the role of symbolic functioning in the process of ego development."[52] Fowler even states his belief that Erikson's influence on him has been "more pervasive and more subtle" than that of Piaget and Kohlberg, that it has touched him "at convictional depths that the structural developmentalists have not addressed."[53] At the same time, however, Fowler has dropped the Eriksonian "Prototypical Challenges with Which Faith Must Deal" from his original set of variables in stage analysis. Erikson's psychosocial stages have also been eliminated from the schematic tables in which Fowler correlates his stages with those of other developmental theories.[54]

Erikson is included in *Stages of Faith*'s fictional conversation with Piaget and Kohlberg, but rather than attempt an integration, Fowler now prefers to speak of the "interplay" between structural and psychosocial stages, and to indicate "optional correlations" between structural equilibrations and psychosocial crises. His emphasis in this interplay is not so much on the experience of psychosocial crises conditioning the possibility of structural stage transition, as on how a person's structural stage will influence the way a psychosocial crisis is experienced.[55] The explanation for this change may be that Fowler has decided that Erikson's "existential" challenges and stages do not fit well with his own structural approach.[56] In any case, the seven variables included in Fowler's recent work are clearly structural and heavily cognitive.[57] This transition in Fowler's writings is particularly interesting when contrasted to Kohlberg's explicit and increasing dependence on Erikson in his later, revised work, especially for his analysis of adult moral development.[58] The fact is that Kohlberg has taken initial steps to integrate Erikson with his own structural approach to the development of moral reasoning in just the way one would expect Fowler to integrate Erikson with his analysis of faith, given his stated conviction about the fusion of knowing, feeling, and valuing in faith. Fowler's recent writings do give greater attention to the "Role of Symbols" as a distinct variable in faith analysis, though his treatment of symbols continues to remain heavily cognitive.

The problem I am pointing to is clearly evident in one of Fowler's later essays. Referring to a chart entitled "Faith: The Structural-Developmental Approach; A Summary Taxonomy of Structural Competences by Stage," which includes six variables but no mention of Erikson's challenges or stages, Fowler says:

> As one examines this chart reflectively, it may seem that the dynamic which lies at the heart of faith—namely, a centering affection, an organizing love, a central object of loyalty and

trust—is missing. And this is true. To note this is to be reminded again of the formal and structural focus of this stage theory. It is this formal character which gives the theory the possibility of being applied to a variety of different religious traditions with a variety of *contents* as regards prescribed beliefs, values, attitudes and behaviors.[59]

To note this is to be reminded not only of the theory's structural focus, but also of its strongly cognitive emphasis. This passage also suggests a confusion between "contents" and the "dynamic which lies at the heart of faith." It seems to presume that a structural approach, in order to maintain its general applicability to the contents of any tradition, must *not* engage the "dynamic which lies at the heart of faith." But is it necessary to omit consideration of the dynamic element in order to maintain general applicability? An affirmative answer is in order only if one is interested in following a strictly *cognitive*-structural approach. However, if one's approach is generally structural, with cognitive-affective-evaluative-committed faithing as its object, then to omit the dynamic is neither necessary nor desirable. The validity of a structural analysis of a cognitive-affective-evaluative-committed faithing depends first of all on a holistic approach—an approach which attends not only to the structure of the cognitive dimension, but also and just as much to the *structure* of faith's fundamental trust and loyalty, its "centering affection," and its "organizing love."

Clearly, in the concrete, these latter aspects always involve content, just as cognitive aspects do. But my concern here is with their structure. It may be that the affective dimensions of faithing are shaped or given their form by cognitive structure. This is the position Fowler ascribes to Kohlberg, and rejects as inadequate for an analysis of faith. On the other hand, the affective dimension of faith may have its own intrinsic structure, correlated with cognitive structure. Or, as we have seen Kohlberg suggest, the cognitive and affective dimensions may have a common structural base.[60] In either of the latter cases, the affective dimension will be explicitly represented, not "missing," in a holistic structural analysis. Rather than being tied to the "contents" of one tradition, such a holistic structural approach would be fully appropriate to every tradition, for all traditions of faithing have affective (love, trust, loyalty) as well as cognitive dimensions. To ignore the affective "dynamic which lies at the heart of faith," then, in order to remain generally applicable to various traditions, is neither necessary nor valid. Any structural approach which would truly do justice to faithing must attend explicitly to both the affective and cognitive dimensions of this integral personal reality.

Apart from the issue of content, it is not clear why Fowler steers clear of the non-cognitive dimensions of faith (love, trust, etc.), for in the same article he talks about "qualitative transformations in the person's structures or patterns of thinking, valuing, committing and believing."[61] These, along with feeling, are precisely the structures which an adequate analysis of faith must attend to, and not restrict itself to the structure of faith-knowing alone.

An important first step in this direction is the distinction Fowler has more recently made between two kinds of knowing: the logic of rational certainty and the logic of conviction. The logic of rational certainty, which Fowler identifies with Piaget's understanding of cognition, "aims at objectivity understood as a knowing free from all particular or subjective investigation. Its truths need to be impersonal, propositional, demonstrable and replicable."[62] Fowler finds this logic a misleading ideal for moral and faith knowing, not because these forms of knowing are not interested in objectivity, but because in these forms of knowing the self's own constitution is always at stake in an existential fashion. The freedom, risk, subjectivity, and passion involved in this self-constitutive knowing points to the larger, more comprehensive cognitive structuring activity of which the logic of rational certainty is only a part: the logic of conviction.

At the heart of this logic of convictional knowing in which the self is existentially constituted through its crucial value choices and actions is the esthetic dimension of "images, symbols, and synesthetic fusions of sense and feeling." This is a knowing steeped in the "so-called 'regressive' movements in which the psyche returns to preconceptual, prelinguistic modes and memories, and to primitive sources of energizing imagery, bringing them into consciousness with resultant reconstruals of the experience world."[63] Fowler insists that the logic of conviction does not negate the logic of rational certainty, but he says little about their relationship other than the suggestion that rational certainty is a specialized (critical) knowing within the more comprehensive cognitive orientation of convictional knowing.

In *The Transforming Moment*, which is devoted to "Understanding Convictional Experiences," James Loder, inspired by Michael Polanyi's analysis of tacit knowing, presents as a framework for situating convictional knowing a cognitional theory in which all knowing is understood as transformational. He specifies five steps in the logic of every knowing event, whether it be scientific, esthetic, therapeutic, or religious: (1) *conflict*—a rupture in the knowing context; (2) an *interlude for scanning*—waiting, wondering, following hunches, exhausting possibilities, for a moment or for years; (3) the *constructive act of imagination*—the turning point where with convincing force an insight transforms the elements of the ruptured situation and the perspective of the knower; (4) a *release of bound-up energy* from the unconscious, and an *opening* of the knower to both self and situation as response to being freed *from* conflict and *for* self-transcendence; (5) *interpretation* of the imaginative solution into the original context.[64]

Each pattern of knowing realizes these five steps in its own way, but each is a variation of the same basic logic. Scientific knowing, for example, is not a different *kind* of knowing from esthetic, just a different patterning of the one underlying logic. The shared basic logic common to every knowing is the intrinsic factor unifying all patterns. One need not search for an extrinsic relationship between a logic of rational certainty and a logic of conviction; on the most basic level they share the same logic of transformational knowing, though they realize it in different patterns. For Loder, the convictional experience of religious knowing includes the self in a special, existential way, as in Fowler's interpretation, but beyond the functional self-transformation characteristic of therapeutic knowing, religious knowing—the manifestation of the Holy—is essentially a transformation of all other transformations. It is a transforming negation of that radical, existential negation which is our potentiality for non-being, the "experience of nothingness." The essence of convictional knowing is the self's intimacy with its Source, and in Loder's Christian view the paradigm of this transforming convictional experience at the level of existential negation is the personally appropriated Christ event.[65]

Clearly, Loder draws his detailed portrait of convictional knowing in deep colors, but on a smaller canvas than Fowler's, which in broader strokes would include esthetic and therapeutic as well as religious knowing. Loder's analysis of the logic of all knowing as transformational, however, provides a unifying context for seeing the intrinsic connections between his sense of convictional knowing as religious and all the other patterns of knowing. It provides a valuable complement to Fowler's interpretation of faith. Aspects of both approaches were involved above when we discussed the *symbolic* pattern of knowing, in which experiencing, understanding, judging, and deciding all work together in an undifferentiated way through feeling to express in intrinsically *imaginative* means the self's deepest understanding of its being—its meanings, values, relationships, sources of power.

Despite the above qualifications, Fowler's work is of special interest because he is attempting to interpret, under the rubric of ultimacy, a person's total world-orientation, in which the affective and cognitive are one. And an analysis of such a fully personal orientation to reality, where feeling and knowing and evaluating and committing and loving are all bound together in a single, irreducible whole, is exactly the kind of framework required for grounding our interpretation of conversion in an adequate understanding of the personal subject, and thus of conscience.

Fowler on the Self: Centering and De-Centering

In fact, at one point, Fowler articulates a view of the person very much in line with this study's thesis on self-transcending subjectivity when he says that development in his theory "presumes a self that is involved in a simultaneous process of *centering* and *de-centering*."[66] This twofold process is a version of the bipolar development noted in the earlier presentation of Piaget's theory: in the single interaction of the individual and the total environment both an ever more fully personal self *and* an ever wider, more complex world are created. In terms of self-transcendence, only this gradual transformation of the egocentric infant, without a self or a world, into the genuine, de-centered self of the mature person relating to an objective world makes self-transcendence possible. It creates a true self to be transcended, which is at the same time capable of transcendence, of reaching out beyond itself. In the case-history of Mary's conversion related in *Stages of Faith*, Fowler is poignantly clear on how cruelly destructive even the most well-intended demand to deny self can be when there is no selfhood to deny. As I argued above for self-transcendence rather than self-sacrifice, Fowler advocates transformation rather than negation of the self.[67]

On the self-side of the developmental process, Fowler understands "an increasingly *individuating* self—a self which, as it develops, differentiates itself from a nurturing ethos and gradually, stage by stage, assumes the burden of construing and maintaining for the self a vision of reality, and of taking autonomous moral responsibility within it." As Fowler sees it, then, "this process describes an increasingly centered self—a self with boundaries established by increasingly self-chosen, self-aware investments of trust and loyalty."[68]

Simultaneous with this process of individuation, in Fowler's view, there occurs a "gradual de-centration in the sense that at each stage a more inclusive account is taken of persons, groups, experiences and world views other than one's own. Increasing with each stage there is an effort to find and maintain a mutuality or complementarity with a widened cosmos of being and value."[69] If the adolescent, for example, begins to define herself more sharply through loyalties to new friends and school communities, these loyalties are at the same time stretching her into a larger world of relationships and concerns. Or, if the new father's world is growing as he meets the needs of his infant daughter, he is also defining himself anew through his caring attention.

In the paradoxical process of personal development, then, as the self becomes more individuated, its orientation becomes more universal. Or, the more authentically subjective one becomes, the more genuinely objective one is. As difficult as it is to understand how authentic subjectivity and genuine objectivity are not only different perspectives on one process and increase together, but are in fact identical, they seem preferable terms to Fowler's "centering" and "de-centering," which turn a paradoxical reality into a literal contradiction. Kegan's constructivist model of subject/object differentiation and integration is a particularly illuminating way of explaining the self-transcending identity of subjectivity and objectivity in developmental terms.

While Fowler offers no analysis of the developing self even remotely as concretely detailed and theoretically comprehensive as Kegan's theory, his concern for an adequate understanding of fully personal faith development has led him to recognize the importance of a theory of the self. In particular, Fowler shows the concern of the present study that such a theory truly be of the historical and social self: that it take seriously how character is shaped by previous decisions and actions of our life histories as well as by the images and stories of the communities in which we are formed.[70] All these dimensions of the self are essential to an adequate theory of conversion.

The Integrated Self: Judgment and Action

Fowler's attempt to attend to the developing self's integrated orientation to the world is also important in relation to a question Kohlberg has raised periodically over the years—the question of the connection between moral judgment and moral action. After constructing the 1976 horizontal sequence of logic, social perception, and moral reasoning noted above, Kohlberg added to the sequence the final step of moral behavior. He then merely noted that whether or not even those who reason in terms of postconventional principles will live up to them depends on a "variety of factors."

Although moral behavior has never been the focus of Kohlberg's research, his interest in it has steadily increased. Thus in a 1984 paper he further specifies the horizontal sequence leading to action by distinguishing within moral reasoning a judgment of rightness and a judgment of responsibility, and by including non-moral ego controls (e.g., I.Q., attention, delay of gratification) as a final moment before action.[71] Although Kohlberg's discussion fails to distinguish consistently between judgment, decision, and choice, we may see in this latest sequence some similarity with Lonergan's distinction between understanding, judgment, and decision which we noted in Chapter 1 and will consider in more detail in Chapter 4. With this recent specification of a judgment of responsibility (What should *I* do?), Kohlberg approaches a practical judgment of personal conscience—in contrast to his standard impersonal judgment of rightness—for the first time.

In light of this model, Kohlberg suggests that action can be considered as moral in two different ways. The "personal consistency" approach defines a moral action as one which conforms to what the actor judges to be right. What Kohlberg calls the "universal right" approach defines moral action "objectively" in terms of agreement among postconventional subjects (not an opinion poll; the point of principled judgments of justice is to lead to agreement about conflicting claims). Thus, for Kohlberg, "when both the individual actor's point of view and that of the consensus of principled persons agree, and the action is carried out, we have a clear case of moral action."[72]

Kohlberg's analyses of both laboratory and real life situations finds an increasing likelihood of moral action at each higher stage. Thus, not only are principled subjects more likely than others to make objective judgments of rightness, but are also more likely to make judgments of responsibility and to perform actions consistent with those judgments.[73] In one laboratory experiment, for example, students coming to an interview were confronted by a "drugged" student looking for help. While the percentages of students who "thought they should help" were 36% at Stage 2, 77% at Stage 3, 69% at Stage 4, and 83% at Stage 5, their consistency between action and judgment increased steadily: 25%, 38%, 55%, 88%.[74] Unlike conventional belief that a particular kind of act should or should not be done, principled moral reasoning, according to Kohlberg, will more likely be followed. For Kohlberg, then, not only do form and content begin to merge in postconventional moral reasoning as the universal principle of justice structures welfare concerns,[75] but moral reasoning itself tends to become one with action through judgments of responsibility. This will be reflected in our later discussion of critical moral conversion, in which the whole self—cognitive and affective—is transformed.

While Kohlberg offers various psychological and philosophical suggestions to account for this increasing consistency, I would specify the basic condition for the possibility of action consistently conforming to judgment as the affective and cognitive integration of the whole self. To the degree that action consistently follows judgment, it follows not the judgment of merely conceptual knowing but the convictional judgment made within the symbolic pattern of imaginative knowing and valuing in which the affective and cognitive are integrated as one. In this symbolic pattern, feeling and knowing and loving and deciding all work together in an undifferentiated personal unity to bring forth action. Here decision (or ego controls) is not an extrinsic factor alongside moral judgment, but is so deeply interwoven with it that to judge is to decide is to act. Reflective ethical analysis may play an important auxiliary role, but the fundamental power of the symbolic pattern comes from the center of the person where the affective and cognitive dimensions speak with one voice. All of this is not to say that the symbolic pattern is found exclusively at postconventional stages, nor that it is always true. Neither is the case. Love, after all, is sometimes myopic. But when persons are able to respond to the values in a situation symbolically, as full persons, their judgments and their actions will be as one. Of course this is not our universal experience.

Kohlberg's point is that persons of principled reasoning are able to respond in this fashion more frequently than others. This, I suggest, is because postconventional persons reason, not with borrowed moral rules, but with self-chosen principles. These universal principles have been personally appropriated and have become identified with the person in such a way that what the person judges he or she *should* do is what he or she *wants* to do. Personal moral judgments of principle, and not other situational factors, dominate the decision-making process. In this sense, Kohlberg says, "the basic virtue may be called 'autonomy' as well as 'justice'."[76] This is possible because principled moral reasoning has its source in and flows from the integrated affective-cognitive core of the personal subject. It does not merely represent what the subject *thinks*, but expresses who the subject *is*. And in one important sense, to talk about who the personal subject is is to talk about the subject's faith.

This is why the intention of Fowler's analysis is significant. He is attempting to delineate the developing structures of the whole person's orientation to reality: not just the person as thinking, or as feeling, or as trusting, but the whole person as relating to reality in an integrated, undifferentiated way which includes what we usually distinguish as thinking and feeling and trusting and loving and committing.

Such faithing is not a complete interpretation of a person's relation to reality. As persons we are not simply undifferentiated unities.

We can dissect a Beethoven quartet as well as respond to it in an integrated way as whole persons. An adequate interpretation of the person must include the differentiation and complexity of personal consciousness as well as the integration and unity. But the integrated, active, relational orientation must be at the center of any interpretation of the person, for it is the living source of deeply personal judgments and decisions. When conscience is more than a word, it is the personal subject making these judgments and decisions of value out of a concrete, particular, and fully personal horizon or orientation to reality—an orientation which, when focused on the ultimate conditions of existence, is faith. This is the dynamic self that not only develops, but is radically transformed in basic conversions.

CONSCIENCE AS DEVELOPMENTAL

After this exposition and critical discussion of Erikson, Piaget, Kohlberg, Fowler, and Kegan on personal development, what can we say directly about conscience? Each of the authors makes a definite contribution to an interpretation of conscience, but none of them deals explicitly with conscience in the fully personal sense envisioned in this study. Erikson's adult ethical orientation comes closest perhaps. Piaget's analysis of cognitive development, and Fowler's of faith, do not focus on conscience as such. While Kohlberg's analysis does focus explicitly on moral judgment, and even speaks of Stage 6 as an orientation of principled conscience, his interview subjects are always making detached, third person, observer judgments about dilemma situations in which they are not involved.[77] While such moral judgments are clearly connected with conscience, they do not constitute, even as judgments, the primary meaning of conscience. For, as understood here, conscience is not simply any judgment about moral issues. As judgment, rather, conscience is the actively involved personal agent struggling to reach a concrete understanding and practical judgment as to what course of *action* he or she should take to respond in a creative and fully human way to the values in this particular situation. Kohlberg's recently introduced judgment of responsibility begins to recognize this.

Kohlberg: Principled Moral Judgment

Many important aspects of the practical judgment of conscience are involved, of course, in the moral judgments made about Kohlberg's hypothetical dilemma stories, although in a less personal, more abstract fashion. And we have noted that Kohlberg finds a positive correlation between such moral judgment and action at the principled level. So while Kohlberg's analysis is not of personal conscience judgments in the proper sense, it does help us to understand the developmental nature of conscience in an especially clear way.

Two of Kohlberg's most important contributions to an understanding of conscience are only implicit in his analysis. The first is that development to higher stages, or growth in maturity, of moral judgment has self-transcendence as a fundamental criterion.[78] As one's moral reasoning develops from an egocentric, preconventional orientation, to a social, conventional orientation, and finally to a personal, principled orientation, one progressively moves more and more beyond one's self and one's narrow interests toward ever greater and wider values. And this is the basic reality of conscience: a radical drive of the personal subject to reach out beyond himself or herself to others in the realization of value.

Second, because Kohlberg's analysis focuses on the cognitive dimension of moral development, but also includes the affective as intrinsic to moral judgment, it points to another essential characteristic of conscience: while conscience manifests itself in a judgment of what the subject should do in a particular situation, it is always a judgment of the whole person, integrally cognitive and affective.

Piaget's and Erikson's insights can also reinforce this integral concept of conscience. As judgment, conscience clearly has a cognitive dimension. And it is on this point that Piaget's analysis makes its powerful contribution to an explanatory understanding of conscience, specifying the developing subject's possibilities as well as limitations for cognitive self-transcendence. By coupling Piaget's cognitive analysis with Erikson's psychosocial theory of affective development, and by focusing this stereoscopic perspective on moral issues of value as in Kohlberg's approach, we have the possibility of understanding conscience in some measure of its full personal depth. Kegan integrates these various dimensions in a unified theory of the self, which, with Lonergan, we specify normatively as self-transcending.

However, if we are to realize such a fully personal interpretation of conscience it will be necessary to shift from Kohlberg's third person, external observer model of moral judgment to one centered clearly on the subject in the first person, concretely involved in a particular situation and struggling to reach an authentic judgment on a course of action. Kohlberg's emphasis on justice as reversibility and such formal criteria as impersonal universalization is invaluable in sorting out conflicting values in dilemma situations, and, when operative, guarantees at least a minimal moral "floor" of respect for persons and their rights.[79] This is fundamental to morality, but it is not the whole of morality. As we shift the moral center of gravity from observer judgments about value conflicts to the personal consciences of acting subjects, we must also expand our understanding of justice. If justice as reversibility suggests too much the blind, abstract, passive regulator, our emphasis on the seminal empathy in Kohlberg's understanding of moral reasoning requires a passionate, concrete, activist justice. And because real needs go beyond individual relations, the structure of fully human justice must be social-distributive as well as interpersonal.[80]

Now the scope of morality is the fullest realization of human value in every area of life. Now justice goes beyond the cool, detached calculation of quasi-legal rights to include, as Kohlberg's psychosocial specification of postconventional morality suggests, the warm, committed love and care of Erikson's adult generativity that responds actively to the real, specific needs of concrete persons.[81] Here personal conscience is concerned with how one will most fully realize one's being as an originating source of value through action in the world. In this engaged role, postconventional moral reasoning, like all genuinely adult knowing, brings its liberating power to bear on the unique reality of the situation. It refuses to sacrifice the concrete personal good to the abstract moral rule. It insists that every value is relative to a context, that human good is realized or destroyed in the full consequences of concrete action, not in the mere observance of abstract rule.[82] At this point the fundamental personal realities of character—vision and virtue—assume their rightful place at center stage. From the perspective of fully personal conscience, then, moral reasoning is not simply the analytic resolution of fictional dilemmas presented to an external judge, but assumes the greater dimensions of creative, imaginative, critical understanding actively engaged in the pursuit of concrete value in the real world.[83] Such is the moral reasoning that will play a central role in our interpretation of conversion.

Gilligan: Care and Responsibility

One important aspect of this concern for a rich, fully personal understanding of conscience has been highlighted recently in Carol Gilligan's study of women's development, *In a Different Voice*. Why is it, Gilligan wondered, that "the very traits that traditionally have defined the 'goodness' of women, their care for and sensitivity to the needs of others, are those that mark them as deficient in moral development"?[84] *In a Different Voice* reports her ten years' experience of listening to men and women talk about themselves and their moral understanding, and of discerning (especially in the accounts of women) a moral voice different from that she hears in the standard developmental theories—a voice stressing not justice and rights, but care and responsibility. By focusing on this distinctive voice of care and responsibility she hears in women, Gilligan hopes to expand our view of human development—a view that is based almost exclusively on the experience of men.

Gilligan develops the morality of responsibility and care principally from her study of twenty-nine women interviewed during the process of making an abortion decision. In these interviews Gilligan not only discerns a different voice, the distinct moral language of selfishness and responsibility which "defines the moral problem as one of obligation to exercise care and avoid hurt," but recognizes in it three perspectives specifying a sequence in the development of care which she sees paralleling Kohlberg's preconventional, conventional, and postconventional orientations. In this sequence the initial focus is on caring for the self to ensure survival. Transitional criticism of this focus as selfish leads to a second perspective characterized by an understanding of responsibility that is fused with a maternal morality of care for the dependent and unequal. Now goodness is equated with care, but a conventional understanding of feminine goodness that identifies care with self-sacrifice and recognizes only others as legitimate recipients of women's care sets up relationships of inequality which can initiate a second transition. Shifting concern from goodness to truth or honesty, a woman may now ask whether it is selfish or responsible to extend care to her own needs. Unless doubts about her own worth prevent a woman from claiming equality, this concern for truth leads her to a third perspective where, by elevating non-violence to "a principle governing all moral judgment and action, she is able to assert a moral equality between self and other and to include both in the compass of care."[85] Gilligan sees this third perspective as a postconventional, self-chosen ethic of universal care.

While for men the moral imperative appears "as an injunction to respect the rights of others and thus to protect from interference the rights to life and self-fulfillment," Gilligan stresses how for women it repeatedly manifests itself as an injunction to care, "a responsibility to discern and alleviate the 'real and recognizable trouble' of this world." Since women's care is initially self-critical rather than self-protective, while men begin by understanding obligation to others in the negative terms of non-interference, Gilligan concludes that "Development for both sexes would therefore seem to entail an integration of rights and responsibilities through the discovery of the complementarity of these disparate views." "To admit the truth of the women's perspective to the conception of moral development," says Gilligan, "is to recognize for both sexes the importance throughout life of the connection between self and other, the universality of the need for compassion and care."[86]

Gilligan stresses the role that contemporary attention to women's rights has played in the transformation of women's moral judgments, "seasoning mercy with justice by enabling women to consider it moral to care not only for others but for themselves."[87] And in a discussion of the basic personal realities of attachment and separation, she emphasizes how their integration—for both women and men—leads to a shift in moral judgment from absolutism to contextual relativity: women's absolute of care being relativized by the perception of personal integrity and equality; men's absolute of equality being relativized by the recognition of individual differences and equity.[88]

The primary significance of Gilligan's work is that it calls our attention to the undeniably central role of care and responsibility in the moral life—a role that has not explicitly received full credit in Kohlberg's perspective. Indeed, in much of Kohlberg's work it has seemed possible to imagine a person of Stage 6 reasoning whose moral life is "correct" but essentially passive, perceiving no *effective* reason for taking responsible initiative in creating value through active care for persons. The "different voice" that Gilligan discerned in women reminds us, then, that all authentic moral reasoning is at once radically affective as well as cognitive—that only such deeply human moral reasoning perceives the concrete personal values that demand a caring response.

Our detailed examination of Kohlberg's position in the preceding pages indicates that it recognizes, in principle, the affective dimension of moral reasoning through its attention to empathy, and that it has, in fact, explicitly acknowledged this dimension by incorporating adult phases of Erikson's life cycle into its view of postconventional morality. Thus Kohlberg's understanding of Stage 6 justice is not the abstract, rationalistic version of justice characteristic of an adolescent ideological orientation. Stage 6 justice cannot be interpreted correctly apart from Erikson's generative care and responsibility. Kohlberg insists that such experience is a condition for the postconventional orientation.[89] Stage 6 justice includes care; it is the structure of care (that is, mature empathy); it does not exist without care. Justice that is truly Stage 6 is not a laissez-faire ethic of non-interference.

Besides the *language* of care which Gilligan clearly discerned in her interviews with women, is there also, as she suggests, an *ethic* of care distinct from that of justice? Or, rather, does Gilligan's sequence of care perspectives in fact reflect the development of a justice structure—for example, in the role women's rights play in the shift to the third perspective? And even within this third perspective, how does one judge between competing claims of care? In what critical sense is this third perspective of care postconventional? Does the inclusion of the self within the spectrum of one's caring really make one's perspective universal? Rather than postconventional, could Gilligan's third perspective simply be a more adequate conventional orientation, freed from the oppression of a distorted understanding of self-sacrifice? These are some of the questions raised by Gilligan's proposal for complementing an ethic of justice with an ethic of care and responsibility.

From a cognitive-developmental perspective, caring responsibility is an essential dimension of Stage 6 justice, but an *ethic* of care that is distinct from and would complement the ethic of Stage 6 justice is neither necessary nor possible. While the abstract, ideological justice of adolescence needs caring responsibility, an ethic of care is an unnecessary complement to a Stage 6 ethic of justice because the mature justice at this normative adult stage is precisely the cognitive structuring of empathy that *is* caring responsibility. This does not mean that Kohlberg has succeeded in elaborating an *ethic* of justice adequate to the fundamental understanding of justice intrinsic to his developmental theory—an understanding that is at once concrete and universal, cognitive and affective. The elaboration of such an adequate ethic of justice remains to be done: an ethic rooted in the responsive justice of intimate love and generative care. For now we can only anticipate, as Piaget did over a half-century ago, an active, compassionate justice whose penetrating eye of equity discerns the real inequality of personal needs and abilities behind the veil of ignorance intended to protect the radical equality of personal dignity.[90]

From the cognitive-developmental perspective an ethic of care is impossible because, again, fully adult responsible caring is the mature form of empathy cognitively structured by Stage 6 justice. As Gilligan points out, care takes different forms in what she sees as a developmental sequence. What she does not emphasize is that these sequential forms of care are differentiated by increasingly complex *cognitive* structures. The affective reality of compassionate, responsible caring may undoubtedly be the radical dynamism of the moral life. But an ethic is a discriminating *ordering* of that dynamism, and, as such, an essentially cognitive enterprise. Caring has no ordering ethic of its own, only the structuring that is justice. As we strive in love to be compassionate in our response to a complex human world, our caring has no automatic pilot; we necessarily turn to justice for direction, for an ordering ethic. But the justice we turn to must be fully human, sensitive to the real needs of concrete persons.[91]

Still, the importance of Gilligan's stress on care must not be underestimated. For even though the reality of Stage 6 justice includes caring responsibility as a constitutive dimension, it remains true that the *language* of justice can be learned and used even by persons whose empathy has never developed into mature caring. The phenomenon is not unlike those people who can facilely speak the language of a special field like psychoanalysis with no more than a superficial understanding of the reality it represents. This explains why the ability of some people to deal with hypothetical stories of justice dilemmas outruns their ability to respond positively to personal values in real situations. The *language* of justice, in other words, can be distorted into passive, abstract word games which have little to do with conscience, with active personal judgment, decision, and action in the concrete world of values. This presents a special problem for a theory of moral development that—perhaps through over-reliance on hypothetical dilemma stories or through excessive concern for the clarity of justice concepts—leaves the affective dimension of morality for the most part implicit, and thus the dynamism of caring responsibility unattended. Such a passive abstract moral posture is not compatible with a mature personal conscience, however. Conscience understood as the drive of the personal subject for self-transcendence is an active, creative conscience, imaginatively striving to interpret experience and to construct a concrete world of meaning and value in its caring response to the actual needs of persons. Our later analysis of conversion presupposes nothing less.

Erikson: Mutuality in Ethical Orientation

Such a dynamic interpretation of conscience has been adumbrated by Erikson in his distinction of the adult ethical orientation from the moral and ideological orientations of childhood and adolescence. In contrast to the internalized prohibitions of childhood and the utopian convictions and totalistic systems of ideas of adolescence, the adult ethical orientation is characterized, as we have noted, by "*a universal sense of values assented to* with insight and foresight, in anticipation of immediate responsibilities. . . ."[92] In another place Erikson describes this adult orientation as a sense of "ideals to be striven for with a high degree of rational assent and with a ready consent to a formulated good, a definition of perfection, and some promise of self-realization."[93]

Although working within the psychoanalytic perspective which commonly identifies conscience with the unconscious superego, in this distinction of child, adolescent, and adult orientations Erikson clearly provides the grounds for interpreting conscience as conscious, self-transcending subjectivity. In Erikson's view the superego is identified with the internalized prohibitions of the child's moral orientation (which later orientations absorb but never fully replace).[94]

As the child grows into adolescence, according to Erikson, the universal good begins to be perceived in ideological terms. For as "the adolescent learns to grasp the flux of time, to anticipate the future in a coherent way, to perceive ideas and to assent to ideals, to take—in short—an *ideological* position for which the younger child is cognitively" unprepared, "an ethical view is approximated, but it remains susceptible to an alternation of impulsive judgment and odd rationalization." As Erikson stresses throughout his exposition of the life cycle, "it is the joint development of cognitive and emotional powers paired with appropriate social learning which enables the individual to realize the potentialities of a stage."[95] Here we see Erikson specifying cognitive development as a critical differentiating factor not only between the morality of childhood and the ideology of adolescence, but also between the latter orientation and its adult ethical successor.

In fact, Erikson follows Piaget's interpretation of cognitive development, which, as we have noted, understands adolescent formal thinking as initially egocentric, requiring a gradual process of equilibration through immersion in the concrete demands of social experience before consistent realistic judgment is possible. Even Kohlberg, who has always placed such great emphasis on the cognitive dimension in his analysis of moral development, has only recently recognized this crucial role of adult experience as a cognitive-structural factor in the constitution of specifically adult moral reasoning.

Only in adulthood, for Erikson, is there the possibility of the truly ethical orientation, based on socially integrated cognitive and emotional maturity. And it is with this adult ethical orientation that Erikson identifies conscience in its normative sense. Rooted in the ego-strengths or virtues of intimate love and generative care, this adult orientation of responsible conscience is characterized most of all by what Erikson calls active mutuality. First realized in the infant's favorable ratio of basic trust over mistrust, mutuality really comes into its own in the loving and caring adults who strengthen themselves as they strengthen others. Erikson sees such initiating love and care in the prayer of St. Francis, who sought not so much to be consoled as to console, to be loved as to love. And it is this active mutuality that informs Erikson's psychosocial reinterpretation of the Golden Rule: "Do to another what will strengthen you even as it will strengthen him—that is, what will develop his best potentials even as it develops your own."[96] Understood in terms of such active mutuality, then, self-realization for the loving, caring adult is self-transcendence.

Erikson's focus on mutuality as a central theme in moral development highlights two aspects of his thought which are crucial for any adequate interpretation of conscience. The first point is that mutuality is rooted in a developing constellation of the various ego strengths or virtues that Erikson specifies as appropriate to each stage of the life cycle. As we have seen, virtue for Erikson does not mean moralistic impositions, but the basic human strengths which empower our active commitment in an interpersonal world of value. Here, especially as epitomized in loving care as integrating its developmental predecessors, we have a psychoanalytic version of the interactional realization of fundamental human powers for spontaneous, facile, even enjoyable creative action which Aristotle saw as the heart of moral life.[97] Taken together as patterning the totality of a person's cognitive-affective life (with its dispositions and attitudes as well as images and structures), virtues constitute the embodiment of dynamic conscience we name character. And here we arrive at our second point about mutuality, which insists that this patterned set of virtues we call character must be understood as developing *relationally*.[98] Virtues or human strengths develop throughout the life cycle in interaction with the human environment. Thus the human adequacy of developing conscience is constantly tested by the concrete reality of the challenging give-and-take that constitutes personal relations. Adult mutuality is not a static goal, but a continuation of the interactional dialectic in which all authentic personal development is rooted.

Thus, by distinguishing a mature "ethical" orientation from the flighty "ideological" orientation of adolescence as well as from the primitive, superego-dominated "moral" orientation of childhood, Erikson's perspective offers the possibility of understanding conscience as an active striving for ideals with "a *universal sense of values assented to* with insight and foresight, in anticipation of immediate responsibilities." Further, by identifying conscience with a mature ethical orientation, Erikson helps us to understand that a fully human conscience is not part of a person's birthright, but an achievement of normative human development, the fruit, as we will see in the next chapter, of moral conversion. There is no need, then, to think that everybody has a "conscience" in the fully human sense of the word, just because everybody seems to have some kind of moral sense.

But in distinguishing a mature conscience from the superego, the unconscious childhood predecessor of the conscience which the mature conscience supersedes but never fully replaces, Erikson at the same time highlights the vitally important role played by the conscience's true partner in the person's unconscious life, the ego, and especially the strength of its identity.

However, although his psychoanalytic perspective emphasizes the significance of the unconscious ego which organizes our experience and safeguards our personal existence, Erikson clearly understands the ego within the context of the entirety of personal existence, including the conscious "I."[99] Indeed, the fundamental thrust of Erikson's approach has been to incorporate what he calls the "inward," "backwards," and "downwards" methodological directions of psychoanalysis with an emphasis on those elements in a person's total existence which lead "*outward* from self-centeredness to the mutuality of love and communality, *forward* from the enslaving past to the utopian anticipation of new potentialities, and *upwards* from the unconscious to the enigma of consciousness."[100] It would be difficult to formulate a better statement of the central realities of self-transcending subjectivity than this articulation by Erikson of the concerns of his own professional commitment.

In Erikson's delineation of a mature ethical orientation, then, there are the outlines of an interpretation of conscience as the creative, future oriented drive of the conscious, active, responsible personal subject, rooted in the unconscious ground of ego strengths, and striving imaginatively for the realization of self-chosen ideals and values, thus effecting a personal movement from self-centeredness to the mutuality of love and communality.

In a word, this is the *existential* conscience of a personal subject making judgments, decisions, and commitments in life situations.[101] The cognitive dimension of this existential conscience is illuminated, but not fully accounted for, by Kohlberg's analysis of moral judgment.

In order to be fully existential, an interpretation of conscience must also include as context an analysis of the personal subject's concrete horizon or orientation to reality. Fowler's analysis of faith, though dominated by the cognitive dimension, provides a valuable structural approach to this orientation of the total person to reality, especially in its interpretation of and relatedness to the ultimate conditions of existence—a relatedness which "informs and qualifies [the person's] relations and interactions with the mundane, the everyday, the world of other persons and things."[102]

Kegan: The Self's Unity

If Erikson's psychosocial view of the adult ethical orientation best suggests the reality of mature, fully personal conscience, and if the structural analyses of Piaget, Kohlberg, and Fowler helpfully explicate the cognitive, moral reasoning, and faithing dimensions of this self-transcending orientation, the integration of these perspectives is most powerfully realized in Kegan's constructive-development focus on the self.

First, by reaching for the fundamental meaning-constitutive activity at the heart of personal development, Kegan is able to disclose the radical unity of the self underlying the cognitive and affective dimensions of conscience. Like the self, conscience—the radical drive of the self to reach beyond itself—is at once irreducibly cognitive and affective in its fundamental unity. And Kegan's neo-Piagetian analysis offers an explanatory theory of development that both illuminates this unity of self (conscience) and justifies the methodological integration of Erikson's psychosocial-functional approach to development with those approaches inspired by Piaget's cognitive-structural orientation.

Second, Kegan's systematic distinction between Stage 3 fusion and Stage 5 intimacy provides an explanatory structural framework for critically understanding the fundamental ethical reality of mutuality that permeates Erikson's virtues of intimate love and generative care. Just as Kegan's understanding of genuine intimacy requires a self no longer embedded in its interpersonal and self-organizational needs, so the love and care of Erikson's mutuality requires a secure identity capable of risking itself. The mutuality of the conscience that loves and cares maturely must be clearly distinguished from the pre-identity interpersonal fusion of selves in search of themselves. The love and care of the Stage 3 interpersonal conscience are sincere, but the self at this stage lacks the strength of self-possession necessary for consistent, sustained self-transcendence. Thus, unlike other perspectives on development, Kegan clearly explains difficult developmental issues that are crucial to an accurate understanding of conscience. He makes clear, for example, why moving beyond Kohlberg's Stage 3 is not a loss of the personal for the abstract social, but a developmental advance toward the possibility of the genuinely intimate relationship of persons in mutuality, and why Erikson's crisis of intimacy must be recognized as coming after the establishment of identity, and not confused with the pre-identity concern for persons that ends in fusion (why, for example, Diane is really farther from intimacy than is Rebecca).[103]

From the ethical point of view, to consider the existential orientation (perspective, attitudes, beliefs, etc.) of the personal subject in its most concrete sense is to attend to character. This means attending to the specific concrete shape that conscience, the radical drive for self-transcendence, has taken through the discoveries, decisions, and deeds of the personal subject's life; in short, to the "sort of person" the subject has created out of his or her own and only life. But, if this creation of the existential personal subject is the result of development, it is highlighted most dramatically at those crucial points in the personal history of a self we call conversions, to which we turn directly in the following chapter.

"I'll stop [drinking] for *you*," [Jessica Fayer] says. "No, it has to be for yourself. You have to choose yourself." . . . We make our choices and then they make us.

John L'Heureux

4

CONVERSION: MORAL, COGNITIVE, AFFECTIVE

Chapter 1 proposed the radical drive of the personal subject for self-transcendence as a foundational interpretation of conscience. Recognizing that the very being of the personal subject is in the process of becoming, Chapters 2 and 3 placed this understanding of conscience in the context of developmental psychology. However, while developmental psychology makes a direct contribution to an understanding of conscience as a developing personal reality, it hardly makes even an explicit reference to the principal topic of this study, conversion. This may seem surprising insofar as both development and conversion ostensibly pertain to the becoming of the personal subject.

Is conversion, then, something altogether different from personal development? Are they totally unconnected? On the other hand, could it be that conversion is not actually a reality in itself apart from development? Perhaps conversion is just another way of naming the process of personal development analyzed by Erikson, Piaget, Kohlberg, Fowler, and Kegan. Their analyses may—at least in principle—exhaust the topic of authentic personal becoming. Or, reversing this last point, might not development itself be in reality a series of conversions? From this perspective, though, one could ask if it is really possible to analyze personal development adequately without an interpretation of conversion. In any event, one might wonder if a psychological analysis, which attempts to interpret development as a spontaneous process of ontogenesis with hierarchical stages unfolding naturally through the individual's interaction with its environment, can really do full justice to truly *personal* development. These are just some of the key questions this chapter will attempt to answer through a critical analysis of the reality of conversion and its relation to personal development.

KIERKEGAARD'S STAGES OF LIFE

Developmental psychologists were not, of course, the first theorists to consider the personal subject in its process of becoming. Modern philosophers and theologians have given serious attention to this dimension of the person rather consistently. Among these, Søren Kierkegaard is certainly one of the most concrete, dramatic, and intensely personal in his treatment of the theme.

Kierkegaard quite clearly views the process of personal becoming as a dialectic of stages. And for him, movement from one stage to another not only involves self-transcendence—as we have seen it does in the psychological theories of development—but also quite definitely requires what can only be called *conversion.* For Kierkegaard's stages are not simply successive steps unfolding spontaneously in the course of one's life, but distinct spheres or levels of existence: the aesthetic, the ethical, and the religious. Transition from one level or stage to the next is realized only through a conscious act of self-committing *choice.*[1]

When a person experiences despair over the radical limitations on the human spirit in a life that (whatever else may be said for it) is governed ultimately by pleasure, he or she is faced with a set of alternatives: *either* remain in despair on the aesthetic level *or,* by an act of deliberate choice, advance to the ethical level of universal moral values. This moral conversion, of course, is always made within a concrete choice. From his own experience Kierkegaard offers as an example the deliberate acceptance of the ethical institution of marriage and its obligations in contrast to the satisfaction of one's passing sexual fancies.

While the ethical stage constitutes a significant advance in self-transcendence, and may find expression in a truly courageous heroism, it does not, according to Kierkegaard, have a realization of sin. The person at the ethical stage believes, in the last analysis, in his or her own moral self-sufficiency.

But just as the aesthetic person can experience despair in the pursuit of pleasure, the ethical person can become aware of sin and guilt as a challenge to moral autonomy. At this point the ethical person is confronted with the decision of faith. Just as despair is overcome only by an act of choice, by a deliberate self-commitment to value, so the agonizing awareness of sin is likewise overcome only by an act of choice, by a deliberate affirmation of one's relationship to God, the Absolute Thou, in a decision of faith. Such faith, for Kierkegaard, is always a venture, a risk, a leap into the unknown, a self-commitment to "objective uncertainty." One "steps out," as it were, over ten thousand fathoms in fear and trembling.

So wide, in Kierkegaard's view, is the chasm between the ethical and religious spheres, that the religious person transcends even the universal moral law in his or her absolute relationship to the Absolute personal God. Kierkegaard presents Abraham as a hero of such faith, but the influence of Kierkegaard's own religious conversion on his difficult decision to break his marriage engagement to Regina Olsen provides a more manageable, if less spectacular, example.[2]

Kierkegaard's position has been presented in this very brief glance simply to introduce a view of personal becoming and life stages significantly different from that of developmental psychology. The point, however, is not to present a choice of *either* development *or* conversion, but to initiate a move to an integrated interpretation of the personal subject's becoming which includes *both* development *and* conversion. In fact, while the developmental psychologists work within a model of development as a natural process of spontaneously unfolding stages, even their own theories, as we have noted, hint that something more is involved.

A striking instance of this is found in Kohlberg's claim that most adults—even those with formal cognitive operations—never advance to the principled stages of moral reasoning.[3] His claim suggests that such a transition may require a radical personal conversion. Let us see, then, where this clue will lead us, as we examine Kohlberg's theory from a new angle.

POSTCONVENTIONAL MORALITY AS EXISTENTIAL

One of the most important and interesting critical discussions of Kohlberg's work is John Gibbs' attempt to clarify its central concept of stage development. Gibbs' critical strategy is based on a fundamental distinction he finds between two groups of Kohlberg's "stages": *natural* stages at the preconventional and conventional levels, and *existential* orientations at the postconventional level.[4]

The specific context of Gibbs' discussion is the relationship of Kohlberg's work to Piaget's developmental stage theory, clearly the single greatest influence on Kohlberg's entire project. Gibbs' critique begins with Kohlberg's claim that the moral judgment stages in his theory satisfy the criteria for stages in the strong Piagetian sense of the term. Stated briefly, Piaget's criteria for stages, as Gibbs understands them, are: (1) evidence of an underlying structure; (2) an upward tendency and stability in development; (3) facilitated development in an experientially "rich" environment; (4) gradual and consecutive sequential movement; (5) common occurrence among species members; (6) realization through spontaneous and essentially unconscious processes.[5]

The central point of Gibbs' criticism is that while there is evidence that Kohlberg's preconventional and conventional stages satisfy all these criteria, his postconventional or principled stages do not. Gibbs claims that the admitted rarity and explicitly reflective character of the postconventional stages argue against their fulfillment of the last two criteria. Gibbs' point is not to deny the existence of what Kohlberg calls postconventional moral reasoning, nor even to deny that there are postconventional stages. His proposal, rather, is that an accurate understanding of moral development requires that Kohlberg's fifth and sixth postconventional stages be recognized as a significantly different *kind* of stage from the first four.

The six criteria for stages listed above relate, according to Gibbs, to four basic features of Piaget's developmental-structural stage theory: holism (underlying structure), constructivism (upward tendency), interactionism (facilitated development), and naturalism (necessarily gradual, common, and achieved through spontaneous and essentially unconscious processes). In Gibbs' view naturalism is the most fundamental of these features: "At the heart of Piaget's theory is a naturalistic theme that human mental development reflects a deep biological significance. Building upon this theme are the assumptions of holism, constructivism, and interactionism." As these themes are interrelated, a correct understanding of Piaget's naturalistic emphasis on the deep biological significance of "normative human behavior" will include the constructionist view on evolution "that human intelligence extends, but does not reduce to, organic regulatory processes and structures."[6]

To repeat Gibbs' basic point now in the specific terms of Piaget's fundamental theme of naturalism, research evidence indicates that Kohlberg's first four stages meet *all* the Piagetian stage criteria and therefore qualify as Piagetian *natural* stages in the fullest sense. However, Kohlberg's postconventional fifth and sixth stages, because they fail to meet the specifically naturalistic criteria of being universal and unconscious, cannot be considered as *natural* stages in the full Piagetian sense, though they may be seen as stages in terms of other criteria.

The naturalism Gibbs recognizes in Kohlberg's first four stages is one of two key themes he finds in Kohlberg's work. The second theme is existentialism. Both are among the most fundamental themes in modern psychology. While naturalism argues that "the development and expression of human behavior reflect spontaneous constructive processes reflective of life in general," existentialism argues that "awareness of self and efforts to come to terms with this awareness are keys to understanding the human phenomenon."[7] Gibbs' claim is that moral development in Kohlberg's theory will be understood more accurately if stages one through four are seen as *natural,* and stages five and six as *existential.* Gibbs is able to point to suggestions of this distinction in Kohlberg's more recent work where Kohlberg admits, as Chapter 2 noted, that the construction of the postconventional stages "seems to require experiences of personal moral choice and responsibility usually supervening upon a questioning period of 'moratorium.' "[8] As Gibbs understands it, "postconventionality is the existential experience of disembedding oneself from an implicit world view and adopting a detached and questioning posture."[9] Clearly, this definition does capture an important aspect of the postconventional orientation, but Stage 4½ alone already fulfills the requirement of detached questioning. What Gibbs' definition does not grasp is the fundamental moral insight and commitment involved in self-chosen universal principles.

Whereas Kohlberg views his postconventional, principled stages as "natural structures" out of which ethical theories may be systematically constructed, Gibbs sees them not as natural stages but as reflective, philosophical formalizations based on implicit achievements of earlier, natural stages.[10] In particular, Gibbs understands the social contract ethic of Kohlberg's fifth orientation (he uses "orientation" as a general, descriptive term, reserving "stage" for those orientations which satisfy all the Piagetian criteria) as a highly formal theory informed by the pragmatic intuition that "*a priori* rational people must simply temper their desires with the recognition that others want their lives and freedom as they themselves want theirs." In Gibbs' view, the social perspective taking involved in the meta-ethics of Kohlberg's fifth orientation "does not seem to go beyond that necessary for the natural moral stage 2." In the social perspective taking required for the meta-ethics of orientation 6's ideal role taking, says Gibbs, "*a priori* rational people must be capable of moderating their immediate interests and reconstructing them into ideal or mutual sentiments." Such third-person perspective taking and the meta-ethics of orientation 6, then, according to Gibbs, are those of the Stage 3 rational person.[11]

In summary, then, Gibbs sees persons reasoning from orientations 5 and 6 as philosophers, and understands "the principled orientations themselves as 'constructive systematizations' starting from natural intuitions about morality and human nature." While natural stages subsume and dominate preceding ones, Gibbs claims that "formal ethical philosophies [i.e., moral reasoning of orientations 5 and 6] may override but do not eliminate the relevance of the natural stages of moral judgment." Stages 3 and 4 possess a maturity that is of permanent significance for everyday life. Gibbs' fundamental objection to Kohlberg's view of all six orientations as natural stages is that it "fails to take into account the crucial distinction between implicit theories-in-action [natural Stages 1–4] and detached reflections upon one's theories-in-action [orientations 5–6]." On the other hand, and this is Gibbs' central positive contention, "explicitly distinguishing the existential and naturalistic themes in Kohlberg's theory permits each theme to assume an important role in his work on the development of moral judgment."[12]

EXISTENTIAL ORIENTATION AS SELF-CHOSEN

The preceding review of Gibbs' "constructive critique" of Kohlberg's theory clearly shows that Gibbs' distinction between two types of stages or orientations has identified an important issue in Kohlberg's interpretation of moral development. As noted in Chapter 2, Kohlberg deals with the existential dimension of principled morality himself in his consideration of adult development. In so doing, however, he takes a significantly different tack from that of Gibbs. Kohlberg's approach is to account for principled moral reasoning as a distinctively adult reality by reinterpreting the concept of structural stage in a broad enough way to include the existential experiences of personal moral questioning, choice, and responsible action—realities excluded from his earlier view which denied the existence of a *structurally* distinctive adult morality. Gibbs moves in a deliberately opposite direction by defining the concept of stage in such narrowly Piagetian terms that Kohlberg's fifth and sixth stages are considered no longer as true natural stages but as existential orientations of a reflective, meta-ethical character.

The intention here, however, is not to arbitrate the differences between Kohlberg and Gibbs, but to reach the most adequate understanding of moral development.[13] If a stage in the full sense must be universally found, then Kohlberg's fifth and sixth stages do not qualify. But, even in Piaget's own theory of cognitive development, it is not clear that the full realization of the formal operational stage is found universally.

Gibbs' second key point about the spontaneous and unconscious nature of stages is more complicated. Gibbs claims that stages in the full sense are *implicit* theories-in-action rather than detached, *explicit* reflections upon one's theories-in-action. By interpreting Kohlberg's principled stages as "constructive systematizations" of reflective, philosophical meta-ethics, Gibbs easily places the principled stages or orientations in the category of detached, explicit reflections upon theories-in-action rather than that of implicit theories-in-action. Gibbs' interpretation on this point deliberately contradicts Kohlberg's explicit understanding, and Gibbs does not argue for his interpretation but simply asserts it in one sentence. The question which remains, then, is whether or not principled moral reasoning should be understood as necessarily explicitly reflective, philosophical meta-ethics.

The answer to be proposed here is clearly negative, but it will be developed within the context of a positive alternative interpretation of Kohlberg's principled moral reasoning based on an understanding of moral conversion derived from the critical methodological thought of Bernard Lonergan.

Perhaps the most significant point about Gibbs' critique is what he does after drawing the natural/existential distinction and emphasizing the importance of the existential theme, which he says is in Kohlberg's theory but not clearly distinguished there. Although he makes very brief references to such existentialist sub-themes as meaning, authenticity, and self-actualization, as well as to such existentially oriented psychologists as Viktor Frankl, Rollo May, and Abraham Maslow, Gibbs explicates the existential theme he finds in Kohlberg not along these lines but almost entirely in terms of formal meta-ethical philosophies. This perspective echoes Gibbs' interpretation of Kohlberg's Stage 6 as an orientation "justifying moral prescriptions or evaluations by appeal to the results of ideal role taking."[14] Here, and with Kohlberg's other stages, Gibbs is on target in emphasizing the "orientation" character of stages and in stressing "justification" as their central element. Gibbs misses the bull's-eye in his interpretation of Stage 6, however, by sighting exclusively on the "appeal to the results of ideal role taking" as the stage's defining element.

While the moral point of view of any rational person (ideal role taking) is clearly part of Kohlberg's characterization of Stage 6, an accurate interpretation of this stage must focus sharply on the defining element of "following self-chosen ethical principles," universal principles of justice.[15] In order to emphasize the existential theme of Kohlberg's postconventional, principled moral reasoning, especially that of Stage 6, the following analysis will focus on its "self-chosen" character. If there is anything "existential" about postconventional moral reasoning it is precisely the fact that the Stage 6 person reasons in terms of, and justifies moral evaluations or prescriptions by appeal to, critically *self-chosen* principles. The person of conventional moral reasoning, on the other hand, appeals to the uncritically *assumed* rules of the given social system as justification. This is a crucial difference, one that Gibbs unfortunately neglects in his interpretation of the existential theme in Kohlberg's theory.

SELF-CHOSEN PRINCIPLES, SELF-CREATION, AND CRITICAL MORAL CONVERSION

Self-chosen ethical principles are an essential part of the existential process of authentic self-creation in which Bernard Lonergan has identified the ground of a contemporary empirical theology—the personal reality of conversion. In Lonergan's view, authentic self-creation demands conversion: conversion which, in its fullest realization, is affective, cognitive, moral, and religious.[16] For the purpose of illuminating the existential theme in Kohlberg's interpretation of moral development, this chapter will concentrate on the personal realities of moral, cognitive, and affective conversion.

Conversion, in Lonergan's view, is the "about-face" by which a person moves into a radically new horizon. More than a direct continuation or expansion of previous horizontal development, conversion is a vertical move which "begins a new sequence that can keep revealing ever greater depth and breadth and wealth." As lived, conversion "affects all of a man's conscious and intentional operations. It directs his gaze, pervades his imagination, releases the symbols that penetrate to the depths of his psyche. It enriches his understanding, guides his judgments, reinforces his decisions."[17]

Moral conversion is basically a shift in the criterion of one's decisions and choices from satisfactions to values. In living up to the norm established by moral conversion, one will opt for what one judges to be "the truly good, even for value against satisfaction when value and satisfaction conflict."[18] Such basic moral conversion should be seen as independent of the other conversions, inasmuch as this shift of criterion does not necessarily presuppose a cognitive, affective, or religious conversion. It would, however, definitely presuppose some significant level of affective and cognitive development. In fact, to be understood properly in its full existential reality, moral conversion in the sense of a shift of criterion for decision must be interpreted in the concrete context of personal development.

For Lonergan, personal development is to an important degree a process of self-creation. When authentic, this self-creation is a personal realization of the radical dynamism of the human spirit for self-transcendence. Central to this process of self-creation is the fact that "by deliberation, evaluation, decision, action, we can know and do, not just what pleases us, but what is truly good, worthwhile."[19] In other words, the moral subject is "at once practical and existential: practical inasmuch as he is concerned with concrete courses of action; existential inasmuch as control includes self-control, and the possibility of self-control involves responsibility for what he makes of himself."[20]

Self-control, however, can be rooted in the ground of quite different personal realities. If that ground be mere selfishness, says Lonergan, "then the process of deliberation, evaluation, decision is limited to determining what is most to one's advantage, what best serves one's interests, what on the whole yields a maximum of pleasure and a minimum of pain."[21] On this ground, one lives one's life, effectively, within Kierkegaard's aesthetic sphere.

But self-control can, at the opposite pole, proceed rather from a concern with value; and in the measure that one's living is a response to value, in that measure one effects a real self-transcendence. In every decision, every action, every achievement that is a response to value—and not the mere gratification of personal desire—one moves beyond one's self, transcends one's self in a real way. Insofar as one achieves such real self-transcendence, one becomes a source, a principle of "benevolence and beneficence, capable of genuine collaboration and of true love."[22] But it is one thing to transcend oneself in response to value once in a while. It is another to do it consistently. Only after many years of development does there emerge in the conscious human subject the *sustained* self-transcendence of the virtuous person.

A crucial factor in this long process of self-creating personal development, clearly, is the transformation of horizon, the shift in criterion of choice named moral conversion. Of course, one does not need to be morally converted to realize self-transcendence in particular choices. Still, moral conversion is a special instance of moral or real self-transcendence in the sense that moral conversion provides the programmatic base for the conscious, deliberate development of the sustained moral self-transcendence of human authenticity. Kierkegaard's aesthetic stage has now been transcended, and one takes up the challenge of living the ethical life.

If moral conversion is the beginning of a deliberate movement toward an ever more complete authenticity, however, it only occurs well along the way in a lengthy process of fundamental cognitive and affective development that forms the condition for its very possibility. The fact is, as Chapter 2 detailed, that a normative personal conscience

is never given as an accomplished fact. From the earliest years of childhood even the most primitive moral sense must be developed. Indeed,
the sense of responsibility only begins to emerge at around the age of
three as the child gradually moves into the world mediated by meaning
and regulated by values. If the child is said to have reached the "age
of reason" by seven, it must also be added that, as important as the
emergence of judgment is, the reason reached by the seven year old is
only the first floor of a structure of cognitive operations whose completion will take many more years.

The child must be "persuaded, cajoled, ordered, compelled to do
what is right."[23] But as the subject's very being is becoming, a measure
of autonomy gradually appears. And because becoming is a matter of
increasing the number of things that one does, decides, and discovers
for oneself, the young subject, resenting adult interference, soon
wants to do, decide, and discover more and more for herself or himself, despite the fact that one's desire for doing for oneself quickly outruns one's ability to reasonably judge and responsibly decide for
oneself. This fact accounts for much of the tragic quality of human life,
for, as Lonergan explains, "man develops biologically to develop
psychically, and he develops psychically to develop intellectually and
rationally. The higher integrations suffer the disadvantage of emerging later. They are the demands of finality upon us before they are
realities in us." Unfortunately, during this process of self-development
"one has to live and make decisions in the light of one's undeveloped
intelligence and under the guidance of one's incomplete willingness."[24]

Still, despite the time and pain involved, one does gradually grow
in knowledge and develop one's response to value; one becomes more
and more oneself. And as one does in fact develop, one is left to exercise freely his or her "ever advancing thrust toward authenticity."[25]

Precisely in this developing drive toward authenticity lies the possibility of moral conversion. For within this long and gradual process
of personal becoming and increasing autonomy the subject may reach
that crucial point, that existential moment when he discovers that his
judging and deciding affect himself no less than the objects of his judgments and decisions; that it is up to himself to decide for himself what
he is to make of himself.[26] In such a discovery one recognizes oneself
as an originator of value who creates himself in every deed, decision,
and discovery of his life, for the subjective effects of these personal acts
accumulate as habits, tendencies, and dispositions determining the
concrete shape of one's very subjectivity, the "sort of person" one is,
one's character. Such a discovery demands that the subject, through a

radical exercise of his fundamental, vertical freedom, take hold of and responsibly choose himself precisely as the originating value he has recognized himself to be.

This choice of oneself as a free and responsible creator of value is not forced; indeed, it can be a difficult one. But if one does make it, it establishes an entirely new personal horizon specified by value as the criterion of decision and choice, a criterion, indeed of one's living. Of course, even before this conversion, before this discovery and choice of oneself as responsibly free, and the consequent reorientation of one's priorities and values, the subject has been creating himself. The essential point of moral conversion is that after it occurs, the self's creation of itself is open-eyed and deliberate. In light of it, and by virtue of it, "autonomy decides what autonomy is to be."[27]

The fact that, before moral conversion, the personal subject made herself what she is, without any significant awareness of what she was doing, offers no escape from responsibility after conversion. For now it is, to an important degree, possible for the subject to re-create herself in the light of better knowledge and fuller responsibility. To refuse the opportunity of such re-creation means, ultimately, the assumption of responsibility, whether she wants it or not, for whatever she had inadvertently made of herself before discovering her responsible freedom.[28] When, for example, women's liberation means something serious, it means at least this: a woman who finally discovers herself amidst all the patterns of inauthenticity which have hitherto defined her life must now opt for her own responsibility. She must authentically create a future out of her past—whatever that past has been, and whatever forces have shaped it. She will need support. People do not create themselves by themselves alone, but they must do it *for* themselves.

In contrast to the open-eyed, deliberate subject, there is the drifter. In Lonergan's description, the drifter has not yet found himself. He has not yet discovered his own deed or his own will or his own mind, and so he is content to do, choose, and think what everybody else is doing, choosing, and thinking.[29] The point is not that drifters are evil. As with Kierkegaard's aesthetes, the problem with drifters is not that they go about deliberately doing evil; the problem is more that they do nothing very deliberately. Either they have never discovered the meaning of human authenticity in themselves, or, if they have, they have never summoned the courage to opt for it—to choose themselves as free and responsible.

Having sketched this brief profile of moral conversion, we must now draw a basic distinction, which Lonergan does not make explicitly, between *critical* moral conversion and *uncritical* moral conversion. For the shift in criterion of decision from satisfaction to value, which constitutes moral conversion, can be made critically or uncritically.[30] In other words, in moral conversion one can *critically* recognize and accept the responsibility of discovering and establishing one's own values (in dialogue with one's community), or one may merely turn *uncritically* toward and accept some *given* set of values of whatever conventional source. Moral conversion in this second, uncritical sense is clearly a real enough conversion (from satisfaction to values). For many people it could follow very naturally from religious motivation. This uncritical moral conversion first appears in adolescence when formal operations make possible a clear distinction in the good between value and "what is good for me." Despite the intrinsic limitations of adolescent development, then, some degree of uncritical moral conversion is found in this period.

If the shift in criterion represents the object-pole of moral conversion, however, it is rooted at the subject-pole in the existential moment when we discover for ourselves "that it is up to each of us to decide for himself what he is to make of himself."[31] Though discovery of the moral self is common enough during the adolescent blossoming of identity, it is also limited by the socially defined nature of identity during this period. As Kohlberg points out, it is only later, in the context of adult moral experiences of irreversible decision and responsibility for others, that an affectively and cognitively more developed *postconventional* subject can discover itself precisely as postconventional. Then a truly critical moral conversion is involved, for in this genuinely adult context the existential discovery that it is up to each of us to decide for ourselves what we are to make of ourselves presupposes at least an *implicit* cognitive conversion. Critical moral conversion involves, in other words, a subject's tacit but nonetheless real recognition and choice of self as criterion of the real and the truly good in her or his own self-transcending judgments and choices.

COGNITIVE CONVERSION

In the fully explicit, philosophical sense, cognitive conversion is the "radical clarification and, consequently, the elimination of an exceedingly stubborn and misleading myth" by which a person spontaneously assumes that "knowing is like looking, that objectivity is seeing what there is to be seen and not seeing what is not there, and that the real is what is out there now to be looked at." But if cognitive conversion eliminates this myth of naive realism, it does so because it consists essentially in what Lonergan calls the "discovery of the self-transcendence proper to the human process of coming to know," the recognition and appropriation, in other words, of the radical dynamism and structure of one's own cognitive capacities and operations.[32]

To appreciate the significance of cognitive conversion and its relationship to moral conversion, it is necessary at this point to consider in some detail the structure of the basic operations which constitute the conscious intentionality of the personal subject. This consideration will simultaneously provide the basis for personal verification of the study's twofold thesis on self-transcendence as the criterion of authenticity: genuine objectivity is self-transcending subjectivity; self-realization is self-transcendence.[33] The double goal of this consideration is possible because Lonergan has explicated the dynamic core of self-structuring conscious and intentional operations precisely as oriented toward self-transcendence. And it is through crucial reflexive instances of these self-transcending operations that the personal subject realizes moral and cognitive conversion.

In the initial consideration of the conscious subject in Chapter 2, it was noted that as the subject develops, increasingly complex dimensions of his or her world unfold: to the original world of immediacy there is added not only the world mediated by meaning, but also the world constituted by meaning. Related hierarchically through sublation, these successive worlds become structural dimensions of the adult subject's world, where they are objective correlatives of the conscious operations, which originally gave them rise.[34]

As the subject awakes from a sleep where dreams have already begun to anticipate the demands of the day, questions at once begin to probe the sensitive images, feelings, and memories which put him or her in touch with the immediate environment.[35] "What's that piercing noise?" "Where am I?" "What am I doing here?" These are only the first in an endless series of questions by which the intelligently conscious subject seeks to make sense of experience. In response to this questioning search for meaning there sometimes occurs understanding. Answers are proposed: "That's my travel alarm." "This is my new Cambridge flat." "I start my research project today." Beyond the practical questions of everyday life, there are the further questions of the scholarly researcher, the scientific experimenter, the philosopher or theologian. And since all knowing is an active construction of meaning, as Piaget has so persuasively shown, their answers differ from the symbolic expression of poets, composers, and sculptors only in kind, not in creativity. Every world of meaning is a created world, those of engineers and politicians no less than those of cinematographers and preachers. Insights occur in many different patterns of understanding. While their frequency and depth and range of significance may vary from person to person, they are experienced in one way or another by everyone. Just about all of us have some memory, however distant and fleeting, of having finally gotten the point about something. Maybe it was as simple as catching on at last, after long struggle, to the now habitualized trick of tying one's shoelaces. Then there are those of us who wear loafers! Most of us, however, stand in awe of those who always have the right word at the right time, who prepare a delectable dinner with seemingly artless grace, or who make breakthroughs in science, business, or law appear routine.

It is also true, as Lonergan says, that insights are a dime a dozen. Some people are bubbling over with a lot of bright ideas that never really pan out. And so, spontaneously, just as we ask what and how and why, we also cast a critical eye on the latest brainstorm and ask for verification. "Is it really so?" "Will it work?" "What evidence is there?" When we are not being rash, then, we are satisfied not with just any meaning, but are driven to insist on correct meaning, on sufficient evidence, on what is really the case. Unless we are plagued by unreasonable doubt, we issue an affirmative judgment whenever the critical process of reflective understanding has marshalled evidence sufficient to warrant assent, to transform a conditional meaning into one that is "virtually unconditioned."[36] Then we claim actually to know something of reality, with more or less probability.

This process is most systematic in scientific method, but it occurs, though less explicitly, every time the pertinent critical questions are answered and a reasonable judgment is made. It may happen in the definitive stroke of a painter's brush or in the cocking of a quarterback's arm as surely as in the experimenter's verification process, for patterns of judgment are as varied as those of understanding. Judgment marks a key stage in the human process of self-transcendence, then, for when judgment is correct, one's *thinking* about the universe is transformed into a *knowing* of the universe as it really is. Lonergan relates this point to the subject's worlds by explaining that though the personal subject always lives in a world inasmuch as being human is being-in-the-world, the world in which the subject lives is not always a world that really exists.[37]

If we experience the desire to know the universe, we also experience the need to act in it. So, beyond those questions for intelligence by which we reach out for meaning, and beyond those for critical reflection by which we attempt to establish true meaning, there are also questions for deliberation by which we seek to determine what is to be done. When the personal subject is oriented in a practical direction, in other words, understanding regards not just what is, but also what might be. But a possible course of action grasped by practical insight is not automatically translated into action. Practical reflection scrutinizes it from every angle, not the least important of which is that of probable consequences. Still, even consequences are factual, and one may ask how desirable they would be in terms of the human good. Practical reflection, then, moves from the realm of fact into that of *value*, as the personal subject deliberates about the goodness of a possible course of action. As factual questions of practical reflection are answered by judgments of fact, evaluative questions of deliberation are answered by judgments of value. But practical deliberation is directed not just to the knowledge of value but also, and especially, to the realization of value in action. In deliberation, the personal subject asks, "Is *this* course of action, beyond all personal pleasure or pragmatic advantage, truly valuable and one *I* should follow?" Ultimately, if the answers to these questions are affirmative, he or she must also face what can be the most difficult question of all: "What am I going to do about it?" This question demands neither a judgment of fact nor a judgment of value, but a *decision*. And because this question is pressed by the same drive for self transcendence which urged the questions for understanding and judgment, it is realized concretely as an exigence for self-consistency in knowing and deciding, as an imperious demand that decision conform to a person's best judgment of what he or she *should* do.[38]

This is the structure, then, of the personal subject's radical drive for self-transcendence: the questions for intelligence, critical reflection, and deliberation which concretely embody the drive, and the responding operations of understanding, judging, and deciding which effect it. As conscious, these questions and operations also specify distinct levels of consciousness in the "I," the personal subject: empirical, intelligent, reasonable, and responsible. Questions for understanding transform the empirically conscious subject into the intelligently conscious subject; questions for critical reflection transform the intelligently conscious subject into the rationally conscious subject; questions for deliberation transform the rationally conscious subject into the responsibly conscious subject. Because each of these levels takes up the preceding levels into itself, the fully conscious existential subject is empirically, intelligently, and rationally as well as responsibly conscious. Thus, if the several levels of conscious intentionality are distinct, they are also interrelated and interdependent insofar as the drives for meaning, for truth, and for value are successive stages in the unfolding of the single dynamism of the human spirit for self-transcendence.[39]

Now this radical drive of the personal subject for self-transcendence, it must be stressed, is a dynamism of the *whole* person. Far from being intellectualist as the foregoing cognitive-structural sketch might suggest, the personal drive for self-transcendence is affective at its very core. Lonergan insists that our feelings—our joys as well as our sorrows, our fears as well as our desires, our remorse as well as our peacefulness—all give "intentional consciousness its mass, momentum, drive, power." Because of these and countless other feelings about the past and future as well as the present, about missed chances as well as anticipated opportunities, and especially about, for, and with other persons, "we are oriented massively and dynamically in a world mediated by meaning."[40]

One cannot imagine the experience of insight without the joyful satisfaction, even ecstatic excitement that accompanies it (as classically captured in Archimedes' "Eureka!"), or the hopeful, enthusiastic anticipation, not to say intense, determined desire that precedes it.[41] If this is the case at the cognitive levels, it is all the more so at the level of evaluation and deliberation. For here values are grasped by the personal subject in feelings themselves. Feelings, however, are ambiguous, responding to the agreeable and disagreeable as well as to the valuable. Sometimes the agreeable and the valuable coincide, and self-transcendence comes easily. But sometimes the valuable is disagreeable, and self-transcendence means overcoming the disagreeable for the sake of doing the valuable. Thus, while feelings are the source of values, as an ambiguous source they require critical discernment.

Yet, when feelings do respond to value, we can be moved effectively toward self-transcendence, for as whole persons, and not just knowers, we respond, as Lonergan says, "with the stirring of our very being when we glimpse the possibility or actuality of moral self-transcendence."[42] Feelings, indeed, can be so deep and so strong that they give shape to a person's horizon, and direction to his or her life.

Just as a person's whole life can be consumed by hatred, so it can be pervaded and driven by love. When a person falls in love he or she not only performs loving acts, but is a being-in-love. Beyond the acts there is a fully personal state of being-in-love which is the dynamic source of every loving act. As self-transcendence is the meaning of each dimension of the personal subject, this self-transcending experience of being-in-love realizes in its fulfillment and self-actualization the meaning of the whole personal subject.

If this fulfillment is obviously the goal of our consciously free and responsible actions as well as of our intelligent and reasonable questioning and spontaneous sensitivity, it also completes the person in a deeper sense. For self-transcendence is first of all the goal of the deepest recesses of the *psyche,* whose images trigger our questioning intelligence, as well as of the *soma,* whose spontaneous interpersonal empathy is familiar to everyone who has ever instinctively reached out to catch a stumbling companion. Even in the most opaque dimension of personal reality, then, through nerves and brain, our flesh and blood spontaneously live out symbolic meanings and carry out symbolic demands. Though the personal subject is not without conflicts at every level, the drive for self-transcendence, then, is truly a *radical* drive which heuristically unifies the entire reality of the personal subject in its dynamism, and integrates it in its fulfillment.[43]

Now cognitive conversion, as noted above, consists essentially in discovering and taking possession of one's own questioning and cognitive operations as dynamically structured and oriented toward self-transcendence. When this is done explicitly, the personal subject makes the factual judgment of self-affirmation which lies at the heart of transcendental method, constituting a personal verification of the thesis on self-transcending subjectivity. For each person can reflexively direct the cognitive operations as intentional to the operations as conscious, and reflect on and verify not only the existence of his or her own experiencing, understanding, and judging, but also the *structured* dynamism of these cognitive operations. One can, in other words, attend to one's experiencing, understanding, and judging; one can understand the unity, relations, and immanent norms of one's experienced experiencing, understanding, and judging. One can also affirm the reality of one's experienced and understood experiencing, understanding, and judging—affirm concretely, that is, the fact that one does perform these operations as experienced and understood, that one is, in this sense, a knower. We can do this because cognitive structures develop to the point where formal operations can reflect not only on concrete operations, but on themselves as well. The subject not only mediates and constitutes meaning, but can appropriate the mediating and constituting structure itself. Fully critical cognitive conversion is the conscious appropriation of the realistic structural development of knowing in the mature adult that dialectically relates formal operations to concrete contexts.[44]

The appropriation of cognitive conversion is not something that happens in its fullness all at once, of course. Occasionally we observe distinct facets of this deeply personal process manifesting themselves. An example which emphasizes the fact that cognitive conversion is not restricted to the rarefied atmosphere of ivory towers is that of Vic Braden, whom millions of athletically inclined Americans know as television's humorous tennis instructor. What many people who have enjoyed Braden are not familiar with, however, is the personal journey which led to his position as tennis' most popular and successful teacher.

Raised in a poor family of seven children in Monroe, Michigan, young Vic fully expected to follow his father into the paper mill when he was old enough to work. A job on the railroad was the only other possibility he could imagine. A good athlete, Braden learned to play tennis when some local men decided it would be better to teach him the game than have him outside the fence running off with their stray balls. Tournaments soon put him in contact for the first time with boys who talked about going to college. This raised his aspirations, but so set was Braden "in his belief that he and his family were ignorant lower class, that it was not until years later when he was at Kalamazoo College that he finally comprehended that intelligence was not necessarily a reflection of economic status."[45] The moment of this insight remains clear to Braden because he still vividly recalls standing in the middle of a Monroe street a few days later, screaming at his younger brother Paul who had dropped out of school: "We're not dumb, Paul! I've learned. We're not dumb! We're not dumb!" Paul went on to an eventual graduate degree, and Vic, rooted in the discovery of his own mind—a discovery that still enchants him—created a new life for himself.

The point, of course, is not that Braden suddenly became more intelligent, but that he discovered and took possession of the intelligence which was always his. He appropriated his own mind and thereby transformed his life through its creative power.

Shifting our focus from the discovery of one's intelligence to the appropriation of reflective judgment, we can consider two aspects of the issue only alluded to above: rashness in judgment and obsession with certitude.

One cannot ask for a better example of rashness, or the pronouncement of judgment on insufficient evidence, than the classic picture etched in exquisite detail by Jane Austen in *Pride and Prejudice*. Indeed, a central theme in the novel, originally titled "First Impressions," is precisely the movement from the error of prejudiced rash judgment to the discovery of truth. Forced to face the facts by the power of Mr. Darcy's famous letter, Elizabeth Bennet not only reverses her original judgments of Darcy and Wickham, which had been unduly influenced by the one's proud manner and by the other's crafty charm, she also makes the vastly more important and humbling discovery of *herself* as she recognizes and acknowledges the personal demands of truth.

> She grew absolutely ashamed of herself. Of neither Darcy nor Wickham could she think without feeling that she had been blind, partial, prejudiced, absurd.
> "How despicably have I acted!" she cried; "I, who have prided myself on my discernment! I, who have valued myself on my abilities! who have often disdained the generous candor of my sister, and gratified my vanity in useless or [blameable] distrust. How humiliating is this discovery! yet, how just a humiliation! Had I been in love, I could not have been more wretchedly blind. But vanity, not love, has been my folly. Pleased with the preference of one, and offended by the neglect of the other, on the very beginning of our acquaintance, I have courted prepossession and ignorance, and driven reason away, where either were concerned. Till this moment I never knew myself."[46]

In most cases, cognitive conversion occurs in the context of personal relationships, as it did for Elizabeth Bennet. Of course, the story of Elizabeth's personal discovery points up only one dimension of cognitive conversion. Moving from the eighteenth century English world of Jane Austen to the global vision of the twentieth century American theologian, John Dunne, we can consider another, perhaps more difficult, dimension of conversion in the interpersonal context.

Dunne suggests that whenever we love a person, there is a good chance that we will also hate that person, because a person who can cause great joy in our life also can—and usually does—cause great pain. Thus, in a deep personal relationship there is often simultaneously hope and disappointment, confidence and fear, trust and mistrust, affection and resentment.

So powerful is the desire for an unambivalent relationship of pure, unadulterated love, that we are tempted to end a relationship rather than live with its intolerable uncertainty. We all know how in these situations imagination can seduce us with various forms of victory for the dark side: at one moment we would secure the relationship by controlling the other, at the next moment the ambiguous friend is transformed into the clear enemy or the mere acquaintance, and so it goes on. At bottom, says Dunne, all of this is a "hunger and thirst for certainty, for certainty at almost any cost. It has the self-defeating quality that the pursuit of certainty always seems to have: the more desperately one seeks for certainty the more intensely one is plagued by uncertainty."[47]

It is difficult to admit the reality of ambivalence in our relationships because our love would have us deny the dark side and expect unadulterated love from the other person. So personally shattering is the insight into ambivalence that it is usually resisted with all one's strength. Such insight is possible, though, and it has the power of liberating us from unrealistic expectations and even self-righteousness. If insight into ambivalence is not to result in the negativity discussed above, however, it must be an insight which recognizes the necessarily self-defeating nature of one's pursuit of certainty.

To surrender the pursuit of certainty, of course, is never an abstract, "intellectual" affair. Our insistence on unambivalent certainty in relationships is not purely intellectual, but a concrete demand of our whole being, and its surrender must therefore be a fully personal surrender. In reality, then, conceptual knowledge of the self-defeating nature of our pursuit of certainty is inadequate. To effect a surrender of this pursuit's demand for the unambivalent requires a deeply and fully personal insight. This insight realizes—in a way that is at once both cognitive and affective—not only that the pursuit is intrinsically self-destructive, but that its surrender can only be achieved in fully personal forgiveness. Rooted in a grasp of the light as well as the dark side of the ambivalence in our relationships, this forgiveness liberates us for the pursuit not of certainty and security but of understanding and truth. Such a conversion is difficult to maintain, for, against our preference for the familiar, the pursuit of understanding would push us into the new and unknown. But given its head, such a cognitive conversion can effect a deeply personal transformation, forcing us to confront the need for certainty and security in every area of our lives.

Clearly, then, cognitive conversion occurs not only in the highly differentiated intellectual pattern of theoretical understanding, but also—and most importantly—in the more undifferentiated personal pattern of understanding I characterized in Chapter 3 as symbolic. In this pattern experiencing, understanding, judging, and deciding all work together through feeling to create the appropriate concrete images for discovering and communicating the deepest personal meanings of one's world. Cognitive conversion in this symbolic pattern might, in light of our earlier discussion of the imaginative embodiment of understanding, be appropriately called conversion of the imagination. By reason of its deeply personal and undifferentiated nature, it is closely associated with the affective conversion we will examine later in this chapter, for feeling and imagination are inextricably linked in a symbolic world that recognizes no divorce. This is why all personal conversions are so intrinsically dependent on the quality and vitality of the symbols and stories available in one's community. Genuine mutuality, for example, will never be more than wishful thinking as long as our imaginations are dominated by symbols and stories of control and competition rather than lured by those of care and cooperation.

Ultimately, of course, conversion to the pursuit of understanding is the point of entry into our lives of genuine mystery. The implications of cognitive conversion of the imagination for religious understanding, then, are enormous, as we will see in a following chapter.

Central to the possession one takes of oneself as a knower in full cognitive conversion, of course, is the specific realization that the criterion of the real is the "virtually unconditioned" of one's own judgment. This insight is the basis for an explicit cognitive conversion's elimination, as noted above, of a fundamental myth about reality and objectivity as well as human knowing. In simplest terms, this myth overlooks the distinction between the world of immediacy and the world mediated by meaning. While the myth that knowing is essentially taking a look at a reality that is "already-out-there-now," and that objectivity is taking a good look and seeing that reality clearly, may do justice to the world of immediacy, it does not—to use its own terms—offer even a glimpse of the world mediated by meaning. For the world mediated by meaning is known not just by taking a look, but by the integrated personal and communal process of understanding and judging the data of both internal and external experiencing that is proper to fully human knowing. From this understanding of knowing one can move to a recognition of reality as what is not only given in experience but also organized and extrapolated by understanding and affirmed by judgment. Likewise, objectivity can be understood in terms of the criteria not only of eyesight and the other external senses but of all experiencing, understanding, and judging. Through a philosophically explicated cognitive conversion, then, one recognizes that an adequate understanding of knowing, objectivity, and reality must take account not only of the world of immediacy but also of the complex process from that world to the world mediated by meaning.[48]

Still, the essence of cognitive conversion is not in its philosophical explication and elimination of the "myth of the given" but in the prior personal performance which grounds the philosophical objectification. The essence of cognitive conversion is one's recognition and grasp of oneself as a knower whose own self-transcending judgments—not some external norm—constitute the criterion of the real.

It is precisely this appropriation of oneself as the criterion of the real in one's self-transcending judgments that distinguishes a critical moral conversion from one that is uncritical. For moral conversion is a dual choice on the fourth level of responsible consciousness: a choice of value as criterion for decision and a choice of oneself as a free and responsible originator of value. But as moral conversion is a transformation of the whole person, and as the moral level of consciousness sublates the cognitive levels, the fundamental cognitive character of a person's moral conversion will be determined by whether or not he or she is cognitively converted. Insofar as a person has taken possession of his or her knowing, then, the shift to value as criterion for decision will be a shift not only to values but to values *critically* discovered and established by a subject who has recognized and chosen himself or herself not only as a creator of value through decision and action but as the very criterion of value in his or her self-transcending judgments. This is the person for whom value takes a particularly sharp existential edge as it opens the mind and lures the spirit toward unrestricted goodness wherever found.

This distinction between critical and uncritical moral conversions, then, is rooted in a basic differentiation within the fundamental structure of conscious operations. For, like every choice, the choice of value over satisfaction as criterion for decisions, and the choice of oneself as responsible, is only as good as the understanding and judgment from which it proceeds. As noted, the fourth level of consciousness itself involves two moments, two different kinds of responses: judgments of value on the one hand and decisions or choices on the other. One's decisions or choices are critical insofar as they proceed from realistic judgment, authentic insofar as they conform to objective judgment. Thus a moral conversion proceeding from an intelligent grasp and reasonable affirmation of one's own dynamism for self-transcendence is a truly critical self-appropriation.

Moral conversion as simply a shift in criterion for decision from satisfaction to value, however, lacks such critical self-knowledge. Thus while such conversion may be adequate for living in the cultural peace of a homogeneous society with uncontested values, still its conventional values—however true and sincerely believed they may be—are held uncritically. Under the onslaught of cultural pluralism, such a conversion will fall like a town without walls. The facts of contemporary life dictate that critical self-appropriation, which was once a moral luxury, is now for many a necessary component of authentic human living. For in a complex world of competing moral values, the person without critical self-appropriation is like most of us simple folks in the hands of the proverbial used-car salesman—going around kicking tires with no more purpose than the desperate hope that they might secretly tell us what to do!

While such a critical moral conversion is ideally based on a fully articulated, philosophical version of cognitive conversion, the implicit or tacit intellectual realization spelled out above is sufficient as well as necessary to ground a critical moral conversion. Indeed, given the rarity of philosophically articulated cognitive conversions, this implicit cognitive conversion would appear to be the usual basis for a critically grounded moral conversion. In the same way, while postconventional moral reasoning can be given explicitly reflective, philosophical expression in a systematic ethical theory, it is the practical reasoning in terms of self-chosen universal ethical principles of justice, not their philosophical articulation, which constitutes postconventional morality.

Cognitive conversion is, of course, the master key to fundamental clarification of philosophical issues in the physical and human sciences. But in our personal lives, its deep significance lies in the existential appropriation of oneself as a free, responsible, and self-constituting originator of value who in one's own self-transcending judgments and choices is the criterion of the real and the truly good. In this existential context, the basic realization, more than its technical philosophical expression, is of paramount importance.

There is, indeed, no place more appropriate for cognitive conversion than one's personal moral life, where seemingly impossible choices can strip an honest person of every so-called "objective" criterion, leaving one morally naked to the conventional world. If one resists the easy choice of the latest fad in ready-to-wear "designer" fashions, gives reasonable and responsible intelligence its head, and follows it courageously, one discovers that even the hottest designer's collection offers only conventional answers for standard sizes, and that the custom fitted response of the authentic subject is not to be found on any rack.

This negative discovery that the perfect fit for the truly personal moral life is not hanging on some ready-to-wear rack, and that the pursuit of it there only results in the inauthenticity of endless bad fits, can lead one to the positive discovery that in the moral life one must be one's own tailor, regardless of the brilliance of one's favorite designer. Such ruthlessly honest pursuit of one's intelligence can lead, in other words, to the discovery of one's own self-transcending subjectivity as the only available objective criterion of meaning and value for one's life. Insofar as one makes this discovery, moral conversion is not simply a shift to value but a truly critical appropriation of oneself. In this critical moral conversion, then, the shift is first of all to oneself as finally the only one a person can authentically turn to in a fundamental moral crisis. In this critical turn to oneself is grounded the shift to value as criterion for decision not just as the adoption of some given conventional values but as the critical appropriation of personally discovered and affirmed values.

In summary, then, while moral conversion in the simplest sense of a shift to value as criterion for decision is independent of and presupposes no cognitive conversion, the deeper critical moral conversion that constitutes full moral autonomy necessarily involves cognitive conversion, either explicitly or, as in most cases, implicitly.

CONVERSION TO POSTCONVENTIONAL MORALITY

Having distinguished moral conversion in its critical and uncritical forms, let us now direct this distinction back to Kohlberg's theory to show the significance of the existential theme which Gibbs has identified as characterizing its postconventional, principled stages.

Focusing first on uncritical moral conversion, it is clear from the very meaning of conventional moral reasoning that an uncritical shift from satisfaction to value as criterion for choice occurs at Kohlberg's third and fourth stages of moral reasoning. Indeed, adolescence is not an uncommon time for a person to turn from excessive concern with obedience-punishment and pragmatic self-interest to a genuine desire to be and to do good, interpersonally and socially. Development in both the cognitive dimension (formal operations) and affective-psychosocial dimension (both mutuality of Interpersonal relations and identity-formation and fidelity), as explained in Chapter 2, ground the morally self-transcending subject's possibility for conversion in this period.[49] From this perspective, though Kohlberg rightly stresses the cognitive dimension, he also needs to emphasize these affective realities as necessary conditions for the transition to conventional morality, just as he has specified the condition of responsible caring for the postconventional shift. Because of the developmental limitations of the adolescent's affective and cognitive resources, however, the desired good, while understood as value rather than simple self-satisfaction, is identified uncritically in terms of interpersonal and social *givens*, as we have seen. Thus, though our emphasis has been on critical moral conversion and the postconventional orientation here, we can see how basic, uncritical moral conversion and the transition to conventional moral reasoning both point to the same reality of personal transformation. This identification, of course, like the one we are about to make between critical moral conversion and the postconventional orientation, is intelligible only in the context of the argument in Chapter 3 that moral reasoning is radically both affective and cognitive. In this sense one's moral reasoning is not what one merely understands conceptually, but what one actually uses in making life decisions. A person's conscience is structured by conventional moral reasoning only if that person is *committed* to conventional values, only if, that is, he or she has been morally converted. This means, of course, that the use of conventional moral reasoning in the concrete situations of real life is rarer than it is in the hypothetical dilemmas of research interviews, where moral distance and abstractness considerably reduce the demand for personal commitment, thus allowing the luxury of inexpensive gift subscriptions to conventional values *for others*.

To thus identify uncritical moral conversion with development to conventional moral reasoning as actually structuring one's affective-cognitive consciousness is to extend (and thereby transform) Gibbs' thesis on the existential character of postconventional morality back to conventional morality. For even an uncritical moral conversion is a deliberate *choice* of value as criterion for decision, and thus not simply spontaneous and unconscious as Gibbs insists natural stage transition must be, but existential. Gibbs, however, explicitly defines conventional moral reasoning as natural, not existential. We avoid the apparent contradiction here if we understand that the one transforming process has two dimensions: one unconscious and spontaneous, one conscious and deliberate. As unconscious and spontaneous the process is the natural restructuring of moral consciousness called stage transition. As conscious and deliberate it is the existential choice of value called moral conversion.

Gibbs is correct in distinguishing the existential dimension of moral development from the natural. It is not necessary, however, to relate them in an exclusive, "either/or" fashion: conventional stages are natural; postconventional orientations are existential. These two dimensions, rather, are better understood as simultaneously characterizing both conventional and postconventional moral consciousness. After all, whatever may be true of the transition from one logical-cognitive stage to another, there is no reason to think that the transformation of moral reasoning, which focuses on value, should simply occur in an unconscious and spontaneous way. All our experience of moral transformation, in fact, suggests conscious struggle as well as unconscious gift.

Indeed, the fact that transition to a new moral stage occurs in the context of the previous stage's functional inadequacy, or breakdown, is strong theoretical reason to expect the unconscious restructuring process to occur in conjunction with the conscious choice of value in moral conversion. James Loder's analysis of convictional knowing, which we discussed in Chapter 3, also points toward this correlation of moral conversion and stage transition. Loder explicitly interprets the transformational logic of convictional knowing as the governing factor in the stage transition process: scanning, constructive act of imagination, release and openness, and interpretation all respond to the conflict of functional negation.[50]

In this context of distinguishing unconscious/conscious, natural/existential dimensions in the one reality of moral transformation, we can turn to the issue of *critical* moral conversion now and recall how Kohlberg has pointed out that moral judgments of a Stage 6 principled conscience require such complex affective and cognitive development, along with a depth of personal experience, that—even in the small minority of people who reach it—the psychological maturity for such a principled conscience emerges only in young adulthood, at the earliest. Taking a clue from this point, one can argue—and this is the chapter's basic thesis—that the realization of a fully personal conscience characterized by Kohlberg's Stage 6 principled reasoning is substantially identical to a critical moral conversion.[51] The key to understanding this identity lies in seeing the *self*-chosen, universal ethical principles of Kohlberg's Stage 6 as constituting the critical dimension of moral conversion. Unlike the assumed rules of conventional moral reasoning, which are rooted—at Stage 4—in societal authority, ethical principles are chosen at Stage 6 on the *self*'s authority, because one has become personally convinced of their moral truth, as well as of one's own radical obligation as a responsible person to make such ultimate judgments and choices for oneself. Thus, in contrast to the conventional moral rules of uncritical conversion which one is socialized to accept, principles at Stage 6 are chosen autonomously, with open, critical eyes. Though Kohlberg does not attend to the correlative personal transformation necessary at the subject-pole, the realization of an orientation of self-chosen, universal principles definitely constitutes a critical moral conversion. That ethical principles be chosen at all clearly requires a moral conversion; that universal principles be chosen on the *self*'s authority requires that the moral conversion be critical.

Of course, the fact that principles are chosen at Stage 6 on one's own authority as a responsible person does not necessarily mean that the values earlier accepted on society's authority are rejected. The same values may be substantially reestablished on a new, critical basis. From a structural perspective, the postconventional stages, in subsuming lower stages, preserve their positive advances and eliminate only their limitations. An example of this is the member-of-society perspective of Stage 4. Persons at Stages 5 and 6 have moved beyond the member-of-society perspective, but only in the sense of relativizing it, not in the sense of eliminating it. A relativized member-of-society perspective, in fact, is essential for principled moral reasoning—a point which makes Gibbs' claim that Stages 5 and 6 are, respectively, only philosophical versions of the perspective-taking of Stages 2 and 3 difficult to accept.[52]

On the other hand, as structural limitations are left behind in the development to postconventional morality (the closed absoluteness of the member-of-society perspective, for example), so also are limited understandings of values transcended. Thus, for example, a person at Stage 6 will find himself or herself at odds with a society's conventional view of patriotism as "my country, right or wrong."

From one important angle, Kohlberg's interpretation of Stage 6 can be seen as explicating the critically converted conscience's structure of reasoning. The moral reasoning of the critically converted conscience at Stage 6 is universal, impersonal, consistent; it is rooted in the intrinsic dignity of the person and in fully reversible justice as normative for relationships among persons. The universalizing demand works against both self- and group-serving deceptions. This is particularly important in establishing a critical definition of the authentic or humanly normative conscience, for even the unconverted person—indeed, especially the unconverted—will appeal to his or her conscience as the final word. Still, postconventional reasoning is the *structure* of committed, loving care of real persons in the complexity of concrete situations. Converted from the illusory pursuit of certainty to the open-ended search for the concrete good, its universalizing intent appreciates the relativity of human reality as well as the limits of its own perspective. Understood in this sense, postconventional reasoning's middle name is humility—the cognitive dimension of the fully personal humility which presses for continuing conversion.

Kohlberg has identified his moral Stage 6 with the ethical orientation of caring responsibility which emerges from the successful resolution of the crisis of generativity at Erikson's seventh stage. While there are similarities, this identification needs serious qualification in terms of conversion.[53] Erikson's ethical orientation does offer a considerably more integrated, explicit view of conscience than does Kohlberg's Stage 6, as Chapter 2 noted. But, unlike Kohlberg's Stage 6 reasoning, nothing about Erikson's ethical orientation demands a critical moral conversion. The crisis of generativity is only an occasion for critical moral conversion. Erikson's ideal ethical person has experienced moral conversion, but may just as easily be at the conventional level of moral reasoning as at the postconventional. Precisely the same point is to be made, of course, about the person at Kierkegaard's ethical stage; moral conversion is present by definition, but this conversion may be critical or uncritical. Even Kierkegaard's reference to rational norms can be easily contained by conventional morality, which admits of highly sophisticated logical reasoning.

At the same time, however, in order to appreciate the existential theme of postconventional morality, one must view it from the perspective of self-creation, and especially the existential moment of that process I have called critical moral conversion. Gibbs correctly points to the existential theme as dominant in Kohlberg's principled morality. He emphasizes the formal, reflective, philosophical dimension of principled reasoning, however, and not its *self*-chosen character. Thus he is able to do full justice neither to the existentialist theme nor to the radical difference between what he calls the first four "natural" orientations in Kohlberg's theory and the last two "existential" orientations. In contrast, I have interpreted both conventional and postconventional morality as existential, while specifying their difference in terms of the postconventional critical moment. In order to do real justice to the existential theme of Kohlberg's postconventional morality, as well as to the *critical* difference between the conventional and postconventional, one must interpret moral development in the context of the self-creation of the concrete personal subject. And in doing this, one must highlight the possibility that within this process of spontaneous, natural self-creation there may occur that existential moment when we critically discover that it is up to each of us to decide for ourselves what we are to make of ourselves. Such a move will also establish a *critical* link between Kohlberg's analysis of moral reasoning and the more existential first person concerns and orientation found in the active mutuality of Erikson's ethical caring and responsibility, and in the open, committed involvement in the world of Fowler's Conjunctive Faithing.

Is conversion necessary for moral development? Yes, in the development to both conventional and postconventional moral reasoning, conversion is necessary; in the latter case, critical moral conversion. Conversion is the conscious, existential dimension of the single transformational reality which in its unconscious, natural dimension is the restructuring that constitutes stage transition. Conversion itself is neither spontaneous nor unconscious, thus in this sense not natural. But, in a different sense of the word, when a person experiences a radical existential crisis in the human environment of value, moral conversion is necessary for normative development to continue, and thus may be thought of as natural. In this sense of the authentically human, the natural and the existential become one. Now the definition of conscience can be given a further normative specification. Conscience is the radical drive of the personal subject for self-transcendence—and it is more; mature, truly adult conscience is the self-transcending drive of the morally converted personal subject, and preferably as converted in a critical fashion.

As appealing as moral conversion may appear on paper, and as attractive as its ideal of personal autonomy may be, the hard truth is that moral conversion is not easy; one does not just wake up one morning in a new moral world. Indeed, it is extremely difficult to overcome the resistance with which the psyche spontaneously responds to the possibility of conversion, of moving into a radically new horizon.[54] For horizons define not abstractions but the concrete shape of one's living. And to contemplate a radical change in the style of concrete living that for many years has more or less successfully integrated the significant elements of one's personality—unconscious as well as conscious, practical as well as interpersonal—is, as Kierkegaard describes so vividly, to invite an experience of anxiety or dread.

The spontaneous and powerful resistance generated by this dread necessarily attempts to defend the challenged horizon from within. It employs a logic based on its own meanings and values, and unimpeachable on its own grounds. From the perspective of logic, then, conversion to a radically new horizon is a non-logical leap. It must be effected, therefore, not by logical argument alone, but also (and especially) dialectically by symbolic means which do not attack logical defenses directly but tunnel to the center of the established horizon's fortress, to its imaginative and affective ground, the "heart" of the subject. Thus, while moral conversion is principally a matter of *discovery* and *decision,* it is predicated on the "3rd D" of *desire:* one's *choosing* of oneself as an originating value rests not only on the explicitly cognitive element of *recognizing* the human call to responsibility, but also on the affective dimension of *feeling* in the demand to respond to this call a joy over the prospect of growth toward more authentic life. The transformation of desire becomes a central issue as we now turn to the "continuing" nature of conversion.

As difficult as such a leap of conversion may be, however, it is more a beginning than an end. To be morally converted is not to be morally perfect. Conversion must be ongoing. As Lonergan puts it, "it is one thing to decide what one is to make of oneself . . . it is another to execute the decision. Today's resolutions do not predetermine the free choice of tomorrow, of next week, or next year, or ten years from now. What has been achieved is always precarious: it can slip, fall, shatter. What is to be achieved can be ever expanding, deepening. To meet one challenge is to effect a development that reveals a further and graver challenge."[55]

Beyond bringing the meaning of personal responsibility into sharp focus, the challenge of moral conversion also highlights in an intensely personal fashion the ideal of authentic human living, as well as the distance between that ideal and one's present achievement. Thus moral conversion is significant not so much as an achievement but as a call to commitment. For insofar as moral conversion reveals how drastically limited one's effective freedom really is, one must commit oneself to the endless task of continuing conversion.[56] Through critical interaction with one's community, one must persist in eradicating personal prejudices and biases, in developing one's knowledge of human reality, in opening oneself to further possibilities, in ruthlessly examining the authenticity of one's responses to values. For if, as Lonergan says, "moral knowledge is the proper possession only of morally good men," these are the very ones who realize that far from implying a possession one has for oneself, this title entails an obligation one has to others.[57] If the challenge of moral conversion is so demanding as to seem impossible, then what are the real possibilities of *living* a morally converted life? In a word, the answer, as we shall see in the following section, is rooted in the reality of *love*.

AFFECTIVE CONVERSION

A person is affectively self-transcendent, as we noted earlier with Lonergan, when the isolation of the individual is broken and he or she spontaneously acts not just for self but for others as well. Further, when a person falls in love, his or her love is embodied not just in this or that act or even in any series of acts, but in a dynamic state of being-in-love. Such being-in-love is the concrete first principle from which a person's affective life flows: "one's desires and fears, one's joys and sorrows, one's discernment of values, one's decisions and deeds."[58] Falling-in-love, in other words, is a more or less radical transformation of a person's life: affective conversion.[59] Such conversion turns one's self, shifts one's orientation, from an absorption in one's own interests to concern for the good of others. If moral conversion is the recognition of the possibility, and thus the felt challenge, of becoming a living principle of benevolence and beneficence, affective conversion is the transformation of personal being which actualizes that possibility, which makes effective response to that challenge a reality. Rooted in the peaceful joy and bliss of affective conversion, therefore, is the concrete possibility of overcoming moral impotence, of not only being able to make a decision to commit oneself to a course of action or direction of life judged worthwhile and personally appropriate, but of being able to execute that decision over the long haul against serious obstacles.[60]

The reality of falling-in-love, of course, has as many versions as there are love stories.[61] There is the beaming love of young parents for their newborn child; there is the love of sons and daughters for mothers and fathers which grows through years of responding to the wonders of parental self-transcendence. Such familial self-transcendence grounds the possibility, too, of the intimate love between a woman and a man—from the boundless dreams and reckless self-giving of young lovers to the gentle touch and knowing smiles of a peaceful couple remembering a half-century through which they have grown together in each other's love.

Life, of course, is made of more than love stories. Right alongside are ugly tales of hatred and brutality, misunderstanding and resentment, indifference and bitter disappointment—tales which too often end without a hint of forgiveness, reconciliation, hope. At the end of a century that has witnessed human atrocities of the most staggering proportions, a story that ignores the full potential of the human heart for evil is less credible than a fairy tale.[62] Still, if life is not an innocent story in which prince charmings and fairy godmothers always emerge triumphant, there are indeed instances of self-transcending love. As the lives of individuals as different as Martin Luther King and Mother Teresa of Calcutta remind us, when the mutual love of families and friends is authentic it does not remain absorbed in an *égoisme à deux* or three or more, but reaches out beyond itself to the neighbor, not to "humanity," but to the concrete person in need, whoever or wherever that person is.

Now, as imaginatively suggestive as the phrase "falling-in-love" is, without further precision it is far too ambiguous to provide a critical understanding of affective conversion. "Love" simply means too many very different things to adequately ground so central a human reality as affective conversion. Erich Fromm speaks of five loves (brotherly, motherly, erotic, self-love, and love of God); Paul Tillich lists four (libido, eros, philia, and agape), as does C.S. Lewis (affection, eros [distinguished from venus], friendship, and charity); the Scholastics specify three (*concupiscentia, benevolentia,* and *amicitia*); Anders Nygren and Denis de Rougement insist on the dichotomy of two loves, eros and agape, while Martin D'Arcy and Robert Johann, following Augustine and Aquinas, attempt their synthesis; the fundamental unity of love, finally, is maintained by George Tavard.[63]

By "love" Lonergan clearly means the active, other-oriented principle of beneficence and benevolence, but this meaning is confused by his use of the phrase "*falling*-in-love," with all its connotations of passivity and sentimentality. A critical interpretation of affective conversion demands a careful examination of affectivity in general and of love in particular.[64]

Cognitive Interpretations of Affectivity

Lonergan's interpretation of affectivity focuses on feelings as sources of value. Distinct from feelings of directly physiological origin, feelings capable of disclosing value are *intentional* responses of the whole person. Such fully personal feelings arise out of cognitive activities like perceiving and imagining, and are thus related not just to causes and ends but to intentional objects as responses.[65]

Although this interpretation of feeling as intentional response is based directly on Dietrich von Hildebrand's (and indirectly Max Scheler's) rather distinctive phenomenological analysis, it relates very positively to the major line of contemporary psychological theories of emotions which stresses their *cognitive* character.[66] Indeed, its roots in the *philosophia perennis* are manifest in the work of Magda Arnold, the principal psychological proponent of the cognitive theory of emotions, who explicitly derives her fundamental approach from Aristotle and Aquinas.[67]

This link to the philosophical tradition can be discerned in Arnold's definition of emotion as "a felt tendency toward anything appraised as good, and away from anything appraised as bad."[68] In this view of emotion, whatever is perceived, remembered, imagined will be appraised; if the object is appraised as desirable or harmful, an action tendency is aroused. Arnold regards the physiological changes that are so impressive in emotion as ancillary to the felt action tendency; both originate from the appraisal. In Arnold's vocabulary, emotions aim at possession or avoidance of objects, while the term "feeling" designates "those affective states where the psychological reference is principally to the subject."[69] Feelings reflect the individual's inner state of functioning.

An essential dimension of this perspective on emotion is what Arnold calls affective memory. Distinct from modality-specific memory such as visual or auditory, affective memory is "the living record of the emotional life history of each person." Unlike modality-specific memory which is usually lost quickly, affective memory is always at our disposal, and in appraisals it relives the original acceptance or rejection (a dog-bite in early childhood, for example) in a new but similar situation. Though appraisals organize emotions, and emotions organize the actions they urge, from the perspective of the person emotions can be perceived as interfering and disturbing if they urge in a direction different from that indicated by deliberate judgment. But, as the diabetic who resists the temptation of the delicious but dangerous dessert exemplifies, even the intuitive appraisal leading to strong desire is not necessarily final. Intuitive appraisal produces an action impulse, but in the end it is the motive established by conscious judgment and deliberate decision that determines action.[70] In Arnold's perspective, then, emotions are cognitive in a twofold sense: they depend on cognitive activities for their objects, and they are fundamentally constituted by intuitive appraisals which are not only cognitive but evaluative.

Richard Lazarus also holds that emotions and cognitions are inseparable. He assumes that emotions arise from how a person construes the outcome of his or her transaction with the environment.[71] In this view, cognitive processes "create the emotional response out of the organism-environment transaction and shape it into anger, fear, grief, etc."[72] Extending Arnold's basic cognitive approach, Lazarus argues that the pattern of arousal observed in emotion derives from impulses to action generated not only by the individual's appraised situation, but also by the evaluated possibilities available for action. An important part of the cognitive dimension of emotions, in other words, are the reappraisals based on feedback processes. Along with direct actions (attack, avoidance), reappraisals constitute the basic coping processes available to the individual. Lazarus also stresses the beliefs, attitudes, etc. of the individual as important conditions of appraisals along with situational factors.

Among psychologists offering a cognitive interpretation of emotions, James Averill is distinctive for his social constructivist view. For him, not only do cognitive structures provide the basis for the appraisal of stimuli, but the functional significance of emotional responses is to be found largely within the sociocultural system. With regard to subjective experience within emotion, Averill makes the important claim that a person interprets his or her own experience as emotional much as an actor interprets a role "with feeling."[73] The passivity commonly associated with emotions, for example, is not intrinsic to the response, according to Averill, but is an interpretation. Here, then, we have a view of emotions as cognitive not just in the sense of being dependent on cognitive activities, or even of incorporating appraisal as a constitutive component, but as essentially an act of creative interpretation of experience.

Of course, if emotions are radically cognitive, we should not be surprised that they have been interpreted developmentally. Silvano Arieti, for example, has distinguished three orders of emotions.[74] First order emotions, elicited by a direct or impending attack or by a threatened change in homeostasis, require minimal cognition: tension, appetite, fear, rage. Second order emotions are elicited by cognitive symbolic processes: anxiety, wishing, security, anger. Finally, according to Arieti, third order emotions are related to language and concept development and refer to past and future as well as present: depression, love, joy, hate. Thus, to take one example, there is a developmental sequence, specified in terms of greater cognitive sophistication, of rage, anger, and hatred.

Perhaps the most comprehensive (and ambitious) psychological interpretation of emotions as cognitive is Joseph de Rivera's structural theory, which focuses on the *movement* of emotion. "The experience of emotion reflects the *transformation* of our relation to the world—to the persons, objects, events, and actions that are important to us."[75] These transformations are the movements of emotion, and each type of emotion reflects a kind of transformation. For de Rivera, though we feel ourselves being moved (from within), such transformation is not a passive reaction to a stimulus, but a transaction between person and environment, a way of organizing the relation between the person and the other so that the response itself gives meaning to the situation. Emotions are ways of perceiving situations (anger, for example, is a challenge—against what is—to what *ought* to be) in which a person unconsciously "chooses" organizations, interpretations, and thus transformations of his or her being-in-the-world, leading to specific behavior.

Following Piaget, de Rivera insists that these organizations, these ways of transforming object relations, are not isolated mechanisms but parts of a whole, of a *structure*. The basic unit of emotional analysis in this structure is not the individual but the *dyad* of person and other. De Rivera outlines a fundamental set of twenty-four interrelated emotions specified according to dimension (belonging, recognition, being), direction of movement (toward other, self; away from self, other), and object of movement (self, other). For example, looking at "belonging" emotions, with the other as object, we have love (toward other), desire (toward self), anger (away from self, against other), and fear (away from other). This impressive synthesis is too complex to present in its entirety, but even this brief look at the interrelationships of four emotions should suggest its explanatory power for distinguishing and integrating the transformations of the structured emotional whole that is the person.

Affectivity as Constitutive of Identity

Psychologists are not alone in their emphasis on the cognitive dimension of emotion. Indeed, it is a contemporary philosopher, Robert Solomon, who has been most insistent on this theme over the course of two books and several articles.

The aim of Solomon's major study, *The Passions,* is to return to the passions the central and defining role in our lives. "Our passions constitute our lives," says Solomon; they alone provide our lives with meaning. Emotions, he argues, are "the very core of our existence, the system of meanings and values within which our lives either develop and grow or starve and stagnate." Focusing on the cognitive theme in particular, Solomon stresses that emotions are "our own *judgments,* with which we structure the world to our purposes . . . and ultimately 'constitute' not only our world but ourselves." As judgments, then, emotions are both evaluative and constitutive. They are the source of most of our values. Our emotions would transform the world. Indeed, emotional expression is an attempt to make the world the way it *ought* to be.[76]

Solomon aims at a marriage of the passions and reason in a new romanticism, in which the passions are illuminated, enlightened by reflection, supported by deliberation. For unlike other judgments, emotions are unarticulated, unreflective, undeliberated. Because they are already made when we come to reflect on them, emotions can appear to happen to us.[77] But it is Solomon's basic point to insist that we make our emotions—we make ourselves angry, we make ourselves depressed, we make ourselves fall in love—and thus we are responsible for them.

As judgments, emotions are not only evaluative and constitutive, they are also distinctively self-involved. The judgments that constitute our emotions are the ones especially important to us, the ones concerning objects, events, people in which we have invested ourselves. But emotions are self-involved not only because they are important to us; all emotions are either explicitly or implicitly *about* us, about our selves. Whether emotions are directly and obviously about our selves, as in pride or shame, or about another person, as in anger or pity, Solomon argues, the self is always involved in a process of constituting itself. Anger may be focused toward the other person, but it always involves a judgment that the self has been offended or violated.[78]

In the most fundamental sense, according to Solomon, the self-involvement of emotions is rooted in the fact that, whatever their immediate, particular objects, the ultimate object of emotional judgments is always our personal sense of self-esteem.[79] Even an emotion about another person constitutes an intersubjective identity in which we attempt to maximize self-esteem: one may become the "defender of right," for example, in anger.

Through our emotions we not only interpret the world but constitute our world, "projecting our values and passing judgments on ourselves and other people, our situations and the various 'intentional objects' in which we have invested our interests."[80] Because this constituted world is *our* world, our emotions are not just projections, but *projects*. Emotions are not only directed toward intentional objects, they are suffused with intentions to act, to change the world that is into the world that ought to be. In its constitution of our personal world, every emotion is a "personal ideology," a set of "hopes and desires, expectations and commitments, intentions and strategies for changing our world," and often enough *the* world. And all the ideologies of our emotions, with their various strategies, have a common goal: the maximization of self-esteem, which Solomon sees as the ultimate goal of all subjectivity.[81]

The full import of Solomon's theory of emotion appears when he turns to the particular emotion of love. Here we clearly see the self-involved, constitutive character of emotion as judgment—indeed, even as decision and choice—in all its personal intensity. One of the main purposes of Solomon's *Love: Emotion, Myth and Metaphor,* in fact, is to stress the connection between romantic love and self-identity, to argue that romantic love is the search for and creation of self-identity.[82]

In Solomon's view, love is not just an attitude we direct *toward* another person, it is an emotion—a world—we *share* with him or her. Love is like all emotions insofar as their ultimate goal is the maximization of self-esteem; for though love is concerned about an other person, it is ultimately about the creation of self. But unlike other emotions, in which the self is often set in opposition to or in isolation from others, the self that is created in love is a *shared* self. In love, Solomon argues, we transform ourselves, but since the self transformed in love is a shared self it is at odds with, even contradictory to, our previous individual autonomous selves. Still, romantic love is not a *union* of shared identity, but a *dialectic* between this ideal of merger and the individual identity and free autonomy which love presupposes. The essence of love, says Solomon, is in the "impossible desire" revealed in the "constant struggle between our sense of individuality and our sense of a 'union'." In sum, "love is a process of transformation, a sometimes violent alteration of self that is always torn between our ideologically all-pervasive need for independence and autonomy and our equally all-pervasive obsession with romantic love and shared identity."[83] Recall Kegan's distinction between fusion and intimacy.

Again, in line with his general analysis of emotion, Solomon wants to insist that love is something we actively *do,* not some passive thing that happens to us. Despite all the sentimental rhetoric to the contrary, we do not *fall* in love; we rather judge, decide, choose to love. Thus, we are responsible for our loving. Solomon's point is that we do not simply come upon and fall captive to, but that we *constitute* the charms and virtues of the person we *choose* to love. Love, like other emotions, is a set of constitutive judgments, in this case "to the effect that we *will* see in this person every possible virtue, ignore or overlook every possible vice, celebrating faults as well as charms in the context of his or her total personality." The virtues and charms lovers "discover," then, are actually created through interpretation. It is the interpretation that is discovered. Even the parameters of one's love are a set of self-legislated ideals and standards. Like the other emotions, love establishes a framework, a set of standards within which we commit ourselves, and "to which the world, other people, and, most importantly, our Selves are expected to comply."[84]

Deciding to love means many things, says Solomon, but most of all it means that "one stops thinking in terms of self-interest as the criterion for making decisions."[85] It means ceasing to think of independence as the ideal of self-identity. Paradoxically, it means dropping the goal of self-esteem, despite love's very strategy of maximizing self-esteem. Ideally, of course, in the shared self of the loveworld, to maximize the self-esteem of one's lover is to maximize one's own self-esteem.

Much of what masquerades as love—dependency, possessiveness, for example—is not love at all. For Solomon, "Love is intimacy and trust; love is mutual respect and admiration; love is the insistence on mutual independence and autonomy, free from possessiveness but charged with desire; love is unqualified acceptance of the other's welfare and happiness as one's own." Love is not possessiveness; love only begins where possessive desire ends. Love is not dependency; love is an emotion of strength. Those who think they need love the most are the least likely to love, because though they may be ready to give themselves, they have so little self to give. And neither, according to Solomon, is love self-love. Self-love is not love at all, but idolatry. In self-love one loves merely the *image* of the self, not the self; the self as object, not as subject.[86]

We have already noted Solomon's aim to bring the emotions and reason together in a new romanticism, a union in which the emotions are illuminated by reflection, supported by deliberation. Emotions are unreflective, but they are connected by a "logic" (and by a common object) to our reflective judgments about them—and thus the possibility of their transformation. Indeed, as Solomon stresses, reflection on our emotions is not just a detached commentary *about* them; reflection transforms our emotions. Reflection can undermine erroneously based emotions; and reflection can also reinforce or even create emotions. But reflection is not always the answer; often expression or even the transformation of our world (even *the* world) is necessary.[87]

Love in innocence and love reflected bear little resemblance. Because of this, says Solomon, many people, unaware of love with experience and commitment, lose innocent love and despair of ever finding it again. Fascination with innocent love, unaware of its commitment to a certain kind of seeing and sharing, blinds us to its naiveté and unpreparedness for coming disappointments, whereas reflective love, cognizant of its commitments as commitments, is not only prepared but *chooses* to face the inevitable problems of love. It is not love lost, says Solomon, but only innocent love lost—with its myths of passivity and perfection—that cannot be recaptured. "We never knew enough to *make* it our own in the first place." If love can be naive, it can also—like other emotions—be inconsistent and arbitrary in its predetermined resolutions (tendencies which have contributed greatly to the emotions' tarnished reputation). But, says Solomon, "rendered reflective and maintained consistently, it is the same predetermined and 'before the fact' resoluteness that stands at the foundation of all love and respect, all ideals and values, all relationships and senses of community." Who we are, and what our world is, he claims, is the "collective and systematic resultant of all our various judgments . . . our judgments of value and our judgments of status, our judgments of power and our judgments of responsibility, our judgments of trust and our judgments of intimacy." Adapting a line from Shelley, Solomon says "the emotions are 'the unacknowledged legislators of [our] world'."[88]

For Solomon, then, emotions are not only radically cognitive, but through unreflective interpretation, judgment, decision, and choice they are also fundamentally constitutive of our human world. Emotions are not essentially at odds with reason; rather, in reflection lies the possibility of emotional transformation. If emotions have in common the power of self-creation, romantic love is singular in that its creation is a radically transforming re-creation of a shared self in a shared world with a shared interest.

Romantic Love: Passion and Decision

The self-transforming power of romantic love is also central to the theological analysis of Rosemary Haughton's *The Passionate God*. Haughton's thesis is that we can make sense of how God loves by looking at the way people love, particularly the way of love called passionate. By "passionate" Haughton means to evoke something "in motion—strong, wanting, needy, concentrated towards a very deep encounter." For her "passion" also means a certain "helplessness, a suffering and undergoing for the sake of what is desired and, implicitly, the possibility of a tragic outcome."[89]

Haughton's analysis of romantic passion is worked out within an interpretative context whose fundamental model of reality is that of "life as given and received in exchange, without ceasing, forever." Here "life" means a complex, moving web of interdependence, an endless flowing of love. Reality is exchanged life, and this is love. But the exchange can be interrupted, blocked, and if the obstacle to the exchange is to be overcome, and a new sphere of experience entered, a *breakthrough* is needed. Haughton argues that romantic love is rooted in the fact that love is experienced not simply as a natural exchange of life (as in ordinary sexual feeling, for example), but as concentrated on one point at a weak spot (picture a water dam) where "it is enabled to break the highly defended barriers between two conscious and complex human beings."[90] By "weak spots" Haughton has in mind such widely ranging human phenomena as physical beauty, shared enthusiasms or commitments, even death. Through such realities, Haughton argues, the dynamism of romantic love smashes through ordinary awareness and creates the exchange of a spiritual power that not only penetrates the lovers and moves them into a more exalted sphere of experience, but reaches through and beyond them.

Romantic love is bodily, sexual (though not necessarily genital) love; it is concentrated on the experience of passion; it is not platonically "spiritual." But as fully human love, it is a radical realization of spirit in the flesh. In this passionate love, Haughton stresses, lovers come to self-awareness in the awareness of the beloved; they are defined in the very exchange of life that is love.

In Haughton's characterization romantic love, because fully physical, is *particular,* through one person, not humanity. And because one's whole energy is concentrated on a point, it is *single;* it happens once, with one person. Romantic love is also *painful;* there is a longing for completeness neither achieved nor possible, despite the breakthrough. In this love one experiences the stupor of a *halo of glory,* a sense of not being able to perceive clearly what one sees. And this is a love, Haughton emphasizes, that is peculiarly open to *corruption.* Most significant, though, is that romantic love *changes the face of reality.* The lovers themselves have a glow, but even more important is the way this glow transforms the world: people appear more lovable, compassion is easier, generosity and tender feelings seem to be nearer the surface.[91]

Haughton discerns four key moments in the pattern or sequence of Romantic breakthrough.[92] First there is *remote preparation,* probably a lenghty process of vague restlessness, desire, longing (adolescence, for example) which creates a situation for *immediate preparation,* the weak spot or vulnerable point. Here something happens which "shakes the person loose from normal expectations and settled attitudes"—a book, a vacation, a disaster, an encounter with "the" person. Whatever the occasion, when it occurs there is recognition, and the response to it transforms vague longing into intense passion: "the thrust of the whole personality towards the strange 'home' it perceives." But the recognition is so profound, so complete as to be ineffable, and is thus experienced as a gap, a void. Passion is the thrust which leaps that void, without guarantee or even knowledge; it is a leap of faith. The actual *breakthrough,* then, is this difficult, painful self-giving—across a gap of "un-knowing"—toward an intensely desired wholeness. The final moment identified by Haughton involves followthrough. How will the *language* of an individual's community help that person to interpret the experience of breakthrough? This element of communal language is vital because on the question of interpretation depends the crucial issue of what one will *do* about the breakthrough.

The question of action points to what Haughton takes to be the most important element of Romantic doctrine, the element that the French originators of courtly love referred to as *amour voulu*. Romantic passion might seize one unawares, they acknowledged, but they had only contempt for one who allowed himself to be swept away by it (*amour fol*), for the ultimate betrayal of love was the self-indulgent lover who surrendered not to love but to mere emotion. In contrast, the poets of courtly love maintained that only a *commitment* to love—absolute, unconditional, permanent—could count as a proper response to the *revelation* of love. In practice this meant the painful, often humiliating "service" the sworn knight rendered to his lady. In Haughton's interpretation of courtly love, then, *amour voulu* is "a 'giving back,' in free but completely uncompromising dedication, of that which has been freely and undeservedly received." She admits that one who sees romantic passion not as "willed love" but as "dominating emotion" will find this understanding of love as commitment and dedication strange. On the other hand, she thinks it will be useful to those who are trying to "understand what Jesus meant when he spelt out the meaning of love not as mystical invasion but as acts of practical service."[93]

Haughton's view of romantic love as *amour voulu* clearly goes beyond that of Solomon, whose most recent account rejects commitment of any kind as the very opposite of love, not its fulfillment.[94] But just as clearly, her interpretation reflects the essence of Solomon's understanding of love as not only a creative transformation of oneself and one's world but as itself open to transformation through reflection and deliberation.

Indeed, Haughton's analysis of conversion in her *Transformation of Man* characterizes it precisely as a radical breakthrough of *love*. Transformation only occurs within a context of formation, she maintains, within the "personality formed through time-conditioned stages of development." But formation is always a matter of fairness, order, self-interest, whereas transformation is a response to the "demand for the decision to love." Conversion is a giving of love, a giving of self in love, a "personal decision of self-surrender."[95]

In asserting that "transformation occurs in the moment of self-surrender to love," Haughton takes her stand within a virtuous circle. For only the individuated self, distinguished in self-awareness, is capable of self-giving. But real self-knowledge, which weakens the defenses against the outside world, can only be accepted by one who has experienced himself or herself *as loved*. So loving requires self-surrender; but self-surrender requires being loved. "Self-awareness as separate is the prerequisite of self-giving love," but the required awareness of self as separate is the genuine self-knowledge of humility; "it is not the withdrawal of pride that defends the beleaguered citadel but the confidence of being valued that makes openness possible without fear."[96]

The transforming decision of love is a "total gift of the whole person," unconditional and unreflective. It is not just a decision to behave differently, but a faithful "commitment to the unknown." "[O]nly the knowledge of *being loved* has the power to set free into faith," says Haughton; alone each of us is helpless. Therefore "Someone already transformed by love is needed, in order to convey an assurance of love sufficiently strong to penetrate the defences of the flesh in another and let loose the power of the spirit," Haughton explains. "This is the work of the community of love." The point to be stressed here is that the support of love must be simply for the sake of love, with its radical given-ness, at-riskness. Support given out of self-confidence is possessive, it wants to control growth. "Support given for love is willing to see the support no longer needed," it has its source not in oneself but in the power of love shared, which is never possessed but always given.[97]

This, indeed, is the fundamental point of Haughton's *Love*, which seeks to distinguish genuine love from its counterfeit. The basic problem in specifying the nature of love, as Haughton sees it, is that if love simply means even the rather advanced notion of a "drive towards, or desire for, a wider, deeper, more important 'beyond' in human life," it can include the demonic devotion of a Hitler as well as the compassionate devotion of a Mother Teresa. Some further, critical specification is needed. In her reading of the mystics especially, Haughton discerns a fundamental criterion: "you can tell genuine love because it opens out and gives itself." In contrast, "You can recognize false 'love' because it encloses itself, and seeks to grow by grabbing and snatching and keeping." The attempt to possess is anti-love, while real love is not only the desire for the "other" or "beyond," but the impulse to give oneself to that "otherness." It may be impossible to draw this line neatly through complex human experience, but the distinction does provide a standard for judgment. Love is genuine to the degree that it is open, self-giving, generous; false to the extent that it is closed, possessive, controlling.[98]

Mystical love's attachment to something beyond the human helps Haughton to recognize that *all* genuine love "actually reaches further than the human object." "Love that stops short at its human object," she explains, "is liable to become anti-love, because it depends on the existence of its object as *lovable*, that is, as a sort of object of worship."

If necessary, it will *force* the beloved to remain lovable. The possessive mother who wants a dependent child to cherish is only the most obvious example of this "love" syndrome that takes its immediate object as its god and becomes anti-love, often destroying the beloved and warping the lover.[99]

But genuine love refuses to worship a limited good, no matter how lovable. It remains responsive to the demand of the call for "something more," the demand to "leave all things," to "go out," to "give oneself." If love goes beyond its immediate object, it is also experienced as originating beyond one's very self and existing beyond one's control; one experiences oneself as almost literally seized by the power of love's demand. Yet the power of the demand is felt so forcefully not because it comes from the outside as a foreign invader, but precisely because it is the fundamental drive, the activity of the spirit of one's person, arising from the depths of one's very being. The demand of such a drive can be resisted, but only at the cost of destroying something of one's deepest reality—thus the sense of being *seized*. Response to this demand, on the other hand, creates the person, says Haughton, for it means going beyond ourselves to others in responding to situations that call for love, thereby actually becoming the self-transcending persons we are capable of being.[100]

Personal Transformation: Desire, Commitment, Service

Clearly, there are important differences between the reflections on love of Haughton and Solomon. But both make up a source from which we may draw some basic points of interpretation. First, love is passionate; it is not a bloodless act of cerebral will. Second, as emotion, love is not blind, it has a cognitive character. Love is a passionate interpretation, judgment, decision, choice—unreflective and therefore undifferentiated (feeling, knowing, choosing are one). Third, though unreflective, love can be influenced, even transformed by reflection. Fourth, and perhaps most important, love, though a passionate desire, must be distinguished clearly from *possessive* desire. Solomon says love begins where possessive desire ends. Haughton names possessiveness anti-love. Both reflect the fundamental distinction we saw earlier in de Rivera's structural theory of emotion between love (self moving toward other: giving) and desire (self moving other toward self: getting).

I have thoroughly reviewed the interpretations Solomon and Haughton give of love because of the striking possibilities they offer for understanding the dynamics of affective conversion. By paying serious attention to the passionate reality of Romantic love they have managed to transcend the tangles of the usual theological discussions of love which revolve upon the relation between eros and agape. Indeed, they have disclosed at the heart of an authentic human love a single source from which spring the movements of both desire and self-giving. Desire and self-giving are not identical, but neither are they inevitably at odds with each other. Indeed, George Tavard insists that human love is inseparably other-desire and self-gift. Desire can be possessive, but it need not be.[101] Self-giving can be personally destructive, but this is not necessary. Eros, as Paul Tillich has shown so clearly, can be desire for value: the true, the good, the beautiful.[102] And as Haughton points out, self-giving can be the fulfillment of the self-transcending person. In fully human love, the two movements specified by de Rivera as desire and love reinforce each other in the single drive for value that moves a person beyond him or her self. Far from being necessarily at odds, then, genuine desire and authentic self-giving become one in the realization of self-transcendence. As Robert Johann argues, eros can be *desire for generosity.*[103]

Despite the self-transcending possibilities of desire, however, Haughton is acutely aware of how easily desire can distort itself into indulgent possessiveness. Thus while the intense *passion* of desire is necessary for authentic love, it is not sufficient. Truly human love also requires what the courtly poets called *amour voulu*: the deliberate self-giving of the lover in the decision of commitment. By transforming passion into a definitive orientation, such decision constitutes the whole person in terms of a love reaching for ultimate value, and commits her or him to express this being-in-love in action for the good of the beloved.[104]

What light, finally, does this analysis of love contribute toward clarifying the fundamental reality of affective conversion? The major point I want to emphasize is the twofold character of affective conversion—its dual dimensions. Affective conversion must be understood as a matter of *both passion and commitment.*

Affective conversion belongs to the interior world of feeling—one falls-in-love; but it is not simply a matter of passion. Again, affective conversion requires deliberate decision—one commits oneself to the beloved; but it is no ethereal, disembodied act of will. Because affective conversion is a transformation of the whole person, it involves both intuitive passion and deliberate commitment.

Affective conversion does mean "falling-in-love," with all the specifications of that phrase we have examined in the views of Haughton, Solomon, and the cognitive interpreters of emotion. One *"falls"*-in-love precisely because love is passionate—the unreflective desire to give oneself in which the self is experienced as passive and helpless because the desire is experienced as originating and existing beyond—and therefore outside the control of—the reflectively conscious self. Haughton reminds us that, in the case of love, beyond the reflectively conscious self means not external to the person, but from within the interior depths of the person, the drive of the spirit of one's very being for self-transcendence. Unless one passionately falls-in-love, unless one unreflectively desires to give oneself in a way that involves one's own meaning and value—indeed, one's identity and self-esteem—then one can expect the deliberate, reflective decision to love and will the good of another, though sincere, to be at best a beautifully crafted, highly polished veneer, unlikely over the long term to stand up under the hard knocks and constant pressure of tough, everyday use. Affective conversion is a reorientation of the whole person, but especially of those prereflective desires which must support our reflectively conscious decisions, choices, and loving commitments.

If reflective commitment to love be merely surface reality when unsupported by prereflective passion, it is also true that feeling needs the guidance and stability of reflective commitment. Passion is neither blind nor weak, but it is often near-sighted and short-lived. We may not be able to *make* ourselves fall-in-love at will, but when it happens that we do desire to give ourselves passionately, reflection and deliberation can, as Solomon argues, both illuminate and strengthen our prereflective responses. "Since emotions are aroused by appraisal, and appraisal depends on what is experienced, remembered, imagined," Arnold explains that we can have at least indirect control over our emotions by using our imagination to influence appraisal.[105] Along the same line, Lonergan, while recognizing that feelings are fundamentally spontaneous inasmuch as they do not lie under the command of decision, points out that "once they have arisen, they may be reinforced by advertence and approval, and they may be curtailed by disapproval and distraction. Such reinforcement and curtailment," he suggests, "will not only encourage some feelings and discourage others but will also modify one's spontaneous scale of preferences."[106] Both Donald Gelpi and Paul Philibert have illuminated this crucial area by stressing Carl Rogers' process approach to the appropriation of affectivity.[107] Reflection, as Solomon further insists, not only considers emotions, but, through criticism and reinforcement, transforms them.

Affective conversion *is* the transformation of our deepest life of feeling. Without the radical reorientation of our passionate desires from obsession with self-needs to concern for the needs of others, there is no affective conversion. But because fundamental conversion is always a fully personal reality, affective conversion is not exclusively a matter of passion, feeling, emotion. The centrifugal reorientation of the passionate desires of our affective life, having been nudged and coaxed, briefed and guided by reflection, finally needs to be thoroughly personalized in the decision of commitment to love. Such commitment is powerful when it crystalizes the other-centered reorientation of feeling. Still, loving commitment is directed toward service; the criterion, then, for passionate commitment to others, for authentic affective conversion, lies in action.

The transformative influence of reflective criticism and deliberate commitment on our feelings notwithstanding, the principal operator of affective conversion remains the symbol. The carriers of meaning in the internal communication between mind and heart and body, symbols are images that evoke feelings and are evoked by them.[108] Thus, if affective development and conversion effect a transvaluation of symbols, it is also the case that they are initiated by the transforming symbols communicated externally through various intersubjective, artistic, religious, and, especially, personally incarnated embodiments. In all these and other forms, imaginative symbols of self-transcendence speak to the internal tensions, incompatibilities, conflicts, struggles, destructions of our psychic life inaccessible to the logical discourse of reflection. Only concrete, undifferentiated symbols speak the natural language of the prereflective heart (where feeling, knowing, and choosing are one). Both prereflective, undifferentiated symbols and the logical discourse of critical reflection are related to feeling, but whereas reflection is the distant cousin that speaks a foreign language, imaginative symbols are "family," and affective conversion is first of all a family affair. This significance of the symbol has recently been rediscovered in an important way by those ethicists who stress the role of story in the formation of character.[109]

If we add active service to the two dimensions of affective conversion already discussed, we can summarize the essence of affective conversion by saying that it is "signed" in the other-centered transformation of feeling effected by symbols and guided by reflection, "sealed" in the deliberate decision of commitment to love, and "delivered" in the action of loving service.

Affective Conversion in Developmental Context

Of course the radical reorientation of desire that constitutes affective conversion must be understood within the context of the self's affective development. Indeed, just as we have interpreted moral conversion as intrinsic to the very process of moral development, so, too, in order to understand clearly the structure and dynamics of affective conversion, we must recognize how this radical transformation of desire fits into the course of personal development. We must see how it occurs within and as a part of the pattern of affective development, not as an extrinsic, arbitrary event independent of developmental context. Especially illuminating in this regard are the developmental patterns traced by Erik Erikson and Robert Kegan.[110]

In the functional terms of psychosocial development, Erikson specifies love and care as the virtues emerging from the successful resolution of the crises of intimacy and generativity. These are adult crises which follow normatively upon the adequate negotiation of the adolescent crisis of identity. Erikson's point is not that love and care, intimacy and generativity are not present in some form throughout the entire life cycle. His point, rather, is that they can be highlighted as *crises* only in the adult who has established a distinct identity. Only the person with the strength of such an identity has the confidence to risk giving itself in intimacy. And only the person who has taken this risk, found a fuller self in intimacy, and emerged from the crisis strengthened in love is prepared to venture the further gift of self demanded by generativity's caring responsibility.

If we transpose the intimate love and generative care of Erikson's life cycle into the constructive-developmental terms of Kegan's neo-Piagetian perspective, we can place affective conversion into an even more powerfully explanatory systematic context. As we saw in some detail in Chapter 2, Kegan traces personal development in terms of the basic process of self/object differentiation and integration. This process can be viewed as the successive objectifications of increasingly complex dimensions of personal needs: sensorimotor needs, impulsive needs, self-interest needs, interpersonal needs, identity needs. Such a pattern of self/object differentiation and integration provides a developmental context for a systematic interpretation of affective conversion as a radical, transformational shift from obsessive concern for self-needs to loving, caring, responsible concern for the needs of others.

From this perspective each stage transition represents the creation of a new set of needs at the subject-pole, more highly differentiated and complex than the previously dominant set that has now been shifted over to the object-pole. Though the self is still subject to needs, the more highly differentiated needs at each new stage allow for a greater degree of affective self-transcendence. Interpersonal needs, for example, clearly place significant limits on Kegan's Stage 3, but the mutuality of this stage just as clearly represents a definitive gain in self-transcendence over imperialistic relations characteristic of Stage 2 self-interest needs.

Within this pattern of development, affective conversion, though prepared for at every stage, can be identified precisely as the conscious dimension of the structural transition from Kegan's Stage 4 to Stage 5, from the Institutional self to the Interindividual self. The transformation involved in this stage shift is not just another important developmental transition, but a radical breakthrough in desire, an about-face of feelings, an affective conversion. For the only need that the affective self is now *subject to* is the radical human need for self-transcendence. All other needs of the self still exist, but they have been "put in their place" at the object-pole. The drive for affective self-transcendence—for intimate love and generative care—now "dominates" at the subject-pole. And this drive for affective self-transcendence that is liberated at the Interindividual stage can be effective because now, unlike at earlier stages, there exists a self capable of sharing its very self with others, of committing itself fully to others in love. The Interindividual self recognizes that its genuine fulfillment consists in giving itself, that authentic self-realization lies only in the self-transcendence of love.

Obviously, to say that affective conversion occurs within a developmental context is not to say that affective conversion merely happens in the ordinary course of things. Experience suggests exactly the opposite: the possessiveness of the self's needs, not self-giving love, dominates in the ordinary course of things. But conversion is precisely a radical reorientation of the ordinary course. When conversion does occur, it breaks through at that point where development would otherwise stop, the self being satisfied with a more or less comfortable organization of its affairs (the Stage 4 Institutional self). Conversion is the breakthrough or turning which enables a transformed self to continue developing in a new, more deeply human direction (the Stage 5 Interindividual self). Thus, even as understood within the pattern of personal development, affective conversion occurs not as an ordinary matter of course, but only as the extraordinary culmination of the various contributing factors discussed above, including reflective criticism and, especially, the prereflective influence of powerfully imaginative symbols of self-transcendence.

In such affective conversion from the possessiveness rooted in obsessive concern for one's own needs to the self-giving of intimate love and generative care of others lies the possibility of actually living the morally converted life (critical or uncritical). Instances of moral self-transcendence do occur in persons who have not experienced affective conversion, but possessive need is not the best soil for the morally converted life. A consistent pattern of sustained moral self-transcendence, a flourishing moral life, requires the richer loam of affective conversion.

CONVERSION AS SOCIAL COMMITMENT

Now that we have established that development to the highest stages of moral reasoning demands critical moral conversion, and that affective conversion is necessary for effectively living out a moral conversion, we must ask ourselves a crucial question. Do moral, cognitive, and affective conversions really have anything at all to do with the hard reality of everyday life in the concrete world? Are they not all too theoretically detached, abstracted from the real, practical world? Or at best individualistic? And in either case, therefore, ultimately egocentric? Perhaps; certainly there have been enough conversions which seem essentially private, sealed up in an airtight interiority, without any perceptible effect on the larger world.[111]

Still, when these lines were first being written, Pope John Paul II was visiting the poverty and strife-ridden countries of Central America. And one recalled the key role that liberation theology is playing in the movement for social revolution in Latin America. For anyone aware of the seminal contribution Paolo Freire has made to this revolutionary movement, summarized in his *Pedagogy of the Oppressed*, it is not an exaggeration to say that the transformation of unjust social structures is rooted in the personal reality of critical moral conversion. A brief consideration of Freire's contribution will illuminate the intrinsically social character of the drive for self-transcendence, the socially practical significance of cognitive conversion, and the relationship between cognitive and moral conversion.

For Freire, one of the distinguishing traits of being human is the ability to stand off from the world, to objectivize the surrounding reality. As they so objectivize the world, humans are "able to act consciously on the objectivized reality." Yet in spontaneously approaching the world, their "moral, basic attitude is not a critical, but an ingenuous one." To be human, then, is to be aware of the world, to be dialectically related to it. But this spontaneous grasp of the world in consciousness is not a critical grasp. The further development of consciousness, what Freire calls conscientization, goes "beyond the spontaneous phase of apprehension of reality to a critical phase," where the personal subject, by grasping consciousness itself, takes an "epistemological stance."[112] At this point, however, the subject is really still a subject-in-expectancy. An authentic grasp of consciousness entails a critical insertion into history. Men and women must not only grasp themselves in their role as historical subjects, making and remaking the world, they must also choose and commit themselves in that role through historical action. Education for liberation must lead to this discovery, make this choice possible.[113]

Freire, of course, is writing in a context of the most thoroughgoing economic, political, and social oppression. Still, the root cause, in terms of which his pedagogical prescription is shaped, is alienation. And alienation is not restricted to the impoverished of Latin America; if anything, alienation, in one form or another, is the human condition—thus the universal need for self-appropriation. For in its most radical sense alienation is the subject's estrangement from his or her own creative and responsible drive for self-transcendence. As a result, the world—with its social, political, and economic structures—is not the dynamic, transformable product of human creation, constituted by meaning, but to a significant degree becomes a statically objectified, reified facticity, over against the individual: "You can't beat city hall." The greatest legitimator of the status quo, as we know, is the power which has the strongest hold on the lives of people, and for many this has been religion. Freire recounts how as a child in northeast Brazil he knew many priests who went out to the peasants saying: "Be patient. This is God's will. And anyway, it will earn heaven for you."[114] Things are the way they should be, the way God made them. The divine right historically claimed in an explicit way for the crown is only symbolic, then, of a divine establishment that has been implicitly, but nonetheless persuasively, asserted for the whole order of things.[115]

Freire's consciousness raising prescription would lead the oppressed to see that their plight is a result of the world they live in; that this world is structured; that its structures are not eternally fixed, but as humanly created can be humanly transformed; and that their liberation depends on their committed participation in the transformation of their world. Although the specific ingredients will change according to time and place, this is a universally human prescription: critical reflection and action.

It is not a prescription everyone will fill perfectly; consciousness raising comes in many degrees. Insofar as one achieves some success in overcoming one's estrangement from the world of human creation, though, and deliberately engages in its ongoing transformation, one also succeeds in effecting a reunion with the source of one's authentic creativity in the radical drive for self-transcendence. If the reflection of the historically committed subject is to be sufficiently critical, so too must his or her discovery and appropriation of self be critical: a critical moral conversion. Freire does not call conscientization a conversion (though he does speak of a radical "conversion to the people" by a member of the oppressor class),[116] but it is interesting that Peter Berger correctly identifies conscientization as a conversion, and faults it for being precisely that![117]

Three points can be drawn from Freire's view to further specify conversion. First, moral conversion has a social dimension. Some moral conversions occur in an explicitly social context. Those which begin in an individual context, however, must not remain private; they must expand to include the reality of social structures. Here cognitive conversion is important, for a critically converted subject will feel more urgency to pursue systematically the causes of injustice from the individual heart to the social structures which embody the human good—or evil. Moral conversion must be prepared to deal with human values and disvalues wherever they exist—not just on the familiar, relatively comfortable interpersonal grounds of the home field, among family, friends, and associates.

Second, moral conversion, as Freire insists so emphatically, must extend to the sphere of action, or it is not moral conversion. The armchair convert, to use a homely expression, is "just bumping his gums." He may have nice sentiments, but likely with a touch of the righteousness of one who has never really committed himself to a project and failed. He may be bubbling with answers, but they may amount to no more than recipes for impractical idealism. The sentiments and ideas of the uncommitted are not to be taken too seriously. Critical moral conversion is the appropriation —the discovery and choice—of oneself not just as a knower as in self-affirmation, but as one who experiences, understands, judges, *and* decides to commit oneself to action. It is the discovery and choice of oneself as a free and responsible person whose very authenticity lies in following the experienced exigence to decide and act consistently with one's intelligent and critical reflection. It is not the discovery and choice of oneself as an ivory tower philosopher or a Monday morning quarterback.

Third, in terms of Freire's explanation of conscientization as a movement from spontaneous consciousness to critical reflection, conversion in general can be understood as a movement from the instinctively spontaneous to the reflectively personal. Moral conversion shifts one's criterion of decision from the spontaneous impulse to respond in terms of satisfaction to the intelligently adopted policy of taking one's stand on reflectively affirmed value. Cognitive conversion is also a shift in criterion, a shift in the criterion of the real: from the instinctive "already-out-there-now" of biologically extroverted spontaneity to the reflectively grasped "virtually unconditioned" of intelligent and reasonable judgment. And affective conversion reorients one's desires from an instinctive obsession with self-needs to a reflectively guided personal concern for the needs of others. But what about religious conversion; does the same fundamental pattern of a shift from the instinctively spontaneous to the reflectively personal characterize this deeply personal transformation? This basic question is explored in the following chapters as we consider the reality of Christian conversion.

But, first, to conclude this chapter we return to its original question: What is the relationship between development and conversion? A brief and tentative answer can now be suggested.

First of all, conversion requires previous development. Radical cognitive conversion requires the fullest degree of cognitive development—not just formal operations, but formal operations capable of reflecting back on and taking possession of themselves precisely as self-constituting. Moral conversion demands cognitive and affective, as well as moral, development as its springboard—formal operations and the affective foundation of psychosocial identity together grounding the reasoning of conventional morality. In terms of even the earliest scheduling, then, neither moral nor cognitive conversion will be found before adolescence. And critical moral conversion, even more stringent in its developmental demands, will not be found before young adulthood.

Indeed, as I have argued, development and conversion are so closely linked that Kohlberg's account of moral reasoning development—integrating the affective and the cognitive—involves conversion at its major transitions to the conventional and postconventional levels. More than natural continuous expansion from egocentric to interpersonal and social awareness, development to conventional moral reasoning involves a conscious desire and deliberate option for the good as distinct from the good-for-me. And postconventional moral reasoning, more than a development from concrete, particular rules to abstract, universal principles, involves a radical revolution in the very locus of moral authority. Initiated by a relativizing of conventional morality, the fullness of this revolution is based on the personal subject's critical discovery and appropriation of his or her drive for self-transcendence.

Finally, of course, as even critical moral conversion is not an end but a beginning, conversion requires not only previous but also consequent development, especially in the affective dimension, whose own conversion is finally necessary for moral conversion to be lived effectively. And, as we have just seen, this affective conversion itself requires the development necessary for an Institutional self secure enough in its identity that it can risk sharing itself in intimate love and generative care.

Conversion and development, then, though clearly distinct realities, are intimately connected. The adolescent and adult crises of psychosocial development occasion and provide the necessary existential conditions for conversions as well as for major structural stage transitions. In turn, *optimal* resolution of psychosocial crises requires conversion, as, for example, the critical moral conversion necessary to fully realize all the possibilities of adult generativity. And key structural shifts occur as the unconscious counterparts to conscious conversions, as, for example, in the correlation of the shift to the Interindividual stage with affective conversion. At key points, then, development requires conversion, and conversion always occurs within a developmental process.

Does the converted person's *reflectively personal* stance toward value, truth, and loving care ever itself become *instinctively spontaneous*?[118] One would like to consider this a human possibility; certainly its approximation is what we mean by virtue. Still, conversion is never total nor secure, but must always be ongoing—seeking the full realization of that joyful, peaceful love which lures us. In Chapters 5 and 6 we will follow the Christian version of that search.

Remember that you were a slave in the land of Egypt, and the Lord your God brought you out of there.

Dt 5:15

5

CHRISTIAN CONVERSION: THE MORAL DIMENSION

Chapter 4 established the drive for self-transcendence of the critically converted subject as normatively definitive of personal authenticity. As fundamentally important as critical moral conversion is, however, it provides no explicit policy or concrete program for the realization of the human good, let alone specific courses of action. Even Stage 6 moral reasoning offers no more definite specification of the criterion of value than the universal principles of justice and the intrinsic dignity of the person.[1]

Concrete, historical human persons do not live and act on the strength of universal, abstract ideals of the human good, however. The concrete personal conscience responds to value as embodied in concrete, affective images, symbols, and stories. As one appropriates these living carriers of value by decision and action as well as through feeling and understanding, one's moral consciousness gradually takes concrete shape, one becomes a certain "sort of person," one creates one's "second nature," one's character.

Indeed, history can to some degree be seen in terms of conversions to one or another cultural incarnation of a system of values. The last two hundred years alone, whether in France or America, in Russia or Germany, in China or Iran, provide a breathtaking assortment of conversions to radically different systems of value. And Andrew Boyle's recent *Climate of Treason,* detailing how sympathy for Communism turned some Cambridge University students in the 1930's into Soviet spies while many of their fellow Englishmen were finding no great difficulty with Fascism, shows powerfully and all too frighteningly that *the* system of true human value does not come stamped

158

with a capital "V," and that its counterfeits are as deceptive as it is elusive.[2]

In any consideration of conversion and value systems, of course, one must rank Christianity among the most important, if only in sheerly quantitative terms. This chapter will consider Christian conversion as one particular way moral conversion is realized concretely in individual lives in terms of very specific personal and communal values. To speak of Christian conversion as moral conversion, of course, is not to deny that Christian conversion is more than moral conversion. In fact, our discussion will focus on the multidimensional experience of Thomas Merton in order to concretize the meaning of Christian conversion in personal terms. We will first review the critical period of Merton's young manhood, and then reflect on his experience in terms of development and conversion. This course will allow us to see how Merton's discovery of a loving God in Jesus Christ transformed the cognitive, affective, moral, and faith dimensions of his life. After situating Merton's youthful conversion experience in developmental terms, we will turn to psychological and theological interpretations of conversion in order to consider how his experience may be appreciated as a fundamental decision, a radical reorientation of life in terms of the values concretely embodied in the person of Jesus. But first we should look at the experience itself.

MERTON'S YOUTHFUL CONVERSION

While the history of Christianity is filled with accounts of remarkable conversions, perhaps the best documented conversion we have is the contemporary story of Thomas Merton's personal journey of transformation. As the detailed narrative of a conversion process extending over some thirty years, Merton's story provides a strikingly vivid and sharply focused example of the complex dimensions of Christian conversion.

This is not the place to tell again the story of Merton's life, something the autobiographical and biographical writings have done with some thoroughness. The emphasis here will be on the conversions, the transformative turning points in that life. We shall leave to *The Seven Storey Mountain* and the biographies, then, the details of Merton's childhood and adolescence with his maternal grandparents on Long Island (his mother died when he was six, in 1921), with his father in Bermuda and France, and with his peers in boarding schools in France and England, and pick up his story in 1934 as he sailed back to America after a year at Clare College, Cambridge.[3]

The Children in the Market Place: Communism and Collapse

Merton's father had died in 1931, and the last few years of school at Oakham and now at Cambridge had been particularly difficult. As he returned to the United States Merton was in the middle of an extended period of self-centered licentiousness:

> The death of my father left me sad and depressed for a couple of months. But that eventually wore away. And when it did, I found myself completely stripped of everything that impeded the movement of my own will to do as it pleased. I imagined that I was free. And it would take me five or six years to discover what a frightful captivity I had got myself into. It was in this year, too, that the hard crust of my dry soul finally squeezed out all the last traces of religion that had ever been in it. There was no room for any God in that empty temple full of dust and rubbish which I was now so jealously to guard against all intruders, in order to devote it to the worship of my own stupid will.[4]

This is a description written years later in the monastery. But there seems to be more to it than just a monk's exaggeration of past sins. In fact, Merton was leaving England upon the "recommendation" of his guardian, who had had to intervene to extricate Merton from a romantic affair that had come to unintended fruition.[5]

Merton had been reading widely for several years, and during the past few years, especially, in Freud and Marx. Now, during the voyage to the States, in the peacefulness of an evening's calm sea and fall of snow, his involvement in Communism seemed to give him an interior peace. He was, as he put it later, "in the thick of a conversion. It was not the right conversion, but it was a conversion. Perhaps it was a lesser evil. I do not doubt much that it was. But it was not, for all that, much of a good. I was becoming a Communist."[6] His commitment to Communism may have been immature, but it was "about as sincere and complete a step to moral conversion as [he] was then able to make. . . ."[7]

Merton's reflections on his conversion to Communism depict a movement towards Erikson's ideological orientation and Kohlberg's conventional morality in a way that concretizes very forcefully some key aspects of what we have called "uncritical moral conversion."

> A lot of things had happened to me since I had left the relative seclusion of Oakham, and had been free to indulge all my appetites in the world, and the time had come for a big readjustment in my values. I could not evade that truth. I was too miserable, and it was evident that there was too much wrong with my strange, vague, selfish hedonism.
>
> It did not take very much reflection on the year I had spent at Cambridge to show me that all my dreams of fantastic pleasures and delights were crazy and absurd, and that everything I had reached out for had turned to ashes in my hands, and that I myself, into the bargain, had turned out to be an extremely unpleasant sort of a person—vain, self-centered, dissolute, weak, irresolute, undisciplined, sensual, obscene and proud. I was a mess. Even the sight of my own face in a mirror was enough to disgust me.[8]

Despite this candid description of life at the aesthetic stage, Merton had been reading not Kierkegaard, but Marx. So, now, as he turned to a personal inventory, it was only natural that he would project his own spiritual condition into the sphere of economic history and class struggle, concluding that it was not he who was to blame for his unhappiness, but society, "the selfishness and irresponsibility of the materialistic century" in which he lived.

Still, if Merton's self-knowledge was something short of perfection at this point, he did seem to have a real enough desire to turn toward value. Beyond his admittedly superficial understanding of Marxism and the idea that the Communists were sincerely trying to do something about the injustice and suffering in the world, there was at the root of this conversion experience Merton's

> own personal conviction, the result of the uncertain and misdirected striving for moral reform, that I must now devote myself to the good of society, and apply my mind, at least to some extent, to the tremendous problems of my time.
>
> I don't know how much good there was in this: but I think there was some. It was, I suppose, my acknowledgment of my selfishness, and my desire to make reparation for it by developing some kind of social and political consciousness. And at the time, in my first fervor, I felt myself willing to

make sacrifices for this end. I wanted to devote myself to the causes of peace and justice in the world. I wanted to do something positive to interrupt and divert the gathering momentum that was dragging the whole world into another war— and I felt there was something I could do, not alone, but as the member of an active and vocal group.[9]

Merton found this group at Columbia University, where he had decided to continue his education. Although Columbia was not the hotbed of Communism which some had made it out to be, Merton soon met among the undergraduates many Communists or Communist sympathizers, who controlled the college newspaper and had influence on the student government and other publications.

Merton attended meetings, sold pamphlets and magazines, gave a speech on "Communism in England" (which he knew nothing about), picketed against Fascism at Columbia's *Casa Italiana*, took the Oxford Pledge against fighting, and signed up as a member of the Young Communist League (with the party name of Frank Swift). But "this campus Communism was more a matter of noise than anything else," as Merton later viewed it, "at least as far as the rank and file were concerned," and Merton's part in the world revolution lasted only about three months. In fact, he walked out in the middle of his first Young Communist Meeting—the discussion centered on a comrade whose father would not allow him to attend meetings—and, finding a bar, "got a glass of beer and lit a cigarette and tasted the first sweet moment of silence and relief." And that was the end of his "days as a great revolutionary." He decided it would be wiser if he "just remained a 'fellow-traveller'."[10]

Looking back on the episode many years later, Merton could say the truth was "that my inspiration to do something for the good of mankind had been pretty feeble and abstract from the start. I was still interested in doing good for only one person in the world—myself."[11] Perhaps; it is possible that this "conversion" was no conversion at all, merely a velleity, or a convenient rationalization: the selfishness and irresponsibility of materialistic society was to blame for his unhappiness, not himself. But it is also possible that the author of *The Seven Storey Mountain* was being too harsh in his judgment of the young Merton. Conversions are personal, but not individualistic; they need the nourishing environment of a vital community endowed with transformative symbols and language.[12] If this is true of conversions generally, it is especially the case with youthful conversions to conventional morality. For, as we noted earlier, these conversions, unlike their distant postconventional relatives, lack the intrinsically persuasive empowerment of self-chosen, critical principles. They are by definition externally oriented, and stand in particular need of extrinsic support. Whatever Merton's personal disposition, there is no sign that his Communist associates ever provided this kind of nurturing context of growth for him. In any event, this "conversion," though short-lived, was at least a beginning, a recognition that the self-centered life of pleasure is a dead-end.

Whatever the exact nature of this "moral conversion" (Merton later also called it a "half-conscious semi-conversion"), the episode was only a brief and partial interruption of an otherwise steady, continuous process of personal disintegration: "In 1935 and 1936, without my realizing it, life was slowly, once more, becoming almost intolerable."[13]

On the surface, though, Merton's life was wonderfully exciting: he was at the center of an "intellectual ferment" which everyone at Columbia sensed the campus to be experiencing in a special way that year. One sobering moment that impressed Merton during the rush of the year's hectic activity was the proximity of two events: a visit to the city morgue as part of the Contemporary Civilization course followed by the police discovery in a Brooklyn canal of the body of one of his fraternity brothers who had been missing for two months. Ten years later the author of *The Seven Storey Mountain* still had a vivid memory of the bodies of those who, like his fraternity brother, had died, as he put it, of contemporary civilization.

Nevertheless, during that year Merton was so immersed in activities that he had no time to think much about such things. He seemed to be in fine condition, enjoying great success. But if a full load of courses, involvement in the *Review,* the *Jester,* the *Spectator,* and the yearbook, jobs at Rockefeller Center, and cross country running left little time for reflection, they caused no serious interference with Merton's dedication to the social life: pulsating nights and early mornings in dark, deafening nightclubs, devoted to drinking, smoking, and jazz. One got caught up in a "strange, animal travesty of mysticism," bound to a sea of bodies, with the "rhythm jumping and throbbing in the marrow of your bones." But the night would end, and, as the day was beginning for everyone else, one finally had to go home:

> The thing that depressed me most of all was the shame and despair that invaded my whole nature when the sun came up, and all the laborers were going to work: men healthy and awake and quiet, with their eyes clear, and some rational purpose before them. This humiliation and sense of my own mis-

ery and of the fruitlessness of what I had done was the nearest I could get to contrition. It was the reaction of nature. It proved nothing except that I was still, at least, morally alive: or rather that I had still some faint capacity for moral life in me.[14]

In 1936–1937, first Merton's grandfather and then his grandmother, with whom he was living, died. He would later reflect on how these deaths brought their atheist grandson to prayer. During the same period Merton was undergoing a death of his own: the fundamental condition for conversion. One day on the Long Island train, under the strain of his life, Merton simply collapsed into a spinning vertigo. Doctors were able to help his body with a diet and medicine. He later supposed the problem was a nervous breakdown, connected with gastritis and a developing stomach ulcer. He had pushed more than his body too far, though, and more than a diet and medicine was required for his moral health. The doctors could not treat the fear that was eating out his insides. He would later picture himself at this time as a true child of the modern world, totally absorbed in himself:

> Here I was, scarcely four years after I had left Oakham and walked out into the world that I thought I was going to ransack and rob of all its pleasures and satisfactions. I had done what I intended, and now I found that it was I who was emptied and robbed and gutted. What a strange thing! In filling myself, I had emptied myself. In grasping things, I had lost everything. In devouring pleasures and joys, I had found distress and anguish and fear.[15]

"Such was the death of the hero, the great man" he had wanted to be. Externally he had almost everything he wanted, but he was bleeding to death from interior wounds. Kierkegaard himself could hardly have written a better scenario for the decline and fall of the aesthetic hero. With his personal foundations shaking, and so much of his life crumbling, Merton was ready for new possibilities. The formation which had made him who he was could no longer sustain him; radical transformation was necessary.

> If my nature had been more stubborn in clinging to the pleasures that disgusted me: if I had refused to admit that I was beaten by this futile search for satisfaction where it could not be found, and if my moral and nervous constitution had not

caved in under the weight of my own emptiness, who can tell what would eventually have happened to me? Who could tell where I would have ended?

I had come very far, to find myself in this blind-alley: but the very anguish and helplessness of my position was something to which I rapidly succumbed. And it was my defeat that was to be the occasion of my rescue.[16]

With a Great Price: God and Baptism

Looking back on this period, Merton would see the next year and a half as a time when the groundwork for his conversion was being put in place. In large part this groundwork was intellectual, and it would be accurate to interpret Merton's transformation during this period as a version of cognitive conversion: the recognition of God's reality.

Of the several cognitive pieces making up this conversion mosaic, the first was Merton's "accidental" discovery of Etienne Gilson's *Spirit of Medieval Philosophy* in February 1937. Although he had enrolled in a course on French Medieval Literature, and in that sense was interested in Catholic culture, the last thing Merton was interested in reading in those days was anything even smacking of officially approved Catholic philosophy or theology. So after purchasing the Gilson volume as what he took to be a series of lectures in history given at the University of Aberdeen, and not a study in Catholic philosophy, he felt more than a little "ripped off" when on closer examination he came upon the despised *Imprimatur* and *Nihil Obstat*. Despite this reminder of the Inquisition and all the other things he feared about the Catholic Church, he read the book, and he was never the same again. This Neo-Scholastic philosophy of God was the first understanding of the Christian God he had ever encountered which was not a simplistic anthropomorphism. And its concept of *aseitas*, "the power of a being to exist absolutely in virtue of itself," along with the insight that Infinite Being transcends all concepts, would "revolutionize" his whole life.

> I had never had an adequate notion of what Christians meant by God. I had simply taken it for granted that the God in Whom religious people believed, and to Whom they attributed the creation and government of all things, was a noisy and dramatic and passionate character, a vague, jealous, hidden being, the objectification of all their own desires and strivings and subjective ideals.
>
> The truth is, that the concept of God which I had always

entertained, and which I had accused Christians of teaching to the world, was a concept of a being who was simply impossible. He was infinite and yet finite; perfect and imperfect; eternal and yet changing—subject to all the variations of emotion, love, sorrow, hate, revenge, that men are prey to. How could this fatuous, emotional thing be without beginning and without end, the creator of all?

It was a great relief for Merton to discover that no idea or sensible image could contain God, and further that we must not be satisfied with such knowledge of God. As a result he not only developed a respect for Catholic philosophy, but, most importantly, recognized the definite meaning and cogent necessity of Catholic faith.

> If this much was a great thing, it was about all that I could do at the moment. I could recognize that those who thought about God had a good way of considering Him, and that those who believed in Him really believed in someone, and their faith was more than a dream. Further than that it seemed I could not go, for the time being.[17]

All this gave Merton the desire to go to church, and he began attending the local Episcopal church at home on Long Island. At the same time, other things were happening, mostly in connection with a group of friends at Columbia, friends Merton connected in one way or other with his favorite professor, Mark Van Doren. In fact, it was during this year that Merton was taking—because he had accidentally (again) stumbled upon it—Van Doren's course on Shakespeare. It was the best course Merton ever had in college, and it did him the most good, for it was the only place where he "ever heard anything really sensible said about any of the things that were really fundamental—life, death, time, love, sorrow, fear, wisdom, suffering, eternity." Van Doren discussed all these aspects of drama—of free, human, moral acts—in ways, as Merton said, that "made them live within us, and with a life that was healthy and permanent and productive."[18]

One of this group of friends was Robert Lax, who possessed "a kind of natural, instinctive spirituality, a kind of inborn direction to the living God." It was Lax who introduced Merton to another book which would make a central contribution to the process leading up to his conversion: Aldous Huxley's *Ends and Means*. Merton wrote an article on this book, and recognized that the essay represented a conversion in him as much as the book represented a conversion in Huxley.

Central to Huxley's book, as Merton later summarized it, was the conviction that "Not only was there such a thing as a supernatural order, but as a matter of concrete experience, it was accessible, very close at hand, an extremely near, an immediate and most necessary source of moral vitality, and one which could be reached most simply, most readily by prayer, faith, detachment, love."[19]

Huxley argued that because of immersion in the material and animal in their nature, humans were incapable of replacing the evil means of war and violence with the good means appropriate to the desired good ends. Liberation from the subjection to these inferior elements of nature required prayer and asceticism.

The very thought of asceticism required a complete revolution in Merton's mind. But he was taken with Huxley's claim that through detachment one's spirit could be freed for an experienced union with the absolute and perfect Spirit, God. In *The Seven Storey Mountain* Merton characterized this contribution to his conversion as a revelation: "My hatred of war and my own personal misery in my particular situation and the general crisis of the world made me accept with my whole heart this revelation of the need for a spiritual life, an interior life, including some kind of mortification." That he would immediately add the following comment about mortification is an indication of the complexity of the "heart": "I was content to accept the latter truth purely as a matter of theory: or, at least, to apply it most vociferously to one passion which was not strong in myself, and did not need to be mortified: that of anger, hatred, while neglecting the ones that really needed to be checked, like gluttony and lust."[20]

On the academic front, Merton had completed his bachelor's degree in February 1938, and immediately begun graduate courses in English. During the spring of that year he searched for a good master's thesis subject, and finally one day in the library he made the important personal rediscovery of the *Poems of William Blake*. As a child, Merton had been introduced to Blake's poetry by his father. And as a young man he had continued to read and admire Blake, without really knowing what to make of him. But now the time was right, and he immediately knew he had the topic of his master's thesis: Blake's poetry and religious ideas.

Through many months of refreshingly hard work on "Nature and Art in William Blake," Merton finally discovered the key to Blake: his "reaction against every kind of literalism and naturalism and narrow, classical realism in art, because of his own ideal which was essentially mystical and supernatural." Through this insight Merton was able to realize that beyond the aesthetic dimension, Blake's poetry "represented a rebellion against naturalism in the moral order as well." In what he called a "revelation," Merton saw that, far from glorifying passion, natural energy, for their own sake, Blake was glorifying "the transfiguration of man's natural love, his natural powers, in the refining fires of mystical experience." In Blake Merton found "moral insight that cut through all the false distinctions of a worldly and interested morality." Although Merton had always been anti-naturalistic in art, he now realized that he had been a pure naturalist in the moral order. Now, thanks to Gilson, and Blake, and Jacques Maritain, in whose *Art and Scholasticism* he discovered a compelling understanding of virtue, things were beginning to change. He later used the classical image of the divided soul to describe his experience during these months: "No wonder my soul was sick and torn apart: but now the bleeding wound was drawn together by the notion of Christian virtue, ordered to the union of the soul with God."[21]

In a certain way all of these influences toward conversion were concretized for Merton in the person of a Hindu monk named Bramachari. An acquaintance of Seymour Freedgood, another of Merton's very close friends at Columbia, Bramachari had been traveling around the United States for a few years by this time, having arrived—penniless—just too late for the World Congress of Religions at the 1933 World's Fair in Chicago, to which he had been sent by his superior. Especially interested in oriental mysticism after reading Huxley's *Ends and Means*, Merton had eagerly anticipated Bramachari's visit with Freedgood. Merton was impressed by the monk's genuine spirituality from their first meeting, and they quickly became good friends. Merton's vivid pages on Bramachari in *The Seven Storey Mountain* several years later indicate rather clearly how much he was influenced by the simplicity and detachment of this man who personified in the flesh so much of what Merton had been encountering in books. Ironically, though, Merton especially remembered this Hindu monk for recommending to him *The Imitation of Christ* and St. Augustine's *Confessions*.

The influences of books and friends were working together nicely now, and, in Merton's own estimation, the groundwork of his conversion was more or less complete by the beginning of September 1938. Not just the cognitive, but the affective, moral, and faith dimensions of development seemed prepared for transformation.

As Blake worked himself into my system, I became more and more conscious of the necessity of a vital faith, and the total unreality and unsubstantiality of the dead, selfish rationalism which had been freezing my mind and will for the last seven years. By the time the summer was over, I was to become conscious of the fact that the only way to live was to live in a world that was charged with the presence and reality of God.[22]

By Merton's own calendar, again, it had taken about a year and a half, beginning with his reading of Gilson's *Spirit of Medieval Philosophy*, for the transformation of the self-described atheist into "one who accepted all the full range and possibilities of religious experience right up to the highest degree of glory."[23]

The difficulty involved in interpreting this kind of personal event is exemplified clearly in the difference between two separate reflections Merton made on this period of his life. At one point, immediately following the passage quoted above about Blake working into his system, and the consequent realization of the need of a vital faith, Merton qualified the statement by saying that it was still "more an intellectual realization than anything else," that it had not yet penetrated to the roots of his will. The autobiographer expanded on this point in Scholastic categories: "The life of the soul is not knowledge, It is love, since love is the act of the supreme faculty, the will, by which man is formally united to the final end of all his strivings—by which man becomes one with God."[24]

At another point in the autobiography, however, Merton, commenting on the same period—the end of the summer, the beginning of September 1938, when he was accepting all the possibilities of religious experience—wrote: "I not only accepted all this, intellectually, but now I began to desire it. And not only did I begin to desire it, but I began to do so efficaciously: I began to want to take the necessary means to achieve this union, this peace. I began to desire to dedicate my life to God, to His service."[25]

In some real sense, then, the affective dimension was beginning to play an active part in Merton's process of transformation. But that it had not yet realized itself in strong conviction, had not yet, as Merton put it, "struck down into the roots of my will," is evident in the fact that Merton was already dreaming of mystical union when, according to his later judgment, he was not even keeping "the simplest rudiments of the moral law," so "completely chained and fettered" was he by his sins and attachments.[26]

Still, even if the goal was not reached all at once, he was taking steps. A key step at this point was his decision, in response to an urge (now a strong, gentle voice) that had been building in him for some time, to attend Mass for the first time in his life.

So, on a beautiful Sunday morning, having passed up his usual weekend visit with his girl friend on Long Island, he made his way to the Church of Corpus Christi near Columbia. He stayed only for the sermon, but this straightforward exposition on the Incarnation, tinged with Scholastic terminology, was just what he most needed to hear that day. For after so many years of hardened refusal, he was now ready to listen, having been beaten, as he put it, "into the semblance of some kind of humility by misery and confusion and perplexity and secret, interior fear, and my ploughed soul was better ground for the reception of good seed."[27]

The author of *The Seven Storey Mountain* did not want to speculate at any length on whether this sermon was the occasion of his "being justified, that is, receiving sanctifying grace in his soul as a habit, and beginning, from that moment, to live the divine and supernatural life for good and all," but his description of the feelings he experienced as he left the church indicate that this moment was certainly an extraordinary one in his process of spiritual transformation:

> Now I walked leisurely down Broadway in the sun, and my eyes looked about me at a new world. I could not understand what it was that had happened to make me so happy, why I was so much at peace, so content with life. . . .
>
> All I know is that I walked in a new world. Even the ugly buildings of Columbia were transfigured in it, and everywhere was peace in these streets designed for violence and noise. Sitting outside the gloomy little Childs restaurant at 111th Street, behind the dirty, boxed bushes, and eating breakfast, was like sitting in the Elysian Fields.[28]

Merton's reading became more and more Catholic—Joyce and the Jesuits especially attracted him. Still, after his first attendance at Mass, life returned to its normal patterns; Merton did not even return to Mass for a while. According to his autobiographical report, it took news of the Nazi occupation of Czechoslovakia (in some unexplained way) to "form and vitalize [the] resolutions that were still only vague and floating entities in [his] mind and will."[29]

Sometime in mid-September, following up his interests in the Jesuits, Merton borrowed a biography of Gerard Manley Hopkins from the library. While reading about the young Hopkins at Oxford writing to J.H. Newman at Birmingham for counsel about his indecision on becoming a Catholic, Merton's own question stepped to center stage:

> All of a sudden, something began to stir within me, something began to push me, to prompt me. It was a movement that spoke like a voice.
>
> "What are you waiting for?" it said. "Why are you sitting here? Why do you still hesitate? You know what you ought to do? Why don't you do it?"
>
> I stirred in the chair, I lit a cigarette, looked out the window at the rain, tried to shut the voice up. "Don't act on impulses," I thought. "This is crazy. This is not rational. Read your book."[30]

But the voice persisted, it would not leave him alone. "What are you waiting for? . . . Why are you sitting there? It is useless to hesitate any longer. Why don't you get up and go?" Merton tried to tell himself it was absurd. But, suddenly, he could bear it no longer. Putting down his book, he got into his raincoat, and went out into the rain, heading toward Broadway: "And then everything inside me began to sing—to sing with peace, to sing with strength and to sing with conviction."[31]

At the rectory he simply said to the priest, "Father, I want to become a Catholic." Instructions followed over the ensuing weeks, and Merton made the "Mission" with the men of the parish in October. He even had thoughts during this period about becoming a priest, but decided it best to let the idea rest for the time being, and did not mention it to anyone.

As November began, Merton could think of nothing else but "of getting baptized and entering at last into the supernatural life of the Church." Finally, towards the end of the first week in November, his instructor told him that he would be baptized on November 16, and he left the rectory that evening "happier and more contented" than he had been in his life.[32] On the appointed day at Corpus Christi Church, Merton, surrounded by his close friends, was baptized, made his confession, and participated in his first Mass as a Catholic.

The Waters of Contradiction: Desert and Vocation

Following a joyous after-Mass breakfast with his friends, Merton heard the interior voice again, once and for all: "The land which thou goest to possess is not like the land of Egypt from whence thou camest out. . . . For my thoughts are not your thoughts, nor your ways my ways, saith the Lord. . . . Seek the Lord while He may be found, call upon Him while He is near. . . ."[33]

In retrospect, knowing how difficult the climb he had begun actually turned out to be, Merton said that he heard all this, but was not able to understand. "Perhaps, in a way, there was a kind of moral impossibility of my doing what I should have done, because I simply did not yet know what it was to pray, to make sacrifices, to give up the world, to lead what is called the supernatural life."[34]

The fact is that, after the initial glow faded, the year following Merton's baptism was not a good one. In his own later judgment, he continued to live pretty much as he had before his baptism: for himself. At the time, however, Merton did not appreciate the reality of his situation. To some degree, the experience of conversion had deceived him. Because of the "profound and complete" conversion of his intellect, because he believed in God and the teachings of the Church, Merton thought he was completely converted, even a zealous Christian. It took some time for him to realize that conversion of the intellect is not enough—that heart or, as he says, will must follow. In the meantime, Merton's treasures remained earthly ones: success and reputation as a writer.[35]

One could not ask for a nicer example of moral impotence: the radical inability to sustain development, to bring decision into line with one's best judgment, to act consistently in the long term in accordance with one's decisions, with one's commitments. Moral conversion, in other words, even Christian moral conversion, is in the first place a challenge. Only in the second place, after completing an arduous course, is it achievement. And that successful response to the challenge of moral conversion, which must be affective as well as cognitive, demands not just a significant measure of affective development, but a radical affective conversion. One must fall in love; one's being must become a being-in-love.

Some months passed after the baptism; Merton took his M.A. and began studies for the Ph.D., with the intention of writing a dissertation on Hopkins. One spring night, in the middle of a conversation, Bob Lax suddenly asked Merton, "What do you want to be, anyway?" Merton gave what he thought was the "correct" answer: "a good Catholic." But Lax knew how inadequate this was, and told his friend that he should want to be a saint. Confused, Merton told him he could not be a saint. His confusion was not dispelled by Lax' provocative response: "All you have to do is desire it." By the summer Merton came to accept this principle, but only filed it away with his other principles, and did nothing about actualizing it in his life.[36]

By the end of the summer of 1939, however, things began to happen. In the wider world, events were ominously building toward war in Europe. And even before the news of the bombing of Warsaw, these developments touched Merton in a very personal way with a sobering recognition: "I myself am responsible for this. My sins have done this. Hitler is not the only one who has started this war: I have my share in it too. . . ."[37]

Fall came, school began again, and then there was a day extraordinary even in Merton's not so ordinary life. Merton had been up all night with a couple of friends, and after a few hours' sleep back at his place, they brought in some breakfast, and talked and listened to jazz on the record player. "Somewhere in the midst of all this," a startling idea came to him: "I am going to be a priest." Even the autobiographer could not say what caused it, but it was "not a thing of passion or of fancy. It was a strong and sweet and deep and insistent attraction that suddenly made itself felt, but not as a movement of appetite towards any sensible good. It was something in the order of conscience, a new and profound and clear sense that this was what I really ought to do."[38]

Merton was alone again that evening, and after dinner, accompanied by a book on the Jesuits, he felt drawn to visit the nearby Jesuit Church of St. Francis Xavier. The church was dark and locked, and he was about to leave, when something prompted him to try a basement door. It opened, and he found himself in a lower church, in the middle of a Benediction service. Kneeling, he fixed his eyes on the Blessed Sacrament in the monstrance as the people sang the *Tantum Ergo*. Suddenly it became clear to him that his whole life was at a point of crisis: everything was hanging upon his decision. He sensed that his whole life was suspended on the edge of an abyss, an abyss of love and peace—God. He knew it would be a blind, irrevocable act to throw himself over, but he also sensed the consequences if he should fail to act—and he had had enough of that life. "So now the question faced me: 'Do you really want to be a priest? If you do, say so . . . '." As the hymn was ending, the priest raised the monstrance: "I looked straight at the Host, and I knew, now, Who it was that I was looking at, and I said: 'Yes, I want to be a priest, with all my heart I want it. If it is Your will, make me a priest—make me a priest'." What he had done with those last four words, the power of the decision they represented, did not escape him; a new course was set.[39]

Magnetic North: Franciscans and Failure

So, the decision was taken. But it would require two full years to bring the decision to life. The next step came rather quickly, though, and before many days had passed Merton decided, with the advice of one of his favorite teachers, Dan Walsh, a visiting professor of philosophy at Columbia, to pursue his vocation with the Franciscans. Merton's initial contact with the Franciscans was positive, and he was encouraged in his desire to become a friar. As he left the monastery on 31st Street after his first visit, his heart was full of happiness and peace. The autobiographer would later comment: "What a transformation this made in my life! Now, at last, God had become the center of my existence. And it had taken no less than this decision to make Him so." Various devotions deepened his sense of peace during the following months, and one month he even devoted an hour each day to making St. Ignatius' *Spiritual Exercises* on his own, finding much value in the contemplations, but only puzzlement in the Ignatian notion of indifference.

After Easter 1940, during a vacation-pilgrimage to Cuba, the consolations Merton had been experiencing so regularly during the past year came to something of a peak. For Merton, life in Catholic Cuba, with all its churches and opportunities for piety, was like that of a spiritual millionaire. Here he experienced "a way into a world infinitely new, a world that was out of this world of ours entirely and which transcended it infinitely, and which was not a world, but which was God Himself." During Sunday Mass at the Church of St. Francis in Havana, the children at the front of the church burst out with a sudden and triumphant shout of *"Creo en Diós"* at the Consecration. Then, as Merton vividly recalled years later, "as sudden as the shout and as definite, and a thousand times more bright, there formed in my mind an awareness, an understanding, a realization of what had just taken place on the altar, at the Consecration: a realization of God made present by the words of Consecration in a way that made Him belong to me."[40]

Merton felt as if he "had been suddenly illuminated by being blinded by the manifestation of God's presence." This awareness ignored all sense experience and imagination to strike directly at the heart of truth, establishing a concrete and immediate contact of loving knowledge between Merton's intellect and the "Truth Who was now physically really and substantially before [him] on the altar." The awareness lasted for only a moment, but it left an unforgettable joy and peace. After it, his first articulate thought was: "Heaven is right here in front of me: Heaven, Heaven!"[41]

Upon his return to New York in June, Merton learned that he had been accepted to enter the Franciscan novitiate as a postulant in August. Everything seemed set, and he left the city to spend the summer upstate with his old friends. What he did not know was that during that summer, with just a few weeks to go before entering the novitiate, he would see his vocation fall to pieces.

One evening, while reading the ninth chapter of the Book of Job, Merton was "amazed and stunned" by a series of disturbing lines which struck deep: "If He examines me on a sudden who shall answer Him?" Suddenly, the peace he had known for six months was gone. Merton did not doubt his desire to become a priest, a Franciscan, but now, remembering who he was, who he had been, he was overwhelmed with an agonizing question: "Do I really have that vocation?"[42] He immediately returned to the city and spelled out his doubts to his Franciscan friend, Father Edmund. A day later, with the help of Father Edmund's kind advice and the blow from a devastating confessional experience with another Franciscan, Merton was convinced that he had no vocation to the cloister. Of his tremendous misery, he needed no convincing.

True North: Patience and Silence

The misery was not debilitating, though, and before long Merton had made a decision: if he could not live in the monastery as a monk, he would live in the world as if he were a monk in a monastery. He would read the Divine Office each day, join a Third Order, and try to get a teaching position at a Catholic college. He did secure a job teaching English at St. Bonaventure's, as he had hoped, and the 1940–41 school year turned out, in so many ways, to be the most fruitful, perhaps, of his life up to that point.

In the winter of 1941 the question of the military draft came up for Merton. As things ultimately turned out, he failed to pass the physical examination, but in the meantime he had to ask himself some serious moral questions about participating in the war. Eight years before he had taken the Oxford Pledge against fighting in any war— an oath, he would judge, made mostly on the basis of emotion. Since then, he had "developed a conscience," and now felt a moral duty to take a clear position. Merton's decision, worked out in terms of just war theory, was that, while he could not absolutely refuse to go if called to a war of self-defense, neither could he participate in the indiscriminate slaughter of non-combatants. Application as a non-combatant objector—for service in something like the medical corps—was his solution.

From the army's point of view, Merton's bad teeth settled the question.[43]

Already during this peaceful year, Merton had sensed the need to make a retreat. His plan was to spend Holy Week and Easter at the Trappist monastery his friend Dan Walsh had told him about—Gethsemani. The experience with the monks was a powerful one for him, and, of course, rekindled his desire for the cloistered life. Inspired by one of the Retreat Master's stories, the last thing Merton did before leaving Gethsemani was to make the Stations of the Cross, asking at the last station "for the grace of a vocation to the Trappists, if it were pleasing to God."[44]

The Sleeping Volcano: Harlem and Gethsemani

The power of the retreat experience was still working in him during summer school at St. Bonaventure's when Merton was struck (almost down a case of stairs, as he put it) by the force of another powerful experience: the Baroness de Hueck. Merton happened upon the baroness one evening as she was giving a talk to the summer school community, telling about the work at Friendship House in Harlem. Merton's two or three weeks' stay at Friendship House after the end of summer school opened his eyes to the reality of poverty as they had never been opened before. He was not back at St. Bonaventure's too many weeks when a surprise visit by the baroness occasioned Merton's decision to leave St. Bonaventure's at the end of the semester in order to give himself to the work of Friendship House.

This decision had hardly been made, however, when the question of the priesthood came back more strongly than ever. On the day after Thanksgiving, Merton met with Mark Van Doren at the Columbia Faculty Club to discuss a manuscript. Van Doren repeated a question which others, including the baroness, had been raising during the last several days: "What about your idea of being a priest?" Merton tried to shrug it off, but knew he really could not. Within a week he suddenly found himself—thanks to a compelling imaginary experience of hearing the great bell at Gethsemani calling him—with a vivid conviction: "The time has come for me to go and be a Trappist." It was clear, powerful, and irresistible. Now things began to move quickly: a chat with his Franciscan friend, Father Philotheus, strengthened Merton against his old doubts; a letter to Gethsemani announced his arrival with the hope of admission; a letter to the draft board secured a delay in their renewed interest in him; Pearl Harbor was attacked; permission was given for an early departure from the college; and Merton was off to Gethsemani. The first phase of a lifelong conversion process had come to term. "I was free. I had recovered my liberty. I belonged to God, not to myself: and to belong to Him is to be free. . . ."[45]

MERTON'S CONVERSION: A DEVELOPMENTAL ANALYSIS

Merton's spirtual journey to Gethsemani offers us several opportunities to reflect on significant affective, cognitive, moral, and faith dimensions of development and conversion. Clearly, Merton's Christian conversion had a strong cognitive dimension—so powerful, in fact, that Merton was deceived into overestimating its efficacy, as we have seen.

Cognitive Transformation

From his adolescent atheism Merton traces his journey of cognitive conversion through encounters with Gilson and Huxley, Blake and Maritain first to an intellectual appreciation of the Christian God and then finally to personal belief in this God. The explicitly intellectual component of this belief, and of Catholic Neo-Scholastic theology generally, provided the cognitive foundation for conversion which Merton had previously lacked, and had failed to find, for example, in his flirtation with Communism.

From a developmental perspective, there seems to be no question about Merton's advanced cognitive status. Exceptionally perceptive, even his reflective power of self-criticism was extraordinary for a young man. What Merton required for Christian conversion, then, was not greater or more sophisticated cognitive abilities, but a liberation of his intelligence for a more authentic grasp of reality. If Gilson provided him with his first intelligible, coherent concept of God, Huxley, Blake, and Maritain together brought Merton to the insight that allowed him to break out of his closed, naturalistic realism in order, finally, to be able to embrace that God. Whatever the ultimate philosophical merit of these perspectives, they did open Merton's horizons to the supernatural, and, by thus exploding the former limits of his world, revolutionized his thinking and eventually his life.

Affective Transformation

But this embrace of God, as we have noted, is never a purely intellectual affair. It is, rather, a fully personal reality, at once thoroughly affective and thoroughly cognitive. The author of *The Seven Storey Mountain* was as acutely aware of this as anyone could be, and he rightly stressed, along with his intellectual journey, the long and difficult course of development in his affective life that led him to ever greater transcendence of himself, and finally to conversion.

Two examples from Merton's early life are to the point: his involvement in Communism and his attraction to Friendship House.

We noted that while the author of *The Seven Storey Mountain* described the young Merton's participation in Communism as a moral conversion, his final estimate of the episode was that his "inspiration to do something for the good of mankind had been pretty feeble and abstract from the start." Pretty much an isolated individualist in 1935 as he entered Columbia after some difficult, lonely school years in England, he was really interested only in doing good for himself, despite his weak attempt at something more. In contrast, the affectively converted person is not primarily interested in the abstract "good of mankind," but in responding to the specific needs of concrete, flesh and blood people.

When we turn our consideration to Merton's attraction to Baroness de Hueck's Friendship House in Harlem six years later, however, just before his decision to go to Gethsemani, we get a quite different picture. Here we see Merton dealing with the injustice of society by responding to the real needs of suffering people he had worked with and knew as individuals. Events quickly conspired to lead Merton along a different path, toward an end which he perceived as greater, so there is no story of "Merton at Friendship House." How such a story might have turned out is not the point here, however, for there is no reason to doubt that his commitment to Friendship House was much more like his decision for Gethsemani than it was like "Frank Swift's" decision for the Young Communist League.

Without intending a pun, the difference is best understood, I think, in terms of six years of *friendship*. Despite all the difficulties and uncertainties of his years of confusion in New York, one constant that stands out clearly is the importance in Merton's life of his friends. Merton the autobiographer saw the hand of God very clearly at work in the small group of friends that formed during those student days at Columbia. Together these truly good friends provided the support each needed to realize themselves in moving beyond the boundaries of their narrow, private worlds. All the prods to sanctity were not as explicit as Bob Lax's suggestion that Merton should desire to be a saint, but, as we have seen, even the most common doings of his friends were important: a recommendation of Huxley's book at one right moment, an introduction to Bramachari at another. It does not seem accidental, either, that this group of friends had a special relationship to Mark Van Doren. A life of self-transcendence does not grow and flourish into conversion without the nourishment of a strong model. Perhaps more than anyone else, Van Doren was such a model for the young Merton. Bramachari and Dan Walsh, and certainly the baroness, were important. But the quiet influence of Van Doren on Merton's intellectual, moral, and affective life appears to have been singular in the depth of its effect. It does not seem inappropriate that in the end it was Van Doren's question to him about the priesthood that finally brought Merton to his decision.

"Falling-in-love," it must be stressed, refers not to an easy soap-opera sentimentalism, but to a radical personal capacity for self-transcendence, for reaching out beyond oneself to the good of others. While the personal dynamic state of "being-in-love" is normative for authentic human living, the affective dimension of the personal subject is clearly developmental, as detailed in Chapter 2. No one familiar with Erikson's pattern of psychosocial development, therefore, will expect normative affective development, and thus the possibility of effective, sustained self-transcendence, in an adolescent, for example. If ethical capacity, in Erikson's view, is the criterion of identity, it is the criterion of identity not as an adolescent crisis but as an adult consolidation. Reversing the lens, we can see that a successful resolution of the identity crisis is a condition for mature ethical capacity, which is to say, for the intimate love of the young adult and the responsible caring of the generative adult. For only a person confident in his or her identity can risk losing that identity in going out to others. While one can fall in love with anything from puppy dogs to God, the meaning here is the normative one of an adult joyous love that is caring and responsible.

In our sketch of Merton's spiritual journey from Cambridge through the period in New York and finally to Gethsemani, we saw the sharply etched lines of an identity crisis that required several years of difficult negotiation for Merton to bring it to a basically successful, if not perfect, resolution in his conversion and decision for the priesthood. If the end of one's twenty-seventh year seems a bit late to be finally getting a real purchase on one's identity, we must remember that Merton had bitten off a very large piece to resolve. He would be satisfied with nothing less than the full commitment of himself in fidelity to the Truth he finally discovered to be God. A modest crisis with an easy resolution was not for Merton; after all, his was an identity reaching out for the Ultimate.

A central factor in Merton's identity resolution, of course, was his very discovery of God—the discovery of a living God to whom Merton reached out in an affective self-transcendence which for the rest of his life would continue to deepen through even the most difficult days and darkest nights. Such a loving relationship would go a long way— if not the whole way—toward resolving the critical issue of intimacy in Merton's life. In all, Merton's experience manifests most lucidly the structure of affective conversion as a shift from the instinctive, spontaneous egocentrism of self-absorption to the personal, reflective caring for others of self-giving love.

Moral Transformation

Having considered the cognitive and affective dimensions of Merton's conversion, we must turn now to see how they came together to effect transformation in his moral life. For, clearly, Merton's years in New York constituted a period of sustained development in his moral judgment and decision-making powers. He was, after all, engaged for much of that time in an almost single-minded effort to reach a decision—not just an important decision in his life, or even about his life, but a decision constitutive of his very life, of the kind of person he would be.

Earlier we considered points of contrast between Merton's conversion to Communism and his Christian conversion. In focusing now on Merton's moral development, it may be helpful to examine the two specific moral judgments he made about war in those different conversion contexts.

In 1935 Merton, along with several hundred others participating in a Peace Strike meeting in the Columbia gymnasium, solemnly took the Oxford Pledge against fighting in any war. The basic attitude of the meeting's speeches, as Merton later reported, was that there was no justification for any kind of war by anybody, and if a war did break out, it would be the result of a capitalist plot and should be resisted. This was exactly the kind of position that appealed to his mind at that time. "It seemed to cut across all complexities by its sweeping and uncompromising simplicity. All war was simply unjust, and that was that. The thing to do was to fold your arms and refuse to fight. If everybody did that, there would be no more wars."[46] The Pledge was strongly supported by the Communists, of course. The next year, when the Spanish Civil War broke out, Merton was no longer actively involved in Communism, but Communists who had taken the Pledge were now either fighting against Franco or picketing anybody who did not see that the war in Spain was a holy crusade for the workers against Fascism.

Reflecting on all this, the author of *The Seven Storey Mountain* admitted that the Pledge could not have been intended by him (or probably the others) as anything more than a public statement, as in his (and their) mind there was no real basis of moral obligation or principle of justice. In fact, Merton saw his younger self and Communist associates as unprincipled opportunists, who recognized no law but their own wills.[47] This stinging judgment from the monastery in terms of Stage 2 instrumental-relativism may not be fully justified, but the simplistic, ideological character of Merton's 1935 judgment on war seems evident enough.

In contrast, six years later, as Merton is moving toward his decision for Gethsemani in 1941, the character of his judgment on war is significantly more nuanced. If Merton's earlier, unconditional objection to war had been based mostly on emotion, his response to the draft in 1941 was the product of a conscience carefully formed in just war theory and rooted in a sense of moral duty. Assessing America's anticipated participation in the war as both defensive and necessary, Merton judged that he could not absolutely refuse to go if drafted. But though the intent of the war would be necessary self-defense, and thus morally legitimate in purpose, there still remained the crucial question of means. Though Merton had little doubt that the indiscriminate slaughter of non-combatants in modern war was immoral, the morality of the means was the most difficult for him to decide. In fact, he did not have to decide it. For, fortunately, as the monastic autobiographer still interpreted it several years later, the draft law left him a loophole: he could apply as a non-combatant objector. In this way he would be able to "avoid the whole question" and follow what seemed the much better course. Setting aside the "practically insolvable question of co-operation," Merton saw service in something like the medical corps as an opportunity to perform works of mercy, to overcome evil with good.[48]

Placed next to his participation in the Oxford Pledge, the reasoning leading to Merton's moral judgment here is clearly superior. In the Oxford Pledge we saw Merton taking a simplistic, absolute stand based more on the abstract, totalitarian logic of ideology than on a perceptive understanding of the concrete realities of the situation. And while his enthusiasm for Communist ideology represented a desire to move beyond egocentric interests to a concern for value, we also noted how, according to the autobiographical interpretation, this short-lived enthusiasm conveniently masked a continuing fundamental self-interest.

By 1941, however, Merton had, as he put it, developed a conscience. Now it was his genuine, tested commitment to value, wedded to intelligence that demanded careful, realistic analysis of the concrete situation, that motivated and guided his decision, not an emotionally charged will whose final norm was self-interest.

If the significant development and conversion in Merton's moral reasoning and decision-making powers between 1935 and 1941 is apparent, however, the limitations of his moral development as manifested in his 1941 decision on the draft should also be clear. In 1935 he had "borrowed," for his own purposes, the Communist ideology on peace. In 1941 his morality is still "borrowed," but this time from standard Catholic moral theology: the just war theory. Merton's application of this theory to his situation was fairly sophisticated, to be sure, but the theory's warrant for Merton lay finally in the Church's authority. Evidence of this is found, for example, in Merton's failure to pursue and resolve the seeming discrepancy between his interpretation and "the mind of the Church" on the meaning of the gospel teaching, "Whatsoever you have done to the least of these my brethren, you did it to me." In Merton's understanding, it was "not the mind of the Church that this be applied literally to war—or, rather, that war is looked upon as a painful but necessary social surgical operation in which you kill your enemy not out of hatred but for the common good." For Merton, this was "all very fine in theory." Whatever difficulties it involved in practice he was willing to avoid by using the legitimate option of the non-combatant objector. This also avoided a personal confrontation with traditional Catholic moral theology. The mind of the Church and civil law combined nicely for Merton into a satisfying conventional solution, which gave him "an ineffable sense of peace."[49]

The fact, of course, which even Merton the autobiographer did not fully realize several years later, is that under the surface of this conventional solution a radical challenge to the traditional just war theory was beginning to take shape. Its development into an autonomous principled morality would require many years, but the seed was growing and already beginning to make its subterranean presence felt in 1941. Merton's stated objection to the war, and thus his explicit reason for application as a non-combatant objector, was the indiscriminate slaughter of civilians through the ruthless bombing of open cities. His own words, however, show that he was really concerned not just about that modern barbarism, but about being involved in any killing: he would "willingly enter the army" so long as he "did not have to drop bombs on open cities, or shoot at other men."[50] Clearly, Merton only *thought* he agreed with the just war theory. The truth is that he had only borrowed it; he would never really own it. Whatever the real limitations of Merton's moral development at this point in his life, though, what seems indisputable are the real gains he had made. By 1941 Merton had not only "developed a conscience," as he put it, he had also committed himself to Christian values in a solidly conventional way through a fundamental (but uncritical) moral conversion.

Faith Transformation

We have considered significant cognitive and affective developments in Merton during the crucial years of young adulthood, and how they combined to effect a profound transformation in the moral dimension of his life. But while Christian conversion touches the moral dimension deeply, as a full personal reality it clearly involves even more than the moral dimension. In order to do at least some justice to this "more than," we must now turn to the personal reality Fowler calls "faithing," the constructing of and relating to an ultimate environment of meaning.

For anyone attempting an interpretation, a conversion to Roman Catholicism such as Merton's is a complex, ambiguous reality, despite the fact that faithing in such an instance is explicitly religious. On the one hand, such a Christian conversion is clearly a deliberate, personal choice of value, a decision, indeed, constitutive of one's character, definitive of one's very being. On the other hand, conversions to Catholicism are often characterized by a marked dependence on the authority of the Church. Merton, clearly, is no exception here. We have just seen, for example, how Merton's acceptance of the official Catholic teaching on the just war overshadowed his own incipient pacifist intuitions.

Through the lens of a cognitive-developmental stage theory of faithing, however, Merton's conversion is brought into sharp focus by Fowler's description of Stage 4 Individuative-Reflective Faith. Several defining elements in this fourth stage of faithing aptly characterize Merton during the conversion period. Clearly, Merton takes seriously the burden of responsibility for his own commitments, life-style, beliefs, and attitudes. His identity is taking on a clear measure of self-definition. And he expresses his intuitions of ultimate coherence in explicit, conceptual systems of meanings. All these aspects of Merton's faithing point unambiguously to Stage 4. However, the picture loses a good bit of its clarity when we consider the stage-defining element Fowler calls "Locus of Authority." In Fowler's perspective, for a fully realized Stage 4 not only must previous tacitly held values be reflectively criticized, but one's source of authority must be shifted from outside the self to an "executive ego" within the self.[51] Fowler recognizes that many persons complete only half of this double move. Merton seems to be an example of one of the two possibilities of partial transition: critical distancing from a previous assumptive value system without the emergence of a fully critical executive ego as internal authority. Merton certainly is able to make his values explicit and achieve critical distance from them. But in committing himself to a new value perspective he chooses an "ideologically established perspective" in dependence on the authority of the Church. This authority is deliberately chosen, not simply assumed as at Stage 3, but it remains external. So while Merton's new Christian faith is personally appropriated, it is not the *critically* self-chosen faith of a fully postconventional orientation. Merton's faithing has moved toward Stage 4 in his conversion, but it will remain transitional for some years. Christian conversion at this point in development may be conceptually sophisticated, affectively rich, and personally profound, yet despite even its reflective distance it will be fundamentally uncritical because tied to an external authority. And as personally authentic and life transforming as Merton's 1938–41 Christian conversion was, I am suggesting that it was essentially an uncritical conversion to given, radically unquestioned Christian values and beliefs on the authority of the Catholic Church.

Preceding pages have discussed, in order, Merton's cognitive, affective, moral, and faith transformations. The fact, of course, is that during the 1938–41 period Merton experienced only one conversion—extended in its realization to be sure, but still one conversion: a single Christian conversion with cognitive, affective, moral, and faith dimensions.

CONVERSION: PSYCHOLOGICAL INTERPRETATIONS

Having analyzed the various dimensions of Merton's Christian conversion in developmental terms, we shall now turn our attention to some significant modern interpretations of conversion in order to further clarify our understanding of Christian conversion, and in particular to illuminate the meaning of conversion in Merton's youthful experience. For this purpose the only place to begin, really, is with the classic modern account of conversion presented by William James at the turn of the century in his *Varieties of Religious Experience*. After a brief examination of this psychological perspective on conversion, we will focus it on Merton's experience.

William James: Conversion of the Divided Self

James sets his consideration of conversion in the context of two quite distinct existential orientations: "the healthy-minded, who need to be born only once, and . . . the sick souls, who must be twice-born in order to be happy."[52] The once-born live in a naturally good, one-storied universe where life's pluses and minuses are reckoned straight-forwardly, and happiness and religious peace consists in keeping to the plus side of the ledger. In contrast, the twice-born live in the mystery of a double-storied universe, where the naturally good is not only insufficient, but false; it keeps us from the true good, and must be renounced if one is to enter true, spiritual life.

The twice-born person suffers notably from a temperamental discordancy, an "incompletely unified moral and intellectual constitution." But to one degree or another, personal development for everyone consists in unifying the inner self, by transforming the chaos of feelings and impulses into a stable system of subordinated functions. In the religiously sensitive, says James, the unhappiness of this struggle will take the form of "conviction of sin," of "moral remorse and compunction, of feeling inwardly vile and wrong, and of standing in false relations to the author of one's being and appointer of one's spiritual fate."[53] One's interiority is the ground on which two deadly hostile selves battle, one actual, the other ideal.

> To be converted, to be regenerated, to receive grace, to experience religion, to gain an assurance, are so many phrases which denote the process, gradual or sudden, by which a self hitherto divided, and consciously wrong inferior and unhappy, becomes unified and consciously right superior and happy, in consequence of its firmer hold upon religious realities. This at least is what conversion signifies in general terms, whether or not we believe that a direct divine operation is needed to bring such a moral change about.[54]

James explains this phenomenon in terms of the aims, ideas, and objects which form diverse, relatively independent, internal groups and systems within a person's consciousness. Each aim elicits a certain kind of interested excitement, and brings together a collection of subordinated ideas. The presence of one such group may totally dominate, excluding others from the field of consciousness. Everyone has had the experience of being engrossed in some particular interest, as well as that of changing interests, with the consequent shift of groups of ideas between the central and peripheral parts of consciousness. Conversion means that a group of religious ideas, aims, and interests moves from the periphery to the center of one's consciousness, constituting the habitual center of one's personal dynamic energy.

James outlines two ways that this shift of center, or conversion, may occur: the conscious and voluntary way of volitional conversion, and the unconscious and involuntary way of conversion by self-surrender. The volitional conversion consists of gradually building up a new set of moral and spiritual habits, though there will always be critical points of especially rapid growth. And even in the most voluntary, gradual process of regeneration there comes a point when the personal will must be given up, when self-surrender becomes indispensable.

Not surprisingly, though, James finds the sudden, dramatic conversion experience, in which self-surrender dominates, much more interesting than the gradual, voluntary type. Self-surrender is necessary because personal will remains centered on the actual, imperfect self, which, though struggling away from acutely felt sin, only dimly imagines the positive ideal. Surrender of personal will makes space for the ideal self to emerge from its subconscious incubation and become the center of consciousness, of one's life. The self-surrendering character of conversion can be so strong, indeed, that the convert has the experience of being a passive spectator, undergoing a miraculous process performed from above, often accompanied by voices, lights, visions.

Realizing that some individuals have larger marginal regions of consciousness than others, and that these persons are naturally more susceptible to having their focal consciousness abruptly unbalanced by the instantaneous invasion of subliminal influences, James sees no reason to presume that the origin or cause of the sudden conversion is more supernatural than that of the gradual conversion. Indeed, James is interested in judging conversions not by their origin, but empirically, by their fruits for life. And by this test, James finds that, aside from preeminent saints, the instantaneously converted are as a class indistinguishable from so-called natural persons. For James, "the real witness of the spirit to the second birth" is to be found not in voices, visions, and other supernatural effects, all explainable in natural terms, but "only in the disposition of the genuine child of God, the permanently patient heart, the love of self eradicated. And this, it has to be admitted, is also found in those who pass no crisis, and may even be found outside of Christianity altogether."[55]

The Varieties of Religious Experience clearly established a well-defined place for conversion in the psychology of religion. Key aspects of James' definition of conversion have become "standard operating assumptions" in its study: (1) the identification of a common phenomenon—prescinding from the necessity of direct divine operation—described by a variety of phrases, some more psychological, some more theological; (2) the fundamental concept of a self, divided (but capable of being united) in the experience of value conflict between the actual self and ideal self; (3) the process-in-time character of both sudden and gradual conversions.[56]

One of the most problematic aspects of James' analysis, however, is his unqualified endorsement of E.D. Starbuck's conclusion about the typical age for conversion. James asserts: "Conversion is in its essence a normal adolescent phenomenon, incidental to the passage from the child's small universe to the wider intellectual and spiritual life of maturity."[57] Starbuck's study at the end of the nineteenth century showed that young people, usually between fourteen and seventeen, manifested common symptoms, whether inspired by evangelical practices or simply as part of normal adolescent growth: brooding, depression, morbid introspection; sense of incompleteness, imperfection, sin; anxiety about the hereafter; distress over doubts. And, as James points out, in both groups, those evangelically inspired and those not, "the result is the same—a happy relief and objectivity, as the confidence in self gets greater through the adjustment of the faculties to the wider outlook." The essential distinction between the two groups, according to Starbuck, is that the conversion experience intensifies but shortens the period of adolescent storm and stress by bringing the individual to a definite crisis.

Starbuck's adolescent converts tended to exaggerate both their preconversion sinfulness and their postconversion virtue. A young man of sixteen reported: "My mind was in a state of great anxiety. The fleshly mind was all aflame, and my guilt was hideous to me. Because I belonged to church I felt myself a hypocrite." And a young woman described her postconversion state: "I was a new creature in Christ Jesus. Everything seemed heavenly rather than earthly: everything was so lovely. I had a love for everybody. It was such a blessed experience. Going home I walked on the curbstone rather than walk or talk with ungodly people." The young man's reference to the "fleshly mind" points to the intimate connection—especially for Starbuck's Victorian converts—between adolescent "conviction of sin" and emerging sexual impulses, a factor James does not emphasize.[58]

Whatever the particular cause of the conflict, however, James' interpretation of conversion as conflict resolution does constitute a significant contribution. Resolution of adolescent conflict is no doubt a real conversion, and one whose significance must be taken into account by any adequate interpretation of conversion. Indeed, some seventy-five years after James, the conversion of adolescence continues to receive fresh psychological interpretation. Of particular interest for purposes of the present study is V. Bailey Gillespie's recent attempt to locate conversion within Erikson's life cycle in his *Religious Conversion and Personal Identity*.

Conversion and Identity

Gillespie's main purpose is to relate what he calls religious conversion to "its secular counterpart—identity." After reviewing the conclusions of the major psychological treatments of conversion since the work of Starbuck and James, he proposes a definition of religious conversion, stressing function and process, which has a strong family resemblance to James' definition. Religious conversion, for Gillespie, is a personal change, as most writers insist, but a change characterized by four constituent elements: (1) self-unification; (2) positive personal effects; (3) intensity of ideological commitment; (4) sudden or gradual decision. The internal unification process of the emerging self includes wholeness, integrity, reorientation. The effects of religious conversion, then, are always experienced by the self as positive. Whether emphasizing traditional Christian or more subjective qualities of religion, religious conversion involves a "perceived 'confrontation' and a resultant intense commitment to an ethical, creedal, or ideological frame-work," with growth as the usual result. And in religious conversion, whether gradual or sudden, decision to change is crucial; it sets an orientation from which all of life is viewed.[59]

Again like the turn-of-the-century pioneers in the field, Gillespie outlines this personal experience of religious conversion in three phases: (1) preconversion, with questioning, tension, anxiety, and stress; (2) crisis, with the sense of a greater presence, higher control, and self-surrender; (3) postconversion, with its relief, release, assurance, harmony, peace, ecstatic happiness. Whatever the language used, the conflict resolution of conversion, from a functional perspective, is both problem-solving and identity-forming.[60]

This last element of identity-formation is particularly significant for Gillespie inasmuch as the attempt to interpret religious conversion in light of contemporary analyses of identity constitutes his specific contribution to the understanding of conversion. That Gillespie should focus on identity is not surprising, for, like Starbuck and James, he also sees religious conversion as occurring principally in adolescence—precisely the period where Erikson, his primary source on identity, places the crisis of identity. Gillespie qualifies the correlation of religious conversion with adolescence; he does not claim that adolescence has a complete monopoly on religious conversion. But everything in his definition of conversion leads him to further agree with Starbuck and James that adolescence is *the* time for conversion. "Religious conversion experience fits into the kinds of decision-making, maturing, and conflict that is a part" of adolescence. "Religious conversion happens more readily in adolescence," a time when several developmental factors ground "a good possibility of intense change. . . . " And when religious conversion does occur in adolescence, "the change is equally as deep as those coming later in life."[61]

The first thing to be said about religious conversion and identity experience from Gillespie's perspective is that, for all their similarities, they are not the same. Like James, Gillespie affirms that conversion can be gradual or sudden; also like James, he emphasizes the sudden conversion. But identity experience is a lifelong process; thus one aspect of the disparity. Also, Gillespie indicates that religious conversion, unlike identity experience, must include the undefined "presence of the 'holy.' "

Despite this disclaimer, the great weight of Gillespie's analysis goes toward showing how religious conversion and identity experience are practically the same. After all, identity formation may be a process extending through the life cycle, but the essential point of that process is the adolescent identity crisis. As Gillespie puts it: "Religious conversion tends to show up more often in the form of a crisis moment with rapid resolution and is like the crisis of identity experience, but not like the [entire] process of identity formation itself." And if the subject struggling through the identity crisis should "attach some subjective religious quality" to the experience, it could, according to Gillespie, "be construed to be totally equated with religious conversion experience."

Gillespie's position on the relationship between religious conversion and identity crisis is best summed up in his central assertion: "The religious conversion experience provides a turning point in the life of the young person and answers the questions raised when the youth faces the problem of just what he is going to give his life to or for."[62]

Psychological Interpretations and Merton

Whatever else must be said about the theses of James, Starbuck, and Gillespie on conversion and adolescence, it is clear that this last assertion of Gillespie accurately characterizes the young Merton's conversion experience. Without any doubt, Merton's 1938–41 conversion was not only *a* turning point, but *the* turning point in his life. The path ahead would be difficult and require continual redefinition, but the basic direction was set. In contrast to the utter aimlessness of his student days in England, Merton not only had a rather clear answer to the question "to what and for what was he going to give his life" as he made his way to Gethsemani, but he was already beginning to live that answer out in action.

When we consider the course of Merton's personal transformation from the perspectives of James, Starbuck, and Gillespie, it almost seems as though their interpretations of conversion had been worked out with Merton's experience in mind. Recalling a few highlights should make this point obvious.

We might consider first James' characterization of the twice-born person as suffering from "an incompletely unified moral and intellectual constitution," which is experienced as "feeling inwardly vile and wrong." Even our brief review of Merton's preconversion life showed that he was dominated by this kind of experience, not just for months, but for years. (Clearly, Starbuck's reference to sexual activity is not irrelevant here.) Finally, of course, he could no longer stand up under the pressure of the deadly battle going on within him between his actual and ideal selves.

For James, conversion means that the ideal self emerges victorious, which is to say that religious interests move from the periphery to the center of one's consciousness, and become one's habitual, dynamic, center of energy. As a result, the divided, wrong, and unhappy self is unified, and becomes right and happy. Again, Merton's descriptions of his experience from 1938 through 1941 constantly emphasize the happiness, often ecstatic happiness, resulting from the transformation that was occurring in his life. We remember, for example, the euphoria he experienced walking down Broadway in the sun after his first Mass: "I could not understand what it was that had happened to make me so happy, why I was so much at peace, so content with life. . . ." This felt happiness is an emphatic manifestation of Merton's movement toward a "unified moral and intellectual constitution."

Merton's experience clearly exemplifies James' claim that all conversions are characterized by self-surrender. Indeed, when we recall the voice urging Merton to a conversion decision, his experience of illumination at the Consecration in Cuba, and his hearing of the Gethsemani bell, we obviously have an example of James' strong sense of self-surrender, accompanied, even, by voices, lights, and visions. Merton, of course, saw a divine, supernatural hand in his experience, but even judged by James' empirical test—what conversion means in one's life over the long term—Merton's conversion experience is impressive.

The depth of one's self-surrender, of course, is directly related to the depth of autonomy one is surrendering, to the degree of possession that one has taken of one's self. From the developmental perspective, which we are about to return to, the limitations of the self-surrendering possibilities of a conversion connected with a youthful identity crisis are obvious. Kegan's view is especially illuminating here. The resolution of an identity crisis in the transition to the Stage 4 Institutional self does constitute an advance in autonomy. But this newly created Institutional self, sharply emphasizing its differentiation-independence in reaction to the previous stage's excessive integration-inclusiveness, is perhaps the least likely candidate for self-surrender. The very dynamics of establishing identity work against the possibility of profound self-surrender. Later we shall see how further development—to the Interindividual self—makes greater self-surrender possible.

When we turn to Gillespie's Eriksonian interpretation of conversion as identity crisis resolution, we find a model that appears almost custom designed for Merton's experience. The classic three phases of conversion, reaffirmed by Gillespie, are especially apparent in Merton: (1) the years of *preconversion* questioning and stress; (2) the *crisis*, with its self-surrender and sense of a greater presence, resulting first in the decision for baptism and then the priesthood; (3) his overwhelming *postconversion* peace and ecstatic happiness.

Just as clear in Merton's transformation are the four elements Gillespie delineates as constitutive of conversion. In the context of Merton's story as well as our analysis to this point, they are self-evident in the very naming: (1) self-unification; (2) positive personal effects; (3) intensity of ideological commitment; (4) sudden or gradual decision. Merton's descriptions leave no doubt that his was an experience of a divided self being torn in different directions and finally unified in its energy and direction (not totally, but effectively). And even years later he continued to perceive his intense commitment to the Catholic faith not only as a positive personal effect in his life, but as its very meaning.

Perhaps Gillespie's fourth element, sudden or gradual decision, needs more explanation in Merton's case. For the fact is that Merton's decision experience of 1938–41 and the period leading up to it was not either sudden *or* gradual, but both sudden *and* gradual. The basic experience was gradual in that it extended over more than two years in a quite explicit way. Still, within this period there were key moments, at least two of which must be considered crises, to which Merton responded with sudden dramatic decisions.[63]

This last point of decision should be highlighted. Gillespie's interpretation rightly gives it constitutive status in the conversion process. And Merton's experience points up just how central the element of personal decision is in conversion. The emphasis by James and Starbuck and Gillespie on factors like self-surrender and a sense of a greater presence and higher control is valid, but these factors should not be allowed to overshadow the central—indeed, crucial—role that active, positive decision plays in an authentic conversion. In the midst of a myriad of psychic factors, the act of decision makes conversion genuinely personal. Indeed, in the process of self-unification, decision is ultimately constitutive of the self. And because it is, Gillespie is correct in saying that it sets an orientation from which all life is viewed. The conversion decision constitutes the personal subject with a particular standpoint and direction, and this establishes his or her horizon on the world.

We have been concentrating on the identity dimension of the conversion experience, which Gillespie (along with James and Starbuck in other concepts and language) sees as an adolescent phenomenon. With Merton, of course, we have a case of conversion occurring not in the teens but in the mid-twenties. Earlier we noted that Merton had set the identity stakes high. His intelligence, sensitivity, and personal depth admitted of no shallow crisis with a facile resolution. If Merton discovered God in finding himself, it also seems true that he could not discover and take any purchase on his own identity until he had confronted and made at least an initial resolution of the ultimate question of God.

Merton's Christian conversion was not simply the resolution of an identity crisis naively clothed in pious Christian language, as so many of the classic adolescent conversion accounts seem to be. Merton's self-discovery did not occur quickly or easily, but when it did come forth his private mirror of self-satisfied narcissism had been shattered and transformed into the powerful telescope of moral conversion reaching out to the universe of value.

Christian Conversion as Religious

But Christian conversion, as we noted earlier, is not simply moral conversion. While Christian conversion necessarily includes a moral dimension, it is more than a conversion to Christian moral values. An authentic Christian conversion is characterized especially by a specifically religious quality—a relationship to God in the person of Jesus Christ. Our review of Merton's transformation experience has left no doubt about the presence of this religious quality in his conversion. In fact, the difficult struggle of these transformative years in Merton's life can be accounted for by the fact that he had questioned his life as a whole at the deepest level and would settle for nothing less than an integrating answer rooted in ultimate reality. With Merton's discovery of God in his own experience, then, the cognitive, affective, moral, and faithing dimensions finally came together in the unity of a thoroughgoing reorientation of his life—a fully Christian conversion: not a total, absolute transformation of his personal being, but a relationship with Jesus Christ deep enough to give unity to his person and moral direction to his life.

Despite the clearly religious quality of Merton's conversion, I have deliberately avoided calling it a "religious" conversion. This is because I have been using however flexibly—Bernard Lonergan's notion of conversion as an interpretive frame for this study, and Lonergan's definition of religious conversion is very specific. I have already referred explicitly to Lonergan's understanding of affective, cognitive, and moral conversions, though with significant modifications.

Lonergan's notion of religious conversion is both profound and powerful. For him religious conversion, like affective conversion, is a falling-in-love that establishes a person as a dynamic principle of benevolence and beneficence. But in religious conversion, one falls-in-love with God, one is grasped by ultimate concern. Being-in-love with God is "total and permanent self-surrender without conditions, qualifications, reservations." Religious conversion transforms a person into a "subject in love, a subject held, grasped, possessed, owned through a total and so an other-worldly love."[64]

This characterization of religious conversion does not seem to be descriptive of the ordinary religious person's experience—not even the young Merton's. It is precisely because of the profundity and power of this notion of religious conversion that I have avoided it in the present discussion of Merton. Whatever Lonergan's intention, his description suggests, if not perfection, at least the deepest kind of fulfillment. In fact, Lonergan explicitly understands such religious conversion as the proper fulfillment of one's capacity for self-transcendence. This notion of religious conversion, as I will argue in a following chapter, most accurately characterizes not just a person's "turning to God," but the radical reorientation of a person's life in such a way that *God* (not just "religious ideas, aims, and interests") becomes not only a part but the center and principal reality of that life. Precisely because this radical experience is so rare, this understanding of "religious" is uncommon. The ordinary experience of the good Christian or Jew grounds the common meaning of "religious" in the Western world. Still, it is not simply arbitrary to reserve the term "religious conversion" for designating the profound state of being-in-love with God in an unqualified way—with one's whole heart and soul and mind and strength. Rather, in a world where language is regularly debased and trivialized, it is a reminder that the religion of institutions and popular culture is only a distant and dim reflection of divine life for men and women who are truly open to reality—to God.

We have seen that Merton, describing his experience at the time of his first contact with the Franciscans in the person of Father Edmund, asserted that his decision on a Franciscan vocation had brought about a great transformation in him, making God the center of his existence. We must interpret this statement in the context of later developments, however, if we are to assess its meaning accurately.

Less than a year later, just weeks before he was to enter the novitiate, Merton saw his Franciscan vocation fall to pieces. This experience occasioned some sobering reflections by the monastic autobiographer on the spiritual state of the would-be novice: "Since I was so strongly attached to material goods, and so immersed in my own self, and so far from God, and so independent of Him, and so dependent on myself and my own imaginary powers, it was necessary that I should not enter a monastery. . . . "[65]

Perhaps the most revealing and accurate reflection on the transformation of Merton's spiritual life during these crucial years, then, was the autobiographer's insight into the young Merton's hospitalization for appendicitis, in the spring of 1940, midway between the beginning and the end of his Franciscan vocation. Although the patient did not realize it at the time, the monk later saw that the lying in bed and being spoon-fed was symbolic of his spiritual life at the time; "For I was now, at last, born: but I was still only new-born. I was living: I had an interior life, real, but feeble and precarious. And I was still nursed and fed with spiritual milk. . . . Weak and without strength as I was, I was nevertheless walking in the way that was liberty and life. I had found my spiritual freedom."[66]

It seems best, therefore, to reserve the notion of religious conversion for the later transformation in Merton's spiritual life which we will consider in due course. What seems right to stress at this point is the extraordinary transformation realized in Merton's 1938–41 Christian conversion: the discovery of and consequent personal relationship with God which not only transvalued his moral values but reoriented his whole life to the loving service of the God Who is Love. A following chapter will consider how this "new-born," loving relationship would later flower after many difficult years into the unqualified being-in-love of radical religious conversion.

Limitations of Psychological Interpretations

There are still many facets of the reality of Christian conversion which this chapter must consider. Before leaving the perspectives of James, Starbuck, and Gillespie, however, a few comments by way of assessment are in order, for our consideration of Merton's conversion suggests that serious qualifications must be made regarding their interpretations of conversion.

We have already recognized the significant contribution James made through his psychological approach to conversion as conflict resolution. Whether James' endorsement of Starbuck's view of conversion as an essentially adolescent phenomenon is equally helpful is quite another question, however. That conversion commonly occurs in adolescence is uncontroversial enough. Chapters 2 through 4 of the present study have explained the developmental possibility of moral conversion during adolescence. But it is one thing to claim that conversions commonly occur during adolescence, it is an altogether different thing to assert that religious conversion is an *essentially* adolescent phenomenon. The latter claim amounts to establishing the adolescent crisis as the preeminently human crisis, as the deepest existential crisis experienced by the personal subject. If developmental psychology supports the assertion of adolescent conversion, it also presents damaging evidence to the claim for this conversion's primacy in human life. For while the analysis of the affective, cognitive, moral, and faith dimensions of personal development indicates the powerful achievement of adolescence, it just as clearly reveals the serious limitations of that achievement in terms of full personal maturity. The critical moral conversion to the principled reasoning of Stage 6—reached only in young adulthood, if at all—is just one example of personal conversion beyond the limits of adolescence. Even without the evidence of developmental psychology, of course, the case for conversion as essentially adolescent would have to explain the fact that history's great personal conversions have been not adolescent but adult conversions; and in many instances, like that of Pascal, for example, these adult conversions—far from being merely retarded adolescent conversions—have followed upon earlier youthful conversions.[67]

When we consider the specifically religious aspect of these psychological interpretations of conversion, the need for qualification becomes more pressing. Insofar as adolescence is characterized by an explicit crisis of identity and by the resolution of its basic conflicts, one can readily agree with Gillespie—and with Starbuck and James—that adolescence is a common occasion of conversion. The issues of ideology, fidelity, and commitment in the identity crisis, indeed, point to moral conversion. Nothing about Gillespie's analysis, however, demonstrates that adolescent conversion is intrinsically religious. In fact, religious conversion for Gillespie turns out to be nothing more than the resolution of the adolescent identity crisis set in an explicitly religious context. Still, by associating conversion with the identity crisis as detailed so thoroughly by Erikson, Gillespie makes it possible to distinguish the various elements in the conversion experience described by Starbuck and James more clearly, and thus to recognize that they, like Gillespie, were focusing on what is essentially a common developmental phenomenon of adolescence, and only extrinsically religious. If James stressed conversion as the resolution of the subject's conflicts between ideal and actual selves, it remained for Erikson to specify in more precise detail the exact nature of this psychological conflict.

In Gillespie's Eriksonian interpretation, then, as well as in those of Starbuck and James, a basic dimension of Christian conversion is analyzed. This dimension—self-discovery and fidelity at the subject-pole and ideological commitment to values and beliefs at the object-pole—is clearly the moral one. It is not surprising, then, that descriptions in James of persons before their conversions are sometimes reminiscent of Kierkegaard's aesthetic subjects. The unhappy soul of the divided self in James is not unfamiliar with Kierkegaard's despair. Adolescent development makes moral conversion possible, but, of course, such conversion may occur at any point in adult life, too. When such moral conversion is concretely a conversion to Christian values, one can speak accurately of a Christian moral conversion. When this Christian moral conversion coincides with the adolescent resolution of an identity crisis, of course, it is necessarily uncritical, as even Gillespie's description inadvertently suggests: "Religious conversion leads to a formulated faith either implicitly given or endowed to the youth through adults."[68]

While the psychological, and especially Gillespie's Eriksonian, interpretation offers much by way of illuminating Merton's conversion experience, it is important to emphasize that Merton's experience is far deeper and more complex than the typical adolescent instance of conversion. Such interpretations of adolescent conversions are valuable explanations of the fundamental psychological dynamics of youth, but by characterizing adolescent conversions as "religious" they are misleading insofar as they divert attention from the more profound, specifically adult transformations of personal consciousness which are developmentally beyond adolescent possibilities. As I have already claimed in anticipation of our later discussion of religious conversion, not even Merton's 1938–41 conversion realized the full possibilities of adult religious transformation. In this light it is less than helpful to state, as Gillespie does, that when religious conversion occurs in adolescence "the change is equally as deep as those coming later in life." Adolescent conversions may be intense, but there is no developmental support for the claim that adolescent conversions exhaust the depths of transformational possibilities. Adolescence is morally and religiously, as well as cognitively and affectively, an important developmental period, but nothing is gained by crediting it with religious possibilities beyond its power. Serious religious transformations occur during the adolescent years, as the analysis of faith development makes clear, but that same analysis also clarifies the fact that adolescent religious developments are just the threshold to the world of genuinely adult religious possibilities. As a key to this religious world, Erikson's analysis of the older adult's crisis of integrity vs. despair offers much more promise than does his consideration of the adolescent identity crisis.

It may seem odd—perhaps even perverse—to define religious conversion in a way that excludes most people ordinarily thought of as "religious." But the point is not to deny the experience of the millions of persons—children, adolescents, adults—who understand themselves as being somehow religious. I am not suggesting that religious conversion is the criterion for defining persons as religious. By no means; indeed, I will later argue that religious conversion occurs in the religious person.[69] Religious conversion is a special, extraordinary transformation of religious consciousness. Persons who are considered religious in the ordinary sense become so through socialization. In the generalized sense of "faithing," we have seen how personal religious consciousness develops. Perhaps the claim that persons do not become religious through religious conversion will seem less strange if we consider the other fundamental conversions. One does not become intelligent and reasonable through cognitive conversion, or loving through affective conversion, or responsible through moral conversion. Each of these conversions is a special transformation of a previously existing and developing dimension of the person. In the same way, a non-religious person does not become religious through religious conversion; rather, the religious person becomes religious in a new way. From the theory of development and conversion explicated thus far in this study, then, this understanding of religious conversion should appear not as a strange departure, but as a consistent theoretical expansion. It should seem elitist only to those who would insist that religious consciousness is univocal and static, that it is not open to ever deeper developments and transformations.

Christian Conversion from the Psychological Perspective

How are we to understand Christian conversion in this context? I have said that while Christian conversion must be a moral conversion, it is more than moral conversion. It always involves the religious quality of a cognitive and affective relationship with God in Jesus Christ. But if Christian conversion is more than moral conversion, it is also less than religious conversion as I have defined it here. Just as not all Christians have experienced Christian conversion, not all who have experienced the transformation of a relationship with Christ have experienced the radical falling-in-love with God that is religious conversion.

By establishing a personal, self-transcending relationship with God in Jesus Christ that is both affective and effective, Christian conversion, as James might put it, moves Christian truth and value from the periphery to the center of one's consciousness and energy. Merton's conversion to Christianity exemplifies this movement perfectly. But the same shift of consciousness occurs when a born Christian experiences the cognitive, affective, moral, and faith transformation which a new and vital relationship with the person of Christ effects. Though a personal gift of inestimable value, this relationship is to be understood not so much as an end as a possibility. From the convert's perspective, it is the beginning of what may become an unending journey into the personal reality of God—a journey which, after many years of arduous travel, may pass through (but not end in) the radical transformation of unconditional love called religious conversion.

CONVERSION: THEOLOGICAL INTERPRETATIONS

Conversion as Fundamental Option

The understanding of Christian conversion we have constructed from Merton's experience—with the help of psychological interpretations of conversion as conflict resolution—corresponds in many ways to what contemporary theologians have called fundamental option or decision. In fact, some theologians have considered conversion precisely as fundamental decision. Karl Rahner, for example, interprets conversion as "the religiously and morally good fundamental decision in regard to God, a basic choice intended to commit the whole of life to God. . . . " This fundamental turning to God is seen, of course, "as a response, made possible by God's grace, to a call from God."[70]

Joseph Fuchs places this fundamental option of conversion in the explicit context of sin. For him, "conversion is a change in the whole person, for the whole person is a sinner. . . . Conversion means to change the whole thrust of one's life." Because conversion is the disposition of the whole person, it occurs on the deep personal level where one is able to dispose of oneself as a whole. "Just as a person becomes a sinner only on the deep personal level, so it is only there that a sinner can experience conversion." Thus conversion is much more a "turning away from the fundamental orientation to sin" than from any particular definite sin of the past.[71] Still, if conversion is achieved on the deepest level at the center of a person, it is always realized in and through a particular concrete good act. We see clearly here how the context of Christian faith transforms the understanding of moral conversion as a shift from satisfaction to value into a shift from sin to God, emphasizing even more the radical discontinuity and dialectical nature of conversion. Paul Tillich speaks of a "turning away from injustice toward justice, from inhumanity to humanity, from idols to God."[72] While not as deep and thoroughgoing as fully religious conversion, the fundamental redirection of life in Christian moral conversion cannot be overstated.

From this point of view, Rahner insists that conversion is primarily unselfish love of the neighbor, "because only in conjunction with this can God really be loved, and without that love no one really knows with genuine personal knowledge who God is." Most simply, then, conversion is "a resolute, radical and radically conscious, personal and in each instance unique adoption of Christian life."[73] Conversion, Karl Barth points out, "would not be the conversion of the whole man if it did not commence and work itself out at once in the relationship" to the neighbor.[74]

Jesus' Call to Conversion

Turning from sin to love of neighbor points to the central moral dimension of Christian conversion. Jesus' preaching clearly called for moral conversion: "Repent and believe in the Gospel!" But just as Christian conversion is more than moral conversion, so Jesus' call to conversion is more than a call to moral obligation. Jesus' call to repentance is a call to Christian conversion only in the context of its immediately preceding proclamation: "The time is fulfilled and the reign of God is at hand!" As Franz Böckle explains, the order of presentation here is important, since, for Jesus, the demand for conversion follows upon God's anticipatory salvific move.[75] On this point of sequence, Barth insists that the dynamic principle of conversion is the "truth, revealing itself to man, that God is for him, and that—in virtue of the fact that God is for him—he is for God." If the "order were different, and the truth revealed to man were that man is for God, and therefore God for man, the truth would not make us free."[76] As Charles E. Curran points out, the "motive for conversion is the presence of the reign of God in Christ."[77] Christian conversion is the joyous and grateful change of heart that results from hearing the good news of salvation: God's offer of love. This good news of God's salvific love both requires—and makes possible—the joyful change of heart, the grateful acceptance of God's reign of love.

The misery of the sinner, God's offer of love, and the appropriate response of conversion is poignantly depicted in the parable of the prodigal son. Bernard Häring helps us to understand the meaning of conversion here by noting that the Hebrew word for conversion, *shub*, means returning home. The good news is the possibility of returning home to God's unconditional love. To accept this good news, of course, one requires a vivid sense of the wretchedness of sin and the need of redemption. Homecoming is for the homesick. One reaches conversion not through increasing evil, says Häring, but through growing insight into one's sin and into the misery of being cut off from God.[78]

Theological Interpretations and Merton

Häring and the other theologians we have been considering were not writing with Merton in mind. But they might have been. For Merton's experience of conversion concretely exemplifies their theological interpretation of Christian conversion just as vividly as it illustrates the psychological analyses of conversion as conflict resolution. Indeed, the intrinsic religious quality of Merton's experience demonstrates the necessity of a specifically theological interpretation to complement the psychological analysis of genuine Christian conversion. Clearly, Merton's conversion cannot be understood without reference to the complex reality of personal identity. Just as clearly, it cannot be adequately understood *only* in relation to personal identity. More precisely, Merton's identity cannot be understood properly except in religious terms. For him the conflict of the divided self was an ultimate conflict. Merton understood that his decision was a radical decision for the fundamental orientation of his life—a turning from sin to God.

In fact, while Merton's experience supports the view that Christian conversion should be understood as a fundamental option, it also suggests that the reality of fundamental option should be understood much more explicitly as an *experience*. Contemporary theologians commonly assert that an adult has a fundamental orientation or stance either for or against God. From this premise it is argued that this fundamental stance could only have been established through a fundamental option. Therefore every adult has made a fundamental option of one kind or another, whether he or she knows it or not. This view was developed in order to shift the focus of contemporary moral theology away from a preoccupation with individual acts to a more biblically oriented concern with the pattern and direction of a person's whole moral life.[79]

Basic developmental insights, however, require that we specify the meaning of "adult" in a critical way. All chronological adults are not moral adults. By definition, moral adults have made a fundamental option. Many chronological adults of long standing, however, have never come into their moral adulthood. They have never confronted themselves and taken possession of their lives at a deep enough level to make any kind of fundamental decision. These persons merely drift. They are often good people, doing many good things. But to claim for them a fundamental decision about their lives is to deny psychological reality for the metaphysical fantasy of ideology.[80] Rahner is correct in emphasizing the radically conscious character of fundamental Christian decision as a personal experience. There may be good doctrinal reasons for positing the existence of a preconscious determination of a person's life, but such an alleged reality should not be confused with the conscious, experiential reality of personal conversion. People do not stumble into a conversion. Personal conversion involves a conscious, deliberate decision. Many important changes may be occurring in a person's moral and religious life of which he or she is unaware. But, if conversion is to mean anything as an empirical concept, it must be distinguished from such changes, however profound they may be. Biblical witness as well as modern psychological analyses supports the view that only persons who have experienced transformation have been converted. It need not be a sudden, dramatic experience of conversion, but for characterizing someone who cannot identify such transformation in his or her experience, conversion is an inappropriate category. No one has to be told that he or she has been converted![81]

The contemporary theological interpretation of Christian conversion is also corroborated by Merton's experience in its emphasis on the biblical call. More than anything else, Merton experienced his conversion as a response to that call: "And He called out to me from His own immense depths." "How beautiful and how terrible are the words with which God speaks to the soul of those He has called to Himself, and to the Promised Land which is participation in His own life. . . . " "This was the call that came to me with my Baptism, bringing with it a most appalling responsibility if I failed to answer it."[82]

The very structure of Merton's autobiography highlights the fact that he heard God's call at a time of utter wretchedness. Part I's final paragraph sums up the first phase of the conversion process, and anticipates the second: "I had come very far, to find myself in this blind alley: but the very anguish and helplessness of my position was something to which I rapidly succumbed. And it was my defeat that was to be the occasion of my rescue."

Merton prefers the imagery of the Jews being called out of Egypt into the Promised Land, but he is obviously, too, the Prodigal Son. And it was in this condition of anguished helplessness, when, as he would reflect, he "had been beaten into the semblance of some kind of humility by misery and confusion and secret, interior fear," that he was able to recognize the gracious offer of God's own life, which is Love. As he began to accept that offer, he "walked in a new world."[83] As Reinhold Niebuhr emphasizes with St. Paul, "the old, the sinful self, the self which is centered in itself, must be 'crucified' " before the new self that lives in and for others can be born.[84]

Christian Conversion as Love of Neighbor

As we have seen, this gift of God's love was extended first of all through Merton's friends. In the same way, with the help of the baroness, one of Merton's first responses to God's call was concern for the poor of Harlem—for his neighbor. Like Rahner, Dom Marc-François Lacan emphasizes that the faith of Christian conversion must be realized in love of neighbor. Because Jesus, in Matthew's version of the Last Judgment, invites us to see him in the least of the little ones who are his brothers, the Christian is not to ask "Who is my neighbor?" as if some people could be excluded from our love. Christian conversion implies a conversion in the way one sees.[85] So, in the parable of the Good Samaritan, Jesus turns the question around: "How will I show that I am a person's neighbor, whoever that person may be?" "By being merciful." To be merciful is to be perfect like the Father. Lacan points out how in Matthew's version of the Beatitudes the merciful are connected with those who search for justice. But this justice is not simply the human justice of loving those who love us; it is the transformed justice of universal love and forgiveness without limit. The root of this transformed justice is the humility which Jesus, the model of true justice, calls his disciples to: "Shoulder my yoke and learn from me, for I am gentle and humble in heart." Humility, indeed, is at the heart of the new law: "If anyone wants to be first, he must make himself last of all and servant of all." In so doing, the disciple will be imitating the Son of Man, who "did not come to be served but to serve. . . . " It is this loving service of the neighbor in the daily lives of his disciples that Jesus points to in the image of the cross: "If anyone wants to be a follower of mine, let him renounce himself and take up his cross and follow me."

Christian Conversion and the Transformation of Social Structures

Loving service of the neighbor, then, is the concrete form taken by the moral dimension of authentic Christian conversion. In order to specify this moral dimension for the contemporary world more sharply, Gustavo Gutierrez has insisted on the need for a spirituality of liberation which focuses conversion to the neighbor on "the oppressed person, the exploited social class, the despised race, the dominated country." For Gutierrez, Christian conversion means committing oneself to the liberation of the poor and oppressed. It means not only committing oneself generously, but lucidly, realistically, concretely, "with an analysis of the situation and a strategy of action."[86]

Taking his lead from social analysts such as Paulo Freire, Gutierrez emphasizes that the "conversion process is affected by the socioeconomic, political, cultural, and human environment in which it occurs. Without a change in these structures, there is no authentic conversion." All conversion requires a break—and not just in the private sphere of personal piety. "We have to break with our mental categories, with the way we relate to others, with our way of identifying with the Lord, with our cultural milieu, with our social class, in other words, with all that can stand in the way of a real, profound solidarity with those who suffer, in the first place, from misery and injustice."[87] This view was strongly endorsed by the document of the 1971 Synod of Roman Catholic Bishops, "Justice in the World." Because sin exists not only in personal consciousness, but just as powerfully in unjust social structures, the bishops declared: "Action on behalf of justice and participation in the transformation of the world fully appear to us as a constitutive dimension of the preaching of the Gospel, or, in other words, of the Church's mission for the redemption of the human race and its liberation from every oppressive situation."[88]

What, then, is the relationship between the radical personal reorientation I have called Christian conversion, and the transformation of unjust social structures? In 1968 the Roman Catholic bishops of Latin America addressed a key aspect of this question at their Medellín Conference: "The uniqueness of the Christian message does not so much consist in the affirmation of the necessity for structural change, as it does in the insistence on the conversion of men which will in turn bring about this change."[89] On this basis, Peter Henriot answers our question this way: "First personal conversion, then conversion of structures; but no authentic personal conversion without genuine commitment to change structures."[90] Though certainly correct in affirming a connection which insists on genuine social commitment, this view's incompleteness oversimplifies the issue.

Coming at the question from the opposite direction, the bishops of the 1971 Synod stressed that the desire for justice "will not satisfy the expectations of our time if it ignores the objective obstacles which social structures place in the way of conversion of hearts."[91] This point makes clear the inadequacy of any "first, then" sequential connection. Personal conversion does demand the transformation of social structures. But the transformation of social structures is also required for personal conversion. The Gospel calls us to work for both simultaneously. Conversion gives a new sense of how personal and social life must be changed if they are to be faithful to God's love. Ultimately, of course, this private/public dichotomy is untenable; society is not a collection of discrete individuals. Persons are social, through and through; and society is personal.[92] Private conversion is really no conversion. Authentic Christian conversion is fully personal; it is thus shaped by, and shapes, the structures of its social context. This is not meant to discredit partial conversions; persons are not transformed totally in even the most intense moment. The point, rather, is to recognize the limits of any conversion, and to press for its expansion into the fullness of one's life.[93]

Indeed, recognition of the limits of a conversion experience, and the necessity of expanding it, is one way of stating the fundamental Christian insight that conversion is not just a momentary, once-and-for-all experience; that authentic Christian life requires continuing conversion. As Curran points out, the vitality and dynamism of the Christian life demands continual openness to the call of God and neighbor. Even while the Christian shares in the work of bringing God's reign to final perfection, he or she remains a "spiritual schizophrenic," at once just and sinful. Thus the Christian needs continual growth, through the redeeming work of overcoming sin by love, toward complete union with God and neighbor. For if God's reign is already present, the eschatological dimension of Christian faith also insists that neither it nor self-transcendence is ever fully realized in this life.[94] By its very nature then, the reality of Christian conversion is never complete, but always moving toward the open horizon that is absolute future.

Empirical Criterion of Conversion: Doing God's Loving Will

Our brief consideration of the theological perspective on Christian conversion brings us back full circle to William James' psychological approach to conversion. Despite significant differences, both views agree that the ultimate test of a conversion is in its living. James, as we saw, was interested in judging a conversion not in terms of its origin, but empirically, by its fruits for life. And this, finally, is the biblical criterion, too. The mark of Christian authenticity is not saying "Lord, Lord," but doing God's will. And for Jesus, as Hans Küng rightly emphasizes, "God wills nothing but man's advantage, man's true greatness and his ultimate dignity." God's will, then, is nothing for himself; it is simply "man's well-being." Jesus' radical identification of God's will and human well-being means that God cannot be seen apart from men and women. To be for God is to be for one's neighbor. If the "universal and final criterion," as Küng says, is "man's well-being,"[95] then the test of Christian conversion can be nothing else than the empirical one of love for one's neighbor.

For Jesus, of course, the call to love one's neighbor has no limits, as we have noted. To follow Jesus means to be the servant of all. Indeed, a radical transformation is necessary in one's understanding to have any sense at all of what God's will requires of us in our loving commitment to the neighbor's good. Human thoughts are not God's thoughts. It is not an easy saying, therefore, that follows Jesus' rebuke of Peter in Mark's Gospel. To follow Jesus in loving service is to lose one's life. But only the person who loses his or her life in loving service will save it. Therefore, as Lacan points out, to follow Jesus is "to walk in a direction diametrically opposed to that which men spontaneously follow."[96]

Such a radical turn from the spontaneously chosen path to follow God's will in Jesus clearly heads one beyond a moral conversion. The genuine Christian conversion involved in such a following of Jesus quite definitely starts one along the path to the profound reorientation of a life centered in God's love that I earlier called religious conversion. As Rudolf Schnackenburg puts it the greater justice demanded by Jesus was a "religious demand, calling on man to hand himself over to the God who was greater than him and to be subject to him in obedience to his call and in readiness to become pure in heart and radical in action, but also in trust, that he will help and save him."[97] In one's response to Jesus' demand for unconditional service, the reign of God that is still to come becomes a present reality. As Böckle strongly emphasizes, the fundamental decision to respond to Jesus is in the final analysis, of course, a matter of faith, and therefore is a response to a call which is not "simply a demand, but primarily a gift."[98]

When Rahner, discussing this religious quality of Christian conversion, speaks about trustingly accepting one's "existence in its incomprehensibility and ultimate unmanageableness as incomprehensibly meaningful, without claiming to determine this ultimate meaning" or to have it under control, and of successfully "renouncing the idols of [one's] mortal fear and hunger for life," he is pointing to the possibilities in the power of God's gift for the lives of those who risk the first step of response in leaving all behind and following Jesus.[99] Where that faithful response can lead one is the subject of the next chapter.

Christian Conversion and Development

At this point we might return to our earlier question and ask how Christian conversion relates to development. Rosemary Haughton, in her brilliant study, *The Transformation of Man*, argues that formation and transformation have nothing in common, are essentially different. Though they never meet, transformation is dependent upon formation, in that "without the long process of formation there could be no transformation." Still, "no amount of careful formation can transform." Haughton's basic point, then, is that "Transformation is a timeless point of decision, yet it can only operate in the personality formed through time-conditioned stages of development, and its effects can only be worked out in terms of that formation." Within this relationship Haughton sees the dilemma of a contradiction: "good formation . . . is necessary if a person is to be able to respond to the demand for the decision to love. Yet if this formation is really good . . . it may, just because it is good, prevent the person from being aware of the need for repentance and decision." As a result, "no change of heart, no transformation, will be possible," for, in Haughton's view, transformation "can only occur when formation breaks down. . . ."[100]

Haughton highlights a central issue dramatically, but key elements of her formulation require examination. First, developmental theory has made it clear that Haughton is correct in her emphasis on a required breakdown. Even stage change within a developmental pattern is a response to breakdown at a lower level. Here we could not have a better example than Merton. And, of course, in this model the possibility of stage progression at any point is dependent on earlier development, just as Haughton maintains about transformation. But what does developmental theory suggest about Haughton's "contradiction"—that good formation militates against transformation? A person well established in conventional moral patterns, for example, may resist openness to other views, and consequent development. But it makes no developmental sense to suggest that a less developed person would be a better candidate for growth.

The problem here is not one of "contradiction," but of simple human fact. No one wants to change a more or less effective and comfortable pattern of living. Only a serious—in the case of Christian conversion it is perhaps no exaggeration to say *deadly* serious—challenge from one's interaction with the human environment will occasion change. There will, of course, always be some kind of resistance. A child of concrete operations may offer only mild resistance to an educational challenge to move to formal operations. An adult with good reading skills will likely present greater resistance to the change required by "speed reading" methods. It should be no cause for amazement, then, that resistance escalates astronomically when the issue is not reading ability, but the very substance of one's personal moral life—and when the challenge is not to a minor adjustment, but to the total reorientation of one's life. Again, Merton is the perfect example here. At center stage in this existential drama, of course, is personal choice and freedom. And all too many of us, when confronted with the demand of conversion to risk who we are in order to become who we can be, will choose to remain who we are. This is not to say that development works against conversion. Rather, through development we come to the difficult edge of conversion and, rather than risk the dangerous leap, we refuse in favor of the safe and the comfortable. To argue that the better developed person will be less likely to risk the leap is to miss the essential point that the less developed person cannot even be challenged by the same leap, cannot, in other words, face the possibility of Christian conversion in the same serious sense. To give up everything when you have nothing is not the act of a hero, but of a joiner.

To speak of "formation" in Haughton's sense involves more than structural or functional development, of course. Both formation and transformation refer to the concrete totality of the moral person, to character.

Clearly, Christian conversion involves a new set of images, symbols, values constituting the *effective central* interpretative story in one's life. In this sense, Christian conversion brings about a transformation in the concrete shape and texture of one's life, in one's character.

To this extent, Christian conversion, like conversion to any other new story, is clearly a *change in content*. Indeed, for Fowler, change in content is the very meaning of conversion, as distinct from structural stage change, or development. Fowler sees conversion or stage change occurring with or without each other.[101]

Character, the concrete shape and texture of personal conscience, involves more than content, however. Character is also a matter of structure. For, as concretely personal, character involves not just content of a story in a general way, but as specified in this particular person in terms of structural development. Just as the meaning of justice differs developmentally, so, too, for example, does the meaning of love which stands at the center of the Christian story. Fowler has no problem agreeing with this position, despite his identification of conversion with content change.

Discussion in the previous and present chapters has made it clear that Christian conversion involves more than content change. From the perspective of content or story, one must say that Christian conversion introduces not just a new story, but a new *kind* of story, a story with its own intrinsic requirements for cognitive, affective, and moral transformation. Authentic Christian conversion demands that one see, feel, and act in a new way. One must be morally converted, but moral conversion is not first of all choosing new values (content), but choosing value as one's criterion of choice. One must be affectively converted, but affective conversion is not first of all loving someone or something new (content), but letting love become the central reality, the dynamic principle of one's life. One must be cognitively converted, but cognitive conversion is not first of all knowing something new (content) but of understanding—and taking possession of—one's knowing, and thus oneself, in a new way.

The fact, however, that cognitive, affective, and moral conversions occur outside of the Christian context suggests that finally Christian conversion is only a matter of content. But the suggestion is tempting only until one realizes that the essential content of Christian conversion is a unique integration of these three conversions in the Gospel of Jesus. Conversion demands a break—not just with this or that, but first of all and most radically with our total orientation, to the neighbor, and, through the neighbor, to God. The point of Jesus' indirect method of preaching in parables, of course, is precisely this, not to teach a new doctrine, but to turn every doctrine about life and love upside down. In genuine Christian conversion, then, one does not simply learn a new doctrine about life or love (content), but through the life and love of Jesus one begins to understand the paradoxical truth that life is love, that the only truly self-fulfilling life is the life given up—even to death—in loving one's neighbor; through a relationship with God in Jesus one begins to embrace this truth; and through the following of Jesus one begins to live this truth.

Beyond any doctrine, this cognitive, affective, moral reality exists only in the transformed being of those who have experienced cognitive, affective, and moral conversions. Indeed, as doctrinal content alone, this Christian truth is reduced to the dead stuff of catechisms and pious posters, and finally—to the honest eye—is not paradoxical, but simply impossible, absurd.

Christian conversions will differ, of course, according to one's point of personal development. But from this developmental perspective, we can say that Christian conversion requires at least the previous acquisition of basic formal cognitive operations, a successful identity integration reaching toward intimacy, and moral reasoning of a conventional level. Typically, then, Christian conversion would minimally require the development of advanced adolescence. Childhood Christian conversions, for example, make no developmental sense. Even ordinary horse sense should suspect crediting a person we judge too immature for marriage with the ability to commit his or her life fully to God in Jesus. In sum, the peculiar content of Christian conversion requires advanced structural development, just as the higher levels of structural development analyzed by Kohlberg and Fowler dictate content.

From the angle of conversion and content, now, we see again, as we noted from the perspective of development and structure in Chapter 3, that at the highest stages structure and content come together. Any adoption of a Christian perspective that is not accompanied by the minimal personal development specified above is a merely verbal or at best conceptual reality supported by emotional enthusiasm, not the integrated cognitive, affective, and moral transformation of one's personal being that is the authentic Christian conversion demanded by the Gospel. In the terms that we noted in Chapter 4 about cognitive, moral, and affective conversions, in genuine Christian conversion one's being is transformed so radically that one begins to follow Jesus in a direction diametrically opposed to the spontaneous, instinctive way of narcissistic self-fulfillment. One commits oneself to and seriously engages the personally reflective life of love. In Christian conversion, of course, serious commitment does not mean grim determination. As Häring stresses, the good news is the possibility of returning to God's unconditional love; this transformation to a life of love is experienced as a joyous homecoming to the integral life our underdevelopment/sin had been frustrating.

FOLLOWING JESUS TOWARD RELIGIOUS CONVERSION

This chapter has focused on Merton's youthful conversion to Christianity in order to concretize through a specific example the moral dimension of Christian conversion. We have seen how the affective, cognitive, moral, and faith dimensions of Merton's life were transformed through his discovery of God and his response to God's love. Psychological and theological interpretations allowed us to appreciate Merton's conversion as a fundamental decision, a radical reorientation of life in terms of the values concretely embodied in the person of Jesus. Truly Christian conversion, we noted, is never merely moral, but through its response to God's love in Jesus always includes a religious quality. Love of God through love of the neighbor perceived as Jesus is the Christian version of an affective-cognitive-moral conversion which wrenches a person out of self-absorption and throws him or her into a caring love of the least of the brethren. Such a conversion of life, of course, is never finished. So to suggest that Merton's youthful Christian conversion of 1938–41 is only the beginning of what Elena Malits has called his "transforming journey" is not to diminish its reality and significance. It is, rather, to recognize the necessity of following the continuing journey which will bring Merton to the possibility of full religious conversion: absolute surrender in a total, unqualified love of God. For Christian conversion is not just another step along one's set path. It is an about-face which sets one on a new, previously unknown path, following the footsteps of Jesus. To follow Jesus along that difficult path in constant fidelity is not just to learn more about God's love, but to discover the loving God in the depths of one's own being, as Jesus did. Merton, the autobiographer, realized that with his youthful commitment he "had entered into the everlasting movement of that gravitation which is the very life and spirit of God: God's own gravitation towards the depths of His own infinite nature, His goodness without end."[102] The next chapter will explore the effects of that gravitational field on Merton's life.

Life comes without warning.

Lieh Tzu

6

CHRISTIAN CONVERSION: THE RELIGIOUS DIMENSION

Christian conversion is essentially an *invitation* to a life not only dedicated to the love of neighbor but focused and empowered by the mysterious presence of God at its vital *center*. Though it requires the fundamental cognitive, affective, moral, and faith transformations of one's being discussed in the previous chapter, it goes beyond them. Indeed, this radical redirection of human life is less a fulfilling accomplishment than a challenging offer: the gracious offer of God's own loving life, and the challenge to allow that love to move in from the edges and corners of our lives to take possession of our hearts and permeate our very beings. As a cognitive, affective, moral, and faith transformation of our lives, in other words, Christian conversion not only sets us in a direction marked by the prints of Jesus' sandals, but calls us to respond to the demands of the journey with the same radical openness to divine mystery which characterized Jesus' response to his Father.

The life of authentic Christian conversion, then, is not simply a reasonably realistic human life guided by an ideal of love. It is a life struggling with the revolutionary dynamism of Jesus' life of love without limits, a dynamism that explodes every comfortably conventional idea about human life and love. As such, Christian conversion must be seen as the beginning of an ever more profound journey into the mystery of God's love—the journey of religious conversion. Beyond any specific demands of the moral life, this revolutionary journey of divine transformation is the paradoxical reality disclosed in Jesus' parables.

JESUS, PARABLES, AND RELIGIOUS CONVERSION

The Parable as Invitation to Religious Conversion

We referred to Jesus' parables at the end of the preceding chapter, but there the consideration of Christian conversion was limited to a conventional context, which by its very nature is incapable of handling the literally world-shattering potential of the parable. Indeed, from a Gospel perspective, it is the parable's precise design and purpose to shake the foundations of our safe and comfortable world of convention, forcing us to the dangerous edge of the postconventional precipice where reality admits no illusion of security.

In his theological study of story, *The Dark Interval,* John Dominic Crossan points out that parables, when they have not been disguised as pious lessons by the moralisms of conventional preaching, are enigmatic, unpleasant, disturbing, unnerving. Freed from moralistic distortion to hit their target, parables typically provoke a response like this: "I don't know what you mean by the story, but I'm certain I don't like it."[1] The point of "The Good Samaritan" parable is not simply that love means helping a stranger (even an enemy) on the road. If that were the point, a "Good Jew" would have been more effective. But the priest and Levite pass by. The man who proves himself a neighbor is not a "Good Jew" but the *despised* Samaritan. We, for whom "Samaritan" has come to mean "Good Samaritan," must make an appropriate contemporary substitution. But for Jesus' audience the Samaritan in this role was clearly too much to accept.

Parables, Crossan tells us, are meant to challenge, assault, indeed subvert the "way things are" in the secure, comfortable world we have carefully built for ourselves by suggesting that our ways, the "way things are," may not be "God's ways." Unlike the religious myths, stories, and allegories that fundamentally support and legitimate the "way things are," Jesus' parables play the radically religious role of undercutting or delegitimating our world as we think it must be by prodding us to think the unthinkable. "You have built a lovely home, myth assures us; but, whispers parable, you are right above an earthquake fault."[2] Just as most Californians resist thinking about earthquakes, most all of us resist really listening to parables. Because if we did listen, our lives might never be the same again.

If we were to really listen to the parable of "The Prodigal Son," for example, and let it touch us, how could we ever return to and take seriously again the conventional world of common sense where hard work, perseverance, and loyalty—not pleasure seeking, laziness, and dissipation—are rewarded? No, it is much easier to listen with a hard-headed common sense and pass judgment on the father: "Very forgiving and generous, but to a fault, and not really fair."

We simply do not need the kind of disorientation that parables would cause, if given a chance. They would rob us of our solid, secure world without offering a replacement, only vague hints about a world to come—more a nightmare than a dream—in which the despised, poor, weak, and oppressed are given primacy of place over the loved, rich, strong, and oppressing, and in which humility and sacrifice of self-interest are honored, leaving no room for pride and self-righteousness. Unlike pietistic moralisms, then, parables are interested not in comforting but in threatening. Having robbed us of the certainties of our given world, they would leave us at the brink of relativity, naked and totally vulnerable before the divine mystery that is God. No wonder, then, that religion has moralized parables beyond recognition; vulnerability and the courage it demands have never been big items in the religious goods line.

Jesus as the Parable of Religious Conversion

Unfortunately for Christians who would be honest with themselves, however, there remains the stubborn fact that Jesus not only taught in parables but lived a parable.[3] In his life, death, and resurrection Jesus lived out *the* Christian parable which stands before every believer as a challenge to the ultimate religious conversion.

Of course, if Jesus is the parable of the Christian life, and if the parable is essentially an invitation, a challenge to conversion, we are finally led to ask, as Donald Gray has, whether Jesus himself experienced conversion.[4] If conversion is understood, as it often is, as the renunciation of a previous life of sin, it is outrageous, from a Christian perspective, to suggest that Jesus might have experienced a conversion; but there is no reason to limit the meaning of conversion in this way. If one does not attribute a pregiven, static perfection to Jesus, then one may presume that as he advanced in wisdom, age, and grace, he not only experienced normal personal development but also faced the normative human conversion possibilities. If Jesus did, indeed, experience a conversion, there is no direct mention of it in the New Testament. However, contemporary theologians have interpreted some Gospel events as pointing to such an occurrence. John Dunne, for example, sees three key turning points in Jesus' life, all connected with John the Baptist: Jesus' meeting with John, the Baptist's imprisonment, and finally his death.[5]

Was Jesus' baptism by John just a pretense, or did he truly come to John ready to undergo the baptism of repentance? What the Gospel does tell us, Dunne reminds us, is that through the symbolism of voice and vision, Jesus experienced unconditional acceptance from God. Jesus, who did not presume to be his own judge, either to condemn or approve himself, "came ready to accept condemnation of his past and received instead unconditional acceptance."[6] Such an experience of acceptance can clearly effect a profound transformation in a person's life. Indeed, according to Hugh Montefiore, "Jesus' experience at his baptism, so far as it can be recovered from the gospel records, seems in many respects akin to the psychological effects of a sudden conversion. There was a sudden and intense personal experience of God. There was a new awareness of personal status with God, a call to a new way of life and the acceptance of that call. There was, in fact, a re-orientation of his whole personality."[7] While the Gospels supply no data for a truly psychological portrait of Jesus, it seems clear, at least, as Gray points out, that "At the time of his baptism Jesus moved from one life-style to another; he gave up an earlier and long-standing way of life as no longer satisfactory in order to take up a new and perilous way of life that now seemed to him imperative."

Could it be, asks Gray, that Jesus, impressed by John's preaching, had "himself repented, not in the sense of turning away from a life of sin, but rather in the sense of reordering the priorities which had previously governed his behavior?" Is it possible, Gray sums his question up, that Jesus had "undergone a conversion through the ministry of John the Baptist, a conversion which led him to take up a ministry which, at least in the beginning, was understood as a continuation of his teacher's ministry?"[8] There is no historical evidence to answer these questions with any certainty, though an affirmative answer would clearly help us to understand why, for example, the people of Nazareth responded to their home town boy the way they did.

Our point here, however, is not to answer the question of Jesus' conversion with historical certainty, but to ask about its appropriateness. Given the parabolic nature of Jesus' life and teaching as a call to conversion, could anything be more fitting than that his own life be a paradigm of conversion? Could there be any better lesson of the absolute need of conversion than the process that took Jesus from his baptism through the agonizing disillusionment of failure in his ministry to the final defeat of the Cross? The public life of Jesus stands as a monument to the failure and utter defeat of reliance on one's own strength which alone can lead to the surrender of absolute autonomy in the acknowledgment of one's radical dependence on the power of

God. And this, of course, is the core of religious conversion. The story of Job tells us that the conversion of the just person is not from evil to good, but from self-centeredness to God-centeredness: allowing God to take possession of one's being through a free surrender of absolute autonomy.[9] But seen as a process of conversion, nothing shows better than Jesus' life the absolute need of such total surrender, and nothing portrays its efficacy more powerfully than his resurrection. For his own disciples, indeed, conversion can be said to be one with their experience of him risen.[10]

But even if Jesus himself experienced no conversion, no transformation of life, still, his life is full of clues for anyone who would understand the depths of religious conversion. To follow these clues in concrete detail, we will soon turn to the experience of the adult Thomas Merton. But first we must consider the possibility of such religious conversion from the developmental perspective.

DEVELOPMENT TOWARD RELIGIOUS CONVERSION

Chapters 2 and 3 attempted to integrate the cognitive, affective, moral, faith, and self perspectives on personal development. This integration deliberately did not include a relatively new dimension of Lawrence Kohlberg's approach: the possibility of a metaphorical seventh, or religious, stage of development. The present context of religious conversion is the appropriate point to complete that integrated view by correlating Kohlberg's suggestion of a religious "Stage 7" with James Fowler's perspective on adult faith development, Erik Erikson's notion of integrity, Robert Kegan's view of the Interindividual self, and Bernard Lonergan's analysis of religious conversion interpreted as a radical transformation of a person's entire life.

Adult Development and "Stage 7"

The idea of a religious stage of life is not new among psychologists. It has been some fifty years since Carl Jung suggested that the second half of life is defined by its concern with essentially religious questions, questions about the ultimate meaning of life.[11] And, as we have seen, Erikson's psychosocial theory of development, influential for more than a quarter of a century now, specifies its last stage of development in the older person in the broadly religious terms of a crisis of integrity vs. despair. Kohlberg's approach, while developmental, is not that of dynamic depth psychology, but is cut, as we have noted, from the entirely different Piagetian cloth of cognitive-structuralist analysis. That Kohlberg raises the question of a religious stage from this structuralist perspective, then, is a significant step.

During the first phase of Kohlberg's research and theorizing (a period of some fifteen years), he viewed the highest or postconventional stages of moral reasoning as rooted in the radical cognitive breakthrough effected by the emergence of formal operational thought. And he considered these highest stages to be attainable by the adolescent. Even then, of course, he understood advanced cognitive development as only a necessary, not a sufficient, condition for postconventional moral reasoning.

During a second phase, at least since 1973, Kohlberg, now paying more attention to the issue of specifically *adult* moral development, and with new data from empirical studies, has found it necessary to revise his earlier position regarding the age at which postconventional stages are attainable. Now he views the postconventional stages, as we reviewed them in Chapter 2, as first appearing no earlier than young adulthood. In addition to the cognitive development of formal operations necessary for the kind of radical questioning capable of relativizing the "givenness" of conventional morality, Kohlberg now says that the postconventional "construction of principles seems to require [adult] experiences of personal moral choice and responsibility usually supervening upon a questioning period of 'moratorium'."

In contrast to his earlier view which distinguished structural stages very sharply from the Eriksonian stages based on social role-defined developmental tasks, Kohlberg now recognizes that his revised "view of adulthood moral stages linked to experience of personal choice suggests a rapprochement between Erikson's stage theory of adult development" and his own "more cognitive-structural stage theory."

It is in this context of reflection on adult development, theoretical revision, and rapprochement with the functional stages of Erikson's psychosocial theory, then, that Kohlberg finds himself speculating about a "more ontological or religious seventh stage which might correspond to Erikson's stage of integrity-despair."[12]

As Kohlberg understands Erikson's psychosocial theory of personal development, the ideal person resolves the adult crisis of generativity vs. stagnation at the seventh psychosocial stage and becomes a fully *ethical* adult. This ideal, in contrast to the earlier stages of childhood moralism and adolescent ideology, corresponds, according to Kohlberg, to his own postconventional moral Stage 6.[13] Despite this significant degree of normative development, however, there still remains for Erikson's adult a final "task that is partly ethical, but more basically religious (in the broadest sense of the term religious), a task defining an eighth stage whose outcomes are a sense of integrity versus a sense of despair." This crisis of integrity, as Kohlberg sees it, is not the problem of moral integrity, but "the problem of the integration and integrity of meaning of the individual's life and its negative side, despair, which hovers around the awareness of death," what Loder calls the experience of nothingness, existential negation. While he sees the integrity of the self as a psychological issue, Kohlberg asserts that the integrity of the meaning of the self's life is a philosophical or religious question. Thus he characterizes his purely hypothetical discussion of a Stage 7 in his own theory as "primarily an effort to make Erikson's concept of integrity more explicitly philosophical."[14]

This speculative interest in a seventh stage can be seen as Kohlberg's attempt to deal with the fact that while his highest stage of moral development is constituted by universal principles of human justice "which can be defined and justified without reference to a specific religious tradition," the moral heroes he cites as models of Stage 6—from Socrates to Martin Luther King—were also "deeply religious men." This fact raises for Kohlberg a fundamental question about "the relation of the development of religious faith to the development of moral principles."[15]

As Kohlberg understands the structural stages of moral development, even Stage 6 "offers only an imperfect integration or resolution of the problem of life's meaning." Thus, even after the attainment of what Kohlberg calls "an awareness of rational universal human principles of justice," there still remains for a person the fundamental question about the very justification of justice: "Why be just in a universe full of injustice?" For Kohlberg this is equivalent to asking "Why be moral?"[16] In other words, Kohlberg is saying that even the clear perception of universal ethical principles, which overcomes the typical skeptical doubts of moral relativism, cannot finally answer the loudest skeptical doubt of all, the radical question "Why be moral?" While the principled orientations of postconventional morality provide valid rational responses to the late adolescent Stage $4^{1}/_{2}$ moral relativism which sees through the arbitrary "givenness" of conventional morality, these orientations cannot provide adequate solutions to the existential problem, "Why be moral?" Kohlberg views the Stage 5 social contract response, that one pursues one's own happiness within a context of regard for the rights and welfare of others, as essentially a compromise. And while he sees Stage 6 as providing an even more adequate response to moral relativism than Stage 5, Kohlberg admits that its uncompromising recognition of a non-relative ground of value offers a less satisfying answer to the question "Why be moral?" For there is, he says, "a sharper contrast between ethical principle and egoistic or hedonistic concerns than there is between the social contract and hedonism."[17]

Ultimately, an answer to the question "Why be moral?" entails, as Kohlberg sees it, the question "Why live?" or "How face death?" In other words, ultimate moral maturity demands an answer to the question of the meaning of life, a question which is not essentially moral at all, but ontological or religious. Further, according to Kohlberg, not only is the question of life's meaning not an essentially moral question, but it cannot be answered on purely rational grounds, as he claims moral questions can.[18] Still, Kohlberg uses what he calls a purely metaphorical notion of a Stage 7 to point to what he regards as "meaningful solutions" to the religious question which are "compatible with rational science and principled ethics."[19]

All Stage 7 solutions to the religious question involve non-egoistic or non-dualistic contemplative experience. While sometimes expressed theistically in terms of union with God, the essence of this contemplative experience is, as Kohlberg puts it, "the sense of being a part of the whole of life and the adoption of a cosmic as opposed to a universal humanistic (Stage 6) perspective."[20] Kohlberg finds such Stage 7 religious solutions in the writings of the classical religious and metaphysical traditions from Plato to Teilhard.[21] There he sees the cosmic perspective often beginning in the feeling of despair, as one begins to perceive human life as finite from the perspective of the infinite, the meaninglessness of life, for example, in the face of death.

But despair is only the first phase of a cosmic perspective. The resolution of the despair which Kohlberg calls Stage 7 "represents a continuation of the process of taking a more cosmic perspective." This leads to a state of mind in which "we identify ourselves with the cosmic or infinite perspective, itself; we value life from its standpoint." Such a state of mind is temporarily achieved even by people who are not "religious" when, on a mountaintop or before the ocean, they sense the unity of the whole and themselves as part of that unity.[22]

Kohlberg claims that this "experience of unity, often treated as a mere rush of mystic feelings, is also associated with a structure of conviction. . . . One may argue," he says, "that the crisis of despair, when thoroughly and courageously explored, leads to a figure-ground shift which reveals the positive validity of the cosmic perspective implicit in the felt despair."[23]

Kohlberg sees something of a parallel between this structural shift of figure and ground and that involved in the earlier moral crisis of relativism. The relativistic Stage 4 ½ can occur, he says, "only because there is [already] a dim apprehension of some more universal ethical standard in terms of which the cultural code is relative and arbitrary. To thoroughly and consistently explore the crisis of relativism is to de-center from the self, reverse figure and ground, and to see as figure the vague standpoint of principle, which is the background of the sense of relativity."[24] Just as relativism is overcome by an insight into the universal ground of value implicit in relativism, so Kohlberg sees despair being overcome by the contemplative experience of cosmic unity implicit in despair.

Kohlberg suggests that it is difficult to justify the philosophical ad-equacy of Stage 7's logical structure because, as he says, "there is no single Stage 7 ontological-religious structure, no universal religion, as there is in some sense a single Stage 6 structure of universal ethical principle."[25] For this reason Kohlberg asserts that his notion of a re-ligious Stage 7 is not a stage in the strictest structural sense, but must rest more on personal testimony than on structural analysis.

"Stage 7" and Fowler's Universalizing Faith

What are we to make of this development in Kohlberg's thought, this expansion of the notion of personal development from the moral into the religious dimension? As interesting and important as this the-oretical breakthrough is, there appears to be a serious problem with Kohlberg's perspective. The apparent difficulty involves Kohlberg's understanding of the way the religious dimension is related to the moral in personal development.

One easily gets the impression from Kohlberg's metaphorical Stage 7 that the religious dimension is something new added on to a previous achievement in moral development—literally a seventh reli-gious stage added to six existing moral stages. Moral development seems to occur first, independently of any religious influence, along the lines of a strictly secular-humanist model. This, of course, is exactly the way Kohlberg has always explained the development of six stages of moral reasoning: a natural process of cognitive-affective develop-ment through social interaction, without reference to any religious fac-tor. To be sure, Kohlberg never denied the influence of religious ideas on moral development; he simply did not recognize religion as having any intrinsic involvement in the development of the *structure* of moral reasoning. Now religion has been introduced as the culminating "stage" of this natural process of moral development.

While this sequence of "first morality, then religion" may accu-rately represent the development of Kohlberg's own perspective, one must wonder how faithfully it characterizes the development of persons who have been explicitly nurtured in the tradition of a religious community from their earliest years. How is the religious perspective of these persons to be understood in relation to their moral development? Kohlberg, in fact, has recognized the importance of this question by referring in his recent work to the research of James Fowler on faith development, and by reflecting on the relationship of Fowler's structural stages of faith to his own stages of moral reasoning.[26]

What, Kohlberg asks, is the relationship between the development of religious faith and the development of moral principles, between faith stages and moral stages? He answers that it is "almost self-evident that they would roughly parallel one another," because "a considerable portion of a child's orientation to divinity, to the ultimate source, power or being in the universe is a moral orientation." But if we may "expect a parallel development of faith stages and moral stages," the critical question for Kohlberg is "whether moral development precedes (and causes) faith development or vice versa." Although he does not have research data on the question, Kohlberg hypothesizes that "development to a given moral stage precedes development to the parallel faith stage."[27]

From a psychological viewpoint this hypothesis is based on Kohlberg's judgment that the elaboration of a moral stage into an "organized pattern of belief and feeling about the cosmos" takes a considerable amount of time. Philosophically, Kohlberg shares the view that "faith is grounded on moral reason because moral reason 'requires' faith rather than that moral reason is grounded on faith." In Kohlberg's reading of the issue, "those who believe that morality derives from faith usually believe that moral principles are based on divine authority or divine revelation." But, as he sees it, "universal moral principles cannot be derived from faith because not all men's faith is, or can be, the same."[28]

Kohlberg's position on the relationship between morality and faith, then, is that "ultimate moral principles, Stage 6 morality, can and should be formulated and justified on grounds of autonomous moral rationality," independent of faith. At the same time, Kohlberg recognizes that to live up to such moral principles does require faith, and this is why the great models of Stage 6 morality, like Martin Luther King, are also persons of faith. The faith required to live up to Stage 6 moral reasoning, which is what Kohlberg means by Stage 7, does not redefine the Stage 6 moral principles of justice, but "integrates them with a perspective on life's ultimate meaning."[29]

Although Fowler expresses substantial agreement with Kohlberg on the relationship between faith and morality, he does insist on an important difference. Fowler thinks it is a "mistake to assume that faith is or must be an *a posteriori* derivative of or justification for morality. . . . " He argues, on the contrary, that "every moral perspective, at whatever level of development, is anchored in a broader system of beliefs and loyalties."[30] In his view, even the appeals to autonomy, rationality, and universality involved in Stage 6 moral reasoning are expressions of faith, not made prior to faith. For Fowler, then, faith precedes and is a matrix for moral reasoning.

I think that the difference between Kohlberg and Fowler on this important point can be reconciled if the definition of faith is clarified and a basic distinction is made in terms of its development. In my view, Fowler is correct in asserting that moral reasoning at any stage is always rooted in and expressive of a particular faith perspective—of a person's concrete way of construing his or her relationship to the ultimate conditions of reality. This faith may or may not be explicitly religious; it may, for example, be a commitment to autonomous rationality. Fowler has delineated six different structural stages of faith in this wide, but deeply personal, sense. Kohlberg's specific focus on the structure of moral reasoning has not stressed the development of this basic personal orientation to reality, but it is clearly compatible with it.[31]

At the same time, I think Kohlberg is right in claiming that Stage 6 moral reasoning can (and should) be formulated and justified independently of the explicit beliefs of *religious* faith.[32] He is also correct in characterizing his understanding of a religious orientation as a Stage 7, following upon Stage 6 of moral reasoning. This is because he defines this religious orientation not as just any kind of religious perspective, but as a *postconventional* religious perspective.[33] This position fits in quite readily with Fowler's view of faith development, inasmuch as Fowler has recently correlated his six stages of faith with Kohlberg's six stages of moral reasoning in such a way that Fowler's sixth stage of "Universalizing Faith" comes *after* Kohlberg's sixth stage of universal ethical principles.[34] And this Stage 6 Universalizing Faith is described by Fowler in terms very similar to Kohlberg's Stage 7, which is a nondualistic contemplative experience of being part of the whole of life, of identifying with a cosmic or infinite perspective. There is at Faith Stage 6, says Fowler, "a post-critical at-one-ness with the ultimate conditions of one's life and of being generally," and "participation in the Ultimate is direct and immediate."[35]

Once allowances are made for variations in Kohlberg's and Fowler's use of "faith," then, a consistent pattern is evident in the recent work of both: parallel stages of moral reasoning and faith developing together, with the highest moral stage followed by an ultimate postconventional faith stage (Stage 6 in Fowler's sequence, Stage 7 in Kohlberg's). For both, this ultimate faith stage is a reality of mature adulthood. From this angle of parallel stage development, it is clear that for Kohlberg as well as Fowler, Stage 6 moral reasoning is preceded as well as followed by faith orientations, orientations which may or may not be explicitly religious (in any more or less traditional or institutional sense).

Thus it must be said that Kohlberg's understanding of the relationship between morality and faith-religion does not imply that religion appears in the developmental process only after the highest stage of moral reasoning has been reached. Preconventional or conventional "faithing" prior to Stage 6 moral reasoning can and probably will be religious in some explicit way. In Kohlberg's view what is new about Stage 7 is not simply that it is a religious orientation, but that it is a new kind of religious orientation, a postconventional religious orientation radically different from other religious perspectives. And, as Kohlberg sees it, this Stage 7 postconventional religious orientation is "both dependent upon, and demanded by a Stage 6 orientation to universal human ethical principles."[36] This position introduces a critical distinction among religious perspectives which, in my judgment, is crucial for an adequate understanding of the relationship between morality and religion.[37]

"Stage 7" and Lonergan's Religious Conversion

Is Kohlberg right in claiming that a Stage 7 postconventional religious perspective is dependent upon and demanded by Stage 6 moral reasoning? I think he is, for these reasons.

As we have seen, the link between Stage 6 and Stage 7, as Kohlberg understands it, is the question, "Why be just in a universe full of injustice?" or, quite simply, "Why be moral?" This question can be verbalized by a person at almost any point of development, but, in Kohlberg's view, it "cannot arise on a psychologically serious level until a man has attained moral principles and lived a life in terms of these principles for a considerable length of time."[38] In other words, the question "Why be moral?" can only be asked in its ultimate religious sense by a person who has taken possession of his or her self as a free and responsible autonomous moral subject on moral Stage 6, and attempted to live out a serious commitment to justice and the realization of value in a very concrete way for some time.

What Kohlberg is suggesting here, in my judgment, is the key insight that only the person who has critically realized and attempted to live a life of fully human autonomy can truly experience the radical moral impotence constitutive of human existence. Unless one has realized and appropriated one's self as autonomous, one has no autonomous self to move beyond in a religious identification with a cosmic or infinite perspective, or, in the classical Christian understanding, one has no autonomous self to surrender in a loving union with God. In this sense Stage 7 is dependent on Stage 6. But if one does take critical possession of oneself as autonomous on Stage 6, attempts to live an autonomous moral life of value, and inevitably fails, one may realize the radical inadequacy of absolute human autonomy, and, beyond despair, be open to a totally new experience of one's existence. In this sense, Stage 6 may require, demand, and move one toward Stage 7. Serious attempts at moral living powerfully reveal the limits of the human in existential negation.[39]

In Chapter 4 I argued that the movement to postconventional Stage 6 moral reasoning constitutes a critical moral conversion; here I would suggest that realization of the postconventional religious orientation called Stage 7 constitutes a radical religious conversion.

As distinct from moral conversion, in which one shifts one's criterion for decision from satisfaction to value, religious conversion has been specified by Bernard Lonergan as "other-worldly falling in love," as "being grasped by ultimate concern," as "total and permanent self-surrender. . . . " According to Lonergan, a person's capacity and desire for self-transcendence meets joyful fulfillment when "religious conversion transforms the existential subject into a subject in love, a subject held, grasped, possessed, owned through a total and so an other-worldly love." Beyond all other human loving, "religious loving is without conditions, qualifications, reservations; it is with all one's heart and all one's soul and all one's mind and all one's strength." This lack of limitation in religious loving is realized in "other-worldly fulfillment, joy, peace, bliss. In Christian experience these are the fruits of being in love with a mysterious, uncomprehended God."[40]

This description suggests an understanding of religious conversion not just as a process of becoming "religious," but as a totally radical reorientation of one's entire life. In theistic terms, one turns in such a radical conversion not to religion but to God. One allows God to move to the center of one's life, to take it over and direct it. Persons with an explicitly religious perspective, as well as those without such an orientation, are eligible candidates, therefore, for a religious conversion in this radical sense. Indeed, for the person whose faith takes an explicitly religious form, this ultimate conversion may be best understood, perhaps, as a conversion from religion to God.[41]

While Lonergan's description of religious conversion emphasizes the dimension of unconditional love, for present purposes I will focus on the element of self-surrender. For surrender—or, in classical Christian vocabulary, abandonment—clearly contrasts the radical religious attitude to the orientation of absolute human autonomy. One could argue that even most religious people, despite their explicit affirmations about Divine Providence and God's Will, implicitly attempt to make their decisions and live their lives on the basis of an absolute human autonomy. Most of us, who are in some way religious, not only anguish over those aspects of our lives which we cannot control, but harbor the deepest desire to control our lives totally. We have to admit the fact of external limitations on our self-control, but we refuse to admit, even to ourselves, that our interior autonomy is in any way limited, that when the bottom existential line is drawn we are not the absolute masters of our lives. It is precisely this desire for total control which prevents the radical trust necessary for religious conversion. In the illusion of total autonomy, rather, we look for security by trusting finally in ourselves alone.

Of course there is an appropriate moral autonomy and legitimate demand for self-control. But these are *relative* personal realities based not on the illusion of absolute autonomy, but on the exigencies of responsible human freedom. Indeed, religious beliefs are destructive when they work against the legitimate and necessary autonomy of personal responsibility—when, through passive resignation, everything is left to God. In this case, personal autonomy and responsible initiative are subverted by religious false consciousness; under the guise of loving self-surrender religion alienates the self from its true being as a creative and responsible originating value.

Authentic religious conversion, on the contrary, does not destroy genuine personal autonomy, but preserves and transforms it by taking it up into a new horizon of unconditional love and ultimate concern. Only the absoluteness of personal autonomy is destroyed, revealed as an illusion. Kegan's interpretation of the Stage 5 Interindividual self as appropriately balancing the dynamics of differentiation and integration, the yearnings of independence and separateness, provides in a psychological model of distinct identity and deep sharing a way of understanding not just the compatibility but even mutual necessity of authentic human autonomy and unconditional surrender.

The autonomy of Kohlberg's Stage 6 will be relative or absolute, authentic or inauthentic, then, depending on whether or not a person has experienced a radical religious conversion. Such religious conversion is constitutive of Kohlberg's Stage 7 and Fowler's Stage 6, by their very definitions. At the same time, I would add that there is no reason to suppose that the sophisticated cognitive development of critical, postconventional moral reasoning and faithing is necessary for religious conversion. Religious conversion is related to but is not always the culmination of structural development. In the same way, neither is the advanced cognitive development of critical, postconventional moral reasoning and faithing necessary for the psychosocial maturity concretized in the wisdom of Erikson's integrated older adult.

History provides more than enough examples to convince us that persons of thoroughly conventional morality and faith do experience the genuinely religious realization of their finiteness in relation to an infinite God or cosmos. And these persons may authentically surrender themselves and their (perhaps unspoken) desire for absolute self-control to the infinite whole of which they perceive themselves a significant, if finite, part. Unlike the religious conversion of postconventional persons, this conversion is uncritical, but nonetheless authentic in radically relativizing or de-centering the self. The process is the same; the difference lies in the degree and quality of realized personal autonomy that is surrendered.

Egocentrism is essentially the tacit assumption of the self as the center of reality. If authentic development is a process of de-centering, of moving beyond or transcending the self, religious conversion effects the most authentic, realistic self-transformation insofar as it is a radical de-centering of the self.[42] As God is allowed to take over the center of the self, so the self is liberated—at least in principle—from the prison of its illusory egocentrism. It is in this liberation that we experience the concrete meaning of Erikson's wisdom, of the integrity of life's meaning.

While recognizing that integrity and religious conversion do not necessarily presuppose a postconventional orientation, we must realize of course that a person of uncritical integrity and religious conversion remains vulnerable to all the distortions of false consciousness. Though uncritical religious conversion is not as rare as its critical version, it is not as common as the shift from sin to God that we have called Christian moral conversion.

I have focused on the dimension of self-surrender in religious conversion in order to highlight its contrast to absolute human autonomy. But Lonergan is on the more direct track to the heart of the issue in his emphasis on love. For only the reality of falling-in-love, in my judgment, makes it possible for a person to surrender his or her self in any significant degree; and only the total falling-in-love of religious conversion makes an unconditional surrender of self possible. From a Christian perspective, one may say that a person can surrender the illusion of absolute self-autonomy only because one has experienced, and can trust in, the unqualified love of a person, of a personal God.

From Lonergan's perspective of religious conversion as the fulfillment of a capacity and desire for self-transcendence, the total surrender of oneself in love without conditions can be seen as the ultimate realization of a multidimensional process of self-transcendence, of moving beyond the self, of reaching out to other persons. Such self-transcendence, I am claiming, constitutes the fullness of authentic self-realization.

Perhaps the notion of *gift* captures the essential reality of religious conversion best. One is able to surrender one's self, make a gift not only of one's illusion of absolute autonomy but of one's whole life only insofar as one can recognize one's very existence as a gift of love.

If, from Lonergan's perspective, religious loving has its own distinct dimension of other-worldly fulfillment, joy, peace, and bliss, still he recognizes that "holiness abounds in truth and moral goodness." Religious conversion provides a "new basis for all valuing and all doing good." In no way does religious conversion negate or diminish the fruits of moral conversion. "On the contrary," says Lonergan, "all human pursuit of the true and the good is included within and furthered by a cosmic context and purpose and, as well, there now accrues to man the power of love to enable him to accept the suffering involved in undoing the effects of decline."[43]

Because Kohlberg's sixth and seventh stages require moral and religious conversions respectively, I am suggesting that their relationship is also best understood under this same rubric of dialectical sublation. Religious Stage 7 takes up, preserves, and transforms the positive gains of Stage 6 postconventional moral reasoning, destroying only the illusion of absolute human autonomy which may be associated with Stage 6. While a preconventional or conventional religious orientation may distort or subvert moral reasoning as well as support it and provide motivation for its translation into action, a postconventional religious orientation (of the Stage 7 variety) that is at once both critical and rooted in authentic religious conversion preserves the authentically human dimension of morality, and transforms it by taking it up into a cosmic or divine context where the deepest human desire realizes itself most fully.

Here Stage 6's universal principles of justice are not redefined, but, as Kohlberg puts it, are integrated with a "perspective on life's ultimate meaning," and insofar as that ultimate meaning is experienced as love, the principles of justice are transformed by the power of that love into an authentic ethic of love.[44]

How religious conversion takes shape in the concreteness of an individual life becomes the central question of this chapter as we shift our focus to the adult life of Thomas Merton in the following section.

MERTON AT GETHSEMANI

The Early Years

Thomas Merton entered the Trappist Monastery of Gethsemani in December 1941. A large part of his motivation was the idea of expiation: he was leaving the sinful world to devote himself to penance for his sinful life. For this purpose Merton certainly chose the right place. Nothing could have been farther from the world Merton knew than the Gethsemani of 1941, which was not much different from a Cistercian monastery of 1241, except that its life was probably even more austere—all the better for one who felt he had so much to expiate. The monastery's own motivation for its austerity had a somewhat wider scope: nothing less than radical religious conversion. As the author of *The Seven Storey Mountain,* writing in his fifth year in the monastery, tells us, "The monastery is a school—a school in which we learn from God how to be happy." Since "happiness consists in sharing the happiness of God, the perfection of His unlimited freedom, the perfection of His Love," the monastery's primary lesson is love. Learning to love requires the healing of our true nature, "for at the very core of our essence we are constituted in God's likeness by our freedom, and the exercise of that freedom is nothing else but the exercise of disinterested love—the love of God for His own sake, because He is God." And what is the course of instruction? Since truth is the beginning of love, God must cleanse our souls of their lies before giving us this love. "And the most effective way of detaching us from ourselves is to make us detest ourselves as we have made ourselves by sin, in order that we may love Him reflected in our souls as He has re-made them by His Love." This healing and learning is "the meaning of contemplative life, and the sense of all the apparently meaningless little rules and observances and fasts and obediences and penances and humiliations and labors that go to make up the routine of existence in a contemplative monastery." The point of it all is "to remind us of what we are and Who God is—that we may get sick of the sight of ourselves and turn to Him," so that finally "we will find Him in ourselves, in our own purified natures which have become the mirror of His tremendous Goodness and of His endless love."[45]

This, then, is Merton's view of the life he entered upon in 1941 near the end of his twenty-seventh year. Whether or not he understood it in precisely this way at the time he entered, it is an important statement both as an indication of his perspective (and its limitations) during his early years in the monastery, and as a preview of how his understanding of contemplative life would develop over the ensuing years of his continuing conversion.

Most obvious, of course, is the emphasis not only on purifying but also on detesting and getting sick at the sight of the sinful self. Clearly, freedom to love was the goal, but the guilt built into the long struggle toward conversion was not something that would disappear in a few short years. For Merton, self-acceptance would be a very hard-won victory over the powerful forces of self-contempt and negativity that had entered the monastery with him.[46] At the same time, this early statement reveals that Merton was convinced that "at the very core of our essence we are constituted in God's likeness by our freedom," that God will finally be found "in ourselves, in our purified natures which have become the mirror" of his goodness and love. Here we have the line of the contemplative's inner search for God, as well as an adumbration of what would become Merton's fundamental distinction between the true or inner self and the false or external self. Only in the discovery of one's true self could one find God. Indeed, it is as a journey in search of God in the depths of his true self that the continuing transformation of Merton's life toward the fullness of religious conversion can best be understood. As this search for God in the true self was one of Merton's favorite images of his own life, as well as the central element in his view of the spiritual life, we shall enlist it as our primary guide as we follow Merton's journey of religious conversion.

The Seven Storey Mountain is our key point of entry to Merton's first five years in the monastery, just as it was for his pre-Gethsemani life. In his autobiography, we find the young Merton, still aflame with the zeal of his conversion, throwing himself head-first into the monastic life, delighting as a new postulant in every aspect of the monastery: the Advent liturgy, the deeply interior warmth of the Gregorian chant, the childlike smile of an older monk, the complexity of the habit's fifteenth century underwear. The portrait is one of a wanderer who is profoundly relieved finally to be happily and peacefully at home. As Frater Louis, Merton felt that he was hidden in the secrecy of God's protection: "He was surrounding me constantly with the work of His love, His wisdom and His mercy. And so it would be, day after day, year after year."[47]

Of course, the young monk had not perfectly mastered the spiritual life. As a case in point, the autobiographer describes his sense of secret joy and triumph in anticipating a stay in the infirmary with influenza, just a few weeks after his formal investiture as a full-fledged novice in the Order. "Now at last I will have some solitude and I will have plenty of time to pray," he thought. "And to do everything that I want to do, without having to run all over the place answering bells." He could hardly wait to indulge all the selfish appetites that he "did not know how to recognize as selfish because they appeared so spiritual in their new disguise." Immediately, he tells us, he "jumped into bed and opened the Bible at the Canticle of Canticles and devoured three chapters, closing his eyes from time to time and waiting, with raffish expectation, for lights, voices, harmonies, savors, unctions, and the music of angelic choirs." In fact, he got little more than vague disillusionment. As the autobiographer, writing from the realistic vantage point of five years' experience of monastic life, reflected: "All my bad habits, disinfected, it is true, of formal sin, had sneaked into the monastery with me and had received the religious vesture along with me: spiritual gluttony, spiritual sensuality, spiritual pride."[48] There is really nothing extraordinary here, just the misguided ambition of an enthusiastic novice, unaware of his conversion's limits. Already, though, there is the desire for solitude beyond the ordinary possibilities of the Trappist life, a desire which, over the years, will develop crisis proportions.

More serious a problem than any bad habits that Frater Louis brought with him into the monastery, however, was the shadow or double which had followed him into the cloister: Merton the writer. Through the happy autobiographical portrait of peace and contentment there emerges the problematic question of identity. Simple vows had been made after two years of novitiate, and these, the autobiographer thought, should have divested him of the last shreds of any special identity. But the writer had not made the profession, and he was not about to be put off so easily: "He is still on my track. He rides my shoulders, sometimes, like the old man of the sea. I cannot lose him. He still wears the name of Thomas Merton. Is it the name of an enemy? He is supposed to be dead." But he was perfectly alive, this schemer, this business man, always intruding into the monk's silence with new ideas for books and articles. "And the worst of it is, he has my superiors on his side. They won't kick him out. I can't get rid of him." The strongly positive tone and outlook of the autobiography wanes here in the closing pages as Merton reflects on the significance of this shadow identity for his vocation. "Maybe in the end he will kill me, he will drink my blood. Nobody seems to understand that one of us has got to die. Sometimes I am mortally afraid. There are days when there seems to be nothing left of my vocation—my contemplative vocation—but a few ashes."[49]

In his great struggle with the shadow writer, Merton the monk had reason to think that his superiors were somewhat less than helpful. During the novitiate, for example, when Merton's health failed seriously, his superiors switched him from manual labor to the physically less rigorous task of translating French texts on Cistercian life. And it was not long before they were presenting him with writing projects on Cistercian saints and spirituality. Even earlier in the novitiate, Merton had permission to write poetry and personal reflections. Indeed, when Merton's old Columbia friend, Bob Lax, visited at Christmas 1943, he returned to New York with the manuscript for *Thirty Poems*, about half of which had been composed at Gethsemani. Not long after the publication of that first volume, toward the end of 1944, the Abbot told Merton that he wanted him to continue writing poetry. Since this directive seems to have come completely unbidden, it is not difficult to understand why Merton the monk might feel that his superiors were part of a conspiracy against him and his confessor in the struggle with Merton the writer. One realizes how vaguely the battle lines were drawn, however, when the autobiographer, who tells us he "did not care if [he] never wrote another poem as long as [he] lived," describes his profound reaction upon receiving his copy of *Thirty Poems*: "I went out under the grey sky, under the cedars at the edge of the cemetery, and stood in the wind that threatened snow and held the printed poems in my hand."[50]

Neither the monk nor the writer, of course, was ever to triumph completely in this struggle which would continue for years. Despite serious obstacles, both followed their vocations as faithfully as possible. The great irony in this struggle, more than his superiors' support of the writer, is the unique mutual fecundation which occurred as a result. An excellent case could be made for the thesis that neither the life of the monk nor the writings of the author would have been nearly as deep without the other's strength and vitality. On the basis of his earlier life, one can only wonder how much direction or depth the writer would have had without the discipline and prayer of monastic life. At the same time, the poems and journals and essays and books were the natural way for a monk with writing in his blood to secure footholds in his difficult contemplative ascent. Again, one can only wonder how far the monk would have gone without the writer. It seems clear that the monk's disillusioning struggle with the writer was the key factor precipitating Merton's gradual liberation from the romantic ideal of the monastic life which pervades so much of *The Seven Storey Mountain*. The monastery did not free one from the problems the postulant would like to have left behind in "the world"; in many ways the monastery only heightened those problems, and even added some new ones, as Merton would increasingly discover.

Near the end of *The Seven Storey Mountain*, then, we can mark in Merton the beginning of a movement toward the appropriation of his critical intelligence, a movement toward cognitive conversion which would eventually free him, not from the problem of "the world" or of the monastery but from the alienating authority of an illusory monastic world. Though containing only a few hints of this new critical direction among its hundreds of pages which naively condemn the ugliness, duplicity, and sin of the world and glorify the goodness, simplicity, and purity of the monastery, the autobiography, written substantially in 1946, just a few months before Merton's solemn vows, really constitutes a significant turning point. Despite the fundamentally uncritical stance it betrays, it is the first time we hear the monk's own prose voice speaking about his own experience, rather than the dubbed voice of the earlier pious works on Cistercian sanctity. The new voice would have to discover its proper critical pitch, but it was his own, and it had found its sure starting point, personal experience.

In the Belly of a Paradox

What was only hinted at in the autobiography about his continuing conversion became the main theme of Merton's journal, *The Sign of Jonas*, which covered the next several years (from the end of 1946 to 1952), roughly the period from solemn profession through ordination and the first years of priesthood. The journal's theme is in the title: "Like the prophet Jonas, whom God ordered to go to Nineveh, I found myself with an almost uncontrollable desire to go in the opposite direction. God pointed one way and all my 'ideals' pointed in the other." From the very beginning, as we have seen, Merton's romantic ideal of monastic life focused on solitude, even the "solitude" of the infirmary. The monk's struggle with the writer was precisely over this ideal: writing was an obstacle to solitude. Even when he was "doing a little better" at his writing, was "more peaceful and more relaxed," he still felt that "for myself, I have only one desire and that is the desire for solitude—to disappear into God, to be submerged in His peace, to be lost in the secret of His Face." But it continued to be the clear and consistent wish of the monk's superiors that he should write. And as the projects multiplied, Merton felt more and more divided, more and more torn in different directions. Several years later, as he edited the journal for publication, Merton could say that he felt his life to be especially sealed with the great "sign of Jonas the prophet"—the sign of Jesus' resurrection—"because like Jonas himself I find myself traveling toward my destiny in the belly of a paradox." There was not the comfort of such imagery, however, during the ordeal itself.[51]

With the assurance of Father Abbot that his vocation was right, despite his continuing question of whether Trappist vows would mean the renunciation of the pure contemplative life, Merton made his solemn profession in March 1947. He felt that he had done the right thing, and had given himself as best he could to God, but still the questioning did not stop. It intensified. The dynamics of conversion are like that.

Indeed, little more than a month after his profession we begin to hear Merton seriously questioning himself about the manifestation of God's will in the rule and spirit of Trappist life. "Trappists believe that everything that costs them is God's will. Anything that makes you suffer is God's will." Therefore, he goes on, "If we want something, we easily persuade ourselves that what we want is God's will just as long as it turns out to be difficult to obtain. What is easy is my own will: what is hard is God's will." As a result, "We think we have done great things because we are worn out. If we have rushed into the fields or into the woods and done a great deal of damage, we are satisfied."[52]

A week later, on a day he received two new writing assignments from Father Abbot, bringing the current total to "no less than twelve jobs in various stages of completion," Merton was in a mood to put his questions even more pointedly. "Just because a cross is a cross," he asks, "does it follow that it is the cross God intends for you?" And, "Just because a job is a nuisance, is it therefore good for you?" More specifically, "Is it an act of virtue for a contemplative to sit down and let himself be snowed under by activities?" And finally, Merton asks the hard one that gets to the heart of the problem: "Does the fact that all this is obedience make it really pleasing to God? I wonder. I do not ask these questions out of a spirit of rebellion. I would really like to know the answers."[53] In light of the following curious journal entry from the previous day, one might want to interpret this critical attitude as an aberration, resulting perhaps from infection: "We had a moral theology exam and then my chest was X-rayed." But this is no abberration. It fits perfectly into the pattern of Merton's increasing critical self-possession.

From the perspective of faith development, Merton has clearly made a definitive move into Stage 4, taking up official residence, as it were, in this Individuative-Reflective stage of faithing. We shall see later how he will continue to explore the neighborhood of social consciousness, and even invite his superiors to a belated "house-warming," but all that will essentially be a follow-up to this decisive move. What is evident at this point is the clear emergence from Merton's struggle for identity of an autonomous sense of himself and of his own power of judgment. This emergence of what Fowler calls the executive ego has freed Merton from reliance on external authority. It has also given him the ability to distinguish the fundamental meanings and values of his life from the symbols which carry them, as well as the power to distance himself critically not only from those meanings and values, but also from the structure and institutions of society. It would take some time, but in the years to follow every aspect of Merton's romanticized ideal of the monastic life—indeed, of the Christian life—would fall before this power of critical reflection.

After his vows, the rest of 1947 passed without great event. On November 16, the ninth anniversary of his baptism, Merton prayed, "Take my life into Your hands, at last, and do whatever You want with it." He realized that he had not lived like a contemplative, and that he was still trying to run his own life. "I only say I trust You," he prayed. "My actions prove that the one I trust is myself—and that I am still afraid of You."[54] Quite clearly, here, Merton's prayer reveals the distinctive orientation of an authentically religious conversion, as he recognizes that his own orientation remains one of absolute autonomy.

For Merton 1948 was a year of transition. *The Seven Storey Mountain* was finally published toward the end of the summer, an event which was to change his whole life. He was now "an author." At about the same time there was another, quite different change which would also have great effect on Merton's life: the death of one Abbot and the election of another. Merton had felt very close to Dom Frederic. The kind Abbot had not only promoted his writing, he had blessed and guided him through every phase of his monastic formation. Merton could only wonder what the future would hold with the new Abbot, Dom James.

"The World." In August of this year, Merton left the monastery for the first time since his entrance—a simple six hour trip to Louisville accompanying a visiting superior as interpreter. Editing his journal for publication a few years later, Merton recalled that during the drive into Louisville, he wondered how he "would react at meeting once again, face to face, the wicked world." With the benefit of a few years' distance and hindsight, the editor reports the encounter this way: "I met the world and I found it no longer so wicked after all. Perhaps the things I had resented about the world when I left it were defects of my own that I had projected upon it. Now, on the contrary, I found that everything stirred me with a deep and mute sense of compassion." The editor concludes: "I went through the city, realizing for the first time in my life how good are all the people in the world and how much value they have in the sight of God." The tone of this recollection from some four years' distance differs from the journal's low-key report in a revealing way. "Going to Louisville the other day I wasn't struck by anything in particular. Although I felt completely alienated from everything in the world and all its activity I did not necessarily feel out of sympathy with the people who were walking around. On the whole they seemed to me more real than they ever had before, and more worth sympathizing with." But the beauty of the drive seemed to impress Merton more than the people of the city. "It was nice reciting the office in the car and saying the *Gloria Patri* while looking at the woods and fields. But Louisville was boring. Anyway, the whole thing was a matter of obedience. It meant losing a day's work."[55]

Much would happen to Merton between 1948 and 1952 to account for this difference in tone, as we shall see. But even in 1948 the *experience* was there, if not the critical, reflective possession of it.

A few months later, in January 1949, Merton went into Louisville again to apply for citizenship. Though he found the visit to the city dull, the trip did expose him to the kind of raw, shanty poverty in which so many people lived—and the embarrassing contrast to the "poverty" of Gethsemani was not lost on him. Again, experience of the world was forcing Merton to critically reappraise his romanticized understanding of the monastery as an island of purity and sanctity in a world of ugliness and evil. He might be behind the normative schedule for breaking out of the adolescent ideological perspective of idealism described by Piaget and Erikson, but Merton is clearly moving toward the critical realism of mature, adult judgment, toward full cognitive conversion.

Indeed, only a month later this increasingly realistic attitude is explicit in a journal entry for February 20, 1949, where Merton begins to take a critical stance toward the romantic idealism of his autobiography and early poetry. "My complaints about the world in the *Mountain* and in some poems are perhaps a weakness. Not that there isn't plenty to complain about, but my reaction is too natural. It is impure." The "spiritualizing" of this insight takes nothing away from the honesty of his critical self-understanding. "The world I am sore at on paper is perhaps a figment of my own imagination. The business is a psychological game I have been playing since I was ten."[56]

This attitude stands in sharp contrast to that expressed in *Seeds of Contemplation,* Merton's book of spiritual reflections completed in mid-1948. "Do everything you can to avoid the amusements and the noise and the business of man," he advised. "Keep as far away as you can from the places where they gather to cheat and insult one another, to exploit one another, to laugh at one another, or to mock one another with their false gestures of friendship." Also to be avoided are the newspapers, magazines, radio, and popular music of the world. Though Merton admits that "it is possible to live in deep and peaceful interior solitude, even in the midst of the world and its confusion," this was his practical advice for anyone who would lead a contemplative life. He was convinced that "you will never find interior solitude unless you make some conscious effort to deliver yourself from the desires and the cares and the interests of an existence in time and in the world."[57]

False Self/True Self. This contempt for the world was clearly secondary to the principal theme of *Seeds of Contemplation*: discovering God and one's true self. Indeed, it is in *Seeds of Contemplation* that Merton first makes explicit, in a major way, this theme of discovery which had been and would continue to be absolutely central in his own life. This is not to say that the discovery theme was not present in *The Seven Storey Mountain.* Indeed, the autobiography is the story of a journey of discovery. In *Seeds of Contemplation,* however, with the true self/false self distinction, Merton found the apt metaphor for articulating the discovery's transformational pattern.

At the beginning of *Seeds* Merton characterizes the journey of the authentic Christian life as an escape "from the prison of our own selfhood." This view can be accurately understood as paradigmatic of Merton, however, only in terms of his distinction between the true self and the false self. The prison from which one must escape is the false self. This is clear in Merton's emphasis that this escape is the "only true joy on earth" because through it one enters "by love into union with the Life Who dwells and sings within the essence of every creature and in the core of our own souls." The essential core is the true self.[58] For Merton, then, the point is not simply to escape the self, but to escape the false self in order to reach the true self—and God. This is the business of conversion. Some years later, as we shall see, Merton will focus on this distinction in the rewriting of *Seeds.*

"For me," writes Merton, "to be a saint means to be myself." Sanctity, therefore, consists of "finding out who I am and of discovering my true self." The difficulty with this prescription is that "Every one of us is shadowed by an illusory person: a false self." This false self is "the one who wants to exist outside the radius of God's will and God's love—outside of reality and outside of life." Such a self is necessarily an illusion, but for most of us, it is *the* subjective reality. And in this lies the reality of sin, that the false self, "the self that exists only in my own egocentric desires, is the fundamental reality of life to which everything else in the universe is ordered." Because of the illusion of the false self, then, the truth of life is paradoxical: "In order to become myself I must cease to be what I always thought I wanted to be, and in order to find myself I must go out of myself, and in order to live I have to die."[59]

Because God is love, to be made in God's image is to have love as the reason for one's existence. God is not to be found in an isolated individualism, then, but in others. A person, says Merton, "*cannot enter into the deepest center of himself and pass through that center into God, unless he is able to pass entirely out of himself and empty himself to other people in the purity of a selfless love.*" In the circle of love, then, Merton sums up the dynamics of the spiritual life: "If I find Him, I will find myself and if I find my true self I will find Him." The ultimate truth, of course, says Merton, is that I only "discover who I am and possess my true identity by losing myself in Him."[60]

Merton speaks of a "point at which I can meet God in a real and experimental contact with His infinite actuality: and it is the point where my contingent being depends upon His Love."[61] It is this contemplative point of contact, in absolute dependence upon God's infinite love, that is the radical existential rub, of course. For beyond the lip-service of pious sentiment, who is really prepared to admit absolute dependence upon God? Yet it is only at this intersection of absolute contingency and infinite actuality that a person can meet the real God, not an idol of one's own making. The route to this intersection, unfortunately, is not of our choosing. The way to this contemplative experience of God, says Merton, "lies through a desert without trees and without beauty and without water. The spirit enters a wilderness and travels blindly in directions that seem to lead away from vision, away from God, away from all fulfillment and joy." But who can go this route? Even most good, holy people are not up to it. "As soon as they reach the point where they can no longer see the way and guide themselves by their own light," says Merton, "they refuse to go any further. They have no confidence in anyone except themselves. Their faith is largely an emotional illusion . . . a kind of natural optimism that is stimulated by moral activity and warmed by the approval of other men."[62] This is not the stuff of religious conversion.

It is possible to remain content with such faith, and most religious people do. "But when the time comes to enter the darkness in which we are naked and helpless and alone; in which we see the insufficiency of our greatest strength and the hollowness of our strongest virtues; in which we have nothing of our own to rely on, and nothing in our nature to support us, and nothing in the world to guide us or give us light—then," says Merton, "we find out whether or not we live by faith." Only in this darkness of radical dependence and utter helplessness is the "deep and secret selfishness that is too close to us for us to identify . . . stripped away from our souls," says Merton. "It is in this darkness that we find liberty. It is in this abandonment that we are made strong. This is the night which empties us and makes us pure."[63] And, from all indications, this is the night Merton himself would soon come to face in a particularly harrowing way as he continued his own transforming journey of discovery.

Ordination and Crisis. If 1948, the year Merton completed *Seeds of Contemplation,* was on his own account a year of transition, 1949 was definitely a year of crisis. In 1948 he became "an author"; in 1949 the "author" found himself incapable of writing. Looking back at the period a few years later, Merton could identify several reasons for the author's paralysis. Part of the transition of 1948 was his proximate preparation for major orders—aiming finally toward ordination to the priesthood in the spring of 1949. His mind, of course, was focused on this, not on his writing. Also, he had been writing too much—he was tired and stale. Then, too, Merton the monk was ashamed of the fame that *The Seven Storey Mountain* had brought to "the author." And, finally, as if the author's fame were not difficult enough for the monk, it produced its own "mountain," the burden of fan mail, something the monk's life is not designed to handle. Though the fan mail had the positive effect of letting Merton discover the holy lives of many good people in "the world," for whom he felt a sense of responsibility, the demand it made on his extremely limited work time was intolerable.

As these factors piled up, Merton the writer found himself buried. He was attempting to write what he later described as "a great synthesis of the interior life drawn from Scripture and the Fathers of the Church," but early in 1949 he found himself unable to make any progress, and the project ground to a frustrating halt. Then, on the occasion of his ordination to the diaconate in March, he experienced a "deep spiritual reaction against all this involvement" in the business of writing, and decided to stop trying to be a poet. He realized that he had never really been a good poet, and that to continue writing poetry would be to continue perpetrating an illusion; he saw the decision as a movement toward integrity.[64]

The ordination to the diaconate itself was a singular experience, and had the effect on Merton of interior "dazzlement." He had prayed that the diaconate would bring him the strength to trust God completely. "To trust Him—I wonder if I have ever really done that?" Or had he just said a lot of things about God's power and then trusted in himself instead? Two days after the ordination he writes: "Yesterday and the day before I felt as if I had found a new center. Something I could not grasp or understand: but nothing else in the world seemed worth trying to grasp or understand either. So I grasp nothing and understand nothing and am immensely happy."[65] In trust, Merton surely has his eyes on the target of religious conversion.

The following month Merton was back struggling with his theological synthesis of the interior life. But now, even in the anguish of failure, he can write: "when I tell myself 'I am no writer, I am finished,' instead of being upset I am filled with a sense of peace and of relief — perhaps because I already taste, by anticipation, the joy of my deliverance." On the other hand, he continues, "if I am not delivered from writing by failure, perhaps I may go on and even succeed at this thing, but by the power of the Holy Ghost—which would be a greater deliverance." In any case, he concludes, "whatever happens, success or failure, I have given up worrying."[66]

Indeed, so strong was this spirit of indifference that it extended even to Merton's longing for solitude. "Although it half kills me," he writes, "[since the diaconate] I find myself accepting the idea that perhaps I do not have a purely contemplative vocation. I say 'accept.' I do not *believe* it. It is utterly impossible for me to believe any such thing: everything in me cries out for solitude and for God alone." He found the feeling that he may somehow be excluded by God's love from this solitude absolutely terrible: his soul was being torn out at its very roots by love only to be stopped dead against a blank wall. Yet in all this terror Merton found not unrest or rebellion but happiness and peace, by clinging to the love of God. "Somehow," he writes "I have to give up this thing that I love above everything else on earth *because the love of God is greater*."[67] That which seemed to him clearly the most perfect way in itself to love and serve God had to be given up because it was not the one chosen for him by the God Who loves him.

In this spirit of happiness and peace, and sensing the presence of a huge power, Christ the High Priest, awakening in the depths of his soul like a giant, Merton was ordained to the priesthood on May 26, 1949, the Feast of the Ascension. Priestly ordination was, Merton felt, the "one great secret" for which he had been born. Three days after the ordination, Merton is finally able to write in his journal: "I am left with the feeling not only that I have been transformed but that a new world has somehow been brought into being. . . ."[68]

The summer months following ordination were filled with days of great joy. In June, Merton writes: "The Mass each day delights and baffles me at the same time. This beautiful mixture of happiness and lucidity and inarticulateness fills me with great health from day to day." He felt that the straightfaced liturgy forced him to be simple at the altar, but "in the middle of this beautiful sobriety the indescribably pure light of God fills you with the innocence of childhood." So great was the consolation during these months immediately after ordination that even the work of writing was enveloped in the glow: "At the moment, the writing is one thing that gives me access to some real silence and solitude," where God is immediately found.[69]

This period of consolation was marred by one event which Merton records in his journal for July 17. "The chief thing that happened to affect the history of my existence was this: I was on as deacon for the Pontifical High Mass. Everything was going along fairly smoothly, although it was a hot muggy day. But in the middle of the Gospel I passed out." Perhaps it was just the heat and humidity of the day, though during the experience Merton thought the devil might have had a hand in it. Or was it the power of that waking giant within Merton's soul, which would soon make itself felt in much more terrifying ways. Toward the end of the summer Merton's thoughts fixed on the reality of trust and dependence again as he meditated on the rejection of Christ—even by the holy: "we do not really believe in Him because we want to believe only in ourselves. . . . "[70] Merton knows how formidable an obstacle the sense of absolute autonomy is to religious conversion.

On the first day of September Merton began reading the Book of Job. Ten days later he made this entry in his journal: "Once before I read the Book of Job and got the feeling that I was going to begin living it, as well as reading it. This has happened again." It would be more than a year before Merton would know fully just how accurate he had been in this prediction. The period of extraordinary consolation was over, and Merton was entering a stage of his journey for which Job is one of the few authorized guides. Indeed, so radical was Merton's transformational experience during this latter part of 1949 and throughout 1950 that the transformation he had undergone by the time of his ordination paled in comparison. Looking back on this period as he prepared his journal for publication, Merton could therefore say that "Ordination is only the beginning of a journey, not its end."[71]

The actual journal entries for this period offer only oblique hints about the extraordinary experience Merton was undergoing, but the reflections Merton added at the time of publication leave no doubt about its power. "When the summer of my ordination ended," he recalled, "I found myself face to face with a mystery that was beginning to manifest itself in the depths of my soul and to move me with terror." He could not explain what it was. He did suffer much bad health, but this, it seemed to him, was only "an effect of this unthinkable thing that had developed in the depths of my being." Trying to suggest the reality of this terror which he knew was unexplainable, Merton took this tack: "It was a sort of slow, submarine earthquake which produced strange commotions on the visible, psychological surface of my life." Realizing the inadequacy of his effort, he immediately switches from the geological image to the military and back again to the geological: "I was summoned to battle with joy and with fear, knowing in every case that the sense of battle was misleading, that my antagonist was only an illusion, and that the whole commotion was simply the effect of something that had already erupted, without my knowing it, in the hidden volcano."[72]

At the time, it was almost impossible for Merton to write about this transforming experience, but signs of it do appear at a few points in the journal. He noted, for example, how "lonely and small and humiliated" he felt one day, "not even a real person any more." Memory of a liturgical text supported him, but "Otherwise—feeling of fear, dejection, non-existence." Solitude, he reflected, "means being lonely not in a way that pleases you but in a way that frightens and empties you to the extent that it means being exiled even from yourself." And, again, on another day, he writes of solitude. "It is fear that is driving me into solitude. Love has put drops of terror in my veins and they grow cold in me, suddenly, and make me faint with fear because my heart and my imagination wander away from God into their own private idolatry."[73]

And, again, as always, Merton's reflections return to the reality of trust as he contrasts his loneliness to the loneliness of Christ, who was alone because he was God, because he was everything. "I am alone," he wrote, "because I am nothing. I am alone in my insufficiency—dependent, helpless, contingent, and never quite sure that I am really leaning on Him upon whom I depend." And then he pursues the point to the quick. "Yet to trust in Him means to die, because to trust perfectly in Him you have to give up all trust in anything else. And I am afraid of that death."[74]

Just before Christmas 1949, Merton sensed that things were building up to a deep decision: "A wordless decision, a giving of the depths and substance of myself." When the decision came, it was an experience of liberty and neutrality which could not be written down, for, as Merton explained, "There is a conversion of the deep will to God that cannot be effected in words—barely in a gesture or ceremony. There is a conversion of the deep will and a gift of my substance that is too mysterious for liturgy, and too private." From Merton's fleeting, impressionistic clues one gathers that the experience, at its core, was one of belonging to God. "Standing on rock. Present. The reality of the present and of solitude divorced from past and future. To be collected and gathered up in clarity and silence and to belong to God. . . ." The experience was as elusive as it was profound. Only one day after the experience, Merton found himself writing: "I wish I could recover the liberty of that interior decision which was very simple and which seems to me to have been a kind of blank check and a promise."[75]

Merton realized, as we have seen, that to belong to and trust in God required a death in himself. But in this experience he also realized, most significantly, that "To belong to God I have to belong to myself." The necessary death, then, we must understand, is not the death or loss of the self, but of one's absolute trust in and dependence on the self—a death which is all the more painful because there remains a self to suffer it. On the very day that Merton records his profound interior decision, he notes how deeply he was struck in choir by Psalm 54 (55)—"My heart is troubled within me: and the fear of death is fallen upon me. Fear and trembling are come upon me: and darkness hath covered me." He felt he was chanting something he had written himself; it seemed more his own than any of his own poems. Merton knew why there are so few candidates for religious conversion![76]

This postordination darkness of 1949 continued into 1950, though it was not entirely unrelieved. Indeed, in January, despite the difficulty he was having in writing, Merton felt positive enough to sign a long-term contract with Harcourt, Brace for four books—including the theology of the interior life. He sensed that this contract probably meant the final renouncement forever of his dream for a hermitage. God, he wrote, "will prepare for me His own hermitage for my last days, and meanwhile my work is my hermitage because it is *writing* that helps me most of all to be a solitary and a contemplative here at Gethsemani."[77]

The journal was another matter, however; as the darkness continued the journal became more and more difficult for Merton. At times he would write at length and then tear the pages up; at other times he would go for weeks without writing at all. Finally, in April 1950, he stopped the journal, as he thought, for good. An epidemic of influenza had hit the monastery during Lent, and Merton was sick, in varying degrees, for the whole of the spring. During the worst of it he still struggled to get out of bed in the middle of the night for choir, but he felt humiliated by the attention the sickness made him give to himself. "The terrible thing about sickness is that you tend to think you are sick. Your thoughts are narrowed to your own little rag of a body. And you take care of her. My God, forgive me."[78]

Given the bad health Merton suffered throughout the monastery years, one cannot take his judgment about excessive concern for his body too seriously. Indeed, by the fall of 1950 he wound up in the hospital on two different occasions, first for an examination, then for treatment during most of November. There were stomach problems, and the chest x-rays were not good; rest was required. And for a nose problem, there was the surgical removal of bone and cartilage.

Resolution in Compassion. In December 1950, after a good rest in the hospital, Merton was back in the monastery and feeling much better. His writing block suddenly disappeared, and in just a few months he completed his manuscript on the interior life, *The Ascent to Truth*, which he had been unable to get into for the last two years.[79]

All this was surely connected with the fact that in the same month, as Merton wrote in retrospect, "in the depth of this abysmal testing and disintegration of my spirit . . . I suddenly discovered completely new moral resources, a spring of new life, a peace and a happiness that I had never known before and which subsisted in the face of nameless, interior terror." For the first time, now, as Merton would later reflect, he really began to know what it means to be alone. He "discovered that the essence of a solitary vocation is that it is a vocation to fear, to helplessness, to isolation in the invisible God." Having made this discovery, he wrote, "I now began for the first time in my life to taste a happiness that was so complete and so profound that I no longer needed to reflect upon it. . . . It penetrated to the depths below consciousness, and in all storms, in all fears, in the deepest darkness, it was always unchangeably there"—"real and permanent and even in a sense eternal."[80] Tearing out the false self by the roots in religious conversion is painful, but it makes room for God at the center.

Such interior peace would inevitably make itself felt in various areas of Merton's life. In March 1951, he had the occasion to read again, after ten years, his manuscript of *Journal of My Escape from the Nazis.* He noted that one of the problems with the novel was what he now recognized as his fake, "supernatural" solution to the world and the war: "the whole world, of which the war is a characteristic expression, is evil. It has therefore to be first ridiculed, then spat upon, and at last formally rejected with a curse." He now realized that he had actually come to the monastery in order to find his place in the world, and that it would be sinful to waste his time cursing the world, without distinguishing good from evil, and end up failing in his true purpose. The monastery had been the right kind of withdrawal for him, he thought. It had given him perspective, taught him how to live. And now, he felt, "I owe everyone else in the world a share in that life. My first duty is to start, for the first time, to live as a member of a human race which is no more (and no less) ridiculous than I am myself. And my first human act is the recognition of how much I owe everybody else."[81]

A major opportunity to make good on some of this debt presented itself in May 1951 when Merton was appointed to the newly created position of Master of Scholastics. Since late in 1949, he had been giving conferences for the novices and classes on Patristic theology for the scholastics. Now, however, he had responsibility as Spiritual Director for all the young professed students who were preparing for solemn vows and ordination.

Taking on this serious responsibility, Merton felt that he was the one who would be most formed by the new scholasticate. It was as if he were beginning all over again as a Cistercian, but this time as a "grown-up monk" with his eye on the only essential: God. "Thus I stand on the threshold of a new existence," he wrote in June 1951. Not only were the hero and the author of *The Seven Storey Mountain* dead, the man who had begun the journal had died as well. In fact, Merton wrote, "this journal is getting to be the production of somebody to whom I have never had the dishonor of an introduction."[82]

In November, after six months as Master of Scholastics, Merton took time out from the burdens of his heavy schedule to return to his journal and reflect on his experience with the scholastics. "I do not know if they have discovered anything new, or if they are able to love God more, or if I have helped them in any way to find themselves, which is to say: to lose themselves." But he knew that he had made an important discovery: "that the kind of work I once feared because I thought it would interfere with 'solitude' is, in fact, the only true path to solitude."[83] He realized that one must be something of a hermit before the "care of souls" can lead further into the desert, but once called to solitude by God, every path leads to greater solitude, as long as one allows oneself to be led.

The new desert Merton had been led into through his care for the scholastics was what he called the desert of *compassion*. "There is no wilderness so terrible, so beautiful, so arid and so fruitful as the wilderness of compassion. It is the only desert that shall truly flourish like the lily." In this desert of compassion Merton felt more like a "family man" than ever before in his life, and for this reason, he thought, he had finally become a "mature monk."[84]

At the age of thirty-six, then, Merton was beginning to take the Eriksonian task of generativity seriously in a very concrete and immediate fashion. Through his caring responsibility for the scholastics, Merton's spiritual experience was being transformed into the authentic religious shape of compassion. And from his new desert of compassion, Merton, the "mature monk," was able to articulate the essence of religious conversion. "Do you suppose I have a spiritual life? I have none, I am indigence, I am silence, I am poverty, I am solitude, for I have renounced spirituality to find God."[85]

Two years earlier, when Merton had felt that he was about to begin living the Book of Job, he anticipated what he was about to go through himself as he reflected on Job's experience. What Job demanded, he wrote, was not the answer to the question of suffering in general, but the *Divine* answer to his own personal suffering. And the answer was not anything his friends could tell him, for the answer was one that Job had to experience for himself: God. Not through abstract theologies, but only in the concrete presence of God could Job acknowledge his sufferings to be just. "If we are to have Job's answer," Merton wrote, "we must have Job's vision of God."[86] Two years later, in his desert of compassion, Merton was experiencing his own answer. But God's answer is not like our answers. As Merton brought his journal to a close in 1951 with an Epilogue of nocturnal reflections on his life while taking his turn at the silent Fire Watch, he reminds us that God's answer is more like a silent, unanswerable question.

For the four years following the completion of *The Sign of Jonas* in July 1952, we have no published account of Merton's life. Certainly it was a busy period, as Merton continued to have responsibility for the growing number of scholastics. And, as his correspondence clearly reveals, it was also a stormy period. Despite the new meaning of solitude Merton had discovered in his work with the scholastics, it was not long before his earlier desire for physical solitude re-emerged—provoked, perhaps, by the very burden the duties of being Master of Scholastics placed on him.

By 1955 the urge to a life of greater solitude was so strong that Merton made a formal request for permission to transfer to the Camaldolese monastery at Frascati, Italy, where the monks lived very much as hermits. The Abbot, on the other hand, was certain that it was God's will that Merton should remain at Gethsemani, and, characterizing Merton as a fickle neurotic who did not know his own mind, persuaded the Abbot General to insist that Merton remain at Gethsemani for five years with a moratorium on writing, before any request for a transfer would be considered.[87]

Merton accepted the decision, but this protracted, humiliating episode did little to foster his trust in authority. Indeed, along with earlier censorship problems (most recently with *The Sign of Jonas,*) this kind of personal experience helped to hone Merton's critical powers to an even sharper edge. As he was taking a second look at "the world," then, and reassessing his original negative estimate, so too was Merton continuing to take a second and deeper look at the institution and authority of both monastery and church, and radically revising the post-conversion romanticism of his early monastic years.

At the end of 1955—surely one of Merton's most difficult years in the monastery—the third highest office at Gethsemani became vacant when the Master of Novices was elected Abbot of another monastery. For reasons not altogether obvious, Merton, the man who after four years as Master of Scholastics desired the solitude of a hermit, suggested himself for the job. Even more surprising was the Abbot's rather quick decision to accept Merton's suggestion, giving full responsibility for the all-important formation of the novices to a man whose personal stability he had seriously questioned. Merton proved to be a superb Novice Master, but the difficult job was not made any easier by Merton's critical questioning of the very life to which he was introducing the novices. This akwardness was compounded by the fact that many novices had been attracted to Gethsemani by the romanticized version of its monastic life portrayed in *The Seven Storey Mountain,* written by a still naive, young monk in a very different Gethsemani with a very different Abbot.

The Guilty Bystander

Postconventional Social Consciousness. Merton's years as Novice Master are covered by his journal-like volume of reflections published in 1966: *Conjectures of a Guilty Bystander.* The title is indicative of one of the major developments taking place in Merton's life during the late 1950's and early 1960's—an emerging awareness of, concern for, and involvement in the social and political dimensions of life, especially the issues of racism and peace.[88]

In order to understand this emergence of critical social consciousness in Merton the Novice Master we must recall not only the young Merton's concern about Harlem and the outbreak of World War II before he "left the world" for the monastery, but also his positive reassessment of "the world," his profound transformational experience of 1949–1950, and the continuing growth of his critical thinking, especially as connected with the anguish of his strained relationship with the Abbot. Also, we must add to this constellation of factors Merton's relationship of loving care and responsibility for the scholastics and novices. About the latter, Merton reflected, "Certainly, it has been a great gift of His Love to me, that I am their Novice Master. It is very good to have loved these people and been loved by them with such simplicity and sincerity. . . ." About the novice brothers, in particular, he wrote: "I see they have need of me, and I have need of them, and I am glad to do what I can for them."[89]

When Merton had become Master of the Scholasticate in 1951, he predicted that he would be "formed" by the experience as much as the scholastics would be. In one sense, at least, his prediction was totally accurate. This experience of responsibility for the scholastics and novices—concern for their needs and awareness of the impact of monastic structures on their well-being and development—was Merton's preparatory school for later social commitment. It was precisely the kind of experience which Kohlberg claims is a *sine qua non* for development to a postconventional moral orientation. The strong personal security needs that generated Merton's youthful conversion to Roman Catholicism, along with the authority-centered nature of monastic life, had put a drag on the development of his moral reasoning. But Merton's restless spirit would not be tied down, and once he had broken through the monastic walls of conventional morality into the fresh air of critical inquiry, his moral consciousness needed only the fertile ground of existential responsibility for others in order to take root and finally blossom into a postconventional orientation of autonomous conscience. Merton's development was slow, and at times extremely painful, but the roots went deep and laid a sound support system for a conscience of universal ethical principles whose branches would reach to the most important and difficult social problems of his day. Critical moral conversion, after all, is a major personal achievement, and does not come easily.

By this period Merton's understanding of the relationship between the world and his vocation to solitude had reached a high level of critical sophistication. Near the beginning of his *Conjectures of a Guilty Bystander* Merton reflects: "To be a solitary but not an individualist: concerned not with merely perfecting one's own life (this, as Marx saw it, is an indecent luxury and full of illusion). One's solitude belongs to the world and to God. Are these just words?" Having thus distinguished the solitary from the individualist, Merton characterizes the solitary life. "Solitude has its own special work: a deepening of awareness that the world needs. A struggle against alienation. True solitude is deeply aware of the world's needs. It does not hold the world at arm's length."[90]

Merton's distinction here between solitude and individualism is correlative to a distinction in his understanding of his relationship to the world. The world which now is not to be held at arm's length was, not too many years before, in Merton's mind, "the world" to be despised. Then, "the world" was everything that Merton had left behind when he entered the monastery. Over the years, though, Merton discovered how simplistic this world/monastery dichotomy was, as he gradually realized how much of the world he had brought with him into the monastery. Now he recognized that "the world" to be abandoned is more properly a closed, egocentric self-understanding—a set of "servitudes to certain [idiotic and repugnant] standards of value. . .: The image of a society that is happy because it drinks Coca-Cola or Seagrams or both and is protected by the bomb." Merton felt committed by his whole life to protest against this callous, sensual, cruel, hypocritical "world," this "spiritual cretinism which in fact makes Christians and atheists indistinguishable" wherever it exists, outside or inside the monastery. The world of God's creation, on the other hand, is not to be scorned. "True *contemptus mundi* is rather a *compassion* for the transient world. . . . " How deeply this insight was rooted in Merton's affective life is evident in his account of an experience during a visit to Louisville in March 1958:

> In Louisville, at the corner of Fourth and Walnut, in the center of the shopping district, I was suddenly overwhelmed with the realization that I loved all those people, that they were mine and I theirs, that we could not be alien to one another even though we were total strangers. It was like waking from a dream of separateness, of spurious self-isolation in a special world, the world of renunciation and supposed holiness.[91]

Affective and critical moral conversions go well together, and, as the following years demonstrate, make powerful allies.

This new understanding of a truly human world outside the monastery distinct from the evil "world," and of a genuine life of solitude as being positively oriented to this world, is manifested very clearly by Merton's wide range of reading during this period. No longer limited to the standard monastery menu, Merton's appetite—as indicated by references in *Conjectures*—seems almost insatiable: not just Bloy and Bernanos, Gilson and Maritain, Pascal and Von Hügel, but also Barth and Bonhoeffer, Sartre and Camus, Gandhi and Niebuhr.

During this period Merton also developed a great interest in psychoanalysis, in large part, it seems, for personal spiritual and emotional reasons. He read Freud, and, with the advice of Gregory Zilboorg, a prominent Catholic analyst, many other psychoanalytic authors. So strong was his interest that he was even able to persuade Dom James to allow him to attend one of Zilboorg's conferences on psychiatry and religion at St. John's College in Minnesota.[92]

Merton certainly saw limitations in the psychoanalytic approach, but he clearly realized its power to subvert "a complacent and evasive ethic of good intentions." Since for many people morality is nothing else than the cultivation of "good intentions" and "a good conscience," psychoanalysis meant to them the destruction of all morality. But Merton was convinced that "by showing that the righteous 'conscience' may in actual fact be the mask of a brutal, selfish, cruelly unjust, greedy, and murderous unconscious, and by challenging man to bring his *whole* house in order by the humble acknowledgment of reality in all its depths, psychoanalysis can in fact do Christianity a real service."[93]

For Merton Christian faith was first of all a "principle of questioning and struggle." Not only is it necessary to doubt and reject everything else in order to believe in Christ, but that faith itself must risk "intolerable purifications" and testings. Merton therefore perceived the crisis of Christianity to be most acute "where fundamentalist and conservative superstitions seek at all cost to defend the shallow and subjective 'good intentions' and conformity to the superficial legal demand against all deeper understandings of one's real hidden motivations." His conviction was clear that "good intentions" are "only good as long as they are faithfully re-examined in the light of new knowledge, and in the light of their fruits."[94] Once discovered, the critical edge of cognitive conversion is relentless.

In opting against an ethic of subjective "good intentions" and for an ethic focused on "objective results," Merton was not simply arguing against the egocentric subjectivism of a preconventional orientation in favor of the "objectivity" of conventional morality. He saw all too clearly that "good intentions" could find a very comfortable niche in conventional morality. Rather, he was finally beginning to argue forcefully for the principled objectivity of a postconventional moral orientation beyond the limitations of conventional "good intentions," for the necessity of critical moral conversion.

No one seems to have had a greater influence on Merton's appropriation of a principled moral orientation than Gandhi, whose "doing the truth in charity" norm Merton identified with the New Testament standard of doing all things in the name of Christ. In reflecting on Gandhi's ethics, Merton wrote: "Of one thing we must be persuaded: good action is not by any means a mere arbitrary conformity to artificial social norms. To conform is not to act well, but only to 'look good.' " In contrast to this conventional conformity, Merton had no doubt that "There is an objective moral good, a good which corresponds to the real value of being, which brings out and confirms the inner significance of our life when we obey its norms." At times, of course, in order to obey these norms of objective good, it will be necessary to go against social norms. But acting in accord with the norms of objective good "integrates us into the whole living movement and development of the cosmos, it brings us into harmony with all the rest of the world, it situates us in our place, it helps us fulfill our task and to participate fruitfully in the whole world's work and its history, as it reaches out for its ultimate meaning and fulfillment."[95]

Merton regarded freedom for such principled morality as the deepest and most fundamental need of the human person, and therefore as inseparable from authentic religion: "the ability to say one's own 'yes' and one's own 'no' and not merely to echo the 'yes' and the 'no' of state, party, corporation, army, or system." Surely Merton had been through enough in his own life to realize acutely that the "system" in question could just as well be monastic and ecclesiastical as any other. In some instances, of course, there are external attempts to deny this deep personal freedom. But Merton was especially concerned about the enemy within. God gives us the freedom to make our own lives and the grace to live happily in our different situations, but we are ashamed to do so. And the reason, says Merton, is that we need one thing more than happiness: we need approval, which destroys our capacity for happiness. "For in the United States, approval has to be bought—not once, not ten times, but a thousand times over every day." We seek happiness by being "thought of" kindly by others while thinking kindly of them, in "a diluted benevolence, a collective illusion of friendship." Merton calls it an illusion because he realizes that to seek happiness is not to live happily, that one finds happiness by not seeking it. "The wisdom that teaches us deliberately to restrain our desire for happiness enables us to discover that we are already happy without realizing the fact."[96] This is the wisdom that liberates us from our prison of needs to respond to the demands of a principled life of post-conventional morality.

For Merton, nothing illustrated the human necessity of the truly principled orientation of critical moral conversion more than the story—in all its chilling absurdity—of Adolf Eichmann, the sane, honest, respectable man who in his appeal to his moral virtues, to his obedience, brought contempt on all morality. Merton recognized that the condemnation of Eichmann fell not on him alone but on the whole of society. Eichmann had absolutized the relative virtues of conventional morality into unconditional principles. However, it was not the absolutizing of the relative, but his ruthless and fanatical devotion to his pseudo-absolutes that distinguished Eichmann. Merton was probably overly optimistic in his insistence that human decency will never again accept a morality of principles that does not demonstrate an "existential respect for the human reality of each situation," but he was clearly calling for nothing less than a Stage 6 morality of universal, principled justice rooted by its very nature in the dignity of each human person.[97]

The lesson of the Eichmann story was not lost on Merton, who feared that monastic life was excessively oriented to passive obedience and submission to authority, and artificially cut off from authentic concern for the world. Already he was doing what he could to see that he and his novices did not truly become guilty bystanders. For he believed, as he was later to write, that "The monastic community is deeply implicated . . . in the economic, political, and social structures of the contemporary world. To forget or to ignore this does not absolve the monk from responsibility for participation in events in which his very silence and 'not knowing' may constitute a form of complicity."[98] No longer the smug and socially irresponsible recluse who wanted nothing to do with the despicably evil world, Merton is now exercising a morally principled attitude whose responsibility extends to the foundational structures of society.

The social dimension and principled quality of Merton's mature, critically converted moral orientation is probably best illustrated by his commitment to the cause of world peace, especially on the issue of nuclear warfare. In the preceding chapter we noted how Merton dealt with the issue of war back in 1941, just before he entered the monastery. Although he had been personally inclined to view killing in war as insupportable on Gospel grounds, Merton, the new Catholic convert, made his decision to register for the draft on the basis of the Church's officially approved just war theory. His moral reasoning then was clearly an advance over the days of his Communist peace protests, but it was just as clearly conventional, still tied to the authority of the ecclesiastical system.

Twenty years later, however, with the United States and Russia head to head in a nuclear arms race which, after much study and deliberation, he judged to be immoral, Merton took a public, independent stand which directly challenged church as well as government authority. Merton felt that many Christian leaders, in their knee-jerk reaction to the threat of atheistic Communism, were as irresponsible in their enthusiastic support of nuclear overkill as were the pragmatic politicians, for whom the moral issue was irrelevant.

Merton's writing on the response required of a Christian in the face of nuclear threat to the very existence of humanity very clearly manifests an autonomous moral perspective. "We must try to remember that the enemy is as human as we are. . . . [We] must be reminded of the way we ourselves tend to operate, the significance of the secret forces that rise up within us and dictate fatal decisions. We must learn to distinguish the free voice of conscience from the irrational compulsions of prejudice and hate. We must be reminded of objective moral standards, and of the wisdom which goes into every judgment, every choice, every political act that deserves to be called civilized." As Merton specifies the conditions for such a perspective, we recognize the self-creative elements of a critical moral conversion. "We cannot think this way unless we shake off our passive irresponsibility, renounce our fatalistic submission to economic and social forces, and give up the unquestioning belief in machines and processes which characterize the mass mind. History is ours to make: now above all we must try to recover our freedom, our moral autonomy, our capacity to control the forces that make for life and death in our society."[99] A clearer call to postconventional responsibility for our world can hardly be imagined.

There was no doubt about Merton's own response to this call to moral, political authenticity. He became something of a leader within the opposition to the nuclear build-up as he published a stream of articles on the issue. This was not a popular stand to take, especially in the early 1960's, but Merton had to speak out. Even his superiors' attempt to silence him on the topic of peace—the same year as Pope John XXIII's *Pacem in Terris*—had only temporary success; on this issue his voice could not be still. Indeed, before long, this critically converted, autonomous moral voice would be speaking out as one of the early opponents of the United States' involvement in Vietnam. The high-pitched, untrained moral voice of the young Communist which had changed into that of the conventional young Catholic, and had slowly matured through years of monastic silence, had in the early 1960's finally found its authentic postconventional pitch.

Religious Relativization of Autonomy. If it is clear that by the early 1960's Merton had developed an autonomous principled moral consciousness in touch with the fundamental social and political realities of the time, it is equally clear that he understood this moral autonomy to be in no way absolute. Indeed, Merton saw the illusion of absolute human autonomy as perhaps the fundamental distortion of human living. "Man, thinking of himself as a completely free autonomous self, with unlimited possibilities," he wrote in *Conjectures*, "finds himself in an impossible predicament." True, it seems that "He is 'as a god' and therefore everything is within reach. But it turns out that all that he can successfully reach by his own volition is not quite worth having." The fact of the matter, Merton emphasizes, is that "What he *really* seeks and needs—love, an authentic identity, a life that has meaning—cannot be had merely by *willing* and by taking steps to procure them."[100]

Rather, Merton is persuaded, "The things we really need come to us only as gifts, and in order to receive them as gifts we have to be open." We have to embrace "the natural readiness, the openness, the humility, the self-forgetfulness that *renounce absolute demands, give up the intransigeant claim to perfect autonomy*, and *believe in life*." Therein, of course, lies the rub. But the Merton who insists on responsible moral autonomy has no hesitance in saying that "In order to be open we have to renounce ourselves, in a sense we have to *die* to our image of ourselves, our autonomy, our fixation upon our self-willed identity."[101]

The spiritual bottom line, for Merton, then, is "the surrender that seeks faith in God as a gift that is not our due, and that is willing to suffer great indigence and peril while waiting to receive it."[102] This demands the recognition that one is not absolutely alone, that one lives by and for others, that one is not free to live and die for oneself alone. We would cling to our absolute autonomy, though, in order to protect our illusion of absolute freedom. In *New Seeds of Contemplation* Merton exposes this self-defeating illusion by zeroing in on the paradoxical and liberating truth of human freedom: "[A]s long as you pretend to live in pure autonomy, as your own master, without even a god to rule you, you will inevitably live as the servant of another man or as the alienated member of an organization. Paradoxically, it is the acceptance of God that makes you free and delivers you from human tyranny."[103]

When Merton speaks of "acceptance of God" here, he means much more, of course, than the superficial acknowledgment of God which all too many religious persons call faith. The surrender of one's claim to absolute autonomy demands the total trust in God which comes only from the radical personal transformation I have called religious conversion.

Merton's reading in Protestant theologians, especially Dietrich Bonhoeffer, helped him to understand the problem of absolute autonomy and ultimate surrender in the explicit terms of conversion. In its simplest and most obvious form, the great Christian issue is the conversion of the sinner to Christ. But the genuine grace of the Protestant Reformers, in Merton's mind, was to raise the question of conversion in its most radical form—the conversion not of sinners but of "the good," of those who are "tempted to believe in their own goodness and their own capacity to love," and who therefore "think they have no further need to be saved and imagine their task is to make others 'good' like themselves."[104]

The Protestant theologians may have been thinking primarily of the surface piety of the good bourgeois Christian, but Merton's reflection on the archetypal good man, Job, and on his own experience following ordination, had brought the truth of their fundamental insight home to him in the most vivid way. Even the authentically good person may very well be living the illusion of absolute, autonomous independence. Conversion to a morally good life is finally not enough. "For conversion to Christ is not merely the conversion from bad habits to good habits, but *nova creatura*, becoming a totally new man in Christ and in the Spirit." Responsible moral autonomy is required of the Christian, in other words, but there is more. Authentic moral autonomy must be relativized in the surrender in faith of its illusory claim to absolute independence. For Merton this is central to the basic Christian faith that "he who renounces his delusive, individual autonomy in order to receive his true being and freedom in and by Christ is 'justified' by the mercy of God in the Cross of Christ."[105] And this is the Christian version of radical religious conversion.

Merton discusses both the necessity of realizing moral autonomy and the necessity of renouncing delusive, individual autonomy, but he discusses them separately, without clearly distinguishing or relating the autonomy in question in each case. My suggestion of religious conversion as a relativizing of the absolute is not present in Merton's own discussions.

The True, Inner Self. Where we can get a clue of how Merton *might* have understood the relationship of these different perspectives on autonomy, however, is in his fundamental distinction between the true self and the false self, briefly considered earlier. Returning now to this basic theme in Merton's interpretation of the spiritual life should also help us to understand why surrender of autonomy is so difficult, even—or especially—for the genuinely good person.

In 1960 when Merton sat down to revise *Seeds of Contemplation* he realized that too much had changed in his life in the dozen years since the first writing to allow anything short of a "completely new book." The first book's ideal of isolated solitude had been exploded by Merton's relentless search for reality. Solitude now was face to face with the reality of the world. In *New Seeds,* therefore, God's will is understood much more concretely as the demands of truth and justice, mercy and compassion, for the rights and needs of others. Merton now thematizes the tragic anguish of doubt he has experienced in such authentic solitude—how deep, inexpressible certitude of genuine contemplative experience "mercilessly examines and questions the spurious 'faith' of everyday life, the human faith which is nothing but the passive acceptance of conventional opinion."[106] And in place of the earlier contempt for the world there is now the clear recognition that obstacles to our union with God are not in the world of his creation, but in the gods of our own false selves. Even the saint takes a natural interest and enjoyment in the created world. Thus the earlier distinction between true self and false self becomes sharper. No longer must we simply escape from the prison of our *selfhood;* more precisely, it is from the prison of our *false self* that we must be liberated through religious conversion.

The false self is now further specified as the superficial consciousness of the external self, which is irreducibly opposed to the "deep transcendent self that awakens only in contemplation." The superficial "I" of the external self is our empirical self and our individuality, but it is not our real self, not the "hidden and mysterious person in whom we subsist before the eyes of God." The external self is not spiritual, not eternal, but frail and evanescent. Contemplation is precisely the awareness that the superficial "I" of this external self is really "not I" which occurs in "the awakening of the unknown 'I' that is beyond observation and reflection." In the contemplative experience, says Merton, there is no superficial Cartesian *cogito* and no *ergo* but only *Sum,* I am. He means this, of course, not as a "futile assertion of our individuality as ultimately real, but in the humble realization of our mysterious being as persons in whom God dwells. . . ."[107]

To say that we are "born in sin," Merton explains, means precisely that we come into the world with a false self. As an effect of what Christians call the "fall," each of us is alienated from our inner self which is the image of God. Our true inner self, the "person," must be saved from that "abyss of confusion and absurdity which is our own worldly self," the external, empirical self, the ego. "The person must be rescued from the individual."[108]

Merton does use strongly judgmental language about the external self in claiming that "The creative and mysterious inner self must be delivered from the wasteful, hedonistic and destructive ego that seeks only to cover itself with disguises." But his last word on the subject at the end of New Seeds is the advice that "we must not deal in too negative a fashion even with the 'external self,' " which, though unsubstantial, is not by nature evil. Even the unsubstantial appearances of transient existence are ineffably valuable as the media in which we apprehend the presence of God in the world. Although Merton cautions us to remember that we are more than the external self we appear to be, he recognizes that God respects our ego, and that we must "act, in our everyday life, as if we were what our outer self indicates us to be."[109] Indeed, if we create the true self working together with God, as Merton maintains, then it is precisely the empirical "I" or external self which is called to the responsibility of sharing with God in this self-creation.

If we associate the at least implicit claim to absolute autonomy with the false, external self, and if we understand authentically human, relative autonomy as proper to the true, inner self, we may be able to secure a useful vantage point within Merton's perspective from which to distinguish and relate the two autonomies he discusses, and thus reach a clearer understanding of religious conversion. One major obstacle to the successful execution of this tactic remains, however: an adequate understanding of the relationship between the true and false self. Merton's spatial images of inner and outer are initially helpful but finally offer little to understanding. At times, for Merton, the true self, though hidden, already exists, and is to be discovered. It is not merely an ideal self that we imagine. Still, we must actively create the true self together with God, in Merton's view.

An important clue as to how the relationship between these different selves is to be understood is found in one of Merton's major, but unpublished, studies on contemplation, "The Inner Experience." In this 1959 manuscript, Merton points to the wholeness of the inner self by stressing that it is "not a part of our being, like a motor in a car." Rather, the inner self is "our entire substantial reality itself, on its highest and most personal and most existential level." The inner self, Merton continues, is "like life, and it is life: it is our spiritual life when it is most alive." And the life of the inner self can communicate "a new life to the intelligence in which it lives, so that it becomes a living awareness of itself. . . ." As a fundamental form of life, the inner self "evades every concept that tries to seize hold of it with full possession." Still, the reality of this life is not inaccessible to us, as "every deeply spiritual experience, whether religious or moral, or even artistic, tends to have in it something of the presence of the interior self."[110]

Merton's characterization of the inner self as the "highest and most personal and most existential level" of our being suggests that his understanding of the reality of the inner self (as well as of the external self and the relationship between them) can be illuminated by reference to Bernard Lonergan's analysis of the personal subject's radical drive for self-transcendence as it manifests itself on successive levels of consciousness. If we identify Merton's image of the true, inner self with Lonergan's drive for self-transcendence which is sometimes realized in reasonable judgment, responsible decision, faithful commitment, and genuine love, we can understand how Merton's true self is both already existing (though hidden) and to be created. In simplest terms, the true self exists as *drive* for self-transcendence, but is still to be fully created as an *actually* self-transcending person (though each of us is somewhere along in the process). In this view, of course, the false, external self is simply the personal subject regarded precisely as failing in self-transcendence. There is no unnecessary multiplication of selves, just the personal subject responding or failing to respond to its fundamental dynamism for self-transcendence.

Within Lonergan's analysis, then, Merton's true self is the personal subject fully alive on the highest level of responsible, existential, indeed, religious consciousness. In its deepest sense, the true self is this fully conscious personal subject as cognitively, morally, affectively, and especially religiously converted. While even the subject who has experienced critical moral conversion may cling to the illusion of absolute autonomy, the true self is most fully realized in its surrendering to God's love in religious conversion the claim of absolute autonomy. That this correlation of Merton's true self with Lonergan's self-transcending subject is accurate at least as a first approximation is supported by Merton's reflections in "The Inner Experience." Paradoxically, he says, though the inner "I" is the sanctuary of our most personal solitude, the "awakening of the inner self is purely the work of love, and there can be no love where there is not 'another' to love. Furthermore, one does not awaken his inmost 'I' merely by loving

God alone, but by loving other men."[111] We will continue this consideration of the true, inner self and its correlation with self-transcending subjectivity in the following section's discussion of Merton's Zen experience, as we attend to the nature of the "I" and its relationship with God.

First, however, we might pause to bring together basic aspects of our discussion on the religious dimension of Christian conversion. At the end of Chapter 4 I suggested that the common pattern of moral, cognitive, and affective conversions can be found in the shift from the instinctively spontaneous to the reflectively personal. On the basis of the present discussion, I would now suggest that religious conversion, too, can be understood in terms of this same basic pattern. Christian religious conversion is a fundamental shift from the instinctive but illusory assumption of absolute autonomy, the spontaneously defensive posture of radical, self-sufficient egocentrism, to the reflective openness and personal commitment of love in the total surrender of self to God. The realistic recognition that one's very being is a gift of love prompts the loving gift of one's entire life.

The Zen Hermit

The 1960's were years of much physical suffering for Merton, as one problem after another made its mark on his deteriorating health. In 1966 he finally underwent surgery to fuse two vertebrae in an attempt to deal with one of his most painful conditions. Despite prolonged bad health, however, Merton persevered in his journey of conversion. Most significant at this point in Merton's journey was an emotional involvement with a young nurse that began during his hospitalization. Though short-lived, this experience was overwhelming, and seems to have secured for Merton his ability to love and be loved.[112]

One of the most important developments of the 1960's for Merton was the establishment of a "hermitage" at Gethsemani. Back in the 1950's the Abbot had suggested that something like this might be possible as a solution to Merton's intense desire for physical solitude. Nothing came of the idea, though, until 1960 when a small cinder-block house was constructed some distance from the monastery buildings for use as an ecumenical meeting place. Merton received permission to spend time at the house. At first the time was very limited, but then more and more was allowed, until he was actually living there by 1965. In that year, as part of monastery reorganization, he was relieved of his duties as Novice Master because of his bad health. Even then the building had no plumbing or electricity, and was heated only by a fireplace; but for Merton it was the hermitage he had long desired, and the peaceful solitude it offered more than made up for its physical shortcomings.

But the monk seeking contemplative solitude was still not alone. Merton's determination not to write books notwithstanding, the writer continued to produce articles, collections, and revisions in prodigious numbers. Though a final settlement may never have been reached, by the early 1960's Merton seems to have arbitrated a fairly successful compromise between the demands of monk and writer—a contract he could realistically live with in peace. In the Preface he wrote for the 1962 *Thomas Merton Reader,* he observed that for him most of the hardship of monastic life had been connected with writing. But, in contrast to earlier years, he no longer wanted to deny the writer: "It is possible to doubt whether I have become a monk (a doubt I have to live with), but it is not possible to doubt that I am a writer, that I was born one and will most probably die as one." Merton still found this fact disconcerting, even disedifying, but he now accepted it as his vocation: "It is what God has given me in order that I might give it back to Him." Having suffered through years of painful negotiations with monk and writer, Merton could now see his writing in the authentically religious terms of "accepting life, and everything in life as a gift, and clinging to none of it. . . ."[113]

Indeed, Merton now realized and accepted the fact that his whole life was almost totally paradoxical. "It is in the paradox itself, the paradox which was and still is a source of insecurity, that I have come to find the greatest security. I have become convinced that the very contradictions in my life are in some ways signs of God's mercy to me. . . ." Merton knew that peace does not come in the realization of one's fondest dreams. "Paradoxically, I have found peace because I have always been dissatisfied. My moments of depression and despair turn out to be renewals, new beginnings." Merton, having persisted through many years of agonizing tensions, without capitulating to the easy but simplistic solution, realized that only in struggling do we find peace: "All life tends to grow like this, in mystery inscaped with paradox and contradiction, yet centered, in its very heart, on the divine mercy."[114]

In a letter a few years later, Merton viewed this paradoxical character of life from the perspective of what we earlier called cognitive conversion. Reality is paradoxical, of course, only in terms of our expectations. We expect, even *demand,* that reality be simple, clear, certain. But reality refuses to cooperate. We suffer, Merton thinks, "from the disease of absolutes. Every answer has to be the right answer and, not only that, the final one. . . . All uncertainties are intolerable. But what is life but uncertainties and a few plausible possibilities? Even the life of faith, in practice, is full of contingencies, and rightly so. That is why it is a life of faith. And its certainties are dark, not absolutely clear."[115]

This more relaxed style of Merton's cognitive stance, at greater ease with paradox and uncertainty, was the fruit of many influences at work over a long period—contemplation, surely, being not the least. One of the most important influences on Merton's continuing cognitive conversion, however, was his Zen experience. As Merton's reading expanded into different areas during the 1950's, one of the new areas of sharpest interest was the spiritual wisdom of the Orient—especially Zen.[116] If the most obvious results of Merton's voracious reading in this new area took the form of essays and books (and permission for a secret 1964 trip to New York to visit the aged and ailing Zen scholar, D.T. Suzuki), the most significant, perhaps, was the ongoing transformation of Merton's critical consciousness.

The personal events we traced through the 1950's, and especially Merton's clearly autonomous, principled stance on moral issues, particularly that of peace, leave no doubt that Merton had experienced a cognitive conversion leading to the radical appropriation of his own critical power. Moreover, because this critical cognitive conversion was experienced by a contemplative poet in a context that was not only intrinsically moral but fundamentally religious, there was no possibility of its taking the rationalistic shape of absolute autonomy. Merton was a man who breathed the air of divine mystery. He took critical possession of his autonomous mind, but, with paradox and contingency in his blood, he was immune to the reductionist illusion of an imperialistic rationalism. Merton's converted intelligence was a critical mind that was in search of and would settle for nothing less than the one true Absolute which is *mystery*.

Transcendent Experience in Pure Consciousness. Zen was particularly attractive to Merton, the contemplative influenced by the western tradition of apophatic or negative theology, because of its power to disclose the limits of rational consciousness.[117] Perhaps the area of Merton's thought most clearly influenced by Zen were his ongoing reflections on the true self and the false self. Zen provided him with an even more radical way of understanding the nature of the true self. Merton understood Zen, distinct from Buddhism, as "consciousness unstructured by particular form or particular system, a trans-cultural, trans-religious, trans-formed consciousness." In contrast to the objectified, concept-dominated reflexive consciousness of the isolated

Cartesian ego, Zen, for Merton, is the "ontological *awareness of pure being beyond subject and object,* an immediate grasp of being in its 'suchness' and 'thusness.' " Peculiarly, this non-reflexive, non-self-conscious awareness is beyond the scope of psychological observation and metaphysical reflection. Merton calls it "purely spiritual," having "none of the split and aberration that occurs when the subject becomes aware of itself as a quasi-object."[118]

In order to sharpen the difference between Zen awareness and our ordinary, subject/object understanding of consciousness, Merton says that Zen awareness is "not 'consciousness *of*' but *pure consciousness,* in which the subject as such 'disappears.' "[119] The subject which "disappears" is the false, empirical, ego self. It may be apparent that this perspective is not completely unlike that of Lonergan's distinction between the subject-as-subject and the subject-as-object considered at the beginning of Chapter 2 in which consciousness, as distinguished from objectifying intentionality, is the subject's own non-reflexive *presence* to itself. While this consciousness is the ground of intentionality—objects can be present to us only insofar as we are present to ourselves as subjects—this self-presence of subjectivity ordinarily is lost in our fascination with objects, including, especially, ourselves as objects. In Merton's view, the subject-as-subject emerges on its own terms only in contemplation.

Zen practitioners may not be particularly interested in moving beyond this pure consciousness, but for Merton its special significance is as a "stepping-stone to an awareness of God." Merton could not be more explicit in his contention that "If we enter into ourselves, find our true self, and then pass 'beyond' the inner 'I,' we sail forth into the immense darkness in which we confront the 'I AM' of the Almighty." For Christians there is an infinite gulf between the being of God and the "I" of the inner self, and our awareness of each must be distinguished. Yet, despite this metaphysical distinction, says Merton, in spiritual experience, "paradoxically, our inmost 'I' exists in God and God dwells in it," and in this identity of love and freedom there "appears to be but one Self." The true self is indeed conscious, but it is aware of itself "as a self-to-be-dissolved in self-giving, in love, in 'letting-go,' in ecstasy, in God. . . . " In the emergence of this true self in contemplation, Merton speaks of transcendent experience—"an experience of metaphysical or mystical self-transcending and also at the same time an experience of the 'Transcendent' or the 'Absolute' or 'God' not so much as object but Subject." In this transcendent experience God is realized "from within," but from within a self that is at once lost and found in God. The true self is "no-self" because it is lost in God; inasmuch as it finds its true identity in God, however, it is not an alienated but a transcendent self.[120]

All this is to say that in the transcendent experience there is a "radical and revolutionary change in the subject." For Merton, this radical change in the subject is a "kenotic transformation, an emptying of all the contents of the ego-consciousness to become a void in which the light of God, or the glory of God, the full radiation of the infinite reality of His Being and Love are manifested." Understood in the Pauline sense of a participation in "the mind of Christ," this "dynamic of emptying and of transcendence accurately defines the transformation of the Christian consciousness in Christ."[121] Existential negation is negated in the personal appropriation of the transforming Christ event.

This is the Christian version of religious conversion, the orientation toward transcendent mystery which climaxes one's radical drive for self-transcendence. This culmination of the self-transcending process is an orientation toward mystery because, although conscious, it is not objectified. In mediating a return to immediacy, as Lonergan expresses it, the contemplative subject has withdrawn from objectification to a prayerful cloud of unknowing.[122]

From the critical perspective of self-transcendence, then, Merton's image of the true, inner self, and its relation to the false, external self, takes on some explanatory precision. Through a contemplatively oriented process of self-transcendence, a subject may withdraw from the humanly constructed (false) self-as-object to the originating (true) self-as-subject, where in non-objectified conscious subjectivity God, too, may be experienced as Subject. The true self, then, is the religiously converted self-transcending subject which has mediated a return to the immediacy of its own presence to itself. From the perspective of this interior, transcendent self-as-subject, the self-as-object is external, empirical, and false. As oriented toward transcendent mystery completely beyond the world mediated by meaning, this true, self-transcending subject-as-subject may be drawn completely out of that mediated world into an unmediated cloud of unknowing.

For Merton, the recovery of the true self and the discovery of God present therein occurs in contemplation. This contemplative movement into the true self—or into the deepest center of the self or soul, as he sometimes puts it—must not be understood in any isolated, individualistic sense, however. Even when writing *Seeds of Contemplation* Merton was clear on the paradoxical conditions for passage through the deepest recesses of interiority into the world of the sacred: "*a man cannot enter into the deepest center of himself and pass through that center into*

God, unless he is able to pass entirely out of himself and empty himself and give himself to other people in the purity of a selfless love."[123]

Toward the East: Final Integration. Two simple but for Merton finally significant events occurred coincidentally at the end of 1967. First, Merton received an invitation from Dom Jean LeClerc to attend a major monastic conference in Bangkok during December 1968. At about the same time, a new Abbot was elected at Gethsemani. The new Abbot allowed Merton to accept the invitation to the Bangkok conference, and it became the occasion for an extended Asian journey on which Merton was able to pursue at first hand his great interest in Eastern spirituality. In a paper prepared for a conference in Calcutta, Merton expressed the purpose of his journey as one of communication—aiming finally at communion—with "those in the various religions who seek to penetrate the ultimate ground of their beliefs by a transformation of the religious consciousness," by a "deepening of consciousness toward an eventual breakthrough and discovery of a transcendent dimension of life beyond that of the ordinary empirical self and of ethical and pious observance."[124]

Merton was convinced that such communion would be of singular importance at this moment of crucial choice in human history when we are in grave danger of losing the spiritual heritage of thousands of generations. If global consciousness is to be more than "a vast blur of mechanized triviality and ethical cliché," it must have the mark of what Merton calls the truly universal man—the depth and integrity of inner transcendent freedom.[125]

Writing about the "final integration" of the true self as a state of transcultural maturity, Merton asserts that the "fully born" man "apprehends his life fully and wholly from an inner ground that is at once more universal than the empirical ego and yet entirely his own. He is in a certain sense 'cosmic' and 'universal man.' " Having "attained a deeper, fuller identity than that of his limited ego-self," he is in a way identified with everybody—he is "all things to all men." Having embraced all of life, the finally integrated self passes beyond the limits of specific cultures and experiences, while retaining their universal qualities. In reaching out to all of humanity, the integrated self remains rooted in the concrete human values of friends, community, society, culture. But "he does not remain bound to one limited set of values in such a way that he opposes them aggressively or defensively to others." Having reached to the unifying depths of his personal being, "he has a unified vision and experience of one truth shining out in all its various manifestations. . . . He does not set these partial views up in opposition to each other, but unifies them in a dialectic or an insight of complementarity."

And it is on this point that Merton understands, beyond the individual, personal meaning of discovering one's true self in religious conversion, the imperative social significance of such discovery. For with its unifying view of life, the true self brings "perspective, liberty and spontaneity into the lives of others. The finally integrated man is a peacemaker, and that is why there is such a desperate need for our leaders to become such men of insight." Unfortunately, as Merton knew better than most, the integrating actualization of the true self only follows upon the excruciating pain of the false self's disintegration: "the rebirth which precedes final integration involves a crisis which is extremely severe—something like the Dark Night described by St. John of the Cross."[126]

If dialogue among spiritual traditions has significance in the ultimate terms of world peace, according to Merton, it also has a deeply personal dimension. And this was particularly true of Merton's Asian journey. At first the trip was something of a treasure hunt. "Too much movement. Too much 'looking for' something: an answer, a vision, 'something other.' And this breeds illusion. Illusion that there *is* something else. . . ."[127]

But all this changed decisively in the presence of the giant Buddhas at Polonnaruwa in Ceylon. "[T]he silence of the extraordinary faces. The great smiles. Huge and yet subtle. Filled with every possibility, questioning nothing, knowing everything, rejecting nothing. . . . " As Merton looked at these Buddhas he was "suddenly, almost forcibly, jerked clean out of the habitual, half-tied vision of things, and an inner clearness, clarity, as if exploding from the rocks themselves, became evident and obvious." In this clarity, for Merton, "The rock, all matter, all life is charged with dharmakaya . . . everything is emptiness and everything is compassion." He did not know when he had ever had "such a sense of beauty and spiritual validity running together in one aesthetic illumination." Now, he felt, his Asian pilgrimage had "come clear and purified itself." In sum, he wrote: "I know and have seen what I was obscurely looking for. I don't know what else remains but I have now seen and have pierced through the surface and have got beyond the shadow and the disguise."[128]

Six days later, the morning of December 10, 1968, Merton presented his paper to the monastic conference in Bangkok, stressing that what is essential to monastic life is not the external, institutional structure of buildings, clothes, or even the rule, but the "business of total inner transformation." He insisted, indeed, on the danger of relying on structures. In this context of graced transformation of ourselves into new beings—our true selves—independent of external structures, Merton left his audience with the lesson of authentic religious autonomy for the future: "From now on, everybody stands on his own feet."[129] After lunch he retired to his room and, in mid-afternoon, was discovered there dead (evidently electrocuted by a large fan found on top of his body).[130]

Paradox Revisited. No life can be "summed up" in a book, let alone in a paragraph. Given the depth of Merton's life, even the attempt would be patently ridiculous. More appropriate in conclusion, perhaps, would be a few modest reflections from the perspective of faith development.

One aspect of Fowler's faith development theory that must have struck readers as we moved from Chapter 2's correlation of developmental perspectives, through the course of Merton's transforming journey, is the central theme of *paradox*. Whereas Fowler identifies the power to reflect critically on one's self and one's world as the characteristic strength of Stage 4 faith, he focuses on ironic imagination as the strength peculiar to Stage 5 Conjunctive Faith. If a person is faithful to experience, the neat boundaries and clear distinctions of the critical, conceptual knowing necessary for the self-certainty of Stage 4 will gradually but inevitably give way to a recovery of the deep, imaginative symbolic life in Stage 5's dialectical-dialogical knowing. If Stage 4's energies were directed toward a clear definition and establishment of self-identity, Stage 5's interests are aimed at the reality beyond the boundaries of that self—both within and without. There emerges at Stage 5, then, not only a radical openness to the truth of others, but a parallel openness to the fuller truth of one's own being. Like Kohlberg's Stage 6 principled moral orientation, Fowler's Stage 5 faith is rooted in the experience of irrevocable commitments and deeds, and like Kohlberg's "Stage 7," it too knows the sacrament of defeat. Again, like Kohlberg's principled Stage 6, Fowler's Conjunctive Faith of Stage 5 has an apprehension of justice as a universal principle—beyond the limits of class, nation, or religion. But if Stage 5 faith has a transforming vision of reality, it is also painfully aware of the limits of the existing untransformed world.[131] It is, in Merton's phrase, caught in the Belly of a Paradox.

It is unnecessary to review Merton's adult years again to appreciate how perfectly Fowler's description of Stage 5 faith fits Merton's experience and perception. Commitment of his energies to global peace and justice was constitutive of his very person. And not only in the social arena, but also in the more personal dimension of life, Merton was on intimate terms with the pain of frustration and defeat. Despite this pain, however, his dynamic openness to reality would not be denied. In one direction the Catholic monk moved *out* to the world of Protestant theology, to the secular world of the civil rights and peace movements, and, of course, to the world of the East. He was convinced that this movement toward the world in all its richness, complexity, but also evil was a necessary condition for moving beyond the self in another direction—toward the depths of the inner self, the true person, and finally the reality of God. This inner movement is a long, arduous journey of radical conversion, for which, Merton gradually learned, one must travel light, jettisoning the non-essentials, if one is to survive the rigors of the desert.

On this inner journey the illusions of autonomy that make the false self's life comfortable become luxuries that make the death of the true self certain. One clings to autonomy at the cost of authentic life. This is the paradoxical truth that is perceived only by what Fowler calls the ironic imagination. There is no doubt that Merton the poet always had a special "feel" for the symbolic, but it was only when that "feel" was freed to explore the darkness of the inner life that Merton came face to face with paradox—not just the paradox of being a contemplative monk with a Madison Avenue schedule, but the radical paradox he discovered at the center of his being: only in losing your self can you find yourself. Merton was interested in the psychoanalytic approach to the unconscious, especially in dream analysis, but his contemplative inner journey also took him to a much deeper, richer dimension of personal life beyond the boundaries of the ego—to the immediate reality of the true self.

For Merton, of course, to find the true self in the center of one's being is also to truly discover God—immediately, concretely, experientially. In Christian terms this transcendent experience at the depths of one's subjectivity appears to condition the movement from Fowler's paradoxical Stage 5 Conjunctive Faith to Stage 6 Universalizing Faith. For the rare person of Stage 6 Faith, such transcendent experience grounds the felt sense of ultimate environment that is inclusive of all being.

By actualizing Stage 5's universalizing apprehension of absolute love and justice in one's very life and action, Stage 6 faith answers the radical question "Why be moral, why be just in an unjust world?" by overcoming the paradoxical split between a transforming vision and an untransformed world. In this sense, Stage 6 is not only universalizing, but also *unifying*.

Throughout his adult years Merton explicitly understood his

life—indeed, at its roots, *human* life—as a struggle in paradox. Is he an example of Stage 6 Universalizing Faith, as Fowler has recently suggested?[132] One does not wish to make Stage 6 a pantheon of religious achievers, but the question is as inevitable as it is ultimately unanswerable. On the basis of his own testimony one can certainly make a case that Merton learned to accept in faith the paradoxical reality of his life. And while neither a martyr nor one heedless of self-preservation, as Fowler finds Stage 6 persons often are,[133] Merton in his later years surely offended the sense of prudence, justice, and relevance of many who had found the strange life of *The Seven Storey Mountain's* young monk so enchanting and captivating. If there is an answer to our question it is probably embedded in Merton's extraordinary experience before the giant Buddhas at Polonnaruwa, where he pierced through the surface and got "beyond the shadow and the disguise." Beyond paradox? Perhaps, but we should not expect neat answers to impossible questions.

CONCLUSION: CHRISTIAN CONVERSION

On the basis of biblically grounded theological reflection, a philosophy of self-transcendence, and the perspective of developmental psychology, I have proposed a normative, multidimensional interpretation of Christian conversion, and traced its course in the extraordinary life of Thomas Merton. I conclude now with a brief summary of the interpretation's key points.

Conversion is the transformation of conscience—of the person precisely as valuer. Therefore I first laid the foundation for a critical understanding of conversion in an interpretation of conscience as the radical drive for self-transcendence, the reality drive for understanding, truth, value, love. And this interpretation of conscience was then elaborated within the context of a unified, explanatory theory of the self as a conscious subject developing cognitively and affectively through subject-object differentiation and integration. Here the perspectives of Erikson, Piaget, Kohlberg, Fowler, and Kegan were critically drawn together toward the construction of a holistic view of development as self-transcendence.

Within this pattern of personal development (moral and faith as well as cognitive and affective), I specified conversion as a vertical shift in structure (in contrast to a horizontal change of content) from a spontaneously instinctive to a reflectively personal orientation toward truth, value, and love. Moral, cognitive, and affective dimensions of conversion in this sense of structural shift in orientation were located at key developmental points—the conscious counterparts of unconscious stage transitions and crisis resolutions.

To see what shape these three conversions take when the content of the Christian story is their symbolic context, when they are dimensions of Christian conversion, I examined Merton's rich Christian life. First I considered his early conversion experience as an example of Christian moral conversion. Then, after distinguishing within the developmental pattern a fourth dimension of conversion—a distinctly religious dimension—I engaged this element in the task of interpreting Merton's mature Christian experience and reflections. Christian conversion, then, is the concrete form that a person's fundamental reorientation to truth, value, love, and God takes when it is shaped by the Christian story.

In claiming a normative character for this interpretation, I defined fully religious Christian conversion, for example, as a specifically adult reality, while recognizing the developmental possibility of a basic Christian moral conversion in the resolution of the adolescent identity crisis. The philosophical grounding and developmental empirical control of this interpretation resists the conversion claim based only on manifest content change—however emotionally charged or forcefully expressed it may be.

The personal measure of Christian living, therefore, is the conscience which has experienced a Christian conversion at once cognitive, affective, moral, and religious. Only a person thus converted is fully and concretely sensitive to the loving life of Jesus. In Merton's life we discovered again the fundamental Gospel truth that lies at the heart of Christian tradition: the radical religious conversion of Christian conscience finds its fullest realization in loving compassion—the self-transcending perfection of human empathy and justice. In its total surrender such religious conversion radically relativizes the moral autonomy of Christian conscience.

In turning life and love upside down, however, religious conversion does not destroy the authentic moral autonomy of personal responsibility. Indeed, the criterion of both religious conversion and the development of personal autonomy is self-transcendence. Justice, universalizing faith, generativity, and interindividual intimacy all insist on mutuality as the norm of authentic autonomy. Only the inauthentic notions of absolute autonomy and self-fulfillment are contradicted by the self-transcending love and surrender of religious conversion. Christian religious conversion is not the antithesis but the completion of personal development toward self-transcending autonomy.

NOTES

1. CONSCIENCE AND CONVERSION

1. In addition to the standard biblical dictionaries, see William L. Holladay, *The Root SUBH in the Old Testament* (Leiden: Brill, 1958); Christoph Barth, "Notes on 'Return' in the Old Testament," *Ecumenical Review* 19/3 (July 1967): 310–12; Aloys H. Dirksen, *The New Testament Concept of Metanoia* (Washington, DC: Catholic University of America Press, 1932); William Barclay, *Turning to God* (London: Epworth, 1963), ch. 1, "Conversion in the New Testament," pp. 11–25; and J. W. Heikkinen, "Notes on 'Epistrepho' and 'Metanoeo'," *Ecumenical Review* 19/3 (July 1967): 313–16.

2. See Gerhard Lohfink, *The Conversion of St. Paul: Narrative and History in Acts,* trans. and ed. B.J. Malina (Chicago: Franciscan Herald, 1976); Günther Bornkamm, *Paul,* trans. D.M.G. Stalkes (New York: Harper & Row, 1971), pp. 13–25; and David M. Stanley, "Paul's Conversion in Acts: Why the Three Accounts?" *Catholic Biblical Quarterly* 15 (July 1953): 315–38.

3. See, e.g., Jon Sobrino, *Christology at the Crossroads: A Latin American Approach,* trans. J. Drury (Maryknoll, NY: Orbis, 1978), p. 94.

4. See Paul Aubin, *Le problème de la "conversion"* (Paris: Beauchesne, 1963).

5. A.D. Nock, *Conversion: The Old and the New in Religion from Alexander the Great to Augustine of Hippo* (London: Oxford University Press, 1933), pp. 1–16, 179.

6. See Jean-Marie LeBlond, *Les conversions de Saint Augustin* (Paris: Aubier, 1950). Also see Lawrence J. Daly, "Psychohistory and St. Augustine's Conversion Process: An Historiographical Critique,"

Augustiniana 28 (1978): 231–54; Paula Fredriksen, "Augustine and His Analysts: The Possibility of a Psychohistory," *Soundings* 61 (1978): 206–27; and Robert J. O'Connell, *St. Augustine's Confessions: The Odyssey of Soul* (Cambridge: Harvard University Press, 1969).

7. See Marilyn J. Harran, *Luther on Conversion* (Ithaca, NY: Cornell University Press, 1983); and Harvey D. Egan, *The Spiritual Exercises and the Ignatian Mystical Horizon* (St. Louis, MO: Institute of Jesuit Sources, 1976), esp. pp. 14–23.

8. See F. Ernest Stoeffler, *The Rise of Evangelical Pietism* (Leiden: Brill, 1971); Stanley Ayling, *John Wesley* (Nashville, TN: Abingdon, 1979); Jonathan Edwards, *Religious Affections*, ed. John E. Smith (New Haven, CT: Yale University Press, 1959); Perry Miller, *Jonathan Edwards* (Amherst: University of Massachusetts Press, 1981 [1949]); and Edwin S. Gaustad, *The Great Awakening in New England* (New York: Harper & Row, 1957).

9. William James, *The Varieties of Religious Experience* (New York: New American Library Mentor, 1958 [1902]).

10. See, e.g., André Marc, *Raison et conversion chrétienne* (Paris: Desclée De Brouwer, 1961); Rosemary Haughton, *The Transformation of Man: A Study of Conversion and Community* (New York: Paulist, 1967); and Jean-Claude Sagne, *Conflict, changement, conversion* (Paris: Cerf-Desclée, 1974). For a collection of essays by a variety of theologians and a selected bibliography of classic and contemporary sources, see Walter E. Conn, ed., *Conversion: Perspectives on Personal and Social Transformation* (New York: Alba House, 1978). For an anthology of personal accounts of conversion experiences from Paul to Charles W. Colson, see Hugh T. Kerr and John M. Mulder, eds., *Conversions: The Christian Experience* (Grand Rapids, MI: Eerdmans, 1983). Also see Cedric B. Johnson and H. Newton Malony, *Christian Conversion: Biblical and Psychological Perspectives* (Grand Rapids, MI: Zondervan, 1982); and Robert Duggan, ed., *Conversion and the Catechumenate* (New York: Paulist, 1984).

11. See Bernard Lonergan, "Theology in Its New Context" in his *A Second Collection*, ed. W.F.J. Ryan and B.J. Tyrrell (London: Darton, Longman & Todd, 1974), pp. 55–67, at 67. Also see Gregory Baum, *Religion and Alienation: A Theological Reading of Sociology* (New York: Paulist, 1975), pp. 208–20; Donald Gelpi, *Charism and Sacrament: A Theology of Christian Conversion* (New York: Paulist, 1976); and Avery Dulles, "Fundamental Theology and the Dynamics of Conversion," *Thomist* 45/2 (April 1981): 175–93.

12. See John Henry Newman, *Apologia pro Vita Sua* (Garden City, NY: Doubleday Image, 1956 [1864]), which includes an account

of his first conversion at age fifteen as well as his later conversion to the Roman Catholic Church; Dorothy Day, *The Long Loneliness: An Autobiography* (Garden City, NY: Doubleday Image, 1959 [1952]); and Charles Davis, *A Question of Conscience* (New York: Harper & Row, 1967). Also see Emilie Griffin, *Turning: Reflections on the Experience of Conversion* (Garden City, NY: Doubleday, 1980). Griffin patterns the story of her conversion as a drama in four acts: Desire and Dialectic, Struggle and Surrender, followed by an epilogue on continuing conversion. At each point she frames her own story with reflections on the conversion experiences of C.S. Lewis, Bede Griffiths, Thomas Merton, Dorothy Day, and Avery Dulles. Griffin's pattern may be compared with the classic Puritan schema (conviction of sin, vocation, justification, sanctification, and glorification) employed by A.J. Krailsheimer in his brief sketches of a dozen conversions throughout Christian history: *Conversion* (London: SCM Press, 1980). The reader shares in the experience of conversion through the exchange of letters which constitute Antonia White, *The Hound and the Falcon: The Story of a Reconversion to the Catholic Faith* (London: Virago, 1980 [1965]). Another British author, Graham Greene, stresses the intellectual dimension of belief in God's existence (in contrast to an emotional falling-in-love) in his early conversion to Roman Catholicism in Marie-Françoise Allain, *The Other Man: Conversations with Graham Greene*, trans. G. Waldman (New York: Simon & Schuster, 1983 [original French 1981]).

13. Essays in the following anthologies provide helpful introductions to the new religious movements: Charles Glock and Robert N. Bellah, eds., *The New Religious Consciousness* (Berkeley: University of California Press, 1976); Jacob Needleman and George Baker, eds., *Understanding the New Religions* (New York: Seabury, 1978); Thomas Robbins and Dick Anthony, eds., *In Gods We Trust: New Patterns of Religious Pluralism in America* (New Brunswick, NJ: Transaction, 1980); and Irving I. Zaretsky and Mark P. Leone, eds., *Religious Movements in Contemporary America* (Princeton, NJ: Princeton University Press, 1974).

14. Among the plethora of studies, see J. Stillson Judah, *Hare Krishna and the Counterculture* (New York: John Wiley, 1979); Ken Levi, ed., *Violence and Religious Commitment: Implications of Jim Jones's People's Temple Movement* (University Park: Pennsylvania State University Press, 1982); John Lofland, *Doomsday Cult: A Study of Conversion, Proselytization, and Maintenance of Faith* (2nd ed.; New York: Irvington, 1977 [1966]); James T. Richardson, ed., *Conversion Careers: In and Out of the New Religions* (Beverly Hills, CA: Sage, 1978); Roy Wallis, *Salvation and Protest: Studies of Social and Religious Movements* (New York:

St. Martin's, 1979); and James T. Richardson and Rex Davis, "Experiential Fundamentalism: Revisions of Orthodoxy in the Jesus Movement," *Journal of the American Academy of Religion* 51/3 (September 1983), 397–425. Especially valuable is Steven Tipton, *Getting Saved from the Sixties: Moral Meaning in Conversion and Cultural Change* (Berkeley, University of California Press, 1981).

15. See David Bromley and Anson Shupe, *Strange Gods: The Great American Cult Scene* (Boston: Beacon, 1982), James T. Richardson and David G. Bromley, eds., *The Brainwashing-Deprogramming Controversy: Sociological, Psychological, Legal and Historical Perspectives* (New York: Edwin Mellen, 1983), and Anson D. Shupe and David G. Bromley, *The New Vigilantes: Deprogrammers, Anti-cultists and the New Religions* (Beverly Hills: Sage, 1980).

16. For an excellent review of the anthropological, sociological, historical, psychological, psychoanalytic, and theological literature, see Lewis R. Rambo, "Current Research on Religious Conversion," *Religious Studies Review* 8/2 (April 1982): 146–59.

17. See C.G. Jung's 1930 essay "The Stages of Life" along with "Psychotherapists or the Clergy" in his *Modern Man in Search of a Soul*, trans. W.S. Dell and C.F. Baynes (New York: Harcourt, Brace & World, 1933). Also see Seward Hiltner, "Toward a Theology of Conversion in the Light of Psychology," *Pastoral Psychology* 17 (September 1966): 35–42.

18. See Leon Salzman, "The Psychology of Regressive Conversion," *Journal of Pastoral Care* 8 (1954): 61–75.

19. Gail Sheehy, *Passages: Predictable Crises of Adult Life* (New York: Dutton, 1976). Also see Daniel J. Levinson *et al.*, *The Seasons of a Man's Life* (New York: Knopf, 1978) and Iris Sangiuliano, *In Her Time* (New York: Morrow, 1980). For a general consideration of the relationship of religious conversion to personal crisis, see Paul E. Johnson, *Psychology of Religion* (New York: Abingdon, 1959), ch. 6, "Conversion."

20. The necessity of conversion became a major issue for nineteenth century religious educators, who tended to polarize conversion and nurture; see Horace Bushnell's reaction to revivalist insistence on the need for conversion in his classic *Christian Nurture* (New Haven, CT: Yale University Press, 1967 [1847]). For recent discussion of the issue, see John Westerhoff, "A Necessary Paradox: Catechesis and Evangelism, Nurture and Conversion," *Religious Education* 73/4 (July-August 1978): 409–16; Thomas H. Groome, "Conversion, Nurture and Educators," *Religious Education* 76/5 (September-October 1981):

482–96; and Mary C. Boys, "Conversion as a Foundation of Religious Education," *Religious Education* 77/2 (March-April 1982): 211–24.

21. For my full explication of the necessarily telescoped interpretation of conscience presented here, see Walter E. Conn, *Conscience: Development and Self-Transcendence* (Birmingham, AL: Religious Education Press, 1981).

22. The multiplicity of views is available in a number of convenient anthologies: see, for philosophical, John Donnelly and Leonard Lyons, eds., *Conscience* (New York: Alba House, 1973); for historical and psychological, Curatorium of the C.G. Jung Institute, Zurich, ed., *Conscience*, trans. R.F.C. Hull and R. Horine (Evanston, IL: Northwestern University Press, 1970 [original German 1958]); for psychological and theological, C. Ellis Nelson, ed., *Conscience: Theological and Psychological Perspectives* (New York: Newman, 1973); and, for pastoral psychological, William C. Bier, ed., *Conscience: Its Freedom and Limitations* (New York: Fordham University Press, 1971). Several theological views are discussed in Eric Mount, Jr., *Conscience and Responsibility* (Richmond, VA: John Knox, 1969); and a variety of psychological views are considered in Donald E. Miller, *The Winged-Footed Wanderer: Conscience and Transcendence* (Nashville, TN: Abingdon, 1977). For a discussion of conscience in Peter Lombard, Philip the Chancellor, Bonaventure, and Aquinas, see Timothy C. Potts, *Conscience in Medieval Philosophy* (Cambridge: Cambridge University Press, 1980).

23. See Daniel C. Maguire, *The Moral Choice* (Garden City, NY: Doubleday, 1978), p. 370.

24. See *Gaudium et Spes: Pastoral Constitution on the Church in the Modern World* (par. 16, "The Dignity of the Moral Conscience") in *The Documents of Vatican II*, ed. W.M. Abbott (New York: America Press, 1966), pp. 213–14. Vatican II documents contain several understandings of conscience; for an analysis and attempt at integration, as well as correlation with major psychological interpretations (cognitive-developmental, identification, and learning theories), see Thomas Srampickal, *The Concept of Conscience in Today's Empirical Psychology and in the Documents of the Second Vatican Council* (Innsbruck, Austria: Resch Verlag, 1976).

Conscience as subjective norm had consistently been recognized in the standard Catholic moral manuals, of course: see, e.g., Henry Davis, *Moral and Pastoral Theology* 1 (New York: Sheed and Ward, 1936): 64; and Marcellino Zalba, *Theologiae Moralis Summa* 1 (Madrid: Biblioteca de Autores Cristianos, 1952): 253. For an excellent brief historical survey of Roman Catholic views on conscience, see Charles E.

Curran, *Themes in Fundamental Moral Theology* (Notre Dame, IN: University of Notre Dame Press, 1977), pp. 191–231.

25. See C.A. Pierce, *Conscience in the New Testament* (London: SCM Press, 1955); and Philippe Delhaye, *The Christian Conscience*, trans. C. U. Quinn (New York: Desclée, 1968 [original French 1964]).

26. Paul Lehmann, *Ethics in a Christian Context* (New York: Harper & Row, 1963), p. 327.

27. *Ibid.*, pp. 336, 340–41.

28. *Ibid.*, p. 350.

29. *Ibid.*, p. 353. For a fuller analysis of Lehmann's treatment of conscience, see Conn, *Conscience: Development and Self-Transcendence*, pp. 12–18.

30. C. Ellis Nelson, *Don't Let Your Conscience Be Your Guide* (New York: Paulist, 1978), pp. 3, 79.

31. Maguire, *Moral Choice*, pp. 371, 373. This excellent study of ethical method is particularly impressive in its treatment of the many dimensions of fully human moral consciousness, especially the usually neglected affective and imaginative dimensions.

32. *Ibid.*, p. 372.

33. John Macquarrie, *Three Issues in Ethics* (New York: Harper & Row, 1970), pp. 111–12.

34. *Ibid.*, pp. 114, 115.

35. Although Macquarrie offers no discussion of conversion, he did anticipate the connection I am making between conscience and conversion at the point of authenticity in his early study of Christianity and existentialism: see John Macquarrie, *An Existentialist Theology: A Comparison of Heidegger and Bultmann* (New York: Harper & Row, 1965 [1955]), pp. 126, 139.

36. See Lionel Trilling, *Sincerity and Authenticity* (Cambridge: Harvard University Press, 1972), pp. 1–12. For a more detailed analysis and critique of Trilling's position, see Conn, *Conscience: Development and Self-Transcendence*, pp. 4–7; for an analysis of self-transcendence as criterion of authenticity, see Walter E. Conn, "Bernard Lonergan and Authenticity: The Search for a Valid Criterion of the Moral Life," *American Benedictine Review* 30/3 (September 1979): 301–21.

37. See H. Richard Niebuhr, *The Responsible Self: An Essay in Christian Moral Philosophy* (New York: Harper & Row, 1963). For an excellent survey of prominent theorists on the topic, see Albert Jonsen, *Responsibility in Modern Religious Ethics* (Washington, DC: Corpus, 1968). For critical analyses, also see Walter E. Conn, "H. Richard Nie-

buhr on 'Responsibility'," *Thought* 51 (March 1976): 82–98 and "Michael Polanyi: The Responsible Person," *Heythrop Journal* 17 (January 1976): 31–49.

38. The following discussion is drawn from my contribution to Joann Wolski Conn and Walter E. Conn, "Self-Transcendence in the Spiritual Life: Thérèse of Lisieux" in Robert Masson, ed., *The Pedagogy of God's Image: Essays on Symbol and the Religious Imagination,* College Theology Society Annual Publication 1981 (Chico, CA: Scholars Press, 1982), pp. 137–52. For explicit theological context of this distinction, see David Tracy, *The Analogical Imagination: Christian Theology and the Culture of Pluralism* (New York: Crossroad, 1981), p. 435.

39. Christopher Lasch, *The Culture of Narcissism: American Life in an Age of Diminishing Expectations* (New York: Norton, 1978). For an analysis of the effect of the cultural shift from the ideal of self-sacrifice to that of self-realization on the meaning of love (from "tragic-mythic" to "exchange"), see Ann Swidler, "Love and Adulthood in American Culture" in N.J. Smelser and E.H. Erikson, eds., *Themes of Work and Love in Adulthood* (Cambridge: Harvard University Press, 1980), pp. 120–47, esp. 136–39, "Self-Realization Versus Self-Sacrifice." For a study of the different conceptions of the self constitutive of child-rearing patterns in early America (evangelical: the self-suppressed; moderate: the self-controlled; genteel: the self-asserted), see Philip Greven, *The Protestant Temperament* (New York: Knopf, 1977).

40. Paul C. Vitz, *Psychology as Religion: The Cult of Self Worship* (Grand Rapids, MI: Eerdmans, 1977). Vitz, a convert to Christianity and proponent of "scientific" psychology, finds little practical difference in the last analysis between such theorists as Maslow, Fromm, Rogers, and May, and the purveyors of "pop psychology." Perhaps because an objectified, conceptualized Transcendent is either ignored or viewed negatively, Vitz finds no hint of transcendence in their work.

If narcissism is not really self-love, but a manifestation of self-hatred, as contemporary psychoanalytic literature suggests, it is necessary to challenge the attacks on serious theorists of the self who promote self-acceptance and a sense of self-worth in the therapeutic context. Because impotent selves do not significantly transcend themselves, we cannot in the present cultural context afford the luxury of misunderstanding necessary remedial therapeutic attention to the self as infantile indulgence and self-worship. Of course, the operative understanding of the self remains crucial. Authentic acceptance of oneself means that one accepts not only one's present limitations, but also one's real exigence for self-transcendence. For explicit treatment of self-transcendence in humanistic psychology, see, e.g., Abraham H. Maslow, *Religions, Values, and Peak-Experiences* (New York: Viking, 1970 [1964]), p. 67.

Christopher Lasch helps to clarify this point in his review of the latest contribution to the literature of self-fulfillment: Peter Clecak, *America's Quest for the Ideal Self: Dissent and Fulfillment in the Sixties and Seventies* (New York: Oxford University Press, 1983). Lasch suggests that Clecak errs in equating narcissism with selfishness, for the terms have little in common. "Narcissism signifies a loss of selfhood, not self-assertion. It refers to a self threatened with disintegration and by a sense of inner emptiness. To avoid confusion, what I have called the culture of narcissism might better be characterized as a culture of survivalism. The concern with the self, which seems so characteristic of our time, takes the form of a concern with its psychic survival." Lasch asserts that "genuine affirmation of the self," which "insists on a core of selfhood not subject to environmental determination," has "nothing in common with the current search for psychic survival" (Lasch, "The Great American Variety Show," *New York Review of Books* 31/1 [February 2, 1984]: 36–40, at 39). This thesis is developed in Christopher Lasch, *The Minimal Self* (New York: Norton, 1984). Lasch's important distinction is difficult to grasp until one appreciates the difference we will discuss later between what Erikson calls a "sense of identity" and what everyday speech means by a "strong ego" (which is one form in which the minimal self manifests itself).

41. Daniel Yankelovich, "New Rules in American Life: Searching for Self-Fulfillment in a World Turned Upside Down," *Psychology Today* 15/4 (April 1981): 35–91, at 40 (essay adapted from his *New Rules: Searching for Self-Fulfillment in a World Turned Upside Down* [New York: Random House, 1981], see esp. pp. 3–15, 234–64; quotation in slightly different form at 10–11).

42. Robert Coles, "Unreflecting Egoism," *The New Yorker*, August 27, 1979, pp. 98–105, at 98. See Heinz Kohut, *The Analysis of the Self* (New York: International Universities Press, 1971).

43. See, e.g., Madonna Kolbenschlag, *Kiss Sleeping Beauty Good-Bye* (Garden City, NY: Doubleday, 1979) and Joann Wolski Conn, "Women's Spirituality: Restriction and Reconstruction," *Cross Currents* 30 (Fall 1980): 293–308.

44. Mary Gordon, *Final Payments* (New York: Random House, 1978). See Diana Cooper-Clark, "An Interview with Mary Gordon," *Commonweal* 107/9 (May 9, 1980): 270–73; and LeAnne Schreiber, "A Talk with Mary Gordon," *New York Times Book Review*, February 15, 1981, pp. 26–28.

45. See Sandra M. Schneiders, "The Foot Washing (John 13:1–20): An Experiment in Hermeneutics," *Catholic Biblical Quarterly* 43/1 (January 1981): 76–92, at 84–88.

46. See Reinhold Niebuhr, *The Nature and Destiny of Man* 1 (New York: Scribner's, 1964 [1941]): 150–66; Paul Tillich, *Systematic Theology* 3 (Chicago: University of Chicago Press, 1963): 86–110; Karl Rahner, *Foundations of Christian Faith,* trans. W.V. Dyck (New York: Seabury, 1978), pp. 181–87; Bernard Lonergan, *Method In Theology* (New York: Herder and Herder, 1972), pp. 104–05; John Macquarrie, *Three Issues in Ethics,* pp. 50–59; and David Tracy, *Blessed Rage for Order* (New York: Seabury, 1975), pp. 96–100.

47. For a sustained, detailed argument of this thesis, see Conn, *Conscience: Development and Self-Transcendence.* Though self-realization, self-fulfillment, and self-actualization are sometimes distinguished in the literature, I am considering them here as roughly equivalent. The key distinction in my thesis is between the realization, fulfillment, or actualization of the self which is directly sought, and that which occurs indirectly through self-transcendence.

48. Viktor Frankl, *Man's Search for Meaning: An Introduction to Logotherapy,* trans. I. Lasch (2nd ed.; New York: Washington Square Press, 1963 [1959]) p. 175.

49. Henri J.M. Nouwen, *Reaching Out: The Three Movements of the Spiritual Life* (Garden City, NY: Doubleday, 1975).

50. See essays in Bernard Lonergan, *Collection,* ed. F.E. Crowe (New York: Herder and Herder, 1967), esp. pp. 211–67, and *Second Collection,* esp. pp. 69–86, 165–87. For a detailed synthesis of basic sources, see Conn, "Bernard Lonergan and Authenticity," esp. pp. 312–21.

51. Basic sources are Erik H. Erikson, *Childhood and Society* (2nd ed.; New York: Norton, 1963 [1950]), *Insight and Responsibility* (New York: Norton, 1964), and *The Life Cycle Completed: A Review* (New York: Norton, 1982).

52. Among the vast Piagetian bibliography, convenient overviews of the theory include Jean Piaget, *Six Psychological Studies,* trans. A. Tenzor and ed. D. Elkind (New York: Random House Vintage, 1968 [original French 1964]) and Jean Piaget and Bärbel Inhelder, *The Psychology of the Child,* trans. H. Weaver (New York: Basic Books, 1969 [original French 1966]). For a comprehensive selection and explanatory editorial presentation, see Howard E. Gruber and J. Jacques Vonèche, eds., *The Essential Piaget* (New York: Basic Books, 1977).

53. Basic essays are collected in Lawrence Kohlberg, *The Philosophy of Moral Development: Moral Stages and the Idea of Justice* (San Fran-

cisco: Harper & Row, 1981) and *The Psychology of Moral Development: The Nature and Validity of Moral Stages* (San Francisco: Harper & Row, 1984).

54. The major statement of faith development is James W. Fowler, *Stages of Faith: The Psychology of Human Development and the Quest for Meaning* (San Francisco: Harper & Row, 1981).

55. The principal source for development of the self is Robert Kegan, *The Evolving Self: Problems and Process in Human Development* (Cambridge: Harvard University Press, 1982).

56. For an excellent discussion of the "sort of person" one is and becomes, with special reference to Erikson and the possibilities of personal transformation, see James M. Gustafson, *Can Ethics Be Christian?* (Chicago: University of Chicago Press, 1975), pp. 25–81. A key source on character is Stanley Hauerwas, *Character and the Christian Life: A Study in Theological Ethics* (San Antonio, TX: Trinity University Press, 1975). Also see Hauerwas, "Towards an Ethics of Character" in his *Vision and Virtue: Essays in Christian Ethical Reflection* (Notre Dame, IN: Fides, 1974), pp. 48–67; and Hauerwas, "Character, Narrative, and Growth in the Christian Life" in his *A Community of Character: Toward a Constructive Christian Social Ethic* (Notre Dame, IN: University of Notre Dame Press, 1981), pp. 129–52. Also important on this point are Josef Pieper, *The Four Cardinal Virtues,* trans. R. and C. Winston *et al.* (New York: Harcourt, Brace & World, 1965); and Alasdair MacIntyre, *After Virtue: A Study in Moral Theory* (Notre Dame, IN: University of Notre Dame Press, 1981).

2. PERSONAL DEVELOPMENT THROUGH THE LIFE CYCLE

1. See Eric D'Arcy, *Conscience and Its Right to Freedom* (New York: Sheed and Ward, 1961), p. 4.

2. See Bernard Lonergan, "Cognitional Structure" in *Collection,* pp. 221–39, esp. 225–27; and Walter E. Conn, "Transcendental Analysis of Conscious Subjectivity: Bernard Lonergan's Empirical Methodology," *Modern Schoolman* 54/3 (March 1977): 215–31.

In the distinction between subject-as-subject and subject-as-object Lonergan specifies a "twilight of what is conscious but not objectified," and suggests that this may be the equivalent of some psychological meanings of the unconscious (*Method in Theology,* p. 34). For further specification of this point, also see Lonergan, "Religious Experience" in Thomas A. Dunne and Jean-Marc Laporte, eds., *Trinification of the World: A Festschrift in Honour of Frederick E. Crowe in Celebration of His*

60th Birthday (Toronto: Regis College Press, 1978), pp. 71–83, at 73–74. Compare Lonergan's distinction between conscious and unconscious components in *Insight,* pp. 476–77.

3. See Bernard Lonergan, *De constitutione Christi ontologica et psychologica* (4th ed.; Rome: Pontificia Universitas Gregoriana, 1964) and "Christ as Subject: A Reply" in *Collection,* pp. 164–97.

4. See Bernard Lonergan, "*Existenz* and *Aggiornamento*" in *Collection,* pp. 240–51, esp. 243–44.

5. See Bernard Lonergan, "Metaphysics as Horizon" in *Collection,* pp. 202–20, and *Method in Theology,* pp. 235–37. For an analysis of "world" and "horizon" in Lonergan's works and an attempt at a synthesis, see Conn, "Bernard Lonergan and Authenticity," pp. 303–07.

6. See Lonergan, *Collection,* pp. 243–46, 252–55.

7. See *ibid.,* pp. 222–23. For a developmental life-span consideration of this theme, see essays in Richard M. Lerner and Nancy A. Busch-Rossnagel, eds., *Individuals as Producers of Their Development: A Life-Span Perspective* (New York: Academic Press, 1981).

8. On cognitive structures as unconscious, see Jean Piaget, "Affective Unconscious and Cognitive Unconscious" in his *The Child and Reality: Problems of Genetic Psychology,* trans. A. Rosin (New York: Viking, 1974 [original French 1972]), pp. 31–48; also see Melvin L. Weiner, *The Cognitive Unconscious: A Piagetian Approach to Psychotherapy* (Davis, CA: International Psychological Press, 1975). On the unconscious character of the ego, see Erik H. Erikson, *Identity: Youth and Crisis* (New York: Norton, 1968), p. 218. To repeat an important point of terminology, Lonergan's perspective refers to conscious but unobjectified structures (*Method in Theology,* pp. 14, 18, 34).

9. The threefold structure of the strategy in Chapters 2 and 3 indicates that the developmental understanding of conscience (3) presented here is rooted in established developmental theory (1) as mediated by critical analysis (2). I am not presenting a new developmental theory, but a critically appropriated, integrated version of several established theories. This project is significantly different from either the straight presentation of established theories (see, e.g., Ronald Duska and Mariellen Whelan, *Moral Development: A Guide to Piaget and Kohlberg* [New York: Paulist, 1975] and Mary M. Wilcox, *Developmental Journey: A Guide to the Development of Logical and Moral Reasoning and Social Perspective* [Nashville, TN: Abingdon, 1979]) or the attempt to create a new model of personal development merely prefaced by a discussion of the limitations and weaknesses perceived in established theories (see, e.g., Gabriel Moran, *Religious Education Development: Images for the Future* [Minneapolis, MN: Winston, 1983]).

10. For a complementary developmental approach with a strong empirical base, see Jane Loevinger, *Ego Development: Conceptions and Theories* (San Francisco: Jossey-Bass, 1976). Loevinger attempts a comprehensive view of ego development incorporating both structural and functional perspectives. One may profitably compare her pattern of stages with those presented in this study: *Presocial* and *Symbiotic* stages of infancy; *Impulsive* and *Self-Protective* stages of childhood; *Conformist* stage of adolescence; *Conscientious-Conformist* self-awareness transition (modal for most adults); *Conscientious* stage, *Individualistic* transition, and *Autonomous* and *Integrated* stages of adulthood. Loevinger's emphasis on moral factors results in an ego that is very much like conscience. For Kohlberg's critical comparison of his position with Loevinger's, see Lawrence Kohlberg, "The Meaning and Measure of Moral Development," Heinz Werner Lecture (Worcester, MA: Clark University Press, 1980) and John Snarey, Lawrence Kohlberg, and Gil Noam, "Ego Development in Perspective: Structural Stage, Functional Phase, and Cultural Age-Period Models," *Developmental Review* 3/3 (1983): 303–38, esp. 316–21; for Loevinger's response, see Jane Loevinger, "On Ego Development and the Structure of Personality," *Developmental Review* 3/3 (1983): 339–50. Snarey, Kohlberg, and Noam, "Ego Development in Perspective" also offers helpful comparisons of Kohlberg's view with those of Selman (pp. 312–13), Kegan (pp. 314–16), and Erikson (pp. 321–26).

11. Erik H. Erikson, "Life Cycle," *International Encyclopedia of the Social Sciences*, ed. David L. Sills, 17 vols. (New York: Macmillan, 1968), 9:286–92, at 288. Erikson's most comprehensive chart of the life cycle is in his *Life Cycle Completed*, pp. 32–33; each stage is specified under the following eight headings: Psychosexual Stages and Modes, Psychosocial Crises, Radius of Significant Relations, Basic Strengths, Core Pathology Basic Antipathies, Related Principles of Social Order, Binding Ritualizations, Ritualism.

12. Donald Evans, *Struggle and Fulfillment: The Inner Dynamics of Religion and Morality* (Philadelphia: Fortress, 1981) delineates the life-long struggle between trust and distrust in terms of five constitutive opposites: assurance and anxiety, receptivity and wariness, fidelity and idolatry, hope and despair, and passion and apathy.

13. This early sense of autonomy must be sharply distinguished from the authentic adult autonomy of critical moral conversion; later we note how the "strong ego" which this early autonomy grounds differs from ego identity.

14. Erikson, *Identity: Youth and Crisis*, p. 119. Also see reflections on "Super-Ego and Identity" in Erikson, *Life History and the Historical*

Moment (New York: Norton, 1975), pp. 101–03. Erikson refers to superego and conscience in his discussions of Stage 2 "autonomy vs. shame and doubt" as well as of Stage 3 "initiative vs. guilt": see, e.g., *Childhood and Society,* pp. 252–53, 257; *Identity: Youth and Crisis,* pp. 111, 119; and Erikson, *Toys and Reasons: Stages in the Ritualization of Experience* (New York: Norton, 1977), p. 93.

15. Mark Twain, *The Adventures of Huckleberry Finn* (New York: Grosset & Dunlap, 1948 [1884]), ch. 31, "You Can't Pray a Lie," p. 272.

16. See Jean Piaget, *The Origins of Intelligence in Children,* trans. M. Cook (New York: Norton, 1963 [first English 1952; original French 1936]) and *The Construction of Reality in the Child,* trans. M. Cook (New York: Ballantine, 1971 [first English 1954; original French 1937]). For Piaget's later work on the topic, esp. the relationship between "knowing how" and conceptualization, see Piaget, *The Grasp of Consciousness: Action and Concept in the Young Child,* trans. S. Wedgwood (Cambridge: Harvard University Press, 1976 [original French 1974]) and *Success and Understanding,* trans. A. Pomerans (Cambridge: Harvard University Press, 1978 [original French 1974]). For recent assessment, see George Butterworth, ed., *Infancy and Epistemology: An Evaluation of Piaget's Theory* (New York: St. Martin's, 1982).

For basic presentations of cognitive development in Piaget's generalized theoretical terms of genetic epistemology, see Piaget, *Genetic Epistemology,* trans. E. Duckworth (New York: Columbia University Press, 1970), *Psychology and Epistemology,* trans. A. Rosin (New York: Grossman, 1971 [original French 1970]), and *The Principles of Genetic Epistemology,* trans. W. Mays (New York: Basic Books, 1972 [original French 1970]). The many volumes of the results of Piaget's collaborative research project began to appear in 1957 as *Études d'épistémologie génétique* (Paris: Presses Universitaire de France). On genetic epistemology in relationship to the human sciences and the structuralist method, see Jean Piaget, *Épistémologie des sciences de l'homme* (Paris: Gallimard, 1972) and *Structuralism,* trans. and ed. Chaninah Maschler (New York: Basic Books, 1970 [original French 1968]); also see Hugh J. Silverman, ed., *Piaget, Philosophy, and the Human Sciences* (Atlantic Highlands, NJ: Humanities Press, 1980), esp. Susan Buck-Moss, "Piaget, Adorno, and the Possibilities of Dialectical Operations," pp. 103–37, and the Heideggerian focused William J. Richardson, "Piaget, Lacan, and Language," pp. 144–63. For philosophical critique, see Richard F. Kitchener, "The Nature and Scope of Genetic Epistemology," *Philosophy of Science* 48 (1981): 400–15.

17. Piaget and Inhelder, *Psychology of the Child,* p. 13.

18. *Ibid.*

19. Piaget, *Six Psychological Studies*, p. 16. Also see Thérèse Gouin Décarie, *Intelligence and Affectivity in Early Childhood: An Experimental Study of Jean Piaget's Object Concept and Object Relations*, trans. E.P. Brandt and L.W. Brandt (New York: International Universities Press, 1965); and John McDargh, *Psychoanalytic Object Relations Theory and the Study of Religion* (Washington, DC: University Press of America, 1983).

20. Exceptionally early recognition in English of this epistemological emphasis is found in Wolfe Mays' comparative study, "The Epistemology of Professor Piaget," *Proceedings of the Aristotelian Society* 54 (1953–54): 49–76. The theme is also clearly noted in John Flavell's excellent *The Developmental Psychology of Jean Piaget* (New York: Van Nostrand Reinhold, 1963), esp. pp. 249–61. Also see David Elkind's Introduction to Piaget's *Six Psychological Studies* and Hans Furth's valuable *Piaget and Knowledge: Theoretical Foundations* (2nd ed.; Chicago: University of Chicago Press, 1981 [1969]). More recently, Brian Rotman has presented a full-length study of Piaget's epistemology: *Jean Piaget: Psychologist of the Real* (Ithaca, NY: Cornell University Press, 1977). A comprehensive view is now available in Rita Vuyk, *Overview and Critique of Piaget's Genetic Epistemology, 1965–1980*, 2 vols. (New York: Academic Press, 1981).

Still, Piaget's epistemology has received relatively little attention from a philosophical viewpoint, and Piaget himself has deliberately designated his genetic epistemology as "scientific," distinguishing it rather sharply from philosophical epistemology principally in terms of empirical verification: see Piaget, *Psychology and Epistemology*, pp. 89–99, and Piaget's contribution to a dialogue in Richard Evans, *Jean Piaget: The Man and His Ideas* (New York: Dutton, 1973), p. 34. Part of the citation of the American Psychological Association's Distinguished Scientific Contribution Award presented to Piaget in 1969 read: "He has approached heretofore exclusively philosophical questions in a resolutely empirical fashion and created epistemology as a science, separate from philosophy, but interrelated with all human sciences." For Piaget's view on the relationship between science and philosophy, see his *Insights and Illusions of Philosophy*, trans. W. Mays (New York: World, 1971), esp. ch. 2; the original French version of this book, *Sagesse et illusions de la philosophie* (Paris: Presses Universitaires de France, 1965), occasioned a valuable consideration of both the general question and the particular issue of scientific epistemology by Enrico Cantore in "Science and Philosophy: Some Reflections on Man's Unending Quest for Understanding," *Dialectica* 22/2 (1968): 132–66.

21. See Jean Piaget, *The Moral Judgment of the Child*, trans. M. Gabain (New York: Free Press, 1965 [first English 1932; original French

1932]). Although this descriptive analysis predates Piaget's major explanatory work in cognitive development and epistemology, it did establish the crucial distinction in moral development between a heteronomous orientation of adult authority, unilateral respect, and external constraint and an autonomous orientation of peer cooperation, mutual respect and immanent obligation. For recent work (with a solid empirical foundation) on the developmental importance of the mutuality and cooperation of peer relations in childhood, see James Youniss, *Parents and Peers in Social Development: A Sullivan-Piaget Perspective* (Chicago: University of Chicago Press, 1980).

22. For an analysis of Piaget's epistemology in terms of self-transcendence, see Walter E. Conn, "Objectivity—A Developmental and Structural Analysis: The Epistemologies of Jean Piaget and Bernard Lonergan," *Dialectica* 30 (1976): 197–221. On the key concept of equilibration, see Jean Piaget, *The Development of Thought: Equilibration of Cognitive Structures,* trans. A. Rosin (New York: Viking, 1977 [original French 1975]); for critical assessment, see Sophie Haroutunian, *Equilibrium in the Balance: A Study of Psychological Explanation* (New York: Springer-Verlag, 1983).

23. Unfortunately, based on Piaget's unrelenting insistence on the subject's constructive activity in knowledge (a theme that runs through the entire body of his writings—see, e.g., *Psychology and Epistemology,* pp. 87, 110)—his epistemological position has been generally—and often very loosely—designated as Kantian. For a psychological perspective, see, e.g., David Elkind's Introduction in *Six Psychological Studies,* pp. xi–xii, and his "Measuring Young Minds" in Evans, *Jean Piaget: The Man and His Ideas,* pp. xxii–xli, at xxxv. Among philosophical considerations, see Stephen Toulmin, *Human Understanding* 1 (Princeton, NJ: Princeton University Press, 1972): 419–26, where Piaget is viewed as "adopting in psychology a historicized version of Kantianism. . . . " Also see Richard F. Kitchener, "Piaget's Genetic Epistemology," *International Philosophical Quarterly* 20 (1980): 377–405; and William V. Fabricus, "Piaget's Theory of Knowledge: Its Philosophical Context," *Human Development* 26 (1983): 325–34. For the most sustained interpretation of Piaget as Kantian, see Rotman, *Jean Piaget: Psychologist of the Real.*

This identification of Piaget's epistemology with the Kantian perspective has occurred despite explicit and repeated attempts by Piaget to distinguish his relational "interactionist" position from any simple "a priori" or purely (extrinsic) "realist" view: see, among other places, *The Psychology of Intelligence,* trans. M. Piercy and D.E. Berlyne (Totowa, NJ: Littlefield, Adams, 1966 [first English 1950; original French

1947]), p. 13; *The Origins of Intelligence in Children*, pp. 376–77; *Biology and Knowledge*, trans. B. Walsh (Chicago: University of Chicago Press, 1971 [original French 1967]), p. 327; *The Construction of Reality in the Child*, pp. 349–50, and *Introduction a l'epistemologie genetique* 1 (2nd ed.; Paris: Presses Universitaires de France, 1973); 25–26. On this point, also see Guy Cellerier's helpful study in the "philosophes" series, *Piaget* (Paris: Presses Universitaires de France, 1973), pp. 20–22. The results of a 1969 symposium on the philosophical implications of Piaget's work have been published in Theodore Mischel, ed., *Cognitive Development and Epistemology* (New York: Academic Press, 1971); the most useful collection of studies on the topic, this volume contains a wide variety of views: see esp. D.W. Hamlyn, "Epistemology and Conceptual Development" (pp. 3–24); Stephen Toulmin, "The Concept of 'Stages' in Psychological Development" (pp. 25–60); Bernard Kaplan, "Genetic Psychology, Genetic Epistemology, and Theory of Knowledge" (pp. 61–81); and Marx Wartofsky, "From Praxis to Logos: Genetic Epistemology and Physics" (pp. 129–47). Also see John Farrelly, "Developmental Psychology and Man's Knowledge of Being," *Thomist* 39 (October 1975): 668–95, where Piaget is introduced in support of the Thomistic position on the human "capacity for, and orientation to, a metaphysical knowledge of reality as being. . . ."

For my philosophical assessment of the operative epistemology in Piaget's work, see Walter E. Conn, "Piaget as Critical Realist," *Angelicum* 54/1 (1977): 67–88, and "Objectivity—A Developmental and Structural Analysis," pp. 201–11. One of the most perceptive philosophical interpretations of Piaget's orientation is given by Richard J. Blackwell, "The Adaptation Theory of Science," *International Philosophical Quarterly* 13 (1973): 319–34. Blackwell acknowledges the Kantian constructive subject as central in the knowing process, although he recognizes that for Piaget the functional invariants of cognition are set within an evolutionary context. More importantly, he also recognizes that for Piaget adaptation is a twofold process, that in addition to assimilating whatever is given to existing structures, the knowing subject also modifies and develops cognitional structures by *accommodating* them to recalcitrant givens. Thus, in contrast to Kant, Blackwell speaks not of a "totally amorphous" manifold of sense, but of "dictates of nature" which are described as "being given as structured" and thus necessitating an "adaptational fit" between themselves and cognitive structures. Accurately interpreting Piaget, Blackwell maintains that "the process of construction is carried out through the interaction of . . . the invariant functions of the mind and the dictates of nature . . ." (p. 334). As Blackwell's purpose was to lay the epistemological foundations for a theory of science, he was content to conclude by observing that his "constructive adaptationism" view of knowledge argues "against both a naive philosophical realism and any shadow of idealism in the traditional senses of these terms" (p. 334). Starting from a similar understanding of Piaget's epistemology, I argue in "Piaget as Critical Realist" (pp. 68, 87) that Piaget's "interactionist" theory of knowing (*Psychology of Intelligence,* p. 13) is a psychological and developmental version of a traditional epistemological realism which takes its stand on critical judgment—not between but beyond both a merely empirical realism and an aprioristic idealism (Piaget, *Introduction,* 1:26). For Piaget's view of Aristotle and Aquinas, see *Biology and Knowledge,* p. 55.

24. See Piaget, *Six Psychological Studies,* p. 29.

25. For a comprehensive treatment, see Bärbel Inhelder and Jean Piaget, *The Early Growth of Logic in the Child: Classification and Seriation,* trans. E.A. Lunzer and D. Papert (New York: Norton, 1969 [first English 1964; original French 1959]).

26. Unlike Piaget's study of moral development, which was based on his early descriptive understanding of cognitive development, Kohlberg's work on moral reasoning development has had the advantage of being carried out some forty years later in the light of Piaget's intervening explanatory interpretation of cognitive development. For Piaget's own later synthetic statement on moral development from the heteronomy of unilateral respect to the autonomy of mutual respect, see Piaget and Inhelder, *Psychology of the Child,* pp. 122 27. On the relationship between Piaget and Kohlberg, see Peter Tomlinson, "Moral Judgment and Moral Psychology: Piaget, Kohlberg and Beyond" in Sohan Modgil and Celia Modgil, eds., *Toward a Theory of Psychological Development* (Windsor, England: NFER, 1980), pp. 303–66, esp. 335–38; and Hugh Rosen, *The Development of Sociomoral Knowledge: A Cognitive Structural Approach* (New York: Columbia University Press, 1980). For discussion of background and context, see William Kay, *Moral Development: A Psychological Study of Moral Growth from Childhood to Adolescence* (New York: Schocken, 1968).

27. For a complete outline of the stages, see appendix in Kohlberg, *Philosophy of Moral Development,* pp. 409–12. The most recent interpretative presentation is in Kohlberg, *Psychology of Moral Development,* Appendix A, pp. 621–39.

28. Lawrence Kohlberg, "Moral Stages and Moralization: The Cognitive-Developmental Approach" in Thomas Lickona, ed., *Moral Development and Behavior: Theory, Research, and Social Issues* (New York: Holt, Rinehart and Winston, 1976), pp. 31–53, at 33.

29. *Ibid.* Corresponding to the three major levels of moral judg-

ment, Kohlberg has specified three underlying levels of social perspective: concrete individual, member-of-society, and prior-to-society. In defining these perspectives Kohlberg relies on Selman's work on the development of social perspective-taking; see Robert L. Selman, "A Developmental Approach to Interpersonal and Moral Awareness in Young Children: Some Educational Implications of Levels of Social Perspective-Taking" in Thomas C. Hennessy, ed., *Values and Moral Development* (New York: Paulist, 1976), pp. 142–67. After an initial egocentric position, Selman distinguishes five stages: subjective, self-reflective, mutual, qualitative-system, and symbolic-interaction. He correlates the first four stages with Kohlberg's first four moral stages in Selman, "Social-Cognitive Understanding: A Guide to Educational and Clinical Practice" in Lickona, ed., *Moral Development and Behavior*, pp. 299–316, at 309. Also see William Damon, *The Social World of the Child* (San Francisco: Jossey-Bass, 1977). Compare Michael Siegal, *Fairness in Children: A Social-Cognitive Approach to the Study of Moral Development* (New York: Academic Press, 1982).

30. Kohlberg, "Moral Stages and Moralization," p. 34.

31. *Ibid.*, p. 39.

32. Lawrence Kohlberg, "Moral Development," *International Encyclopedia of the Social Sciences* 10:483–94, at 488.

33. James W. Fowler, "Stages in Faith: The Structural-Developmental Approach" in Hennessy, ed., *Values and Moral Development*, pp. 173–211, at 175.

34. *Ibid.*, pp. 183–85. For a recent, comprehensive description of the stages, see Fowler, *Stages of Faith*, pp. 119–213.

35. Fowler, "Stages in Faith," p. 191.

36. Fowler, *Stages of Faith*, pp. 134, 127.

37. *Ibid.*, p. 140.

38. Kegan, *Evolving Self*, p. 77.

39. *Ibid.*, pp. 81–82.

40. *Ibid.*, pp. 73–110.

41. *Ibid.*, p. 88.

42. Piaget, *Six Psychological Studies*, p. 61.

43. *Ibid.*, pp. 62–63.

44. *Ibid.*, p. 63. See Jean Piaget, *Logic and Psychology*, with an Introduction on Piaget's Logic by W. Mays; trans. W. Mays and F. Whitehead (Manchester, England: University of Manchester Press, 1953); also see Kurt Bergling, *The Development of Hypothetico-Deductive Thinking in Children: A Cross-Cultural Study of the Validity of Piaget's Model of the Development of Logical Thinking* (New York: John Wiley, 1974).

45. Piaget, *Six Psychological Studies*, p. 64.

46. *Ibid.*

47. Jean Piaget, "Intellectual Evolution from Adolescence to Adulthood," *Human Development* 15 (1972): 1–12.

48. Erik H. Erikson, "Identity, Psychosocial," *International Encyclopedia of the Social Sciences* 7:61–65, at 61. Robert Kegan has suggested that Erikson's life cycle needs to be supplemented with an additional stage after industry/inferiority and before identity/confusion: a stage of affiliation/abandonment focusing on "connection, inclusion, and highly invested mutuality" equivalent to Kegan's interpersonal stage (Kegan, *Evolving Self,* p. 87).

49. Erikson, "Life Cycle," p. 290. For a detailed analysis of identity, especially of the relation of ego, self, and conscious "I," see Walter E. Conn, "Erikson's 'Identity': An Essay on the Psychological Foundations of Religious Ethics," *Zygon* 14/2 (June 1979): 125–34. On the relation of identity, formal operations, and insight (in contrast to identifications, concrete operations, and imagination), see Walter E. Conn, "Personal Identity and Creative *Self*-Understanding: Contributions of Jean Piaget and Erik Erikson to the Psychological Foundations of Theology," *Journal of Psychology and Theology* 5/1 (Winter 1977): 34–39.

50. Erik H. Erikson, "Reflections on the Dissent of Contemporary Youth," *International Journal of Psycho-Analysis* 51 (1970): 11–22, at 16.

51. Erik H. Erikson, *Young Man Luther: A Study in Psychoanalysis and History* (New York: Norton, 1958). Also see Roger A. Johnson, ed., *Psychohistory and Religion: The Case of Young Man Luther* (Philadelphia: Fortress, 1977).

52. Kohlberg, "Moral Stages and Moralization," p. 34.

53. *Ibid.,* p. 38.

54. *Ibid.,* p. 36. For an analysis of different understandings of law at preconventional (law-obeying), conventional (law-maintaining), and postconventional (law-making) levels, see June L. Tapp and Lawrence Kohlberg, "Developing Senses of Law and Legal Justice," *Journal of Social Issues* 27/2 (1971): 65–91.

55. Fowler, "Stages in Faith," pp. 184, 197.

56. James W. Fowler, "Life/Faith Patterns: Structures of Trust and Loyalty" in James W. Fowler and Sam Keen, *Life Maps: Conversations on the Journey of Faith,* ed. Jerome Berryman (Waco, TX: Word Books, 1978), pp. 14–101, at 68.

57. James W. Fowler, "The Pilgrimage in Faith of Malcolm X" in James W. Fowler and Robin W. Lovin *et al., Trajectories in Faith: Five Life Stories* (Nashville, TN: Abingdon, 1980), pp. 40–58, at 50.

58. Kegan, *Evolving Self,* p. 95.

59. *Ibid.*, pp. 96–97.

60. *Ibid.*, pp. 73–74, 97–100, 194–97.

61. *Ibid.*, pp. 102–03, 240–41.

62. See *Ibid.*, p. 210.

63. In addition to Piaget, "Intellectual Evolution from Adolescence to Adulthood" and *Six Psychological Studies*, pp. 63–64, 68–69, see Klaus F. Riegel, "Dialectic Operations: The Final Period of Cognitive Development," *Human Development* 16 (1973): 346–70; Patricia Kennedy Arlin, "Cognitive Development in Adulthood: A Fifth Stage?" *Developmental Psychology* 11/5 (1975): 602–06; John M. Broughton, "The Limits of Formal Thought" in Ralph L. Mosher, ed., *Adolescents' Development and Education: A Janus Knot* (Berkeley, CA: McCutchan, 1979), pp. 49–60; Gisela Labouvie-Vief, "Beyond Formal Operations: Uses and Limits of Pure Logic in Life-Span Development," *Human Development* 23 (1980): 141–61; and Deirdre A. Kramer, "Post-Formal Operations? A Need for Further Conceptualization," *Human Development* 26 (1983): 91–105.

64. Erikson, "Dissent of Contemporary Youth," p. 16.

65. Erik H. Erikson, *Gandhi's Truth: On the Origins of Militant Nonviolence* (New York: Norton, 1969), p. 412. Also see Donald Capps, Walter H. Capps, and M. Gerald Bradford, eds., *Encounter with Erikson: Historical Interpretation of Religious Biography* (Missoula, MT: Scholars Press, 1977).

66. Erikson, *Insight and Responsibility*, p. 239.

67. Erikson, *Gandhi's Truth*, p. 251.

68. Erikson, "Life Cycle," pp. 290, 291. Identity as a crisis characterizes adolescence, but only in adult intimacy and generativity does it become a dependable (though always provisional) achievement.

69. *Ibid.* Also see Erik H. Erikson, "On the Generational Cycle: An Address," *International Journal of Psycho-Analysis* 61 (1980): 213–23, and "On Generativity and Identity: From a Conversation with Erik and Joan Erikson," *Harvard Educational Review* 51/2 (1981): 249–69.

70. Erikson, "Life Cycle," p. 291.

71. See Ingmar Bergman, *Four Screenplays*, trans. L. Malmstrom and D. Kushner (New York: Simon and Schuster, 1960).

72. Erik H. Erikson, "Reflections on Dr. Borg's Life Cycle," *Daedalus* 105/2 (Spring 1976): 1–28, at 2; also in Erikson, ed., *Adulthood* (New York: Norton, 1978), pp. 1–31.

73. *Ibid.*, p. 1.

74. Lawrence Kohlberg and Carol Gilligan, "The Adolescent as a Philosopher: The Discovery of the Self in a Postconventional World," *Daedalus* 100/4 (Fall 1971): 1051–1086, at 1072.

75. *Ibid.*, p. 1071. The text reads "normal," but the context calls for "moral"; the same typographical error ("normal" for "moral") occurs in Lawrence Kohlberg, "Moral Education in the Schools: A Developmental View," *School Review* 74/1 (Spring 1966): 1–30, at 22.

76. *Ibid.*

77. Kohlberg, "Moral Development," p. 491.

78. Lawrence Kohlberg, "Continuities in Childhood and Adult Moral Development Revisited" in P.B. Baltes and K. Warner Schaie, eds., *Life-Span Developmental Psychology: Personality and Socialization* (New York: Academic Press, 1973), pp. 179–204, at 194.

79. *Ibid.*, p. 196. For Kohlberg's earlier view, that though there is "adult movement toward integration in the use of moral structures," there are "no adult stages in the structural sense," see Lawrence Kohlberg and Richard Kramer, "Continuities and Discontinuities in Childhood and Adult Moral Development," *Human Development* 12 (1969): 93–120, at 118. See Walter E. Conn, "Postconventional Morality: An Exposition and Critique of Lawrence Kohlberg's Analysis of Moral Development in the Adolescent and Adult," *Lumen Vitae* 30/2 (1975): 213–30, at 227–28. Most recently, Kohlberg has stressed work experience in positions of responsibility as aiding development to principled reasoning (Lawrence Kohlberg with Ann Higgins, "Continuities and Discontinuities in Childhood and Adult Development Revisited-Again" in Kohlberg, *Psychology of Moral Development*, pp. 426–97, at 468).

80. Kohlberg and Gilligan, "Adolescent as a Philosopher," p. 1068. Although Stage 6 has been dropped from Kohlberg's recent scoring manual (1978) because of its statistical rarity (none of Kohlberg's original group of longitudinal subjects—now adults in their thirties—has reached it) and consequent lack of full empirical definition or confirmation (Stage 6 data come mostly from interviews and writings of persons with serious philosophical training), Kohlberg does retain it in his theoretical position: "Its use is speculative, to clarify the philosophic meaning of moral stages and their claim to adequacy" (Kohlberg, "The Implications of Moral Stages for Adult Education," *Religious Education* 72/2 [1977], 183–201, at 195). Most recently, he explains that he continues the postulation of Stage 6 because he conceives his theory "as an attempt to rationally reconstruct the ontogenesis of justice reasoning, an enterprise which requires a terminal stage to define the nature and endpoint of the kind of development we are studying" (Lawrence Kohlberg with Charles Levine and Alexandra Hewer, "The Current Formulation of the Theory" in Kohlberg, *Psychology of Moral Development*, pp. 212–319, at 271). Sub-

jects earlier scored at Stage 6 are now rescored under new stage definitions at substage B of lower stages (5, 4, even 3), characterized by intuition of Stage 5 content and the universalized and prescriptive form of judgment of Stage 6 (*ibid.*). In contrast to substage A, substage B is also more autonomous at each stage (for the latest presentation of these substages, see Lawrence Kohlberg with Ann Higgins, Mark Tappan, and Dawn Schrader, "Appendix C: From Substages to Moral Types: Heteronomous and Autonomous Morality" in Kohlberg, *Psychology of Moral Development*, pp. 652–83).

Clearly, Kohlberg's research and theorizing is an ongoing project. While it is necessary to discuss its present state, I am principally interested in its unchanging general direction, not its changing specific details.

In his civic moral education aims, Kohlberg has "retrenched" from Stage 6 (1968) to Stage 5 (1976) to Stage 4 (1980) goals: see Kohlberg, "Educating for a Just Society" in Brenda Munsey, ed., *Moral Development, Moral Education, and Kohlberg: Basic Issues in Philosophy, Psychology, Religion, and Education* (Birmingham, AL: Religious Education Press, 1980), pp. 455–70, at 456–59. On stage assessment, see James Rest, *Development in Judging Moral Issues* (Minneapolis: University of Minnesota Press, 1979) and "Developmental Psychology and Value Education" in Munsey, pp. 101–29.

81. The distinction between ethical principles and moral rules is essential for understanding the difference between conventional moral reasoning, which uses only moral rules, and postconventional reasoning, which uses principles as well as rules. Responsible action follows practical moral judgments of conscience, which are guided by practical, substantive moral rules. Until recent years the prohibition of abortion was a commonly recognized example of such a moral rule. In contrast, universal ethical principles serve as second order critical norms appealed to when first order substantive moral rules are called into question. On the question of abortion, for example, the relevant second order ethical principle is the sanctity of life. To a large extent, the content of these second order principles is vague or indeterminate, and it is precisely this vagueness or indeterminate character that gives them their power as formal, critical norms in terms of which the validity of substantive moral rules is assessed.

As characterized by Kohlberg, postconventional moral reasoning is philosophical or ethical in the specific sense of critical reflection upon substantive moral rules. However, postconventional moral reasoning, precisely because it is the *moral* reasoning of a person engaged in making a practical moral judgment in a concrete situation, is not the detached, *abstract ethical analysis* of philosophers. Rather, the transition to postconventional moral reasoning involves a *transformation* of conventional moral reasoning which critically grounds or justifies its substantive moral rules in terms of universal ethical principles. Persons of postconventional moral reasoning, then, make practical moral judgments informed by substantive rules critically grounded in universal ethical principles. Clearly, in a pluralistic cultural and social situation like our own, in which an endless variety of conflicting moral values compete on the open market, such *critically* grounded moral rules (and the values they express) are not luxury items, but necessary equipment for *consistent* performance in the struggle for authentic self-transcendence. Still, many persons of conventional moral reasoning do live excellent moral lives by following practical moral judgments based on substantive moral rules which they, unlike persons of postconventional stages, have not grounded critically through ethical reflection, but have accepted without critical questioning.

The above distinction between rules and principles corresponds to the second and third "Levels of Moral Discourse" (expressive-evocative, moral, ethical, and postethical) in Henry D. Aiken, *Reason and Conduct* (New York: Knopf, 1962), pp. 65–87. Here I maintain the following relationship: second order *ethical principles* function as critical *norms* for *first order moral rules* (or substantive moral principles). On the relationship of principles to the foundational moral experience of value, see Maguire, *Moral Choice*, pp. 83–93, 218–22. Kohlberg's own position on this point is less than clear; in "Stages of Moral Development," p. 60, and in Kohlberg, "The Claim to Moral Adequacy of a Highest Stage of Moral Judgment," *Journal of Philosophy* 70/18 (October 1973): 630–46, at 643, he refers to principles in second order terms; in contrast, in a 1980 revision of the latter essay for *Philosophy of Moral Development* he speaks of the application of principles to decision as "direct, not second order" (p. 221).

82. Kohlberg, "Moral Stages and Moralization," pp. 38, 39.

83. Fowler, "Stages in Faith," p. 184, and *Stages of Faith*, p. 182.

84. Fowler, "Life/Faith Patterns," p. 74.

85. Fowler, "Stages in Faith," p. 185.

86. On second naiveté, see Paul Ricoeur, *The Symbolism of Evil*, trans. E. Buchanon (Boston: Beacon, 1969 [first English 1967; original French 1960]), pp. 347–57, "The Symbol Gives Rise to Thought."

87. Fowler, "Life/Faith Patterns," p. 83.

88. *Ibid.*, p. 88. Though persons of Stage 6 faith are likely to have "strongly developed, disciplined mystical sensitivities," it is not necessarily true, conversely, that such mystical sensitivities indicate

Stage 6 faith; indeed, Fowler is careful to distinguish faith stages from stages in traditional "spiritual paths" ("Stages in Faith," p. 204). Nevertheless, Fowler does recognize that at Stages 5 or 6 faith "will take essentially religious forms," and that the "further one moves beyond a Synthetic-Conventional structuring of faith, the more likely one is to exhibit increased commitment in faith" (*Stages of Faith*, pp. 293, 301).

89. Fowler, "Life/Faith Patterns," pp. 91–92.

90. Kegan, *Evolving Self*, p. 104.

91. *Ibid.*, p. 106.

92. Quoted in Erik H. Erikson, "The Galilean Sayings and the Sense of 'I'," *Yale Review* 70 (Spring 1981): 321–62, at 323.

93. *Ibid.*, p. 330.

94. *Ibid.*, p. 331.

95. *Ibid.*, p. 348. For critical discussion of the religious dimension in Erikson's work, see the excellent essays by Donald Capps, Peter Homans, Don Browning, *et al.* in Peter Homans, ed., *Childhood and Selfhood: Essays on Tradition, Religion, and Modernity in the Psychology of Erik H. Erikson* (Lewisburg, PA: Bucknell University Press, 1978) and J. Eugene Wright, Jr., *Erikson: Identity and Religion* (New York: Seabury, 1982).

3. DEVELOPMENTAL THEORY AND CONSCIENCE

1. See, e.g., Jonas Langer, *Theories of Development* (New York: Holt, Rinehart and Winston, 1969); Tran-Thong, *Stades et concept de stade de développement de l'enfant dans la psychologie contemporaine* (6th ed.; Paris: J. Vrin, 1976 [1967]); and Adrien Pinard and Monique Laurendeau, " 'Stage' in Piaget's Cognitive-Developmental Theory: Exegesis of a Concept" in David Elkind and John H. Flavell, eds., *Studies in Cognitive Development: Essays in Honor of Jean Piaget* (New York: Oxford University Press, 1969), pp. 121–70. For a critical comparative discussion of development in the theories presented here from Kohlberg's structural (multisubdomain) perspective, see Snarey, Kohlberg, and Noam, "Ego Development in Perspective." In James W. Fowler, "Stages of Faith and Adults' Life Cycles" in Kenneth Stokes, ed., *Faith Development in the Adult Life Cycle* (New York: Sadlier, 1982), pp. 179–207, Fowler compares psychosocial-life cycle and constructive-developmental perspectives in terms of theoretical focus, research methods, views of development, and concept of stage (pp. 185–86). For philosophical critique of the fundamental notion of development itself, see

Richard F. Kitchener, "Developmental Explanations," *Review of Metaphysics* 36/4 (June 1983): 791–817.

2. See Erikson, *Insight and Responsibility*, pp. 135–38, and *Life Cycle Completed*, p. 76; Jean Piaget, "The General Problems of the Psychobiological Development of the Child" in J.M. Tanner and Bärbel Inhelder, eds., *Discussions on Child Development* 4 (New York: International Universities Press, 1960): 3–27, esp. 15–16; Peter H. Wolff, *The Developmental Psychologies of Jean Piaget and Psychoanalysis*, Psychological Issues 5 (New York: International Universities Press, 1960); and Stanley I. Greenspan, *Intelligence and Adaptation: An Integration of Psychoanalytic and Piagetian Developmental Psychology*, Psychological Issues 47–48 (New York: International Universities Press, 1979).

3. Like the psychoanalytic perspective itself, Erikson's view has received its share of criticism. For cultural critique, see Frederick Crews, "American Prophet," *New York Review of Books* 22 (October 16, 1975): 9–15; and David Gutmann, "Erik Erikson's America," *Commentary* 58 (September 1974): 60–64. Difficulties with Erikson's method considered as phenomenological, especially the problem of validation, are outlined in Jack Tyrus Hanford, "A Synoptic Approach: Resolving Problems in Empirical and Phenomenological Approaches to the Psychology of Religion," *Journal for the Scientific Study of Religion* 14 (September 1975): 219–27. For an example of feminist criticism, see Carol Gilligan, "Woman's Place in Man's Life Cycle," *Harvard Educational Review* 49/4 (November 1979): 431–46. For a comprehensive survey of Erikson's work that presents the most commonly stated objections, see Paul Roazen, *Erik Erikson: The Power and Limits of a Vision* (New York: Free Press, 1976); a more appreciative view is Robert Coles, *Erik H. Erikson: The Growth of His Work* (Boston: Little, Brown, 1970).

For a sampling of the varied critical discussions of Freud and psychoanalysis, see Philip Rieff, *Freud: The Mind of the Moralist* (Garden City, NY: Doubleday Anchor, 1961 [1959]); Paul Ricoeur, *Freud and Philosophy: An Essay on Interpretation*, trans. D. Savage (New Haven, CT: Yale University Press, 1970); Peter Homans, *Theology after Freud: An Interpretive Inquiry* (Indianapolis, IN: Bobbs-Merrill, 1970); Daniel Yankelovich and William Barrett, *Ego and Instinct: The Psychoanalytic View of Human Nature—Revised* (New York: Random House Vintage, 1971); Richard Wollheim, ed., *Freud: A Collection of Critical Essays* (Garden City, NY: Doubleday Anchor, 1974); Frederick Crews, *Out of My System: Psychoanalysis, Ideology and Critical Method* (New York: Oxford University Press, 1975); Roy Schafer, *A New Language for Psychoanalysis* (New Haven, CT: Yale University Press, 1976); Judith Van Herik, *Freud on Faith and Feminity* (Berkeley: University of California Press,

1982); and Adolf Grünbaum, *The Foundations of Psychoanalysis: A Philosophical Critique* (Berkeley: University of California Press, 1984).

4. Critical assessment of Piaget's work covering more than half a century has been enormous. In addition to other references cited, two convenient sources are Linda S. Siegal and Charles J. Brainerd, eds., *Alternatives to Piaget: Critical Essays on the Theory* (New York: Academic Press, 1978) and Geoffrey Brown and Charles Desforges, *Piaget's Theory: A Psychological Critique* (London: Routledge and Kegan Paul, 1979). Of special critical interest is John M. Broughton, "Piaget's Structural Developmental Psychology," *Human Development* 24 (1981): I. "Piaget and Structuralism," 78–109; II. "Logic and Psychology," 195–224; III. "Function and the Problem of Knowledge," 257–85; IV. "Knowledge without a Self and without History," 320–46; V. "Ideology-Critique and the Possibility of a Critical Developmental Theory," 382–411.

5. Research results indicating only thirty percent of adults completing the transition to consolidated formal operations (and fifteen percent showing no formal thought at all) is presented in Deanna Kuhn, Jonas Langer, Lawrence Kohlberg, and Norma S. Haan, "The Development of Formal Operations in Logical and Moral Judgment," *Genetic Psychology Monographs* 95 (1977): 97–188. Piaget, "Intellectual Evolution from Adolescence to Adulthood," pp. 9–10, suggests that all normal adults attain formal operations, but "in different areas according to their aptitudes and their professional specializations. . . . " This suggestion qualifies the demand for rigorous universality in the last of the six conditions for strict universality stipulated by John H. Flavell, *Cognitive Development* (Englewood Cliffs, NJ: Prentice-Hall, 1977), p. 115: "(1) all biologically normal (e.g., non-retarded) adults in all cultures and subcultures (2) can and (3) spontaneously do employ (4) all . . . complex types of post-childhood thinking . . . (5) at a high level of expertise (6) in all problem situations and all content areas where such thinking is applicable." Kuhn *et al.* used the pendulum, correlation, and chemicals problems of propositional logic from Bärbel Inhelder and Jean Piaget, *The Growth of Logical Thinking from Childhood to Adolescence: An Essay on the Construction of Formal Operational Structures,* trans. A. Parsons and S. Milgram (New York: Basic Books, 1958 [original French 1955]). In contrast, Flavell, p. 117, cites the example of the complex reasoning performed by Kalahari Bushmen engaged in hunting.

6. See Kohlberg, "Continuities Revisited," p. 183.

7. Even Piaget, despite his predominant focus on cognitive development, has also given systematic attention to the development of

affectivity, morality, and personality; see, e.g., Piaget, *Six Psychological Studies*, pp. 15–17, 33–38, 54–60, 64–70; Piaget and Inhelder, *Psychology of the Child*, pp. 21–27, 114–29, 149–51; and esp. Jean Piaget, *Intelligence and Affectivity: Their Relationship during Child Development*, trans. and ed. T.A. Brown and C.E. Kaegi (Palo Alto, CA: Annual Reviews, 1981 [original French 1954]). The texts of two brief lectures by Piaget printed in the *Bulletin of the Menninger Clinic* 26 (1962) are particularly pertinent: "The Relation of Affectivity to Intelligence in the Mental Development of the Child," pp. 129–37, and "Will and Action," pp. 138–45. Also see, on the correlation of Piaget's concept of personality (in contrast to self) with Erikson's identity (in contrast to identifications), Conn, "Personal Identity and Creative *Self*-Understanding," pp. 36–38; and, on childhood affectivity, Walter E. Conn, "Cognitive and Affective Foundations of Moral Development: Jean Piaget's Analysis of the Emergence of Concrete Operations and Will in Middle Childhood," *Lumen Vitae* 37/4 (1982): 367–82. For an especially helpful analysis, see Wolfe Mays, "Affectivity and Values in Piaget" in Modgil and Modgil, eds., *Toward a Theory of Psychological Development*, pp. 35–59; also see Philip A. Cowan, *Piaget with Feeling: Cognitive, Social, and Emotional Dimensions* (New York: Holt, Rinehart and Winston, 1978). For a Piagetian inspired approach to affectivity, see Henry Dupont, "Affective Development: Stage and Sequence" in Mosher, ed., *Adolescents' Development and Education*, pp. 163–83.

8. Erik H. Erikson, *Identity: Youth and Crisis* (New York: Norton, 1968), p. 92; also Erikson, *Identity and the Life Cycle*, Psychological Issues 1 (New York: International Universities Press, 1959), p. 52.

9. Don S. Browning, *Generative Man: Psychoanalytic Perspectives* (New York: Dell, 1975 [1973]), pp. 22, 181.

10. Lawrence Kohlberg, "Stage and Sequence: The Cognitive-Developmental Approach to Socialization" in David A. Goslin, ed., *Handbook of Socialization Theory and Research* (Chicago: Rand McNally, 1969), pp. 347–480, at 353.

11. See, e.g., Paul Ricoeur, *Interpretation Theory: Discourse and the Surplus of Meaning* (Fort Worth: Texas Christian University Press, 1976) and *Freud and Philosophy*, pp. 20–37.

12. See Howard Gardner, *The Arts and Human Development: A Psychological Study of the Artistic Process* (New York: John Wiley, 1973), *Artful Scribbles: The Significance of Children's Drawings* (New York: Basic Books, 1980), *Art, Mind, and Brain: A Cognitive Approach to Creativity* (New York: Basic Books, 1982), and "Developmental Psychology after Piaget: An Approach in Terms of Symbolization," *Human Development* 22 (1979): 73–88.

13. Hans Furth, "Symbol Formation: Where Freud and Piaget Meet," *Human Development* 26 (1983): 26–41.

14. See Jean Piaget, "Developmental Psychology: A Theory," *International Encyclopedia of the Social Sciences* 4: 140–47, at 140–41.

15. Jean Piaget, *Play, Dreams and Imitation in Childhood*, trans. C. Gattegno and F.M. Hodgson (New York: Norton, 1962 [first English 1951; original French 1945]), pp. 289, 211.

16. William F. Lynch, *Images of Hope: Imagination as Healer of the Hopeless* (Baltimore, MD: Helicon, 1965), pp. 35, 63, 14, 149.

17. Maguire, *Moral Choice*, p. 189; also see Walter E. Conn, "Ethical Style for the Creative Conscience," *Louvain Studies* 7/3 (Spring 1979): 183–94, where I suggest an understanding of ethics modeled on art criticism as appropriate to the creative character of human action and life.

18. Ray L. Hart, *Unfinished Man and the Imagination* (New York: Herder and Herder, 1968), p. 247.

19. *Ibid.*, pp. 187, 188, 135, 207, 250, 242, 252.

20. *Ibid.*, pp. 216–17, 235.

21. Harold Rugg, *Imagination* (New York: Harper & Row, 1963), pp. 282, 241–43. For a relatively brief statement of Cassirer's exhaustive treatment of symbol, see Ernst Cassirer, *An Essay on Man: An Introduction to the Philosophy of Culture* (New Haven, CT: Yale University Press, 1944); for Langer, especially on the discursive/presentational distinction and on the artistic symbol, see Susanne K. Langer, *Philosophy in a New Key: A Study in the Symbolism of Reason, Rite, and Art* (2nd ed.; New York: New American Library, 1951 [1942]) and *Feeling and Form: A Theory of Art* (New York: Scribner's, 1953).

22. William A. Van Roo, *Man the Symbolizer*, Analecta Gregoriana 222 (Rome: Gregorian University Press, 1981), pp. 186–92, 271–94.

23. For a recent, much needed study of imagination in the moral life, see Philip S. Keane, *Christian Ethics and Imagination: A Theological Inquiry* (New York: Paulist, 1984).

24. Lawrence Kohlberg, "Stages of Moral Development as a Basis for Moral Education" in C.M. Beck, B.S. Crittenden, and E.V. Sullivan, eds., *Moral Education: Interdisciplinary Approaches* (New York: Newman, 1971), pp. 24–92, at 65. To say that lower stage limitations are not taken up and integrated into the structure of higher orientations is not to claim that egocentrism, e.g., is thereby eliminated, but that the limitation does not dominate the higher orientation.

25. See, e.g., Justin Aronfreed, "Moral Development from the Standpoint of a General Psychological Theory" in Lickona, ed., *Moral*

Development and Behavior, pp. 54–69; Fowler, *Stages of Faith*, pp. 101–02; and Paul J. Philibert, "Conscience: Developmental Perspectives from Rogers and Kohlberg," *Horizons* 6/1 (Spring 1979): 1–25, esp. 11–20 ("Kohlberg's Moral Rationalism").

26. Like every influential and popular theory, however, Kohlberg's approach has not suffered from lack of criticism. The following list is only a representative sampler of the many types (several others are mentioned in notes below): William Kurtines and Esther Blank Greif, "The Development of Moral Thought: Review and Evaluation of Kohlberg's Approach," *Psychological Bulletin* 81/8 (August 1974): 453–70; Elizabeth Leonie Simpson, "Moral Development Research: A Case Study of Scientific Cultural Bias," *Human Development* 17 (1974): 81–106; Paul J. Philibert, "Lawrence Kohlberg's Use of Virtue in His Theory of Moral Development," *International Philosophical Quarterly* 15 (December 1975): 455–97; Edmund V. Sullivan, "A Study of Kohlberg's Structural Theory of Moral Development: A Critique of Liberal Social Science Ideology," *Human Development* 20 (1977): 352–76; D.C. Phillips and Jennie Nicolayev, "Kohlbergian Moral Development: A Progressing or Degenerating Research Program?" *Educational Theory* 28/4 (Fall 1978): 286–301; Ralph B. Potter, "Justice and Beyond in Moral Education," *Andover Newton Quarterly* 19/3 (January 1979): 145–55; and the sets of essays, with Kohlberg's statements and responses, in Munsey, cd., *Moral Development, Moral Education, and Kohlberg;* Richard W. Wilson and Gordon J. Schochet, eds., *Moral Development and Politics* (New York: Praeger, 1980), including Kohlberg, "The Future of Liberalism as the Dominant Ideology of the Western World," pp. 55–68; and in *Ethics* 92/3 (April 1983): 468–532. Kohlberg responds to a wide range of specific criticisms in Lawrence Kohlberg with Charles Levine and Alexandra Hewer, "Synopses and Detailed Replies to Critics" in Kohlberg, *Psychology of Moral Development*, pp. 320–94. Finally, for a recent survey, see H. Newton Malony and Donald D. Hoagland, "Moral Development: A Review of Empirical Research," *Religious Studies Review* 10/4 (October 1984): 343–47; and for a variety of recent perspectives, see the essays in William M. Kurtines and Jacob L. Gewirtz, eds., *Morality, Moral Behavior, and Moral Development* (New York: John Wiley, 1984).

27. See, e.g., R.S. Peters, "Form and Content in Moral Education," B. Crittenden, "The Limitations of Morality as Justice in Kohlberg's Theory," and R.S. Peters, "Virtues and Habits in Moral Education" in Donald B. Cochrane, Cornel M. Hamm, and Anastasios C. Kazepides, eds., *The Domain of Moral Education* (New York: Paulist, 1979), pp. 187–202, 251–66, 267–87; also see Craig R. Dykstra, *Vision*

and Character: A Christian Educator's Alternative to Kohlberg (New York: Paulist, 1981), pp. 7–29; Moran, *Religious Education Development*, pp. 67–106; and André Guindon, "Moral Development: Form, Content and Self—A Critique of Kohlberg's Sequence," *Revue de l'Université d'Ottawa/University of Ottawa Quarterly* 48/3 (1978): 232–63.

28. For my earlier criticism, see Conn, "Postconventional Morality," esp. pp. 226–30; more recently there is Walter E. Conn, "Moral Reasoning and Moral Action: A Critical Analysis of Kohlberg's Theory of Moral Development" in J.A. Meacham and N.R. Santilli, eds., *Social Development and Youth: Structure and Content*, Contributions to Human Development 5 (Basel: Karger, 1981), pp. 100–12.

29. Kohlberg and Gilligan, "Adolescent as a Philosopher," p. 1071.

30. Kohlberg, "Moral Stages and Moralization," p. 32.

31. Kohlberg, "Stages of Moral Development," p. 44.

32. Kohlberg, "Stage and Sequence," p. 393.

33. Kohlberg, "Stages of Moral Development," p. 44. Kohlberg is clear that moral stages are cognitive in their structure, but "not in the sense of being free of emotions": see Kohlberg, "The Implications of Moral Stages for Adult Education," p. 188.

34. Kohlberg, "Stage and Sequence," pp. 389–90.

35. Kohlberg, "Stages of Moral Development," p. 51.

36. Kohlberg, "Moral Stages and Moralization," p. 49.

37. Kohlberg, "Stage and Sequence," pp. 393, 394.

38. Kohlberg, "Stages of Moral Development," p. 52. That by "empathy" Kohlberg means a justice-structured empathy is clear from his 1976 remarks on the limitation of empathy as simply feeling for others in Thomas C. Hennessy, "An Interview with Lawrence Kohlberg" in Thomas C. Hennessy, ed., *Value/Moral Education: The Schools and the Teachers* (New York: Paulist, 1979), pp. 211–42, at 237–38.

39. Martin L. Hoffmann, "Empathy, Role Taking, Guilt, and Development of Altruistic Motives" in Lickona, ed., *Moral Development and Behavior*, pp. 124–43; also see Hoffmann, "Development of Moral Thought, Feeling, and Behavior," *American Psychologist* 34/10 (October 1979): 958–66.

40. Kohlberg, "Moral Development," p. 491.

41. Kohlberg and Gilligan, "Adolescent as a Philosopher," p. 1071.

42. Indeed, the worth of even universal principles depends on the *depth of moral insight* with which a given person uses them in discerning the concrete personal values involved in a situation. Such moral insight is symbolic—a radically and fully *personal* reality, at once

and inseparably affective and cognitive. Unlike critical ethical reflection, moral insight is not the exclusive possession of people at postconventional stages of moral reasoning. Though ethically uncritical, persons (especially adults) reasoning at conventional stages can, and in many cases do, realize great depths of moral insight in the concrete circumstances of their lives. Such insight has its source in the wells of rich imaginative and affective experience of persons involved in the life around them and in touch with the life within them. Critical ethical reflection strengthens and sharpens the edge of moral insight for surer movement through the maze of conflicting values and principles. But without concrete, affective-cognitive moral insight, morality is lifeless, nothing more than the mechanical, logical application of conceptual principles to cases. On the central role of affectivity and imagination in the moral life, see Maguire, *Moral Choice,* ch. 6, "Ethics and Creativity," esp. pp. 189–99, and ch. 9, "The Feel of Truth"; on the relation of affectivity to rational moral discourse, see Daniel C. Maguire, *"Ratio Practica* and the Intellectualistic Fallacy," *Journal of Religious Ethics* 10/1 (Spring 1982): 22–39. For an excellent consideration of the various elements in the process of discernment, see James M. Gustafson, "Moral Discernment in the Christian Life" in Gene H. Outka and Paul Ramsey, eds., *Norm and Context in Christian Ethics* (New York: Scribner's, 1968), pp. 17–36. See Karl Rahner on the logic of concrete individual knowledge in his *The Dynamic Element in the Church,* Quaestiones Disputatae 12, trans. W.J. O'Hara (New York: Herder and Herder, 1964 [original German 1964]), pp. 84–170; also see Rahner, "On the Question of a Formal Existential Ethics" in his *Theological Investigations* 2, trans. Karl-H. Kruger (Baltimore: Helicon, 1963 [original German 1955]): 217–34. For Aristotle's classic version of moral discernment in the concrete situation, see the discussion of *phronesis* in his *Nicomachean Ethics,* II, 6.

43. Kohlberg, "Continuities Revisited," pp. 195–96, 198.

44. Kohlberg, "Stage and Sequence," p. 349.

45. Abraham H. Maslow, *Motivation and Personality* (New York: Harper & Row, 1954) and *Toward a Psychology of Being* (2nd ed.; Princeton, NJ: Van Nostrand, 1968 [1962]). For a correlation of Maslow with Kohlberg, see Elizabeth Léonie Simpson, "A Holistic Approach to Moral Development and Behavior" in Lickona, ed., *Moral Development and Behavior,* pp. 159–70, esp. 159–62. In addition to the gratification of basic psychic needs, Simpson emphasizes the cultivation of imagination as a condition for moral development (pp. 163–68).

46. Lawrence Kohlberg, "The Development of Children's Orientations toward a Moral Order: I. Sequence in the Development of

Human Thought," *Vita Humana* 6 (1963): 11–33, at 14. On the function of needs in moral consciousness from the perspective of communicative action and interactive competence, see Jürgen Habermas, "Moral Development and Ego Identity" in his *Communication and the Evolution of Society,* trans. T. McCarthy (Boston: Beacon, 1979), pp. 69–94, at 78, 91.

47. Fowler, "Life/Faith Patterns," pp. 36–37. In the 1980 "Faith and the Structuring of Meaning" Fowler recognizes that Kegan's thesis that meaning-making is prior to and generative of both cognition and affection overcomes, in principle, the false problem of integrating thought and feeling (p. 60); Fowler's 1981 discussion of this issue in *Stages of Faith* (pp. 101–02) stresses the separation in Piaget and Kohlberg but does not refer to the possible resolution in Kegan's thesis.

48. James W. Fowler, "Faith Development Theory and the Aims of Religious Socialization" in Gloria Durka and Joan-Marie Smith, eds., *Emerging Issues in Religious Education* (New York: Paulist, 1976), pp. 187–211, at 191.

49. Fowler, "Life/Faith Patterns," p. 37.

50. *Ibid.,* pp. 37, 18. Fowler's project has received relatively little critical comment. In addition to the papers in Stokes, ed., *Faith Development and the Adult Life Cycle,* see, e.g., Moran, *Religious Education Development,* ch. 6, "Faith Development: Fowler"; Alfred McBride, "Reaction to Fowler: Fears about Procedure" and James E. Hennessy, "Reaction to Fowler: Stages in Faith or Stages in Commitment" in Hennessy, ed., *Values and Moral Development,* pp. 211–18, 218–23; Loder's contribution to James E. Loder and James W. Fowler, "Conversations on Fowler's *Stages of Faith* and Loder's *The Transforming Moment,*" *Religious Education* 27/2 (1982): 133–48: at 133–39: "Reflections on Fowler's *Stages of Faith*"; Craig R. Dykstra, "Transformation in Faith and Morals," *Theology Today* 39/1 (April 1982): 56–64; Thomas Groome, *Christian Religious Education: Sharing Our Story and Vision* (San Francisco: Harper & Row, 1980), pp. 70–73; and C. Ellis Nelson, "Does Faith Develop? An Evaluation of Fowler's Position," *Living Light* 19/2 (Summer 1982): 162–73. Also see John McDargh, "Faith-Development Theory at Ten Years," *Religious Studies Review* 10/4 (October 1984): 339–43.

51. Fowler, "Stages in Faith," p. 178.

52. Fowler, "Faith Development Theory," p. 193.

53. Fowler, *Stages of Faith,* p. 110.

54. See Fowler, "Faith Development Theory," pp. 198–99, 205–06, and "Life/Faith Patterns," pp. 39–41, 96–99.

55. Fowler, *Stages of Faith,* p. 107.

56. Fowler, "Stages in Faith," p. 190.

57. See Fowler, *Stages of Faith,*, pp. 244–45. The variables or aspects of faith are: Form of Logic (Piaget), Perspective Taking (Selman), Form of Moral Judgment (Kohlberg), Bounds of Social Awareness, Locus of Authority, Form of World Coherence, and Symbolic Function.

58. Kohlberg, "Continuities Revisited," p. 180.

59. Fowler, "Faith Development Theory," p. 199; for the chart, see pp. 205–06. The six variables listed here are: Form of Logic (modified Piaget), Form of World Coherence, Role Taking (modified Selman), Bounds of Social Awareness, Form of Moral Judgment (modified Kohlberg), and Role of Symbols.

60. Kohlberg, "Stage and Sequence," p. 389.

61. Fowler, "Faith Development Theory," p. 200.

62. Fowler, *Stages of Faith*, p. 102.

63. James W. Fowler, "Faith and the Structuring of Meaning" in James W. Fowler, Antoine Vergote, *et al., Toward Moral and Religious Maturity: The First International Conference on Moral and Religious Development* (Morristown, NJ: Silver Burdett, 1980), pp. 51–85, at 63.

64. James E. Loder, *The Transforming Moment: Understanding Convictional Experiences* (San Francisco: Harper & Row, 1981), pp. 31 34. For Polanyi on tacit knowing, see Michael Polanyi, *Personal Knowledge: Towards a Post-Critical Philosophy* (New York: Harper & Row Torchbook, 1964 [1958]), for a synthetic presentation and critical assessment of tacit knowing, see Conn, "Michael Polanyi: The Responsible Person," esp. pp. 45–49.

65. Loder, *Transforming Moment*, pp. 164, 123, 164.

66. Fowler, "Faith Development Theory," p. 199.

67. Fowler, *Stages of Faith*, p. 264.

68. Fowler, "Faith Development Theory," p. 200.

69. *Ibid.*

70. Fowler, *Stages of Faith*, p. 105.

71. Lawrence Kohlberg with Daniel Candee, "The Relationship of Moral Judgment and Moral Action" in Kohlberg, *Psychology of Moral Development*, pp. 498–581, at 536–37.

72. *Ibid.*, pp. 523–24, 510. Claiming that justice is a universal principle, Kohlberg takes a deliberate non-relativist position. There is an objectivity to moral reasoning that goes beyond personal opinion. In fact, Kohlberg sees principled moral reasoning, especially Stage 6, as the developmental overcoming of the relativistic Stage 4$^{1/2}$, which, though having perceived conventional morality as only one among many moralities and not absolutely "given," still lacks objective

grounding. Speaking about the Heinz dilemma, for example, Kohlberg says he "would claim that in this situation it is universally morally right to steal the drug" (Hennessy, "Kohlberg Interview," p. 223). By its very definition, then, Stage 6 moral reasoning is objectively grounded in principled justice. This is not to say that conventional moral reasoning cannot be objective. The point, rather, is that, unlike conventional reasoning, postconventional principled reasoning is *intrinsically* objective. Persons at conventional stages can and sometimes clearly do make objective moral judgments. But their objectivity is in a sense "accidental," dependent upon whether the substantive moral rules they borrow from the "given" morality happen to be objective. Conventional morality is a "borrowed" morality, and whatever objectivity it possesses is also borrowed. In contrast, postconventional morality is the orientation of a person whose critically appropriated substantive moral rules have been objectively grounded and justified in personal ethical reflection. Objectivity is a constitutive component of such a critical ethical orientation of (consistent, inclusive, and impartial) *universal* principles. This orientation grounds the consensus of postconventional subjects.

73. Kohlberg with Levine and Hewer, "Current Formulation," p. 261.

74. Kohlberg with Candee, "Moral Judgment and Moral Action," p. 521. Although Kohlberg includes ego controls as the last "follow through" factor in the horizontal sequence before action, he gives them little attention, regarding them as non-moral—as merely working to reinforce whatever one's judgment is: strong ego controls, for example, allow preconventional subjects to cheat, while enabling conventional subjects to follow their conventional moral judgment and refrain from cheating (*ibid.*, p. 559). However, there is a difference, which Kohlberg does not seem to account for fully, between following a judgment that will entail significant personal cost and one that will not. Although Kohlberg once characterized ego controls as "decision capacities," he needs to focus more sharply on the role of *decision* between judgments of responsibility (what one should do) and actions (what one does). The distinction between judgment and decision is crucial, for everyone's experience includes not only instances when reasoning and judgment were clouded or distorted, but also times when one *knew* quite well what one should do, but did not *decide* to do it. Kohlberg's suggestion that ego controls along with judgments of responsibility constitute a psychological analogue to what some philosopher-psychologists have called moral will (*ibid.*, p. 580) may account for the decision-making function, but would then fail to specify ade-

quately one's practical judgment of personal conscience (what I should do).

75. Kohlberg's position is that the development of the very structure of moral reasoning leads—in the limit of Stage 6—to a moral orientation grounded in the central principle of justice: "Our major and most controversial claim is that the only 'true' (stage 6) moral principle is justice." He explains this claim by asserting "that human welfare is always the core of morality but that, at the principled level, welfare considerations subsumed under the heading 'justice' take priority over other 'principles' for considering welfare whenever there is conflict between the two, and that there is no strong 'principle' for deciding between the various welfare alternatives other than justice." At Stage 6, then, structure (or form) and content are one. As Kohlberg says, his "conception of moral principle implies that one cannot ultimately separate form and content in moral analysis" (Kohlberg, "Stages of Moral Development," pp. 62–63, 60). While "concern for welfare consequences" in some way characterizes each stage of moral reasoning, only at Stage 6 are welfare concerns structured by the universal principle of justice: the equality of human rights and respect for the dignity of human beings as individual persons. Empathy structured in any way short of this fundamental principle of justice does not result in consensus of moral judgment.

76. Kohlberg, "Stages of Moral Development," p. 80. For a recent focus on the self in the judgment-action issue, see Augusto Blasi, "Moral Cognition and Moral Action: A Theoretical Perspective," *Developmental Review* 3 (1983): 178–210.

77. On conscience at Stage 6, see, e.g., Lawrence Kohlberg, "Moral and Religious Education and the Public Schools: A Developmental View" in Theodore R. Sizer, ed., *Religion and Public Education* (Boston: Houghton Mifflin, 1967), pp. 164–83, at 171. Kohlberg has not been consistent in his stage designation of conscience; in later writings he refers to conscience at Stage 4: see, e.g., "Moral Stages and Moralization," p. 35, and *Philosophy of Moral Development,* p. 410. These brief references to conscience as Stage 6 or Stage 4 are unsystematic and unexplicated. Kohlberg's only extended explicit discussion of "conscience" is an early examination of the inadequate conceptions of conscience as superego strength in learning-theory and psychoanalytic treatments: see "Moral Development and Identification" in Harold W. Stevenson, ed., *Child Psychology: The Sixty-Second Yearbook of the National Society for the Study of Education, Part I* (Chicago: University of Chicago Press, 1963), pp. 277–332; also see Paul F. Grim, Lawrence Kohlberg, and Sheldon H. White, "Some Relationships between Conscience and

Attentional Processes," *Journal of Personality and Social Psychology* 8/3 (1968): 239–52, for an ego-strength rather than superego-strength interpretation of moral behavior. My approach is not to identify conscience with any particular stage, but to interpret all the moral stages precisely as stages in the development of conscience.

78. See Walter E. Conn, "Moral Development as Self-Transcendence," *Horizons* 4/2 (Fall 1977): 189–205.

79. See Lawrence Kohlberg, "Justice as Reversibility" in Peter Laslett and James Fishkin, eds., *Philosophy, Politics and Society* 5 (New Haven, CT: Yale University Press, 1979): 257–72, and "The Claim to Moral Adequacy of a Highest Stage of Moral Judgment." For a helpful analysis of Kohlberg's view of Rawls as an example of Stage 6 structuring of justice, see Dwight Boyd, "The Rawls Connection" in Munsey, ed., *Moral Development, Moral Education, and Kohlberg,* pp. 185–213. The clearest example of reversibility is the classic procedure for dividing a piece of cake fairly—one person cuts, the other chooses. Kohlberg calls his own version of reversibility "moral musical chairs": "going around the circle of perspectives involved in a moral dilemma to test one's claims of right or duty until only the equilibrated or reversible claims survive"; e.g., in the famous Heinz dilemma, Kohlberg claims that if the druggist imaginatively changed places with Heinz's wife, he would have to admit that her right to life is prior to his right to property (thus, unlike the wife's claim, the druggist's claim is not reversible) ("Justice as Reversibility," p. 262).

80. For a sketch of such an understanding of justice, see Daniel C. Maguire, "The Primacy of Justice in Moral Theology," *Horizons* 10/1 (Spring 1983): 72–85; for an application to the contemporary issue of preferential affirmative action, see Daniel C. Maguire, *A New American Justice: Ending the White Male Monopolies* (Garden City, NY: Doubleday, 1980).

81. See Kohlberg, "Continuities Revisited," pp. 193–201.

82. Despite his insistence on universal principles, Kohlberg is unambiguous in stating that his "conception of principle implies a 'situation ethic' in the sense that it reduces all moral obligation to the interests and claims of concrete individual persons in concrete situations." For Kohlberg, then (and this is a side of his thought which has not been taken into sufficient account), true principles are "guides to perceiving and integrating all the morally relevant elements in concrete situations . . . to the obligating elements in the situation, to the concrete human claims there." In his view, "the case is always higher than the principle, a single human life is worth more than all the principles in philosophy to the man. Principles simply tell us how to resolve

these concrete claims, when claims conflict in a situation, when it is one man's life against another's." In contrast, the universality of principles used as rules of action, whether conceived formally or materially, is "always purchased at the price of ignoring unique elements of human welfare and justice in the concrete situation." Asserting that "moral obligations are towards concrete other people in concrete situations," Kohlberg rejects the "fallacy of treating a principle as elevated above the individual in the situation to which it applies" (Kohlberg, "Stages of Moral Development," pp. 60–61, and "A Reply to Owen Flanagan and Some Comments on the Puka-Goodpaster Exchange," *Ethics* 92/3 [April 1982]: 513–28, at 520–21).

Kohlberg's view is "situational," then, in the sense that, while affirming the universality and objectivity of ethical principles as guides for dealing morally with concrete situations, he rejects the validity of principles understood as universal rules of action. Indeed, Kohlberg is the rare moral thinker who explicitly understands his position in terms of both natural law and situation ethics perspectives (Kohlberg, "Education, Moral Development and Faith," *Journal of Moral Education* 4/1 [1974]: 5–16, at 5). He can do this because he understands natural law in terms of universal principles of justice. And these are the principles which guide us in concrete situations, directing the use of lower level principles or rules to the realization of the interests and claims of the persons in those situations. Only in respecting the concreteness of situations are universal principles truly objective.

"Natural law" here refers to objectivity and universality in morality; "situation ethics" means taking the particulars and the persons of the situation seriously—not an absolute situationalism that recognizes no continuity between situations. For Kohlberg's discussion of the relationship of fact and value, or is and ought, that is fundamental to natural law morality, see his "From Is to Ought: How to Commit the Naturalistic Fallacy and Get Away with It in the Study of Moral Development" in Mischel, ed., *Cognitive Development and Epistemology*, pp. 151–235, esp. 222–26; and Dwight Boyd and Lawrence Kohlberg, "The Is-Ought Problem: A Developmental Perspective," *Zygon* 8 (1973): 358–72, esp. 365–67.

In our earlier survey of the stages of moral reasoning we noted the period of radical relativism Kohlberg calls Stage 4¹/₂. The radical nature of this relativism, which would subvert all morality, is normatively overcome by principled morality. However, the emphasis Kohlberg places on the concrete situation makes it clear that for him the relativity of the specific context is never left behind by principled morality. This situational emphasis shows that, like William Perry and other developmentalists who focus on personal commitment within relativism as a mature moral orientation, Kohlberg understands that authentic insight into the relativity of human reality endures as a constitutive dimension of adult morality. As we pointed out in the discussion of cognitive development, the mature, realistic knowing of the adult is intrinsically related to the concrete context—and mature moral reasoning is no exception. Universal ethical principles may escape the situation in their abstract formulations, but as working principles they exist in relation to each situation. In action, such ethical principles are neither abstract universals nor concrete specifics; they are universals *in* the concrete. Not they, but only principles understood as absolute, substantive rules of action applicable to every situation without exception conflict with the fundamental insight of contextual relativism. See Kohlberg with Higgins, "Continuities Revisited—Again," pp. 432–60; and Carol Gilligan and Lawrence Kohlberg, "From Adolescence to Adulthood: The Rediscovery of Reality in a Postconventional World" in Barbara Z. Preseissen, David Goldstein, and Marilyn H. Appel, eds., *Topics in Cognitive Development 2: Language and Operational Thought* (New York: Plenum, 1978): 125–36. Also see William G. Perry, Jr., *Forms of Intellectual and Ethical Development in the College Years: A Scheme* (New York: Holt, Rinehart and Winston, 1970); Carol Gilligan and John Michael Murphy, "Development from Adolescence to Adulthood: The Philosopher and the Dilemma of the Fact" in Deanna Kuhn, ed., *Intellectual Development Beyond Childhood* (San Francisco: Jossey-Bass, 1979), pp. 85–99; John Michael Murphy and Carol Gilligan, "Moral Development in Late Adolescence and Adulthood: A Critique and Reconstruction of Kohlberg's Theory," *Human Development* 23 (1980): 77–104; André Guindon, "Kohlberg's Postconventional Yogis," *Eglise et Théologie* 12 (1981): 279–306; Gisela Labouvie-Vief, "Dynamic Development and Mature Autonomy: A Theoretical Prologue," *Human Development* 25/3 (1982): 161–91; and Wolfgang Edelstein and Gil Noam, "Regulatory Structures of the Self and 'Postformal' Stages in Adulthood," *Human Development* 25 (1982): 407–22.

83.   In such a holistic view of conscience that integrates the fundamental cognitive and affective dimensions (the respective strengths of Kohlberg and Erikson) lies the possibility of establishing the intrinsic relationship between an ethics of principle and an ethics of disposition: see editor's Introduction in Don S. Browning, ed., *Practical Theology* (San Francisco: Harper & Row, 1983), pp. 1–18, at 11–13.

84.   Carol Gilligan, *In a Different Voice: Psychological Theory and Women's Development* (Cambridge: Harvard University Press, 1982), p.

18. For a related approach, distinguishing formal and interpersonal moral perspectives, see Norma Haan, "Two Moralities in Action Contexts: Relationships to Thought, Ego Regulation, and Development," *Journal of Personality and Social Psychology* 36/3 (1978): 286–305.

85. Gilligan, *In a Different Voice,* pp. 73, 74, 90.

86. *Ibid.,* pp. 100, 98.

87. *Ibid.,* p. 149. Recognizing the limitations of her research findings, Gilligan is modest in her claims: any generalization will require much further study (p. 126). Indeed, despite her focus on care and responsibility as voiced by women in her studies, Gilligan disavows any claim of absolute association of this voice with women, of any generalization about either sex, or "about the origins of the differences described or their distribution in a wider population, across cultures, or through time" (p. 2). For Kohlberg's brief comments on Gilligan, see his "Reply to Owen Flanagan and Some Comments on the Puka-Goodpaster Exchange," pp. 513–19.

88. Gilligan, *In a Different Voice,* p. 166. In addition to Gilligan's "In a Different Voice: Women's Conceptions of Self and of Morality," *Harvard Educational Review* 47/4 (November 1977): 481–517, and "Justice and Responsibility: Thinking about Real Dilemmas of Moral Conflict and Choice" in Fowler, Vergote, *et al., Toward Moral and Religious Maturity,* pp. 223–49 (where an ethic of responsibility is contrasted to an absolute ethic, p. 225), see, on the point of relativism especially, her essay with Murphy, "Moral Development in Late Adolescence and Adulthood."

89. Kohlberg, "Continuities Revisited," p. 196.

90. On equity resolving the conflict between love and justice, see Piaget, *Moral Judgment of the Child,* pp. 323–24; on the "veil of ignorance" of the "original position," see John Rawls, *A Theory of Justice* (Cambridge: Harvard University Press, 1971), pp. 12, 136–42; for a more recent statement, see Rawls, "Kantian Constructivism in Moral Theory," *Journal of Philosophy* 77/9 (September 1980): 515–72, at 522–24. For a valuable critical analysis of the relationship between Rawlsian liberalism (with which Kohlberg associates himself) and Christian ethics, see William Werpehowski, "Political Liberalism and Christian Ethics: A Review Discussion," *Thomist* 48/1 (January 1984): 81–115.

91. Gilligan's distinction between justice and care is reflected in Kohlberg's recent distinction between judgments of rightness and judgments of responsibility which we have noted. My different approach is to integrate justice and care in the single moral response of the fully personal judgment of conscience. For Kohlberg's comprehensive response to Gilligan, see Kohlberg with Levine and Hewer,

"Synopses and Detailed Replies," pp. 338–70. For several responses to Gilligan from varied critical perspectives, see the entire issue of *Social Research* 50/3 (Autumn 1983). Also see Mary Brabeck, "Moral Judgment: Theory and Research on Differences between Males and Females," *Developmental Review* 3 (1983): 274–91; and Nel Noddings, *Caring: A Feminine Approach To Ethics & Moral Education* (Berkeley: University of California Press, 1984).

92. Erikson, "Dissent of Contemporary Youth," p. 16. See William W. Meissner, Erikson's Truth: The Search for Ethical Identity," *Theological Studies* 31/2 (June 1970): 310–19.

93. Erikson, *Identity: Youth and Crisis,* p. 222.

94. For a critical analysis of conscience and superego in Erikson, see Walter E. Conn, "Erik Erikson: The Ethical Orientation, Conscience and the Golden Rule," *Journal of Religious Ethics* 5/2 (Fall 1977): 249–66, at 252–55.

95. Erikson, *Insight and Responsibility,* p. 225.

96. *Ibid.,* pp. 232, 233; also see Erikson, *Gandhi's Truth,* p. 413. On active mutuality and the Golden Rule, see *Insight and Responsibility,* pp. 231–36, and Conn, "Erik Erikson," pp. 256–60.

97. See Philibert, "Kohlberg's Use of Virtue," pp. 461–64; MacIntyre, *After Virtue,* ch. 12, "Aristotle's Account of the Virtues"; and Aristotle, *Nicomachean Ethics,* II, 1.

98. See Paul J. Philibert, "The Motors of Morality: Religion and Relation" in Donald M. Joy, ed., *Moral Development Foundations: Judeo-Christian Alternatives to Piaget/Kohlberg* (Nashville, TN: Abingdon, 1983), pp. 87–110, at 97–99.

99. Erikson insists on the necessity of maintaining the unconscious character of the ego: see Erikson, *Identity: Youth and Crisis,* p. 218; also see Conn, "Erikson's 'Identity'," pp. 128–30. Still, the experience of the conscious "I" is fundamental, and even makes self-analysis possible. On English translations of Freud's "Ich" as "ego" and its relationship to "I," see Erikson, *Life Cycle Completed,* pp. 86–88, and Bruno Bettelheim, *Freud and Man's Soul* (New York: Knopf, 1983).

100. Erik H. Erikson, "Autobiographic Notes on the Identity Crisis," *Daedalus* 99 (Fall, 1970): 730–59, at 740–41.

101. For Erikson on "existential identity" and its relation to the "I," see "On Generativity and Identity," p. 261.

102. Fowler, "Stages in Faith," p. 175.

103. Kegan, *Evolving Self,* pp. 96–97. Also see Gilligan, "Woman's Place in Man's Life Cycle," esp. p. 437; and Erikson, "On Generativity and Identity," pp. 262, 266–67. Critical literature on Kegan is not yet extensive: in response to Robert Graham Kegan, "The Evolving Self:

A Process Conception for Ego Psychology," *Counseling Psychologist* 8/2 (Fall 1979): 5–34, there are evaluations in the same issue by Thomas C. Barrett and Vincent A. Harren (pp. 34–39) and by Jane Loevinger (pp. 39–40); also see Snarey, Kohlberg, and Noam, "Ego Development in Perspective," pp. 314–16.

4. CONVERSION: MORAL, COGNITIVE, AFFECTIVE

1. The stages are vividly described by Kierkegaard in *Either/Or* (1843), *Fear and Trembling* (1843), and *Stages on Life's Way* (1845); Princeton University Press, Princeton, NJ, which first published these English translations in 1944, 1941, and 1940, respectively, is now publishing new standard English translations of Kierkegaard's Writings. On irony and humor as the boundary zones between the aesthetic, ethical, and religious, see Søren Kierkegaard, *Concluding Unscientific Postscript*, trans. D.F. Swenson and W. Lowrie (Princeton, NJ: Princeton University Press, 1941 [1846]), p. 448. For a penetrating perspective on Kierkegaard, see David B. Burrell, "Kierkegaard: Language of Spirit" in his *Exercises in Religious Understanding* (Notre Dame, IN: University of Notre Dame Press, 1974), pp. 143–81.

2. On Kierkegaard's relationship to Regina Olsen, see Søren Kierkegaard, *Letters and Documents*, trans. H. Rosenmeier; Kierkegaard's Writings 25 (Princeton, NJ: Princeton University Press, 1978), letters 15–46, 50, 62, 68 and document XXI, "Will."

For a valuable analysis of the relationship of the ethical and religious in terms of Abraham's decision, see Gene Outka, "Religious and Moral Duty: Notes on *Fear and Trembling*" in Gene Outka and John P. Reeder, Jr., eds., *Religion and Morality: A Collection of Essays* (Garden City, NY: Doubleday Anchor, 1973), pp. 204–54.

3. Kohlberg and Gilligan, "Adolescent as a Philosopher," p. 1066.

4. John C. Gibbs, "Kohlberg's Stages of Moral Development: A Constructive Critique," *Harvard Educational Review* 47/1 (February 1977): 43–61, at 44.

5. *Ibid.*, pp. 47–50, 53.

6. *Ibid.*, pp. 53, 52.

7. *Ibid.*, p. 43.

8. Kohlberg, "Continuities Revisited," p. 180.

9. Gibbs, p. 56.

10. *Ibid.;* compare Kohlberg, "Claim to Moral Adequacy," p. 634.

11. Gibbs, p. 56. Among the many critical discussions of Stage 6 from various perspectives, see Don Locke, "The Illusion of Stage 6," *Journal of Moral Education* 9/2 (1979): 103–09; Elizabeth A. Morelli, "The Sixth Stage of Moral Development," *Journal of Moral Education* 7/2 (1977): 97–108; and Dwight Boyd, "An Interpretation of Principled Morality," *Journal of Moral Education* 8/2 (1978): 110–23.

12. Gibbs, pp. 57, 58.

13. For Kohlberg's own response to Gibbs, see Kohlberg with Levine and Hewer, "Current Formulation," pp. 236–49, and "Synopses and Detailed Replies," pp. 372–75.

14. Gibbs, p. 54.

15. See Kohlberg, "Moral Stages and Moralization," p. 35. Perhaps the clearest way to state the basic difference between Stages 5 and 6, while avoiding Kohlberg's problematic references to specific ethical systems (e.g., Stage 5 is utilitarian), is to characterize them as different *personal* responses to the problem of relativism: Stage 5 as a necessary practical response to the perception of all values as totally relative (e.g., individual's right to life); Stage 6 as grounding that response in the radical philosophical recognition of fundamental human values as absolute (e.g., dignity of the person) even though always realized *in relation to* the conditions of a specific context. This approach encompasses Kohlberg's recent recognition of relativism at Stage 5 ("Stage 5½"), the reason why he no longer regards "Stage 4½" as *the* transitional stage, and places quotes around it. See Kohlberg with Higgins, "Continuities Revisited—Again," pp. 440, 480–90. Among possible relativisms I give Stage 4½ primacy of epistemological place because it breaks through the socialized givenness of conventional morality. For an important influence on Kohlberg regarding relativism and types of subjectivism, see James S. Fishkin, *Beyond Subjective Morality: Ethical Reasoning and Political Philosophy* (New Haven, CT: Yale University Press, 1984).

16. For Lonergan's basic statement of intellectual, moral, and religious conversions, see his *Method in Theology*, pp. 237–43. Though Lonergan speaks of "intellectual conversion" to specify the explicit, philosophical appropriation of oneself as a knower, I use the term "cognitive" to emphasize that the conversion transforms knowing in all its patterns and dimensions, not just the intellectual. For Lonergan on affective conversion, see his "Natural Right and Historical Mindedness," *Proceedings of the American Catholic Philosophical Association* 51 (1977): 132–43, at 140–41; also see Walter E. Conn, "Bernard Lonergan's Analysis of Conversion," *Angelicum* 53/3 (1976): 362–404, at 389–90.

Among the many discussions of Lonergan's general notion of conversion, see Charles E. Curran, "Christian Conversion in the Writings of Bernard Lonergan" in Philip McShane, ed., *Foundations of Theology: Papers from the International Lonergan Congress 1970* (Notre Dame, IN: University of Notre Dame Press, 1972), pp. 41–59; Kevin J. Colleran, "Bernard Lonergan on Conversion," *Dunwoodie Review* 11 (January 1971): 3–23; Donal Dorr, "Conversion" in Patrick Corcoran, ed., *Looking at Lonergan's Method* (Dublin: Talbot, 1975), pp. 175–86; and Michael L. Rende, "The Development and the Unity of Lonergan's Notion of Conversion," *Method* 1/2 (October 1983): 158–73.

For some of the critical discussion of various aspects of Lonergan's methodological project, see the essays in Corcoran, ed., *Looking at Lonergan's Method;* in McShane, ed., *Foundations of Theology,* see Charles Davis, "Lonergan and the Teaching Church," pp. 60–75, Langdon Gilkey, "Empirical Science and Theological Knowing," pp. 76–101, Karl Rahner, "Some Critical Thoughts on 'Functional Specialties in Theology'," pp. 194–96, David Tracy, "Lonergan's Foundational Theology: An Interpretation and a Critique," pp. 197–222, and Lonergan's response, pp. 223–34; in Philip McShane, ed., *Language, Truth and Meaning: Papers from the International Lonergan Congress 1970* (Notre Dame, IN: University of Notre Dame Press, 1972), see Robert O. Johann, "Lonergan and Dewey on Judgment," pp. 79–92, Schubert M. Ogden, "Lonergan and the Subjectivist Principle," pp. 218–35, and William J. Richardson, "Being for Lonergan: A Heideggerean View," pp. 272–83.

Useful general orientations to Lonergan's work are David Tracy, *The Achievement of Bernard Lonergan* (New York: Herder and Herder, 1970); Hugo Meynell, *An Introduction to the Philosophy of Bernard Lonergan* (New York: Barnes & Noble, 1976); and Frederick E. Crowe, *The Lonergan Enterprise* (Cambridge, MA: Cowley, 1980).

17. Lonergan, *Method in Theology,* pp. 237–38, 131.

18. *Ibid.,* p. 240.

19. *Ibid.,* p. 35.

20. Bernard Lonergan, "Faith and Beliefs" (mimeographed version of paper presented to the American Academy of Religion, Newton, MA, October 1969), p. 6. On self-creation, also see Lonergan, *Second Collection:* "By his own acts the human subject makes himself what he is to be, and he does so freely and responsibily; indeed, he does so precisely because his acts are the free and responsible expressions of himself" (p. 79); "Just as the existential subject freely and responsibly makes himself what he is, so too he makes himself good or evil and his actions right or wrong" (p. 83).

21. Lonergan, "Faith and Beliefs," p. 6.

22. *Ibid.,* pp. 6–7.

23. Lonergan, *Method in Theology,* p. 240.

24. Bernard Lonergan, *Insight: A Study of Human Understanding* (2nd ed.; New York: Philosophical Library, 1958 [1957]), pp. 625, 627. Integration needs to be understood here not imperialistically (in favor of an abstract intellectualism), but hierarchically in the sense of Erikson's epigenetic principle, so that the rich symbols of the psyche, e.g., are sublated and included in the fabric of the higher integration. See *Insight,* pp. 471–78, on the tension of limitation and transcendence in human integration and genuineness; p. 633, on the autonomy of lower levels.

25. Lonergan, *Method in Theology,* p. 240.

26. *Ibid.*

27. Lonergan, *Collection,* p. 242. Self-creation, of course, is not *ex nihilo;* one creates oneself within given limits of personal biology, psyche, family, culture, history, etc.

28. Bernard Lonergan, "Notes on Existentialism" (mimeographed notes for lectures at Boston College, July 1957), sec. IV, p. 11.

29. Lonergan, *Collection,* p. 242. For an excellent descriptive analysis of drifters, people who go "through life without ever confronting anything but a small portion of their own reality," who "may never have decided anything for themselves," see Eugene Kennedy, *A Sense of Life, A Sense of Sin* (Garden City, NY: Doubleday, 1975), pp. 84, 42.

30. For a more detailed discussion of this distinction, see Walter E. Conn, "The Ontogenetic Ground of Value," *Theological Studies* 39/2 (June 1976): 313–35, at 328–35.

31. Lonergan, *Method in Theology,* p. 240.

32. *Ibid.,* pp. 238–39. According to Lonergan, this philosophical version of cognitive conversion, which he names "intellectual," is very rare. My point is that such explicit philosophical conversion is not required for critical moral conversion; the less rare but still uncommon implicit conversion of cognitive self-possession suffices. Uncritical moral conversion, of course, presupposes no cognitive conversion.

33. For detailed explication of this thesis, see Conn, "Bernard Lonergan and Authenticity," pp. 307–20, and "Objectivity—A Developmental and Structural Analysis," pp. 218–21. A distinction between two related but different forms of self-transcendence is important: if the most obvious form is the way successive levels of consciousness (and dimensions of the subject's world) transcend and hierarchically

incorporate the preceding (developmentally as well as structurally), the really significant form is the objective movement of the subject *beyond* itself that is normatively definitive of this successive transcendence of levels (dimensions) in the subject (see "Bernard Lonergan and Authenticity," p. 311).

34. By sublation Lonergan means that "what sublates goes beyond what is sublated, introduces something new and distinct, puts everything on a new basis, yet so far from interfering with the sublated or destroying it, on the contrary needs it, includes it, preserves all its proper features and properties, and carries them forward to a fuller realization within a richer context" (*Method in Theology*, p. 241). Like Erikson's epigenetic stages, then, hierarchical levels in sublation are simultaneous (lower not destroyed by higher) and mutually conditioning (higher needs and includes lower). Compare "levels of reality" in Michael Polanyi, *The Study of Man* (Chicago: University of Chicago Press, 1959), pp. 46–67.

Although Lonergan (*Method in Theology*, p. 241) does speak of one conversion sublating another (e.g., moral conversion sublating intellectual), it is more precise to speak, as he usually does, of one level of consciousness sublating another (e.g., moral consciousness sublating rational consciousness, with either level being converted or unconverted).

35. Lonergan discusses the structure of conscious intentionality sketched here in several places; for a concise statement, see *Method in Theology*, pp. 6–9, 104–05. For recent discussion of Lonergan's structural analysis, see Marc Smith, "Is There a Thomistic Alternative to Lonergan's Cognitional Structure?" *Thomist* 43 (1979): 626–36. One of the best informed critiques of Lonergan's cognitional theory remains the early work of Edward M. MacKinnon: see, e.g., his three part "Understanding According to Bernard J. F. Lonergan," *Thomist* 28 (April 1964): 97–132; 28 (July 1964): 338–72; 28 (October 1964): 475–522, and "Cognitional Analysis and the Philosophy of Science," *Continuum* 2/3 (Autumn 1964): 343–68 (this issue of *Continuum* with some twenty essays devoted to Lonergan's work was also published as a separate volume: Frederick E. Crowe, ed., *Spirit as Inquiry: Studies in Honor of Bernard Lonergan, S.J.* (Chicago: St. Xavier College, 1964).

36. "To grasp evidence as sufficient for a prospective judgment is to grasp the prospective judgment as virtually unconditioned." A virtually unconditioned has conditions but they are fulfilled. And these "conditions for the prospective judgment are fulfilled when there are no further, pertinent questions." This judgment of the virtually unconditioned occurs within a self-correcting process of learning that

"reaches its limit in familiarity with the concrete situation and in easy mastery of it" (Lonergan, *Insight,* pp. 280–87). Think of the high school mathematics teacher, e.g., who after many years in the classroom has heard every question and now anticipates them, or the experienced auto mechanic who needs no more than the description of a symptom or the sound of an engine to identify the problem.

37. See Bernard Lonergan, "Religious Knowledge" in Fred Lawrence, ed., *Lonergan Workshop* 1 (Missoula, MT: Scholars Press, 1978): 309–27, at 312.

38. For an integrated exposition of Lonergan's different discussions of the complex relationships among practical reflection, deliberation, value, and decision in *Insight* (1957), *The Subject* (Milwaukee, WI: Marquette University Press, 1968), and *Method in Theology* (1972), see Walter E. Conn, "Bernard Lonergan on Value," *Thomist* 40/2 (April 1976): 243–57, esp. 244–51. The key point in the development of Lonergan's thought on this question is his introduction in 1968 of the *transcendental* notion of value; on this point also see Frederick E. Crowe, "An Exploration of Lonergan's New Notion of Value," *Science et Esprit* 29/2 (1977): 123–43. Also see Paul Schuchman, "Bernard Lonergan and the Question of Moral Value," *Philosophy Today* 25 (1981): 252–61. For Lonergan on the differences and similarities of judgments of fact and judgments of value, see *Method in Theology,* p. 37. For critical discussion, see Charles Davis, "Lonergan's Appropriation of the Concept of Praxis," *New Blackfriars* 62 (March 1981): 114–26.

This key structural distinction between one's assessment of a situation and one's deliberation about what he or she should do in the situation is reflected in the way Kohlberg relates judgments of justice and judgments of responsibility in his "Reply and Some Comments," p. 514.

39. For an important discussion of the unity within the levels of consciousness, see Lonergan, *Insight,* pp. 320–28.

40. Lonergan, *Method in Theology,* pp. 30, 31.

41. See Arthur Koestler, *The Act of Creation* (New York: Dell, 1967 [1964]), pp. 87–89, on self-assertive and self-transcending emotions in the act of discovery.

42. Lonergan, *Method in Theology,* p. 38. On the relation of feeling and value and on the distinction of values according to a scale of preference (vital, social, cultural, personal, religious), see *ibid.,* pp. 30–32.

43. See Lonergan, "Religious Knowledge," pp. 313–14.

44. For detailed discussion of self-affirmation see Lonergan, *Insight,* ch. 11, and *Method in Theology,* pp. 13–20.

45. Frank Deford, "Problem Solving Can Be Beautiful," *Sports Illustrated*, May 10, 1976, pp. 83–96, at 93.

46. Jane Austen, *Pride and Prejudice* (New York: Washington Square Press, 1940 [1813]), p. 229.

47. John S. Dunne, *The Way of All the Earth* (New York: Macmillan, 1972), esp. "The Way of Conscious Individuation," pp. 38–49, at 42.

48. See Lonergan, *Insight*, pp. 250–53, 375–84, and *Method in Theology*, pp. 238–39. Also see James L. Marsh, "Lonergan's Mediation of Subjectivity and Objectivity," *Modern Schoolman* 53 (March 1975): 249–61, and "Objectivity, Alienation, and Reflection," *International Philosophical Quarterly* 22 (1982): 131–39; and J.W. Sullivan, "Lonergan, Conversion and Objectivity," *Theology* 86 (September 1983): 345–53.

49. Especially important here is the reality of peer cooperation emphasized by Piaget, *Moral Judgment of the Child*, and Youniss, *Parents and Peers in Social Development*, as well as that of interpersonal affiliation which Kegan suggests as a new stage before identity in Erikson's life cycle (*Evolving Self*, p. 87).

50. See Loder, *Transforming Moment*, pp. 128–33.

51. For the view that moral conversion requires a seventh *moral* stage, see Morelli, "The Sixth Stage of Moral Development," esp. pp. 104–08.

52. Gibbs does not explain why a philosophical version of Stage 2, e.g., would not simply be a type of meta-ethical egoism.

Gibbs refers to the "existential crisis" which sometimes results from "confronting alternative moral viewpoints, and discovering hypocrisy and societal corruption" ("Kohlberg's Stages of Moral Judgment," p. 54), but in this article he does not explicitly discuss Kohlberg's Stage 4½ of moral relativism. To move beyond conventional morality requires an insight into the relativity of any society's values. While that insight is necessary, it does not advance a person beyond the relativism of Stage 4½. To move to postconventional morality in a positive sense, a further insight is necessary to overcome extreme relativism and provide a critical grounding for fundamental human values—a cognitive conversion. Gibbs develops his critique of Kohlberg in terms of the basic natural (standard)/existential thesis in his "Kohlberg's Moral Stage Theory: A Piagetian Critique," *Human Development* 22 (1979): 89–112, where he discusses Stage 4½ but principally as a weakness in the earlier version of Kohlberg's theory.

53. See Kohlberg, "Continuities Revisited," p. 201; something of the necessary qualification is indicated on p. 199 in terms of the cog-

nitive-moral stimulation and conditions required for movement to principled morality.

54. See Lonergan, "Notes on Existentialism," sec. IV, pp. 10–11.

55. Lonergan, *Collection*, pp. 242–43.

56. For Lonergan's distinction between essential and effective freedom, see *Insight*, pp. 619–24.

57. Lonergan, *Method in Theology*, p. 240.

58. *Ibid.*, p. 105.

59. See Lonergan, "Natural Right and Historical Mindedness," pp. 140–41. Lonergan's treatment of affective conversion is clearly the least developed of the conversions; one must rely on his rather brief discussions of falling-in-love, as I do in the present attempt at systematic analysis. While my discussions of the other conversions deliberately introduced innovations into Lonergan's original perspectives, the process here is more clearly one of creative development from a minimal starting point. For a somewhat different version of affective conversion stressing the centrality of decision, see Donald L. Gelpi, *Charism and Sacrament*, p. 17: "Affective conversion is the decision to assume personal responsibility for my emotional growth and development," *Experiencing God: A Theology of Human Emergence* (New York: Paulist, 1978), pp. 179–81 (where eight stages of affective conversion are outlined following the seven stages of therapeutic process in Carl R. Rogers, *On Becoming a Person: A Therapist's View of Psychotherapy* [Boston: Houghton Mifflin, 1961], pp. 125–59), and "Conversion: The Challenge of Contemporary Charismatic Piety," *Theological Studies* 43/4 (December 1982): 606–28, esp. 613–16. Another excellent treatment of affective conversion in Christian terms complementary to the present discussion is William Johnston, *The Mirror Mind: Spirituality and Transformation* (San Francisco: Harper & Row, 1981), esp. ch. 6, "Transformation of Feeling."

Significantly different from affective conversion in the sense developed here, though often confused with it, is psychic conversion: see Robert M. Doran, "Psychic Conversion," *Thomist* 41 (April 1977): 200–36; *Subject and Psyche: Ricoeur, Jung, and the Search for Foundations* (Washington, DC: University Press of America, 1977), and *Psychic Conversion and Theological Foundations: Toward a Reorientation of the Human Sciences*, AAR Studies in Religion 25 (Chico, CA: Scholars Press, 1981), esp. pp. 178–93. In the latter work, Doran explains that this conversion, which releases the capacity for internal symbolic communication (p. 178), has religious, moral, and intellectual conversions as conditions for its possibility (p. 184). To use the terms of the present study, then, it *seems* that psychic conversion would be some form of explicitly critical affective conversion—the extension of cognitive (intellectual) conversion into the domain of preconscious affectivity through the symbolic imagination. Also see Bernard Lonergan, "Reality, Myth, Symbol" in Alan M. Olson, ed., *Myth, Symbol, and Reality* (Notre Dame, IN: University of Notre Dame Press, 1980), pp. 31–37, at 37. Another important treatment of the topic along different lines is Bernard J. Tyrrell's discussion of "psychological conversion" and "conversion from addiction" along with religious and moral conversions in his *Christotherapy II: The Fasting and Feasting Heart* (New York: Paulist, 1982), pp. 10–23. Psychological conversion as a shift from a neurotic to a healthy state (from a sense of being unlovable and worthless to a sense of being lovable and worthwhile) may be a necessary first moment in affective conversion. In relation to this point, see J.A. Meacham, "A Dialectical Approach to Moral Judgment and Self-Esteem," *Human Development* 18 (1975): 159–70.

In my interpretation, conversion is not identical with self-appropriation. I distinguish conversion as the transformation of one's horizon from the critical appropriation of that transformation: only critical versions of conversion are forms of self-appropriation (thus affective conversion may or may not be a form of self-appropriation, but it seems that psychic conversion is by definition). Further, my interpretation does not focus on only one factor (e.g., deciding) as the defining element in all the conversions. While all the basic dimensions, including decision, are involved in every form of conversion, each conversion is specified by a particular element (e.g., as deciding is primary in moral conversion, so understanding and judging play important roles in affective conversion, but to focus on them as definitive is to miss the transformation of desire that is central to affective conversion).

60. On moral impotence as the existential gap between actual and hypothetical effective freedom in terms of incomplete willingness, see Lonergan, *Insight,* p. 627. From this perspective affective conversion is a transformation of willingness. On willingness and the various attempts to escape the exigence for self-consistency in knowing and deciding (avoidance of self-consciousness, rationalization, and moral renunciation), see *ibid.,* pp. 598–600.

61. See Lonergan, *Method in Theology,* pp. 105, 289.

62. For Lonergan on alienation, basic sin, evil, social surd, breakdown, and decline, see *Insight,* pp. 228–32, 666–68, 688–93, and *Method in Theology,* pp. 39–40, 53–55, 117–18, 242–44, 364. For Lonergan's analysis of dramatic, individual, group, and general bias, see *Insight,* pp. 191–206, 218–242. Also see William P. Loewe, "Dialectics of

Sin: Lonergan's *Insight* and the Critical Theory of Max Horkheimer,"
Anglican Theological Review 61 (1979): 224–45.

63. See Erich Fromm, *The Art of Loving* (2nd ed.; New York:
Bantam Books, 1963 [1956]), pp. 38–69; Paul Tillich, *Love, Power, and
Justice: Ontological Analyses and Ethical Applications* (New York: Oxford
University Press Galaxy, 1960 [1954]), pp. 28–33; C.S. Lewis, *The Four
Loves* (London: Collins Fontana, 1963 [1960]); Andrew Nygren, *Agape
and Eros,* trans. P.S. Watson (2nd ed.; New York: Harper & Row
Torchbooks, 1969 [original Swedish 1930, 1936; first English 1932,
1938, 1939; 2nd 1953]), pp. 53–55; Denis de Rougemont, *Love in the
Western World,* trans. M. Belgion (2nd ed.; Garden City, NY: Double-
day Anchor, 1957 [original French 1939; first English 1940; 2nd
1956]), pp. 51–61; M.C. D'Arcy, *The Mind and Heart of Love* (2nd ed.;
New York: Meridian, 1956 [1945]); Robert O. Johann, *The Meaning of
Love: An Essay towards a Metaphysics of Intersubjectivity* (New York: Paulist, 1966), pp. 74–75; and George Tavard, *A Way of Love* (Maryknoll,
NY: Orbis, 1977), p. 66. One of the most valuable integrating theological analyses of love (human loves prepare for agape) is Daniel Day
Williams, *The Spirit and the Forms of Love* (New York: Harper & Row,
1968), where love in the Christian tradition is distinguished as Augus-
tinian, Franciscan, and evangelical (pp. 52–89). Of the many excellent
studies on Augustine, whose caritas synthesis set the terms of the succeeding discussion, see Oliver O'Donovan, *The Problem of Self-Love in
St. Augustine* (New Haven, CT: Yale University Press, 1980), which
considers four aspects of love: cosmic, positive, rational, and benevo-
lent, pp. 10–36. For a valuable analysis of love in Aquinas, see Frederick E. Crowe, "Complacency and Concern in the Thought of St.
Thomas," *Theological Studies* 20 (March 1959): 1–39; 20 (June 1959):
198–230; 20 (September 1959): 343–95, with a perceptive critique of
Nygren at 353–63. For a study informed by the contemporary philosophical perspective, see Gene Outka, *Agape: An Ethical Analysis* (New
Haven, CT: Yale University Press, 1972).

64. In addition to the authors cited here and below, see the following for valuable contextual and critical discussions: James Hillman,
*Emotion: A Comprehensive Phenomenology of Theories and Their Meanings
for Therapy* (Evanston, IL: Northwestern University Press, 1961); Anthony Kenny, *Action, Emotion and Will* (New York: Humanities Press,
1963); J.R.S. Wilson, *Emotion and Object* (Cambridge: Cambridge University Press, 1972); W.W. Fortenbaugh, *Aristotle on Emotion* (London:
Duckworth, 1975); William Lyons, *Emotion* (Cambridge: Cambridge
University Press, 1980); and Robert C. Roberts, *Spirituality and Human
Emotion* (Grand Rapids, MI: Eerdmans, 1982); also see these helpful

6

collections of essays: Bernard Weiner, ed., *Cognitive Views of Human Motivation* (New York: Academic Press, 1974); D.K. Candland *et al.*, *Emotion* (Monterey, CA: Brooks/Cole, 1977); Ashley Montagu, ed., *The Practice of Love* (Englewood Cliffs, NJ: Prentice-Hall, 1975); and Kenneth S. Pope *et al.*, eds., *On Love and Loving: Psychological Perspectives on the Nature and Experience of Romantic Love* (San Francisco: Jossey-Bass, 1980).

65. See Lonergan, *Method in Theology*, p. 30; also see William M. Shea, "Feeling, Religious Symbol and Action" in Masson, ed., *The Pedagogy of God's Image*, pp. 75–95.

66. See *ibid.*, p. 31. Also see Max Scheler, *Formalism in Ethics and a Non-Formal Ethics of Value*, trans. M. Frings and R. Funk (Evanston, IL: Northwestern University Press, 1973 [original German 1913, 1916]), and "Ordo Amoris" in his *Selected Philosophical Essays*, ed. and trans. D.R. Lachterman (Evanston, IL: Northwestern University Press, 1973), pp. 98–135; Manfred S. Frings, *Max Scheler* (Pittsburgh, PA: Duquesne University Press, 1965), esp. chs. 3, 4, 6; Edward V. Vacek, "Scheler's Phenomenology of Love," *Journal of Religion* 62 (April 1982): 156–77; Dietrich von Hildebrand, *Christian Ethics* (New York: David McKay, 1953), ch. 17, "Value Response," pp. 191–243, esp. 191–97, 214–15; and Dietrich von Hildebrand, "The Role of Affectivity in Morality," *Proceedings of the American Catholic Philosophical Association* 32 (1958): 85–95.

67. Magda B. Arnold, *Emotion and Personality* (2 vols.; New York: Columbia University Press, 1960), 1:93–95.

68. Magda B. Arnold, "Perennial Problems in the Field of Emotion" in Magda B. Arnold, ed., *Feelings and Emotions: The Loyola Symposium* (New York: Academic Press, 1970), pp. 169–85, at 176.

69. M.B. Arnold and J.A. Gasson, "Feelings and Emotion as Dynamic Factors in Personality Integration" in Magda B. Arnold, ed., *The Nature of Emotion: Selected Readings* (Baltimore: Penguin, 1968), pp. 203–21, at 210.

70. Arnold, "Perennial Problems," pp. 177, 179.

71. Richard S. Lazarus, Allan D. Kanner, and Susan Folkman, "Emotions: A Cognitive-Phenomenological Analysis" in Robert Plutchik and Henry Kellerman, eds., *Emotion: Theory, Research, and Experience, 1: Theories of Emotion* (New York: Academic Press, 1980), pp. 189–217, at 198, 192.

72. Richard S. Lazarus, James R. Averill, and Edward M. Opton, Jr., "Towards a Cognitive Theory of Emotion" in Arnold, ed., *Feelings and Emotions*, pp. 207–32, at 219.

73. James R. Averill, "A Constructivist View of Emotion" in

Plutchik and Kellerman, eds., *Emotion*, pp. 305–39, at 305. For interpretations of specific emotions, also see Averill and R. Boothroyd, "On Falling in Love in Conformance with the Romantic Ideal," *Motivation and Emotion* 1 (1977): 235–47; and Averill, "Anger" in Richard A. Dienstbier, ed., *Nebraska Symposium on Motivation 1978* (Lincoln: University of Nebraska Press, 1979), pp. 1–80.

74. Silvano Arieti, "Cognition and Feeling" in Arnold, ed., *Feelings and Emotions*, pp. 135–43.

75. Joseph de Rivera, *A Structural Theory of the Emotions*, Psychological Issues 40 (New York: International Universities Press, 1977), p. 35.

76. Robert C. Solomon, *The Passions: The Myth and Nature of Human Emotion* (Garden City, NY: Doubleday Anchor, 1976), pp. xiv, xvii, 229.

77. *Ibid.*, pp. 191–92.

78. *Ibid.*, p. 189.

79. *Ibid.*, pp. 190, 221, 245, 280, 282.

80. *Ibid.*, p. 214.

81. *Ibid.*, pp. 214, 221.

82. Robert C. Solomon, *Love: Emotion, Myth and Metaphor* (Garden City, NY: Doubleday Anchor, 1981), p. 57.

83. *Ibid.*, pp. 131, 142, 146, 147, 276, 277.

84. *Ibid.*, pp. 212, 213, 201, 202–03. Also see Robert C. Solomon, "Emotions and Choice" in Amélie Rorty, ed., *Explaining Emotions* (Berkeley: University of California Press, 1980), pp. 251–81.

85. *Ibid.*, p. 223.

86. Solomon, *Passions*, pp. 337, 359. For a different perspective on self-love, see Fromm, *Art of Loving*, pp. 48–53, where self-love is defined in contrast to selfishness, and affirmed.

Solomon's entire discussion of love, of course, focuses on romantic love, a point that needs emphasis when he states, e.g., that love is not dependent, an obvious characteristic of a child's love. For an analysis that explicitly recognizes need love, see Otto Bird, "The Complexity of Love," *Thought* 39 (June 1964): 210–20, which shows three basic forms of love (gift, appreciative, need) blending to give four familiar types (gift and appreciation: friendship; gift and need: affection; appreciative and need: romantic; gift, appreciative, and need: charity); see Lewis, *Four Loves*, pp. 7–14.

87. *Ibid.*, pp. 414–16, 419, 422.

88. *Ibid.*, pp. 417, 203.

89. Rosemary Haughton, *The Passionate God* (New York: Paulist, 1981), p. 6; for critical discussion of this book, see the Review Sym-

posium with essays by Joann Wolski Conn, Lawrence S. Cunningham, Pheme Perkins, and Brian O. McDermott, and Haughton's response in *Horizons* 10/1 (Spring 1983): 124–40; also see Dennis P. McCann, "Rosemary Haughton: The Passionate Theologian," *Anglican Theological Review* 65/2 (April 1983), 206–13.

90. *Ibid.,* pp. 21, 23, 35, 18.

91. *Ibid.,* pp. 55–57.

92. *Ibid.,* pp. 58–61.

93. *Ibid.,* p. 58. For a Jungian version of the standard interpretation of romantic love in opposition to the committed love of human relationship, see Robert A. Johnson, *WE: Understanding the Psychology of Romantic Love* (San Francisco: Harper & Row, 1983), pp. 99–104. Johnson sees romantic love as a necessary stage in psychological evolution, but insists that it must be clearly distinguished from committed love so that the latter may flourish and that the true significance of romantic love, its spiritual aspiration for inner wholeness and transcendence, may be followed into the interior world of religious experience (pp. 52–58, 131–32). The opposition of these loves is upheld on different grounds in Francesco Alberoni, *Falling in Love,* trans. L. Venuti (New York: Random House, 1983 [original Italian 1981]). On this point M.C. Dillon argues that romantic love and enduring love are mutually exclusive and that taken by themselves neither can be fulfilling; he proposes a third, authentic, love—an active, dialogic, responsible, developing love rooted in the self-transcendence of mutual affirmation: see "Romantic Love, Enduring Love, and Authentic Love," *Soundings* 66/2 (Summer 1983): 133–51. For the classic analysis of the medieval origins of romantic love, see C.S. Lewis, *The Allegory of Love: A Study in Medieval Tradition* (Oxford: Oxford University Press, 1936).

94. Solomon, *Love,* pp. 224–27. By denying commitment in love Solomon wants to emphasize that, whatever commitments may be added, in itself love makes no promises, offers no guarantee of future love. Commitment in this sense of promise of future love is different from the commitment of the self in the very decision of love that Solomon recognizes (*Passions,* pp. 416–17).

95. Haughton, *Transformation of Man,* pp. 32, 34.

96. *Ibid.,* pp, 80, 38, 110.

97. *Ibid.,* pp. 80, 174, 80, 115.

98. Rosemary Haughton, *Love* (Baltimore, MD: Penguin, 1971 [1970]), pp. 170, 173, 174, 175.

99. *Ibid.,* p. 176.

100. *Ibid.,* p. 183.

101. Tavard, *Way of Love,* pp. 66, 92.

102. Tillich, *Love, Power, and Justice,* pp. 30–31.

103. Johann, *Meaning of Love,* p. 74.

104. For an approach that sets the question of love in terms of the relationship between heart and will (will alone; heart alone; heart, then will; or will, then heart), and opts for the priority of will (will, then heart), see Andrew Tallon, "Love and the Logic of the Heart," *Listening* 18/1 (Winter 1983) 5–22, at 8–11. Also see M. Scott Peck, *The Road Less Travelled* (New York: Simon & Schuster Touchstone, 1978), who argues that "Genuine love is volitional rather than emotional" (p. 119). For Peck, love is "the will to extend one's self for the purpose of nurturing one's own or another's spiritual growth" (p. 81). In contrast, falling-in-love is not an act of will, for Peck, not an extension but a collapse of ego boundaries (p. 89). In terms of the present interpretation, Peck may be contrasting the passion and commitment seen here as complementary moments in affective conversion. Indeed, collapse of ego boundaries may be a condition for the self-transcendence of affective conversion.

105. Magda B. Arnold, "Human Emotion and Action" in Theodore Mischel, ed., *Human Action: Conceptual and Empirical Issues* (New York: Academic Press, 1969), pp. 167–97, at 188.

106. Lonergan, *Method in Theology,* p. 32. Also see Richard S. Peters, "The Education of the Emotions" in Arnold, ed., *Feelings and Emotions,* pp. 187–203.

107. See Gelpi, *Experiencing God,* pp. 179–81; and Philibert, "Conscience: Developmental Perspectives from Rogers and Kohlberg," pp. 3–10; also see Rogers, *On Becoming a Person,* pp. 125–59.

108. See Lonergan, *Method in Theology,* pp. 64–67, and *Insight,* pp. 533, 547, 561–62, 723.

109. See, e.g., Stanley Hauerwas, "The Self as Story: A Reconsideration of the Relation of Religion and Morality from the Agent's Perspective" in his *Vision and Virtue,* pp. 68–89, "Character, Narrative, and Growth in the Christian Life," esp. 143–49, and "Constancy and Forgiveness: The Novel as a School for Virtue," *Notre Dame English Journal* 15/3 (Summer 1983): 23–54.

110. For a different but complementary approach to affective development, see Sam Keen, *The Passionate Life: Stages of Loving* (San Francisco: Harper & Row, 1983). Keen traces the unfolding of eros through five stages: the Child, the Rebel, the Adult, the Outlaw, and the Lover. Despite similarities between Keen's pattern and those of Erikson and Kegan (as well as Kohlberg, Fowler, and Loevinger), Keen sees his project as different from the descriptive one he understands the psychologists to be pursuing; his is explicitly the philosophical task

of delineating normative development: "We age in order to become lovers" (p. 30).

111. Near the end of his Preface to *Insight* (pp. xiii–xiv), Lonergan asks, "What practical good can come of this book?" Pointing out that "insight is the source not only of theoretical knowledge but also of all its practical applications and, indeed, of all intelligent activity," he asserts that insight into insight will "reveal what activity is intelligent, and insight into oversights will reveal what activity is unintelligent. But to be practical is to do the intelligent thing and to be unpractical is to keep blundering about. It follows that insight into both insight and oversight is the very key to practicality." Thus, in the common sense world of policies and action in which we live, "insight into insight brings to light the cumulative process of progress," and "insight into oversight reveals the cumulative process of decline." For Lonergan's basic discussion of this issue, esp. the longer cycle generated by the general bias of common sense, see *Insight*, ch. 7, and *Method in Theology*, ch. 2, esp. pp. 47–55. Also see Lonergan, "Dialectic of Authority" in Frederick J. Adelmann, ed., *Authority*, Boston College Studies in Philosophy 3 (The Hague: Nijhoff, 1974), pp. 24–30, and "Theology and Praxis," *Proceedings of the Catholic Theological Society* 32 (1977): 1–16. A particularly helpful analysis of the fundamental social dimension of Lonergan's philosophical method is Gerald A. McCool, "Social Authority in Transcendental Thomism," *Proceedings of the American Catholic Philosophical Association* 49 (1975): 13–23. Of the several valuable essays on this point in Matthew L. Lamb, ed., *Creativity and Method: Essays in Honor of Bernard Lonergan, S.J.* (Milwaukee, WI: Marquette University Press, 1981), see David Tracy, "Theologies of Praxis," pp. 35–51, and Matthew L. Lamb, "Praxis and Generalized Empirical Method," pp. 53–77. For critical discussion, see Davis, "Lonergan's Appropriation of the Concept of Praxis."

112. Paulo Freire, "Conscientisation," *Cross Currents* 24 (Spring 1974): 23–31, at 24–25.

113. For a discussion of such education with a focus on Kohlberg's developmental approach, see Margaret Gorman, "Moral Education, Peace, and Social Justice" in Padraic O'Hare, ed., *Education for Peace and Justice* (San Francisco: Harper & Row, 1983), 157–71.

114. Freire, "Conscientisation," p. 29.

115. One of the most important of contemporary social movements, of course, is the challenge to the male establishment in every aspect of Western life resulting from the critical conversion of feminist consciousness. For a consideration in the specifically theological context of feminist consciousness precisely as cognitively converted, see

my contribution to a CTSA symposium on women's contribution to theology: Walter E. Conn, "Two-Handed Theology," *Proceedings of the Catholic Theological Society of America* 38 (1983): 66–71. Among the many important interpretations of feminist consciousness in theology and spirituality, see Elisabeth Schüssler Fiorenza, "Feminist Theology as a Critical Theology of Liberation," *Theological Studies* 36/4 (December 1975): 605–26; Joann Wolski Conn, "Women's Spirituality: Restriction and Reconstruction," *Cross Currents* 30/3 (Fall 1980): 293–308; Anne Carr, "On Feminist Spirituality," *Horizons* 9/1 (Spring 1982): 96–103; and Denise Lardner Carmody, *Feminism and Christianity: A Two-Way Reflection* (Nashville, TN: Abingdon, 1982).

116.   Paulo Freire, *Pedagogy of the Oppressed,* trans. Myra Bergman Ramos (New York: Seabury, 1970), p. 47.

117.   Peter Berger, *Pyramids of Sacrifice* (New York: Basic Books, 1974), pp. 111–19. Berger does not seem to appreciate the distinction between conversion as imposition of content and conversion as liberation of critical creative intelligence.

118.   See Charles Davis, *Body as Spirit: The Nature of Religious Feeling* (New York: Seabury, 1976), p. 56, for a discussion of the asceticism of achieved spontaneity: the goal of practicing (tennis, or the piano, e.g.) is not to acquire deliberate, rational control, but to move beyond the need for it; see above for pertinent references to Polanyi on the tacit dimension, Ricoeur on second naiveté, and Doran on psychic conversion.

5. CHRISTIAN CONVERSION: THE MORAL DIMENSION

1.   Kohlberg does suggest some content judgments, but they are neither essential to his position nor in most cases argued systematically; for one of his more sustained efforts, see Lawrence Kohlberg and Donald Elfenbein, "The Development of Moral Judgments concerning Capital Punishment," *American Journal of Orthopsychiatry* 45/4 (July 1975): 614–40.

2.   See Andrew Boyle, *Climate of Treason: Five Who Spied for Russia* (London: Hutchinson, 1979).

3.   For Merton's own version of his life, see his *The Secular Journal* (New York: Farrar, Straus & Giroux Noonday, 1977 [1959; written 1939–41, with only slight editing for publication]), *The Seven Storey Mountain* (Garden City, NY: Doubleday Image, 1970 [1948]), *The Sign of Jonas* (Garden City, NY: Doubleday Image, 1956 [1953]), *Conjectures of a Guilty Bystander* (Garden City, NY: Doubleday Image, 1968 [1966]),

and *The Asian Journal,* ed. N. Burton, P. Hart, and J. Laughlin (New York: New Directions, 1973). Of Merton's other works, see the autobiographical novel *My Argument with the Gestapo* (Garden City, NY: Doubleday, 1969 [written 1941 as *Journal of My Escape from the Nazis*]). Of the many biographical and interpretive studies, see esp., in addition to those cited below, Michael Mott, *The Seven Mountains of Thomas Merton* (Boston: Houghton Mifflin, 1984); Monica Furlong, *Merton: A Biography* (San Francisco: Harper & Row, 1980); Elena Malits, *The Solitary Explorer: Thomas Merton's Transforming Journey* (San Francisco: Harper & Row, 1980); and Anthony T. Padovano, *The Human Journey: Thomas Merton, Symbol of a Century* (Garden City, NY: Doubleday, 1982). To focus on Merton's adult years is not to dismiss the importance of his childhood and early adolescence, esp. the impact of the early deaths of his mother and father (see Mott, *Seven Mountains* and Furlong, *Merton*).

4. Merton, *Seven Storey Mountain,* pp. 108–09. The first half of the six division headings in this section (e.g., "The Children in the Market Place") are titles of the corresponding parts of *Seven Storey Mountain.*

5. On this difficult experience, see Mott, *Seven Mountains,* pp. 84–90, and Furlong, *Merton,* pp. 59–60.

6. Merton, *Seven Storey Mountain,* p. 164.

7. *Ibid.*

8. *Ibid.* pp. 164–65.

9. *Ibid.,* p. 170.

10. *Ibid.,* pp. 177, 184.

11. *Ibid.,* p. 184.

12. See Haughton, *Transformation of Man,* pp. 105–15.

13. Merton, *Seven Storey Mountain,* p. 186.

14. *Ibid.,* p. 196. On Merton's Columbia years from the viewpoint of a college friend, see Edward Rice, *The Man in the Sycamore Tree: The Good Times and Hard Life of Thomas Merton* (Garden City, NY: Doubleday, 1970), pp. 19–31.

15. Merton, *Seven Storey Mountain,* p. 203.

16. *Ibid.,* p. 204.

17. *Ibid.,* pp. 213–14. See Etienne Gilson, *The Spirit of Medieval Philosophy,* trans. A.H.C. Downer (New York: Scribner's, 1936 [original French 1932]). For Lonergan's extension of intellectual conversion to the question of God, see *Insight,* ch. 19, and, for later assessment, his *Philosophy of God, and Theology* (London: Darton, Longman & Todd, 1973). Also see Bernard Tyrrell, *Bernard Lonergan's Philosophy of God* (Notre Dame, IN: University of Notre Dame Press, 1974). For Loner-

gan on Gilson, see his "Metaphysics as Horizon" and his review of Gilson's *Being and Some Philosophers* in *Theological Studies* 11 (1950): 122–25.

18. Merton, *Seven Storey Mountain*, pp. 220, 221.

19. *Ibid.*, p. 226. See Aldous Huxley, *Ends and Means* (London: Chatto and Windus, 1937).

20. Merton, *Seven Storey Mountain*, p. 228.

21. *Ibid.*, pp. 247, 248. See Geoffrey Keynes, ed., *Complete Writings of William Blake* (Oxford: Oxford University Press, 1966 [1957]); Merton refers to the Nonesuch Press edition (London, 1927). Also see Jacques Maritain, *Art and Scholasticism*, trans. J.F. Scanlon (London: Sheed & Ward, 1930 [original French 1927]).

22. Merton, *Seven Storey Mountain*, p. 233.

23. *Ibid.*, p. 249.

24. *Ibid.*, p. 233.

25. *Ibid.*, p. 249.

26. *Ibid.*, pp., 233, 249, 250.

27. *Ibid.*, p. 256.

28. *Ibid.*, p. 257.

29. *Ibid.*, p. 260.

30. *Ibid.*, p. 262.

31. *Ibid.*, p. 263.

32. *Ibid.*, p. 269.

33. *Ibid.*, p. 277.

34. *Ibid.*

35. *Ibid.*, pp. 280–81.

36. *Ibid.*, pp. 289–90.

37. *Ibid.*, p. 302.

38. *Ibid.*, p. 307.

39. *Ibid.*, p. 310.

40. *Ibid.*, pp. 343–44.

41. *Ibid.*, pp. 344, 345. For Merton's reflections on this experience at the time, see his *Secular Journal*, pp. 74–78. Merton's first dramatic religious experience of this kind (Rome, 1933), which he called a "conversion," involved real but very short-lived religious fervor (see *Seven Storey Mountain*, pp. 137–45.

42. Merton, *Seven Storey Mountain*, p. 358.

43. *Ibid.*, pp. 376–82.

44. *Ibid.*, p. 402.

45. *Ibid.*, pp. 438, 440, 448.

46. Merton, *Seven Storey Mountain*, p. 180.

47. *Ibid.*, p. 181.

48. *Ibid.*, pp. 376, 378–79.

49. *Ibid.*

50. *Ibid.*, p. 378.

51. Fowler, *Stages of Faith*, p. 179.

52. James, *Varieties of Religious Experience*, p. 140.

53. *Ibid.*, pp. 141, 143.

54. *Ibid.*, p. 157.

55. *Ibid.*, p. 192.

56. See Wayne E. Oates, "Conversion: Sacred and Secular" in his *The Psychology of Religion* (Waco, TX: Word Books, 1973), pp. 92–109.

57. James, *Varieties of Religious Experience*, p. 164. James' references are to E.D. Starbuck, *The Psychology of Religion* (New York: Scribner's, 1899).

58. See Robert H. Thouless, *An Introduction to the Psychology of Religion* (3rd ed.; Cambridge: Cambridge University Press, 1971 [1923]), pp. 113–14.

59. V. Bailey Gillespie, *Religious Conversion and Personal Identity: How and Why People Change* (Birmingham, AL: Religious Education Press, 1979), pp. 47–57.

60. *Ibid.*, pp. 62–70.

61. *Ibid.*, p. 87.

62. *Ibid.*, pp. 199, 200, 171.

63. See Merton, *Seven Storey Mountain*, pp. 262–63, 307–10, and 440 for Merton's decisions on baptism, priesthood, and Gethsemani.

64. Lonergan, *Method in Theology*, pp. 240, 242. I deliberately make the controversial distinction between the moral and religious dimensions within Christian conversion not to undercut the importance of the moral (nor to deny that Christian moral conversion has a religious quality), but to stress the singular power and profundity of religious conversion. The more common approach is to regard Christian conversion as a particular specification of religious conversion.

65. Merton, *Seven Storey Mountain*, p. 353.

66. *Ibid.*, p. 355.

67. See Krailsheimer, *Conversion* on Pascal, pp. 59–69, and several other adult conversions.

68. Gillespie, *Religious Conversion and Personal Identity*, p. 171.

69. See Roger Balducelli, "A Phenomenology of Conversion," *Living Light* 10 (Winter 1973): 545–57, for a distinction between first conversion and second conversion, in which the second is conversion as commonly understood, and first conversion is a hermeneutical model which "delivers the intelligibility" of the result of religious so-

cialization: "the ordinary believer precisely as ordinary, and . . . his religion precisely as taken-for-granted" (p. 546). For a particularly helpful analysis of religious socialization (which Balducelli depends on), see Peter L. Berger, *The Sacred Canopy: Elements of a Sociological Theory of Religion* (Garden City, NY: Doubleday Anchor, 1969 [1967]), esp. chs. 1–2. For an important critique of Berger's basic understanding of religion, see Baum, *Religion and Alienation*, pp. 108–11.

70. Karl Rahner, "Conversion," *Encyclopedia of Theology: The Concise Sacramentum Mundi,* ed. Karl Rahner (New York: Seabury, 1975), pp. 291–95, at 291–92. For critique of Kohlberg in the context of fundamental themes in contemporary moral theology, see Bartholomew Kiely, *Psychology and Moral Theology: Lines of Convergence* (Rome: Gregorian University Press, 1980).

71. Joseph Fuchs, "Sin and Conversion," *Theology Digest* 14 (Winter 1966): 292–301, at 297–98.

72. Tillich, *Systematic Theology* 3, 219.

73. Rahner, "Conversion," pp. 292–93.

74. Karl Barth, "The Awakening to Conversion" in his *Church Dogmatics* 4/2, trans. G.W. Bromiley (Edinburgh: T. & T. Clark, 1958), pp. 553–84, at 563.

75. Franz Böckle, *Fundamental Moral Theology,* trans. N.D. Smith (New York: Pueblo, 1980 [German 1977]), pp. 152–53.

76. Barth, "Awakening to Conversion," p. 579.

77. Charles E. Curran, "Conversion: The Central Moral Message of Jesus" in his *A New Look at Christian Morality* (Notre Dame, IN: Fides, 1968), pp. 24–71, at 27.

78. Bernard Häring, "The Characteristics of Conversion" in his *This Time of Salvation,* trans. A. Swidler (New York: Herder and Herder, 1966 [1964]), pp. 217–28.

79. For a recent example of this approach, see Timothy E. O'Connell, *Principles for a Catholic Morality* (New York: Seabury, 1978), ch. 6, "The Human Person," esp. pp. 64–65. For critical discussion of this position from the perspective of character as fundamentally historic, see Stanley Hauerwas, *The Peaceable Kingdom: A Primer in Christian Ethics* (Notre Dame, IN: University of Notre Dame Press, 1983), pp. 40–41.

80. See Kennedy, *Sense of Life, Sense of Sin,* pp. 106–11, for a perceptive comparison of sinning with loving in terms of the mature, integrated possession of self that both require.

81. In discussing the personal discovery that is intellectual conversion, Lonergan speaks of the memory of its "startling strangeness"

(*Insight*, p. xxviii). My point is simply to generalize this *explicitly* conscious experience to the other conversions.

82. Merton, *Seven Storey Mountain*, pp. 274, 275, 276.

83. *Ibid.*, pp. 256, 207, 257.

84. Reinhold Niebuhr, *The Nature and Destiny of Man* 2 (New York: Scribner's, 1964 [1943]): 108–10.

85. Marc-François Lacan, "Conversion and Kingdom in the Synoptic Gospels" in Conn, ed., *Conversion*, pp. 97–118, at 117 (essay originally appeared in special issue, "La conversion," of *Lumiere et Vie* 9/47 [April-May 1960]: 25–47). For biblical passages in this paragraph, see Lk 10:29, 36, 37; Mt 11:29; Mk 9:35; Mk 10:45; Mk 8:34.

86. Gustavo Gutierrez, *A Theology of Liberation: History, Politics and Salvation*, trans. C. Inda and J. Eagleson (Maryknoll, NY: Orbis, 1973 [1971]), pp. 204–05. For critical discussion of liberation theology, with special reference to Gutierrez and Freire, see Dennis P. McCann, *Christian Realism and Liberation Theology: Practical Theologies in Conflict* (Maryknoll, NY: Orbis, 1981) and the response to McCann in Matthew L. Lamb, "A Distorted Interpretation of Latin American Liberation Theology," *Horizons* 8/2 (Fall 1981): 352–64.

87. Gutierrez, *Theology of Liberation*, p. 205.

88. 1971 Synod of Bishops, "Justice in the World" in David J. O'Brien and Thomas A. Shannon, eds., *Renewing the Earth: Catholic Documents on Peace, Justice and Liberation* (Garden City, NY: Doubleday Image, 1977), pp. 390–408, at 391.

89. Second General Conference of Latin American Bishops (1968), "Medellín Documents: Justice" in Joseph Gremillion, ed., *The Gospel of Peace and Justice: Catholic Social Teaching since Pope John* (Maryknoll, NY: Orbis, 1976), pp. 445–54, at 447.

90. Peter J. Henriot, "Social Sin and Conversion: A Theology of the Church's Social Involvement," *Chicago Studies* 11 (Summer 1972): 115–30, at 128.

91. 1971 Synod of Bishops, "Justice in the World," p. 393.

92. Recognizing the justice structure of care (as discussed above, ch. 3) helps to overcome the dichotomy usually made between care (love) as private and justice as public, thus grounding the possibility of a unified ethics.

93. On the new relation to nature that conversion requires, see John Carmody, *Ecology and Religion: Toward a New Christian Theology of Nature* (New York: Paulist, 1983), esp. ch. 5.

94. Curran, "Conversion: The Central Moral Message of Jesus," pp. 49–50. For a developmental analysis of continuing conversion in

response to life cycle crises from a sacramental-liturgical perspective of ritual, see Mark Searle, "The Journey of Conversion," *Worship* 54 (January 1980): 35–55.

95. Hans Küng, *On Being A Christian*, trans. E. Quinn (Garden City, NY: Doubleday, 1976 [original German 1974]), pp. 251–52. For an analysis of the ethical implications of the call to holiness that is a normative dimension of Christian conversion, see James P. Hanigan, "Conversion and Christian Ethics," *Theology Today* 40/1 (April 1983): 25–35, esp. 31–35.

96. Lacan, "Conversion and Kingdom in the Synoptic Gospels," p. 106.

97. Quoted in Böckle, *Fundamental Moral Theology*, p. 166, from R. Schnackenburg, "De Vollkommenheit des Christen nach Matthäus" in *Christliche Existenz nach dem Neuen Testament* 1:146.

98. Böckle, *Fundamental Moral Theology*, p. 166.

99. Rahner, "Conversion," p. 292.

100. Haughton, *Transformation of Man*, pp. 31–32, 34, 35.

101. Fowler, *Stages of Faith*, pp. 281–86. In his most recent work, Fowler's brief description of conversion as an ongoing process from self-groundedness to vocational existence suggests the understanding of conversion offered here more than his earlier change of content, but he gives no explanation of the relationship between development and the conversion he says fulfills it in the motion of transformation (*Becoming Adult, Becoming Christian: Adult Development and Christian Faith* [San Francisco: Harper & Row, 1984], pp. 138–41).

102. Merton, *Seven Storey Mountain*, p. 274.

6. CHRISTIAN CONVERSION: THE RELIGIOUS DIMENSION

1. John Dominic Crossan, *The Dark Interval* (Niles, IL: Argus, 1975), p. 56 (see esp. chs. 2, 4); also see Crossan, *In Parables: The Challenge of the Historical Jesus* (New York: Harper & Row, 1973) and *Clifts of Fall: Paradox and Polyvalence in the Parables of Jesus* (New York: Seabury, 1980); Sallie McFague TeSelle, *Speaking in Parables* (Philadelphia: Fortress, 1975); and Pheme Perkins, *Hearing the Parables of Jesus* (New York: Paulist, 1981).

2. Crossan, *Dark Interval*, p. 57.

3. See Sallie McFague, "Conversion: Life on the Edge of the Raft," *Interpretation* 32/3 (July 1978): 255–68, at 258.

4. Donald P. Gray, "Was Jesus a Convert?" *Religion in Life* 43 (Winter 1974): 445–55.

5. John S. Dunne, *A Search for God in Time and Memory* (New York: Macmillan, 1969), pp. 9–12.

6. *Ibid.,* p. 10.

7. Quoted in Gray, "Was Jesus a Convert?" p. 449, from Hugh Montefiore, *Awkward Questions on Christian Love* (Philadelphia: Westminster, 1964), pp. 52–53.

8. Gray, "Was Jesus a Convert?" pp. 449, 451.

9. See Marc-François Lacan, "Conversion and Grace in the Old Testament" in Conn, ed., *Conversion,* pp. 75–96, at 95–96 (originally in *Lumiere et Vie* 9/47 [April-May 1960]: 5–24).

10. See Edward Schillebeeckx, *Jesus: An Experiment in Christology,* trans. H. Hoskins (New York: Seabury, 1979 [original Dutch 1974]), pp. 380–85. While in this section, and throughout the chapter generally, I focus on theistic, even Christian versions of religious conversion, this focus should not be understood in any exclusive sense, as we shall see below in discussing Kohlberg's Stage 7; whatever the religious tradition, the issue turns on absolute autonomy.

11. See Jung, "Stages of Life" and "Psychotherapists or the Clergy." Also see Janice Brewi and Anne Brennan, *Mid-Life: Psychological and Spiritual Perspectives* (New York: Crossroad, 1982) for a discussion of the potential of adulthood's middle years for profound conversion.

12. Kohlberg, "Continuities Revisited," p. 180.

13. *Ibid.,* p. 201. It is misleading to say that Erikson's ideal ethical adult corresponds to Kohlberg's Stage 6 inasmuch as Erikson's understanding of ethical maturity does not require postconventional reasoning. The same point applies to Kohlberg's suggestion of correspondence between his Stage 7 and Erikson's Integrity (see "Continuities Revisited," p. 180).

14. *Ibid.,* pp. 201–02. See Loder, *Transforming Moment,* p. 164.

15. Kohlberg, "Education, Moral Development, and Faith," p. 11.

16. Kohlberg, "Stages and Aging in Moral Development—Some Speculations," *Gerontologist* 13/4 (Winter 1973): 497–502, at 500.

17. Kohlberg, "Continuities Revisited," p. 202.

18. *Ibid.* We should not let Kohlberg's stress here on the "purely rational grounds" of morality obscure the attention he gives to the affective element of empathy in moral reasoning, as we saw above in ch. 3.

19. Kohlberg, "Stages and Aging," p. 500.

20. *Ibid.,* p. 501.

21. For discussion of Plato, Marcus Aurelius, Spinoza, Kant,

Dewey, and Teilhard de Chardin, see Lawrence Kohlberg and Clark Power, "Moral Development, Religious Thinking, and the Question of a Seventh Stage," *Zygon* 16/3 (September 1981): 203–59. While the present discussion restricts itself to Christian forms, religious conversion clearly takes shapes that are neither Christian nor theist; for particularly helpful studies on this point in relation to Buddhism, see William Johnston, *The Mirror Mind* and *The Inner Eye of Love: Mysticism and Religion* (San Francisco: Harper & Row, 1978); for a valuable critical survey of literature in which to pursue this question, see Paul F. Knitter, "Horizons on Christianity's New Dialogue with Buddhism," *Horizons* 8/1 (Spring 1981): 40–61.

22. Kohlberg, "Stages and Aging," p. 501.

23. *Ibid.*

24. Kohlberg, "Continuities Revisited," p. 203.

25. Kohlberg, "Stages and Aging," p. 501. From the viewpoint of content there clearly is no single religion just as there is no single morality, but from the structural perspective some qualification of Kohlberg's position may become necessary in light of Fowler's continuing analysis of faith development.

26. For Kohlberg's most extensive consideration of the issue, see Kohlberg and Power, "Moral Development, Religious Thinking, and the Question of a Seventh Stage," pp. 212–33, where faith development is identified with ego development (Erikson and Loevinger) or the development of the unitary valuing activity of the personality that Kohlberg names ethical development. Within this broad matrix Kohlberg distinguishes "two separable spheres, moral judgment and reasoning and religious judgment and reasoning" (p. 226). He considers development of moral reasoning as a necessary but not sufficient condition for the development of religious reasoning. In Fowler and Vergote, *Toward Moral and Religious Maturity*, see Fritz Oser, "Stages of Religious Judgment" (pp. 277–315) and F. Clark Power and Lawrence Kohlberg, "Religion, Morality, and Ego Development" (pp. 343–72).

Clearly, Kohlberg is deliberately relating moral reasoning here to religious reasoning, not to Fowler's faithing. Earlier, in his attempts to relate moral stages with faith stages, Kohlberg sometimes seemed to understand Fowler's stages as stages of explicitly religious faith, rather than stages in the development of the wider (and not necessarily explicitly religious) construing of one's relationship to the ultimate conditions of reality that Fowler clearly intends by "faithing": see Kohlberg, "Education, Moral Development, and Faith."

27. Kohlberg, "Education, Moral Development, and Faith," pp. 13, 14.

28. *Ibid.*, p. 14. Kohlberg clearly seems to be working here with a notion of faith different from Fowler's, stressing the content of faith.

29. *Ibid.*

30. Fowler, "Stages in Faith," p. 209. In his "Moral Stages and the Development of Faith" in Munsey, ed., *Moral Development, Moral Education, and Kohlberg,* pp. 130–60, Fowler stresses that "each moral judgment stage implies and requires anchorage in a more extensive framework of belief and value," not just Stage 6 (pp. 158, 139). For an analysis of conversion in terms of Fowler's stages, see Leroy T. Howe, "A Developmental Perspective on Conversion," *Perkins Journal* 33 (Fall 1979): 20–35.

31. For Kohlberg's recent steps in this direction, see Snarey, Kohlberg, and Noam, "Ego Development in Perspective."

32. For a detailed discussion of this issue which sets Kohlberg (morality) and Fowler (religion) in opposition, and opts for Kohlberg, see Ernest Wallwork, "Morality, Religion, and Kohlberg's Theory" in Munsey, ed., *Moral Development, Moral Education, and Kohlberg,* pp. 269–97, esp. 284.

33. Kohlberg, "Continuities Revisited," p. 202.

34. Fowler, *Stages of Faith,* p. 245.

35. Fowler, "Stages in Faith," pp. 201, 185. Compare Fowler's Stage 6 and Kohlberg's Stage 7 of personal-psychological development with Bellah's final stage of cultural-historical development in Robert Bellah, "Religious Evolution," *American Sociological Review* 29 (1964): 358–74.

36. Kohlberg, "Continuities Revisited," p. 202.

37. For a valuable set of philosophical and theological analyses of this relationship, see the essays in Outka and Reeder, eds., *Religion and Morality.*

38. Kohlberg, "Stages and Aging," p. 500. One will note some similarity here with the insistence of Eastern traditions, especially Buddhism (Eight-fold Path), that moral living precede religious experience or Enlightenment; see Wm. Theodore de Bary, ed., *Sources of Indian Tradition* 1 (New York: Columbia University Press, 1969 [1958]): 99.

39. Though the focus here is on the postconventional, this radical moral impotence and its implications may certainly be adumbrated within the conventional horizon, e.g., of an adolescent. For seminal work in Catholic moral theology on the relation between the moral and religious, see the delineation of "Three Levels of Ethics" (instinct, moral, Christian-religious) in Louis Monden, *Sin, Liberty and Law,* trans. J. Donceel (New York: Sheed and Ward, 1965), pp. 4–16. Mon-

den points out how chronological, moral, and religious maturity do not necessarily coincide: not only may the chronological adult not be morally mature, but the moral adult may not be religiously mature.

40. Lonergan, *Method in Theology*, pp. 240, 242. Lonergan's description of religious conversion is my starting point, but I quite deliberately develop my own version of it, as I have with the other conversions. I attempt to give full force to the profoundly radical nature of religious conversion as Lonergan describes it, and thus see it as a relatively rare occurrence, much less common than Lonergan's linking it with God's gift of grace would seem to have it (*Method in Theology*, pp. 107, 241). Indeed, my interpretation moves religious conversion in the direction of mystical experience, as William Johnston has done in his *Inner Eye of Love*, pp. 59–66. For my fuller discussion of this complex issue, see Conn, *Conscience: Development and Self-Transcendence*, pp. 189–90, 200–01. Also see William J. O'Brien, "A Methodological Flaw in Tracy's Revisionist Theology," *Horizons* 5/2 (Fall 1978): 175–84, esp. 178–81; André Gilbert and Louis Roy, "Le structure éthique de la conversion religieuse d'après B. Lonergan," *Science et Esprit* 32/3 (1980): 347–60; James Robertson Price, "Conversion and the Doctrine of Grace in Bernard Lonergan and John Climacus," *Anglican Theological Review* 62/4 (October 1980): 338–62, esp. 340–47, 354; Antony Archer, "Theology and Sociology: Two Approaches to Religious Conversion," *New Blackfriars* 62 (April 1981): 180–90; and Marc E. Smith, "Can Moral and Religious Conversions Be Separated?" *Thought* 56 (June 1981): 178–84.

41. In one sense, religious conversion may be understood as the recognition of and assent to the fundamental truth of one's being. The shape of a particular conversion—how this truth will be grasped and expressed (the Christian's relationship to God as personal, e.g.)—will depend on the language available to a given person. For an analysis of Christian religious conversion as intersubjective, see Stephen Happel, "Sacrament: Symbol of Conversion" in Lamb, ed., *Creativity and Method*, pp. 275–90.

42. For Piaget's explicit reflections on religion, see Jean Piaget, *La Psychologie et les Valeurs religieuses* (Geneva: Labor, 1922); Piaget, "Immanence et Transcendance" in Jean Piaget and J. de la Harpe, *Deux types d'attitudes religieuses: Immanence et Transcendance* (Geneva: Labor, 1928), pp. 7–40; and Piaget, *Immanentisme et foi religieuse* (Geneva: Robert, 1930). For a Piagetian inspired analysis of faith and religious thinking, see J.-M. Pohier, *Psychologie et Théologie* (Paris: Cerf, 1967).

43. Lonergan, *Method in Theology*, p. 242.

44. For Kohlberg's understanding of the relationship between

Stage 6 morality and *agape*, see Kohlberg and Power, "Moral Development, Religious Thinking, and the Question of a Seventh Stage," pp. 239–43.

45. Merton, *Seven Storey Mountain*, p. 451.

46. On conversion's necessary dimension of self-acceptance in faith, see Jacques Pasquier, "Experience and Conversion," *The Way* 17 (April 1977): 114–22.

47. Merton, *Seven Storey Mountain*, p. 467.

48. *Ibid.*, pp. 469–70.

49. *Ibid.*, p. 497.

50. *Ibid.*, p. 496. See Thomas Merton, *Thirty Poems* (Norfolk, CT: New Directions, 1944).

51. Merton, *Sign of Jonas*, pp. 20, 26, 21.

52. *Ibid.*, p. 49.

53. *Ibid.*, pp. 53–54.

54. *Ibid.*, p. 82.

55. *Ibid.*, pp. 97, 98, 119.

56. *Ibid.*, p. 163.

57. Thomas Merton, *Seeds of Contemplation* (New York: Dell, 1960 [1949]), p. 53.

58. *Ibid.*, p. 16.

59. *Ibid.*, pp. 20, 22, 32.

60. *Ibid.*, pp. 41, 23, 40. For a detailed presentation of Merton on the true self, see James Finley, *Merton's Palace of Nowhere: A Search for God through Awareness of the True Self* (Notre Dame, IN: Ave Maria, 1978).

61. Merton, *Seeds of Contemplation*, p. 25. See Raymond Bailey, *Thomas Merton on Mysticism* (Garden City, NY: Doubleday, 1975), pp. 72–74.

62. Merton, *Seeds of Contemplation*, pp. 146, 163.

63. *Ibid.*, pp. 163–64.

64. Merton, *Sign of Jonas*, pp. 130, 131.

65. *Ibid.*, pp. 170, 171.

66. *Ibid.*, p. 179.

67. *Ibid.*, pp. 175, 176.

68. *Ibid.*, p. 191.

69. *Ibid.*, pp. 197–98, 204.

70. *Ibid.*, pp. 203, 215.

71. *Ibid.*, pp. 231, 225.

72. *Ibid.*, p. 226.

73. *Ibid.*, pp. 243, 248.

74. *Ibid.*, p. 234. See Henri J.M. Nouwen, *Thomas Merton: Con-*

templative Critic, trans. D. Schlaver (San Francisco: Harper & Row, 1981 [1972]), pp. 38–48.

75. Merton, *Sign of Jonas,* p. 246.

76. *Ibid.,* pp. 246, 247.

77. *Ibid.,* p. 263.

78. *Ibid.,* p. 286.

79. Thomas Merton, *The Ascent to Truth* (New York: Harcourt, Brace, 1951).

80. Merton, *Sign of Jonas,* pp. 226, 227.

81. *Ibid.,* p. 312. The novel was published in 1969 as *My Argument with the Gestapo.*

82. Merton, *Sign of Jonas,* p. 317.

83. *Ibid.,* p. 323.

84. *Ibid.,* pp. 323, 324.

85. *Ibid.,* p. 323.

86. *Ibid.,* p. 230.

87. See Furlong, *Merton,* pp. 203–14.

88. On the social dimension, see Frederick Joseph Kelly, *Man Before God: Thomas Merton on Social Responsibility* (Garden City, NY: Doubleday, 1974); and James Thomas Baker, *Thomas Merton: Social Critic* (Lexington: University of Kentucky Press, 1971).

89. Merton, *Conjectures of a Guilty Bystander,* p. 280.

90. *Ibid.,* p. 19.

91. *Ibid.,* pp. 47, 53, 156. For a critical comparison of the "Fourth and Walnut" context in *Conjectures* with that of the original journal, see Mott, *Seven Mountains,* pp. 311–13. On Merton's developing attitude toward the world, see Malits, *Solitary Explorer,* pp. 56–60; and John J. Higgins, *Thomas Merton on Prayer* (Garden City, NY: Doubleday Image, 1975 [1972]), pp. 114–22.

92. See Mott, *Seven Mountains,* pp. 290–98, on Merton's illuminating but painful meetings with Zilboorg.

93. Merton, *Conjectures of a Guilty Bystander,* p. 113.

94. *Ibid.,* pp. 70, 113.

95. *Ibid.,* pp. 118–19.

96. *Ibid.,* pp. 91, 98, 97, 95.

97. *Ibid.,* p. 288.

98. Thomas Merton, *Seeds of Destruction* (New York: Macmillan, 1967 [1964]), p. 7.

99. Thomas Merton, "Introduction" in Thomas Merton, ed., *Breakthrough to Peace* (Norfork, CT: New Directions, 1962), pp. 7–14, at 11.

100. Merton, *Conjectures of a Guilty Bystander,* p. 224.

101. *Ibid.*, pp. 224, 225, 224.

102. *Ibid.*, p. 225.

103. Thomas Merton, *New Seeds of Contemplation* (New York: New Directions, 1972 [1961]), p. 110.

104. Merton, *Conjectures of a Guilty Bystander*, p. 170.

105. *Ibid.*, pp. 169, 115.

106. Merton, *New Seeds of Contemplation*, pp. ix, 12.

107. *Ibid.*, pp. 7, 9.

108. *Ibid.*, p. 38.

109. *Ibid.*, pp. 38, 295, 281.

110. Thomas Merton, "The Inner Experience" (unpublished manuscript at Thomas Merton Studies Center, Bellarmine College, Louisville, Kentucky), pp. 6–7. Though Merton directed that this manuscript not be published as a book, the Trustees of the Merton Legacy Trust have permitted sections to be published in William Shannon, *Thomas Merton's Dark Path: The Inner Experience of a Contemplative* (New York: Farrar, Straus, Giroux, 1981) and, more recently, in a *Cistercian Studies* series, beginning with 18/1 (1983).

111. *Ibid.*, p. 21. See Lonergan, *Method in Theology*, p. 357: "For a man is his true self inasmuch as he is self-transcending."

112. See Mott, *Seven Mountains*, pp. 435–58, for a sensitive presentation based on exclusive access to Merton's private papers.

113. Thomas Merton, "First and Last Thoughts: An Author's Preface" in Thomas P. McDonnell, ed., *A Thomas Merton Reader* (rev. ed.; Garden City, NY: Doubleday Image, 1974 [1962]), p. 17.

114. *Ibid.*, pp. 16, 17.

115. Thomas Merton, Letter to Fr. Chrysogonus Waddell, January 4, 1964, quoted in Furlong, *Merton*, p. 248.

116. This new interest in the East was, of course, really the return of a transformed Merton to an earlier interest, noted in the previous chapter. The younger Merton had concluded that the East had nothing substantial to offer him (see Merton, *Seven Storey Mountain*, p. 230).

117. On the *via negationis*, see Bailey, *Thomas Merton on Mysticism*, pp. 85–88.

118. Thomas Merton, *Zen and the Birds of Appetite* (New York: New Directions, 1968), pp. 4, 23–24, and *Mystics and Zen Masters* (New York: Delta, 1968), p. 14.

119. Merton, *Zen and the Birds of Appetite*, p. 24.

120. Merton, "Inner Experience," p. 11, and *Zen and the Birds of Appetite*, pp. 24, 71–72.

121. Merton, *Zen and the Birds of Appetite*, pp. 72, 75.

122. Lonergan, *Method in Theology*, pp. 342, 77.

123. Merton, *Seeds of Contemplation*, p. 41.

124. Merton, *Asian Journal*, pp. 311, 309–10.

125. *Ibid.*, p. 317.

126. Thomas Merton, *Contemplation in a World of Action* (Garden City, NY: Doubleday Image, 1973 [1971]), pp. 225, 226, 227. In Loder and Fowler, "Conversations on Fowler's *Stages of Faith* and Loder's *The Transforming Moment*," see Fowler's reflections on the death of the egoic self in the context of Loder's negation (pp. 144–45).

127. Merton, *Asian Journal*, p. 148.

128. *Ibid.*, pp. 233, 235, 236.

129. *Ibid.*, pp. 340, 338.

130. See John Moffitt, "Thomas Merton: The Last Three Days" in Martin E. Marty and Dean G. Peerman, eds., *New Theology No. 7* (New York: Macmillan, 1970), pp. 125–34, esp. 131–33; and Rembert G. Weakland's reflections in Paul Wilkes, ed., *Merton: By Those Who Knew Him Best* (San Francisco: Harper & Row, 1984), pp. 159–63, esp. 161–63.

131. See Fowler, *Stages of Faith*, pp. 184–98.

132. *Ibid.*, pp. 201–02.

133. *Ibid.*, p. 200.

INDEX

Included from notes are authors of reference works as well as editors of books which have no designated author. In cases of multiple authors or editors, the name of the first is included.

339